THE CAMPAIGN OF THE MARNE

1914

THE CAMPAIGN OF THE MARNE

1914

BY

SEWELL TYNG

WESTHOLME
Yardley

Originally published by Longmans, Green and Co. in 1935

This edition © 2007 Westholme Publishing, LLC

Westholme Publishing, LLC

Eight Harvey Avenue

Yardley, Pennsylvania 19067

Visit our Web site at www.westholmepublishing.com

First Edition: April 2007

10 9 8 7 6 5 4 3 2 1

ISBN: 978-1-59416-042-4

ISBN 10: 1-59416-042-2

Printed in Canada

To
MY MOTHER

INTRODUCTION

TWENTY years have elapsed since the events described in the following pages. During that time the military operations on the western front between the outbreak of the World War and the middle of September 1914, the period inclusively termed the Campaign of the Marne, have called forth a wealth of literary effort ; but so far no comprehensive account seems to have been published in any English-speaking country. Doubtless this is due, in part, to the relatively limited appeal that military history holds for the general reader, but it is partly due, as well, to the fact that until recently the available documentation has been too incomplete to justify the effort required. Now, however, the record is all but closed ; the belligerent nations have all told their official stories. Successively through the years the memoirs of the chief actors in the drama of 1914 have come to light ; a majority of the leaders have given their judgment of men and events, have said their last word and have passed on. A multitude of personal reminiscences varying in authenticity and interest has become available. Numberless biographies have been written and critiques of arm-chair strategists abound, dealing with different phases of the struggle, analysing its progress and explaining its outcome. It does not seem too early, therefore, to assemble and appraise the data, and it may not appear presumptuous to attempt a complete, impartial account of events as they occurred, which, though not final, may serve at least as a base and guide-post for future writers. Such is the purpose of the present study.

It is perhaps needless to enlarge upon the importance of the Campaign of the Marne. It represents the period within which the General Staffs of the two greatest military powers of Europe put into execution, each to its own discomfiture, the elaborate plans matured during the preceding forty years. From a military stand-point, it constitutes a complete phase, particularly adapted to unity of treatment, during which the opposing forces engaged in a type of operations that did not recur in the course of the next four years. Never before in history and never again in the World War itself were so many battles of the first magnitude fought within so brief a space. It forms, moreover, the transitional link between the wars of the past and the mechanized warfare of our own era. Nor is it solely an object of academic historical interest, for the experiences of the Marne and the lessons to be derived from it are not wholly of the past.   In essence the problems and difficulties that beset both sides were those that must arise again whenever in the initial stages of a great conflict it becomes necessary for large bodies of inexperienced, partially trained forces to take the field equipped with new devices untested under battle conditions, and armed with weapons whose potentialities and limitations they only partially understand.

In the following narrative, an attempt has been made to adhere, so far as possible, to matters of military interest and to avoid the fields of political and economic history, despite their necessarily close relationship.

It will be noted, also, that no reference has been made to the attitude of the German armies towards the civilian population in the territory they invaded and occupied.   The omission is deliberate. History has proved repeatedly that "atrocities" of one sort or another are the inevitable accompaniment of armed invasion, differing through the ages only in kind or degree.   It seems obvious that an honest statement with regard to the actions of the German military authorities in the occupied regions or during the progress of their invading march requires a difficult and exhaustive factual inquiry, the results of which would, in any case, bear only an incidental relation to the subject of the present work.   Accordingly no inquiry has been made, and no opinion is expressed with regard to the so-called "German atrocities" which figured so largely in contemporary stories of the summer of 1914.   While there seems no doubt that the German military commanders generally applied the principles of martial law with a rigour that was unexpected and perhaps unnecessary ; whether their conduct so far exceeded the bounds of legitimate military necessity as to constitute violations of the law of nations, what may have been the extent of such violations, if any, and what justification may have existed for them, are questions to be determined elsewhere.

The author desires to acknowledge his grateful indebtedness to the many friends who have given him unfailing encouragement.   In particular he wishes to record his thanks to Major-General George S. Simonds, U.S.A., formerly Chief of Staff of the 2nd Army Corps, A.E.F., and now Deputy Chief of Staff of the United States Army, Major-General Peter E. Traub, U.S.A. retired, formerly Commander of the 35th Division, A.E.F., Major Wm. F. Freehoff, Captain Ewen C. MacVeagh, Captain John E. Bakeless, Captain F. C. Coulter, Mr. A. C. Sedgwick and Miss Penelope Turle for their helpful advice and constructive criticism in the preparation of this book, to Mr. Carl A. Gage for assistance with the maps, and also to Mr. Ernest C. Oberholtzer whose aid in many ways has been especially valuable.

CONTENTS

APPENDICES

LIST OF MAPS

THE CAMPAIGN OF THE MARNE
1914

THE CAMPAIGN OF
THE MARNE

1914

CHAPTER I

THE SCHLIEFFEN PLAN

THE Franco-Prussian War, which ended in 1871 with the Peace of
Frankfort, brought into being two new political entities. In Germany a nationalistic ardour, born of victory over an ancient foe,
welded twenty-five independent or semi-independent states into an
empire under the stern leadership of Prussia, the most warlike of
them all. In France a desperate and disillusioned people, after a
moment of blazing anarchy and a hesitant consideration of a res-
toration of a Bourbon monarchy, founded a new republic upon
the ruins of their fallen dynastic empire. But these proved no
more than changes in outward forms. Beneath the decorous veil
of stilted formalism called diplomatic usage the course of international politics followed its accustomed channel in an unbroken succession of alliances and counter-alliances, of treaties, notes and
aide-mémoires, all more or less adroitly conceived to further national
or racial aspirations.

For more than forty years the nations of Europe without exception
lavished the military preparations which alone could lend force to
the words of their diplomats and give them point. In France and
Germany alike, General Staffs laid plans for a new conflict which
both recognized must inevitably come. The outbreak of hostilities
in the summer of 1914 brought the opportunity to test the efficacy
of these plans, laboriously devised over so many years, that represented the composite achievement of so many careers, and the opening campaign of the war, the Campaign of the Marne, became not
only the introduction to the bloodiest, costliest war of historic times,
but also the climax to the years of preparation that had gone before.
Its history is the story of six weeks in which all of these plans failed
and in which the product of the best military brains of Europe for
more than a generation fell into the discard. It was a colossal bank-
ruptcy, that doomed millions of men for four years thereafter to

watch each other from burrows in the earth a few yards apart, striking to kill now and again as opportunity offered, not in hate, but soberly, impersonally, with the sense of sacred duty that is the distinguishing badge of "civilized war."

The Prussian tradition of militarism, which had reached its highest expression under the great Frederick and had survived even the dark days of Jena, came into its own again with Sadowa and Sedan, and became the rock upon which the foreign policy of the German Empire was built.

"The soldier and the army, not parliamentary majorities, have welded together the German Empire," declared William II upon his accession to the throne. "My trust is placed in the army."

In truth, from 1871 to 1914, the army enjoyed a favoured position in the German state. Backed by all the weight of the Emperor's personal influence, and relatively immune from civilian interference, its political and social prestige progressively increased. Quickly moulded to the Prussian form, the forces of Bavaria, Saxony and the lesser states soon blended into a homogeneous entity, an Imperial Army, in which their differences of background and tradition continued only as ceremonial survivals.[1]

In theory the Emperor himself, the Supreme War Lord, held the chief command of the military and naval forces of the German Empire, but in practice he exerted even less authority than the President of the United States in the analogous position of Commander in Chief of the army and navy, and in time of war William II exercised hardly more than a back-stairs influence over the forces nominally under his command. The real power over the land armies rested with the Chief of the General Staff of the Army who issued his orders in the Emperor's name and assumed responsibility for the nation's military policy. For twenty years after the Franco-Prussian War, Von Moltke, the victor of Sedan, and his colleague and protégé, Von Waldersee, successively held this post, devoting themselves to the perfection of the most elaborate military organization of modern times, the German General Staff.

"What our sword has won in half a year, our sword must guard for half a century."

Taking these words of Von Moltke as its watch-word the Great General Staff prepared to protect the fruits of victory and if need be to enlarge upon them. With a conscientious thoroughness that soon became proverbial it laid its plans, and in these plans a war on two fronts, in which Germany allied with Austria would simul-

[1] Gen. von Cochenhausen in *Von Scharnhorst zu Schlieffen* (Mittler, Berlin, 1933) has given a valuable account of the growth and development of the German General Staff.

taneously oppose France and Russia, became a favourite hypothesis.

The origins of the plan that governed the operations of the German armies in the summer of 1914, date from the last decade of the nineteenth century. The retirement of Field Marshal von Waldersee in 1891 placed the direction of the German General Staff in the hands of a new chief, one of the outstanding military leaders of modern times, Count Alfred von Schlieffen.[2]

Combining in his person both the virtues and the limitations of the Prussian school of "blood and iron," the new Chief of Staff was a man whose deserved prestige becomes the more remarkable from the fact that he never exercised high command against an enemy. With fierce energy and single-minded intensity, Schlieffen devoted himself to the cause of his country's military welfare, ruthlessly subordinating every other consideration. One of his officers and pupils, General von Kuhl,[3] has told of Schlieffen's custom to send him each Christmas Eve a theme establishing the conditions of an imaginary war for which it thereupon became Von Kuhl's duty to prepare a plan of operations.

"He would have been very much surprised," Von Kuhl writes, "had he not received my completed work on Christmas night. The day after Christmas, he had prepared and I had received a continuation of the study. He considered that holidays and Sundays were days especially created for important work, requiring concentration and quiet, undisturbed by ordinary routine."

A profound student of the theory of war and of military history, Schlieffen became the author of a number of authoritative works, notably a monograph on Cannae.[4] Cold, critical, utterly unsparing either of himself or his subordinates, he possessed none of the qualities calculated to inspire enthusiasm or affection in troops, maintaining his ascendancy by sheer intellectual superiority, but Schlieffen's influence on the mentality of the officers destined to lead the German armies of 1914 can hardly be exaggerated.

The conclusion of the Franco-Russian military alliance of 1893,

[2] Gen. von Freytag-Loringhoven, who received his training under Schlieffen and held a number of important staff assignments during the war, has written an able biography, *Generalfeldmarschall Graf von Schlieffen* (Leipzig, 1920); see also Hugo Rochs, *Schlieffen* (Berlin, 1921).

[3] For twenty-two years before the war, Von Kuhl served on the General Staff eventually attaining the post of Quartermaster-General. During the Campaign of the Marne he became Von Kluck's Chief of Staff and later in the war acted as Chief of Staff to the Group of Armies commanded by Crown Prince Rupprecht of Bavaria. His book, *Der deutsche Generalstab* (Mittler, Berlin, 1920), contains a complete and authoritative account of the pre-war plans of the German General Staff, including an analysis of the Schlieffen Plan and the modifications introduced in it. It should be read, however, in conjunction with the partial French translation and commentary of General Douchy, *Le Grand Etat Major Allemand* (Payot. Paris, 1922). See also Gen. von Einem's *Erinnerungen eines Soldaten*, 1853–1933 (Köhler, Leipzig, 1933).

[4] Schlieffen, *Cannae* (Berlin, 1925).

convinced Schlieffen that eventually Germany would take the field against the combined strength of both powers, and that of the two, France rather than Russia would prove the more formidable adversary. Over the years of his tenure of command, Schlieffen evolved a plan for a rapid campaign to overwhelm the French before the powerful but slow-moving Russian military machine could gain momentum, and this plan, with certain modifications, became the basis of German strategy during the opening weeks of the war.

"A masterpiece of divination. Absolutely sound from any angle from which it may be approached."

Thus in eulogistic phrase, a former Chief of Staff of the United States Army [5] has described the celebrated Schlieffen Plan which the aged Field Marshal, upon his retirement in 1906, turned over to his successor, Von Moltke the younger, in the form of a lengthy memorandum.

A simple formula formed the basis of the Schlieffen Plan, a wide enveloping manoeuvre by a right wing of overwhelming strength, while the left and centre remained temporarily on the defensive. Though the strategy that Hannibal had employed against the Romans at Cannae — an envelopment by both wings — enjoyed great vogue in the Imperial German Army, and Schlieffen himself wrote a treatise upon it, in preparing his plan of operations for war against the French, Schlieffen rejected the "pincers of Cannae" in favour of a simpler conception more suited to the nature of the terrain. In the two decades following the Franco-Prussian War the construction of a series of fortresses at Belfort, Epinal, Toul and Verdun had erected an all but impregnable barrier along the eastern frontier of France and had rendered negligible the chances of a successful German invasion debouching from Alsace-Lorraine, based on the fortresses of Metz and Strasbourg. This difficulty Schlieffen resolved by massing his principal strength on the right wing of the German armies, and advancing boldly across the flat reaches of Belgium and Holland that for centuries have been the favourite battle-ground of western Europe. Thus avoiding the fortified line to the east as well as the obstacles of the wooded Ardennes, Schlieffen oriented the main German attack west of the Meuse River against the relatively undefended northern frontier of France between Dunkerque and Mezières with the objective of encircling the left wing of the French armies and rolling it up from west to east against the line of the Moselle. When this had been accomplished, and the advance of the German armies threatened the French fortresses from flank and rear, then and

[5] Gen. Peyton C. March, *The Nation at War* (Doubleday Doran, New York, 1932). Opinions are not unanimous, however, even in Germany; see for example, Dr. Steinhausen's *Die Gründfehler des Krieges und der Generalstab* (Perthes, Gotha, 1919) and Gothein's *Warum verloren wir den Krieg* (Deutsche Verlags-Anstalt, Berlin, 1919).

then only, would the German centre and left abandon their defensive role and proceed to a frontal attack designed to complete the enemy's destruction.

It was a bold plan which had for its primary purpose nothing less than the elimination of the main body of the French armies within five to seven weeks after the outbreak of hostilities, and the reduction of Germany's most dangerous antagonist to a state of impotence that would allow the German armies to turn their attention to Russia without fear of serious interference.

To accomplish the result he sought, Schlieffen envisaged a force concentrated on the western front amounting to $40\frac{1}{2}$ army corps and 10 cavalry divisions, supported by $26\frac{1}{2}$ brigades of Landwehr. In addition, he planned the formation immediately after the outbreak of hostilities of 6 new army corps of Ersatz troops, constituted from reservists not already assigned to organized units, which would reinforce the first-line armies. While these forces took the field against the French, a skeleton army composed of Reserve and Landwehr units were to hold the Russians in check, with such aid as Austria might afford.

The fortified region of Thionville-Metz served as the hinge for the manoeuvre contemplated by the Schlieffen Plan. Of the seven field armies into which the German forces on the western front were divided, the five concentrated along the borders of Luxembourg, Belgium and Holland were assigned the offensive portion of the program, while the two armies to the east, along the frontier of Alsace-Lorraine between Metz and the Swiss border, remained on the defensive with their strength reduced to the minimum required to hold the enemy in check and to avoid decisive defeat. The relative importance of the offensive right wing and of the defensive left wing in Schlieffen's original conception is illustrated by the fact that the former comprised $35\frac{1}{2}$ army corps and the latter only 5 army corps.

The offensive right wing Schlieffen divided in turn into three major groups, a northern, a centre and a southern group, and a defensive flank guard. Upon the northern group, the two armies on the extreme right of the line, he fastened his particular attention, for to these armies fell the task of delivering the decisive blow upon which the hope of speedy victory depended. To these two armies of the northern group Schlieffen allocated 16 army corps and 5 cavalry divisions, picked from the finest units of the Imperial Army. Foreseeing the likelihood that the Belgian fortresses of Liége, Namur and Antwerp and the French fortress of Maubeuge would be tenaciously defended and so would require the detachment of covering forces of considerable strength, Schlieffen provided for the reinforcement of his northern group from two sources : first, by two army corps withdrawn from the left wing armies as soon as the intentions of the enemy had become sufficiently defined, and second, by a second echelon of the 6 newly formed Ersatz corps.   The function of these reinforcements became the protection of lines of communication, the besieging of fortified positions which could not immediately be reduced and other like secondary missions, thereby relieving the main body of the right wing armies from any necessity of detaching an important fraction of their strength.

With an accuracy demonstrated by events, Schlieffen anticipated the main French concentration between Verdun and Belfort and an initial offensive directed into Alsace-Lorraine.   This offensive, it became the duty of the two German left wing armies to combat by executing a strategic retreat and by offering only enough resistance to keep the enemy occupied and to prevent any serious diversion of his forces, while the five armies of the offensive right wing pursued their advance and made ready to launch their decisive blow. Though the defensive attitude thus prescribed for the two left wing armies necessarily entailed a temporary abandonment of territory, Schlieffen was wholly ready to accept this disadvantage in order to achieve his larger aim.

The cardinal principle of Schlieffen's strategic conception resided in the concentration of the maximum strength in the five armies assigned to offensive operations and in their reinforcement by every available means.   Until the great outflanking movement had been completed, the two German left wing armies constituted no more than a counterfoil for the right.

During the years from 1906 to 1914 the Schlieffen Plan continued as the basis for the war-plans of the German General Staff even after its author had gone into retirement.   When advancing years and increasing physical infirmities made it obvious that Schlieffen could not long continue to perform the arduous duties of his post, the Emperor's choice of a successor fell upon Von Moltke, a nephew of the illustrious Prussian commander.

In the Franco-Prussian War Von Moltke the younger had served gallantly as a lieutenant of Grenadiers, and later after qualifying for staff duty had acted as aide-de-camp to his uncle, the Field Marshal.   At the latter's death he had become for a time the Emperor's personal aide, but during Schlieffen's régime he had not been a member of the select coterie admitted to the inner circles of the General Staff.   Instead, he had served with troops, commanding successively a regiment, a brigade and a division of the Imperial Guard.   It was with some reluctance and considerable misgivings that in 1904 Von Moltke acceded to the Emperor's request and accepted appointment as First Quartermaster-General of the General Staff, thereby becoming Schlieffen's chief deputy, and after a probationary period of two years succeeding him, on January 1, 1906.[6]

However lacking Von Moltke may subsequently have proved in qualities of moral leadership, officers high in authority through the years that he served at the head of the General Staff unite, almost without exception, to praise his soldierly qualities, his keen intelligence and his organizing abilities. Though ill-natured rumour often ascribed Von Moltke's appointment to a vainglorious desire on the Emperor's part to emulate his grandfather by the selection of a Von Moltke as his chief military adviser, Von Moltke the younger exerted an influence far from negligible in building up the German army of 1914. It is said that Schlieffen, a cavalry officer of the old school, for all his high qualities, was inclined to overlook or minimize the effect of mechanical development in modern armament,[7] but Von Moltke did not fall into the same error. The superior tactical training of the German army during the opening battles of the war, its skill in the use of machine-guns and in the technical arms, particularly in heavy artillery, and the development of military aviation were all due in no small measure to Von Moltke's foresight. For his share in the preparation of the magnificent war-machine with which Germany embarked upon the campaign of 1914, Von Moltke's countrymen owe him a debt which too often they seem inclined to forget.

In the domain of strategy he proved less fortunate. Though affecting to adopt the Schlieffen Plan in its entirety, Von Moltke introduced many modifications with unfortunate results and in so doing lost sight of the basic principles that governed its conception.

The first and not the least important of Von Moltke's modifications was his determination to respect the neutrality of Holland. Instead of crossing the corner of Dutch Limbourg that projects into Belgium as Von Schlieffen had planned to do, Von Moltke decided to restrict the German right wing armies to an invasion of Belgium. However praiseworthy from the stand-point of international ethics and of German political and economic policy, this decision involved important military complications, for it necessitated crowding the concentration of two armies into the area around Aix-la-Chapelle, thereby increasing the manifold problems of mobilization and supply at the most critical point of the German line. It required, moreover, the prompt reduction of the Belgian fortress of Liége as an

[6] In a collection of memoirs, posthumously published under the editorship of Countess von Moltke, *Erinnerungen, Briefe, Dokumente 1877–1916* (Der Kommende Tag A. G. Verlag, Stuttgart, 1922), Von Moltke has given a detailed account of events leading up to his appointment as successor to Schlieffen.
[7] See Lieut.-Col. Justrow's *Feldherr und Kriegstechnik* (Stalling, Oldenburg, 1933).

operation preliminary to the main advance of the German armies, instead of allowing them to turn the position from the north as Schlieffen had intended. Though careful plans were made for a rapid and powerful assault against the fortress, it proved an obstacle more formidable than Von Moltke anticipated.

More important still was the alteration in the character of the mission assigned to the two left wing German armies. Unable to reconcile himself to the surrender of German soil, even temporarily, Von Moltke sought to avoid this necessity by limiting the strategic retirement of the VI and VII Armies which Schlieffen had prescribed, and by preparing to meet the expected French offensive with a counter-stroke. To provide the strength necessary for this undertaking, Von Moltke eliminated in 1910 the proposed withdrawal of two army corps from the left wing armies, thus suppressing the principal reinforcement that Schlieffen had provided for the offensive right wing, and likewise he eliminated the second echelon of Ersatz troops, concentrating these forces instead in the vicinity of Metz. In addition, as new legislation made further forces available, Von Moltke assigned them not to the right wing armies but to the left, so that by 1914, the German VI and VII Armies had been increased from the 5 army corps originally contemplated by Schlieffen to 8½ army corps and 6 Ersatz divisions.

When the reorganization of the Russian army after its disastrous experience in Manchuria made it seem advisable to yield to the importunities of Austria and to strengthen the German forces on the eastern front, Von Moltke drew the requisite forces, 4½ army corps and a cavalry division, from the right wing armies.

In short, instead of following Schlieffen's basic conception, Von Moltke not only failed to increase the power of his right wing armies but weakened them, at the same time increasing the difficulty of their task by depriving them of reinforcements and by converting the mission of his left wing armies from a purely defensive to a partially offensive one. As a result when the campaign of 1914 opened the five armies of the German offensive right wing aggregated only 27½ army corps, instead of the 35½ that Schlieffen had planned, with no provision for their reinforcement or for their support from a second echelon.

It seems evident that even before the war Von Moltke was considering an enveloping manoeuvre by both wings, and came close to adopting the classical conception of Cannae that Schlieffen had rejected. When after the initial German successes at Sarrebourg and Morhange, Von Moltke permitted the counter-offensive of the VI and VII Armies to expand into a major operation, the unfortunate consequences more than justified Schlieffen's fears.

Neither Schlieffen nor Von Moltke appears to have taken serious account of the possibility of resolute resistance by the Belgian army, but on the other hand both fully anticipated the appearance of England in the ranks of Germany's enemies, and Schlieffen with astonishing foresight predicted that a British army some 100,000 strong would co-operate with the French on the left of their line. It seems to have been his view, however, as well as Von Moltke's, that the German right wing armies could execute their advance so rapidly and with forces so over-powering as to render British intervention ineffective to save the French from destruction.

Similarly the German General Staff foresaw the probable defection of Italy, the third member of the Triple Alliance, although as late as the fall of 1913 an agreement provided for the co-operation of an Italian army of 3 army corps and 2 cavalry divisions along the Upper Rhine. Von Moltke did not count heavily upon this aid, however, and Italy's declaration of neutrality did not materially affect Germany's war-plans.

Though the Schlieffen Plan as modified by Von Moltke and applied in an emasculated form failed of its purpose and was finally abandoned — not as has sometimes been supposed as a result of the Battle of the Marne, but a full forty-eight hours before the battle opened — it has nevertheless won wide-spread admiration from military authorities. German writers have stoutly averred that had Von Moltke adhered to Schlieffen's original conception, the whole outcome of the campaign and of the war itself would have been altered. An inquiry into such claims would lead far afield into the realm of speculation, and it is a matter that in its nature can never be settled. It is certain that the modifications introduced by Von Moltke contributed largely to the failure of the German plan of operations, but it seems, too, that Schlieffen himself, as well as Von Moltke, under-estimated the capacity of his adversaries, and especially the recuperative power of the French soldier.

Despite the fact that the German plan of operations of 1914 is generally known as the Schlieffen Plan,[8] it may well be doubted whether Count von Schlieffen would have acknowledged the paternity of the final product; surely he would have disputed its legitimacy. It is said that as Schlieffen lay on his death-bed in 1913, his last words were : "Make the right wing strong !"

[8] The term Schlieffen Plan as used herein refers to the Plan of 1905. In 1912 Schlieffen prepared a second plan premised upon a complete reorganization of the German army, and the formation of 51 army corps or Grand Divisions by a combination of Active and Reserve units. As in the earlier plan the main concentration of strength was on the right wing, but this plan, forecasting such a stabilization of the front as actually occurred in the fall of 1914, provided for an offensive extending from Belgium to the Swiss frontier. Inasmuch as Schlieffen's second plan was not adopted, it becomes a matter of merely academic interest.

In Von Moltke's failure to heed his predecessor's dying injunction, may be found one of the primary causes for Germany's defeat in the opening campaign of the war.[9]

[9] Particularly significant among the many discussions and analyses of the Schlieffen Plan are Gen. Gröner's *Das Testament des Grafen Schlieffen* (Mittler, Berlin, 1927) and Lieut.-Col. Förster's *Graf Schlieffen und der Weltkrieg* (Mittler, Berlin, 1921).

CHAPTER II

PLAN XVII

WHILE the German General Staff under the leadership of Schlieffen and Von Moltke matured its plans for the coming conflict, the French General Staff was no less active. The disastrous defeats of 1870 and 1871, which swept away the last vestiges of the military prestige that France retained as a heritage of the Napoleonic era, had shaken to its foundations the confidence of the French people in their army and its leaders, and had brought about a complete reorganization of the French military establishment. But despite every effort to efface the dark memories of Sedan and Metz and to return to the tradition of the armies of Marengo, Austerlitz and Jena, the French General Staff entertained no illusions as to its capacity for offensive action, and Plan I, the first of a long series envisaging war with Germany, which was promulgated in 1880, provided for a purely defensive resistance along the frontier which the loss of Metz had left virtually unprotected.

The completion of the fortifications of Verdun, Toul, Epinal and Belfort, under the direction of General Séré de Rivières, altered the situation, however, and in 1887 the French General Staff discarded its conservative, defensive policy. In a new plan, Plan VIII, it adopted a project for a general offensive directed against Alsace-Lorraine, with the recovery of the lost provinces as the initial and primary objective. Thereafter, throughout the succession of plans developed up to the outbreak of the war, including Plan XVII which governed the concentration of 1914, the offensive remained the keynote of French strategy.[1]

While the German General Staff under four successive leaders, Von Moltke, Von Waldersee, Von Schlieffen and Von Moltke the younger, had been permitted to pursue the preparation of its plans undisturbed, and the German army had received financial and political support in unstinted measure, the contrary had been the case in France. From the beginnings of the Third Republic, the French army became the victim of the vagaries of political influences to an

---

[1] For an analysis and discussion of the various French plans of concentration, see A. Marchand's *Plans de Concentration de 1871 à 1914* (Berger-Levrault, Paris, 1926).

astonishing degree.   The conspiracy of General Boulanger, the wave of anti-Semitism that accompanied the Dreyfus Case, and the anti-clerical crusade conducted under the ministry of General André, all had their effect on the army, and above all on the morale of its corps of professional officers.   Many officers, among whom Foch, a devout Catholic, affords a conspicuous example, found their careers impeded by reasons of birth, religion or political affiliations wholly unrelated to their professional capabilities, and many resigned their commissions in the face of discriminations imposed by political considerations.

The year 1911 proved a particularly turbulent and significant one in the international, political and military affairs of the French nation.   It was the year of the crisis of Agadir that brought relations between France and Germany to a point of highest tension and left the peace of Europe hanging by a thread.   The French plan of concentration then in force, Plan XVI, which had been promulgated two years before by General de Lacroix, followed the traditional policy of establishing the main area of assembly of the French armies near the German frontier preparatory to opening the campaign with an invasion of Alsace-Lorraine, and it took little account of the possibility of a German attack from the north, such as the German General Staff had already determined upon.   To General Michel, Vice-President of the Superior War Council and Commander in Chief designate, the plan seemed fraught with danger.   He had directed the fall manoeuvres of 1910 in the frontier region between Metz and Belfort in which forces representing the German army had been commanded by Galliéni, with Foch as his Chief of Staff, and those representing the French had been commanded by Pau, with De Castelnau as his Chief of Staff, while Joffre had directed the services of the rear.   The result of these exercises, conducted by the most distinguished French commanders, had been a stalemate which convinced Michel that the eastern frontier region was unsuitable for decisive operations by either side.   In the event of war, he concluded, the main conflict would occur not as his predecessors had assumed on the ground fought over in the campaign of 1870, but farther to the north on the historic battlefields of Flanders.

This thought formed the basis of a report that Michel submitted to the Minister of War, General Brun, in February 1911, in which he suggested an extensive regrouping of the French armies by the concentration of approximately 1,000,000 men between Lille and Rethel. and a corresponding reduction in the forces along the eastern frontier.   Though Michel's proposal constituted a radical departure from the conventional theory of the French General Staff, it did not alter the fundamental plan for an offensive at the outset of the campaign; but merely shifted to Belgium the offensive which all previous plans had projected against the German frontier, reducing the latter to a secondary operation.

It is noteworthy that the adoption of Michel's project would have entailed a French advance into Belgium immediately upon completion of the concentration and a violation of Belgian neutrality similar to the one already in course of preparation on the German side under the Schlieffen Plan.

The Michel Plan was not limited merely to an alteration of the bases of French strategy, for it also proposed a complete remodelling of the tables of organization of the army by abolishing Reserve divisions and combining existing Reserve regiments with Active regiments.   The purpose of these drastic changes was to attain a more effective utilization of reserve forces, and the result would have been to double the size of existing infantry divisions and to compel far-reaching modifications in cavalry and artillery units as well.

It was not until July 1911, that the plan came before the Superior War Council for its consideration.   Since February, when Michel had first advanced it, there had been four successive civilian ministries and in July the Minister of War was Messimy — who after several further turns of the political wheel again came into power in the summer of 1914.   Personally dubious of Michel's capacity and convinced after talking with Galliéni that the army generally shared his lack of confidence, Messimy thought little of Michel's plan and sought to obtain his resignation, but the latter refused to submit it, and the action of the Superior War Council upon his plan became a test of his authority.

It was hardly a propitious moment for the consideration of such a proposal.   Agadir had brought France and Germany to the brink of war, and conversations were in progress between representatives of the French and British General Staffs looking towards common action.   It seemed anything but a suitable time to embark upon a complex reorganization of the army or upon a scheme of concentration that might alienate British support by the implication that France was inclined to disregard her duty under the Treaty of 1839 which guaranteed Belgium's territorial integrity.

Only the portion of the Michel Plan relating to the reorganization of the army came formally before the Superior War Council for consideration, and the strategic aspects of the new scheme of concentration received only incidental consideration.   At a stormy session, an account of which, contrary to all precedent, appeared in the press, the Council overwhelmingly voted down Michel's proposals, and Michel found himself in a minority of one, with Galliéni, Pau, Dubail and Joffre, among others, in opposition.   The principal basis for the general dissent seems to have been the delay in the concentration which the combination of Active and Reserve forces suggested by Michel would have caused. Due to the fact that units could not reach their full strength until reservists had joined the colours, it was estimated that six days would be lost and the French concentration would thus fall behind the German and give the enemy an important initial advantage. The defeat of Michel's plan for reorganizing the army was apparently accepted as equivalent to a general vote of lack of confidence, and though the discussion extended to the proposed modification of the zone of concentration, no vote was taken upon it.

The result confirmed Messimy in his opinion and brought about Michel's downfall. By Presidential Decree the post of Vice-President of the Superior War Council which he held was abolished and a new post, that of Chief of the General Staff of the Army was created, of which the incumbent became automatically designated as Commander in Chief in time of war. The task of selecting the first Chief of the General Staff fell to the Premier, Caillaux, the same who was later destined to play a dramatic role in war-time politics, and to Messimy, his Minister of War. The obvious choices were Galliéni or Pau, at the time the outstanding figures in French military circles, but Galliéni felt that he had disqualified himself by the part that he had taken in Michel's overthrow and also by the fact that his service had been mainly with the Colonial Army, while Pau, on being offered the appointment, stipulated that he must formally be accorded full liberty in the selection of general officers and in their assignment to command. This condition amounted in substance to renunciation of civilian control of the army, and Caillaux and Messimy were unwilling to surrender their ministerial prerogatives to one whose political affiliations consisted in large part of elements hostile to the Caillaux Ministry.

A compromise candidate became necessary, and it seemed that Joffre, then the youngest member of the Superior War Council, had all the necessary qualifications. He was only fifty-nine at the time, thus insuring the possibility of continuity in office for at least six years. Like Pau and Galliéni, he was a veteran of the War of 1870, and although his career had been less spectacular than theirs, he had a long record of distinguished accomplishment, including a period of active service in the colonies followed by nearly ten years in France as a division and corps commander. Since 1909, he had been a member of the Superior War Council and Director of the Services of the Rear, a post which had afforded him ample opportunity to gain familiarity with the manifold and complex problems of the mobilization, transportation and supply of field armies.

Although by no means devoid of friends in political circles, Joffre had studiously refrained from becoming conspicuous in controversy or involved in intrigue, and beyond the fact that he was known as a convinced republican, he had not closely identified himself with any party or group. His personal character was beyond reproach, and his temperament seemed calculated to reduce to a minimum the likelihood of friction with his civilian superiors. Accordingly by a decree of July 28, 1911, Joffre became Chief of the French General Staff and assumed the post that led him to the chief command of his country's armies at the outset of the Great War.[2]

For the next three years Joffre justified his selection by maintaining cordial relations with four successive ministries and in return received in practice the authority that Pau had demanded should be formally delegated. His control of the selection of his subordinates in the higher grades became absolute. Without friction but with greatest firmness he dominated the Superior War Council, which ceased in effect to be a deliberative body and became transformed into a medium through which the Commander in Chief transmitted decisions of important policy to his principal subordinates. At sessions of the Council, Joffre's decisions were rarely questioned and never disapproved, and he became in fact as well as in name France's supreme military authority.[3] The responsibility for the conception no less than the execution of Plan XVII, which controlled the concentration and early operations of the French armies in 1914, may be laid to him personally. To his credit it must be said that Joffre never sought to evade this responsibility.

The bases of Plan XVI, which Joffre found in force when he assumed command, had been laid in 1907, and much had occurred in the interval. The rehabilitation of the Russian army and a closer understanding with the British General Staff gave rise to the belief that France could reasonably expect a greater measure of cooperation from the other two Entente Powers, while improved diplo-

[2] A summary but authoritative account of the reorganization of the French army after the Franco-Prussian War and of the preparations of the French General Staff between 1871 and 1914 is contained in the French Official History, *Les Armées Françaises dans la Grande Guerre* (Ministère de la Guerre — Service Historique, Paris), hereinafter cited as *Fr. O. H.*, Tome I, Vol. 1. The Michel Plan and the minutes of the session of the Superior War Council which rejected it appear as Documents 3 and 4 of the Annex to the above volume.

A detailed account of Michel's proposals and of the circumstances leading up to their rejection is to be found in the testimony taken by the Parliamentary Commission which in 1919 inquired into the loss of the Briey mines (*Procés-verbaux de la Commission d'enquête sur le rôle et la situation de la metallurgie en France* — Documents Parlementaires de la Chambre des Deputés de Paris, session 1919), particularly in the testimony of Generals Michel and Messimy.

[3] Gen. Alexandre in *Avec Joffre d'Agadir à Verdun* (Berger-Levrault, Paris, 1933) has given an account of Joffre's efforts to strengthen the French army in the pre-war years.

matic relations with Italy further led to the hope that the latter would be unwilling to follow Germany and Austria into a war involving France and England, so that modifications in the French dispositions for the defence of the Alpine frontier seemed permissible. Improvements of the railroad systems in the eastern zone of concentration made it possible to move the area in which the French armies were to assemble nearer to the German frontier, while on the other hand like improvements in the German railways in the regions adjacent to Belgium, and especially the construction of extensive debarkation facilities east of Malmédy, lent weight to the view that the German armies were planning to march across Belgium and that consequently further provision must be made to meet such a contingency. In the face of these considerations Joffre prepared and soon submitted to the Minister of War a new plan, Plan XVII, that was destined to become one of the most controversial documents of modern military history.

Unlike the Schlieffen Plan, Plan XVII was not strictly speaking a plan of operations, for it did not purport to map out a whole campaign designed to defeat the enemy and achieve final victory, but merely established the method and place of concentration, fixed the composition of the respective armies and declared the Commander in Chief's intention to assume the offensive. While the provisions of Plan XVII necessarily limited the French High Command in the application of its strategy, Joffre took the position that the operations of the field armies after concentration rested wholly within the responsibility of the Commander in Chief, and that a wide margin of discretion should be allowed in any preconceived plan to permit of variations to suit developments.

Discarding the suggestions offered by Michel, Joffre followed in Plan XVII the tradition of Plan XVI and its predecessors by concentrating the main body of the French armies in the region of the German frontier with a view to an offensive operation in Alsace-Lorraine upon the completion of the concentration. Upon the promulgation of a decree of mobilization, Plan XVII provided for the formation of five field armies, two independent groups of Reserve divisions and an autonomous cavalry corps, comprising the major part of the French land forces.

Four armies, the First, Second, Third and Fifth, with headquarters respectively at Epinal, Neufchâteau, Verdun and Rethel, formed the first line and furnished the troops required to cover the mobilization, while another army, the Fourth, with headquarters at St. Dizier, remained in reserve, ready to move into the line either to the left between the Third and Fifth Armies in the event of an enemy advance through Belgium, or to the right between the Third and

Second Armies in the less likely but possible contingency of a German invasion of Switzerland.   The two independent groups of Reserve divisions of three divisions each were placed at opposite ends of the front to cover the flanks of the zone of concentration.   The cavalry corps of three cavalry divisions was to assemble in the vicinity of Mezières, on the left of the front of the Fifth Army, where operating initially under the direct orders of the Commander in Chief, it would be ready to move into southern Belgium in the event that the German right wing armies violated Belgian neutrality.

Though not officially included in Plan XVII, the concentration of the British army, under the transparent pseudonym Army W. (War Office), was provided for by separate understanding with the British General Staff, in the triangle Maubeuge-Busigny-Hirson, with headquarters at Le Cateau.

In addition to the forces assigned to the five field armies, the French Commander in Chief had available four divisions from the Active army, three of them drawn from the North African forces and one, assuming Italy remained neutral, from the southeastern frontier. Of the 25 Reserve divisions which formed the bulk of the French Reserve army, 14 were allocated to the field armies and the balance distributed among the garrisons of the fortresses and fortified towns within the Army Zone.   In principle, garrison troops did not fall within the jurisdiction of the Commander in Chief, except in case of emergency, but during the Campaign of the Marne a substantial proportion actually came under Joffre's command, and frequently participated in operations not strictly of a defensive nature, though no account was taken of them under Plan XVII.

Upon the completion of the concentration, on the thirteenth day after the date of mobilization, Joffre declared in general terms his intention to assume the offensive.

Whatever the circumstances, it is the Commander in Chief's intention to advance with all forces united to the attack of the German armies.

The action of the French armies will be developed in two major operations: one, on the right, in the country between the wooded district of the Vosges and the Moselle below Toul; the other, on the left, north of the line Verdun-Metz.

These two operations will be closely connected by forces operating on the Hauts de Meuse and in the Woevre.[4]

Apart from the foregoing general statement of the Commander in Chief's intentions, which in fact foreshadowed the two great offen-

---

[4] The text of Plan XVII and supplemental data appears in *Fr. O. H.* Tome I, Vol. 1, Annex, Docs. 8, 9 and 10.   See also English translation in Appendix 9 to the British Official History, *Military Operations — France and Belgium* 1914, Vol. 1 (Macmillan, London, 1928), hereinafter cited as *Br. O. H.*

sives in Lorraine and in the Ardennes with which the French armies began the war, Plan XVII did not attempt to prescribe the course of operations after the outbreak of hostilities. It was thus a plan of concentration as distinguished from a plan of operations or a plan of campaign.

The ultimate test of any military plan is its success or failure at the crucial moment when it is applied against the enemy. That Plan XVII failed of its objectives and caused incalculable fruitless sacrifices is beyond dispute ; and the fact that the Schlieffen Plan, as modified by Von Moltke, also proved unsuccessful afforded the French little consolation. The bitter criticism that has been levelled against the pre-war dispositions of the French High Command [5] seems based upon two principal grounds, first, the determination to assume the offensive at the outset of the campaign, and second, the failure to take sufficient account of the sweeping enveloping movement that carried the German armies through Belgium west of the Meuse River and brought the left wing of the Allied armies to the verge of disaster. Though there can be no doubt that in theory, with the wisdom gained after the event, both criticisms are well-founded, there is much to be said in extenuation of Joffre and his officers.

An abiding faith in the efficacy of the offensive had become a primary article in the military creed of the generation of French officers who reached maturity during the years following the Franco-Prussian War ; a natural reaction, perhaps, to the painful memory of the surrender of Bazaine and his army at Metz which survived as a vivid example of the contrary method. As soon as the rehabilitation of the French army permitted, the offensive became and remained the basis of the war-plans formulated by successive commanders.

When Joffre took command in 1911, the cult of the offensive was reaching its zenith. Though he had graduated from the *Ecole Polytéchnique*, Joffre had not received the coveted "brevet," the honour diploma ordinarily essential to open the gateway of rapid advancement in France's peace-time army, and his early training and experience as an officer of engineers in the colonies had been mostly of a practical sort that left little time for study of the theory of war or the principles of strategy. Fully conscious of his deficiency in these fields in which Foch, Lanrezac and others of his contemporaries

[5] Among the many analyses and critiques of Plan XVII and Joffre's early strategy, two may be particularly cited: Lieut.-Col. de Thomasson's *Le Revers de 1914 et ses Causes* (Berger-Levrault, Paris, 1919), and Lieut.-Col. Grouard's *La Conduite de la Guerre jusqu'à la Bataille de la Marne* (Chapelot, Paris, 1922). More controversial and marked by animus is Gen. Percin's *1914* (Michel, Paris, 1919). See also Gen. Revol's *Le Plan XVII* (Payot, Paris, 1920).

excelled, Joffre took pains to surround himself with younger men who had achieved particular distinction as officers of brilliancy and promise. These men, upon whom he relied heavily for advice and guidance, Joffre found in the main ardent devotees of the *offensive à outrance*, which has most often been associated with the name of one of its ablest exponents, Lieutenant-Colonel de Grandmaison, then Chief of the Operations Section of the French General Staff.

Adopting as an axiom that only by offensive action can positive results be achieved and the enemy destroyed, De Grandmaison proceeded to the conclusion that the offensive spirit must be preserved at whatever sacrifice. The enemy must be sought out and attacked, whenever and wherever found. The choice of battle-ground became immaterial, and all incidental risks could be disregarded. Liaison with adjacent units became of minor importance ; advance, flank and rear-guards, indeed all classical precautions, could be ignored as mere dissipations of strength, for an attack was guaranteed from failure, if only it could be conducted swiftly enough and with enough determination. Trenches, barbed-wire and even artillery preparation, with its unavoidable delay, could have no part in such a philosophy in which imprudence became a virtue.

Reduced to the terms of the company and platoon, this doctrine made war a matter of pathetic simplicity ; a series of glorious charges, risky to be sure, but without soul-trying waits and uncertainties, and best of all, without the arduous details more befitting a day-labourer than a fighting man. It was a doctrine of ardent youth and fiery patriotism, with the stirring appeal of a martial bugle. Fervently preached by the most eloquent and brilliant soldiers of France, it is small wonder that in the years just before the war, it had permeated all grades of the military hierarchy and had set its stamp not only upon Army Regulations, but upon the plan of campaign as well.

Inevitably, the theory as taught by De Grandmaison and other high-ranking officers not infrequently reached the point of absurdity, and its misapplication, particularly by officers in the lower grades, led to a reckless disregard of all other tactical considerations too often with tragic consequences. It became responsible, as we shall see, for deficiencies of all sorts in the various arms of the French service, and in the early battles of the war, efforts to apply it cost thousands of lives for no appreciable results. Yet despite its exaggerations and obvious defects it cannot be dismissed as pure folly. The value of prompt and unrelenting offensive action, especially in its moral aspects, has again and again been demonstrated by great soldiers from Napoleon to Foch. It may well be doubted whether without a firm belief in this doctrine the French armies could have found courage to retreat before the enemy for two agonizing weeks, and turning in their tracks over night, launch the offensive that produced the victory of the Marne.

With the idea of the offensive firmly imbedded in the mentality of soldiers and politicians alike, it would have required more influence and more intellectual independence than Joffre possessed to discard the offensive as the basic theme of Plan XVII. The adoption of a defensive policy at any part of the front would necessarily have entailed the surrender at the outset of the campaign of a relatively large area of French territory. A course so contrary to the national temperament and traditions would beyond doubt have aroused such popular and political criticism, that no government or Commander in Chief could have withstood the violence of the storm. Nor could any plan have received the co-operation and support of all ranks that did not require the French armies to seek out the enemy.

The neglect to provide an adequate defence against the manoeuvre of the Schlieffen Plan, however, seems less understandable and less defensible. The failure of the French High Command to prepare for the defence of the northern frontier resulted in the loss, almost without a struggle, of the most valuable industrial region of northern France and compelled Joffre to resort to a hastily improvised regrouping of his forces under the very guns of the enemy. The principal explanation seems to lie in a major miscalculation by the French Intelligence Service with respect to the use that the Germans proposed to make of their reserve forces. The French steadfastly believed that German Reserve corps would not appear in the main line of battle at the opening of the campaign. Had this been true, the German right wing could hardly have been made strong enough to permit of its extension west of the Meuse River ; but it was not true.[6] In fact, the Germans used their Reserve corps on the same footing as the army corps of their Active army, and the three right wing German armies that crossed the Meuse included six Reserve corps, which approximately accounted for the initial numerical superiority of the German right wing over the Allied left.

In point of fact, only some such plan as that suggested by Michel in 1911 would have provided a complete and effective riposte to the manoeuvre of the Schlieffen Plan ; but aside from the practical difficulties that would have beset Joffre, had he attempted to

[6] The Chief of the Intelligence Section of the French General Staff, General Dupont, in his book, *Le Haut Commandement Allemand en 1914* (Chapelot, Paris, 1922), denies that any such miscalculation was made, but his contention is hardly sustained by the reports on the enemy Order of Battle furnished to Joffre by the Intelligence Section during the opening weeks of the campaign ; for example, the report of August 16, 1914 (*Fr. O. H.*, Tome I, Vol. 1, Annex, Doc. 342), which contains no mention of Reserve corps in the German Order of Battle as then estimated by the French Staff. See Appendix V.

adopt the scheme proposed by his immediate predecessor, which had resulted in the latter's downfall, there were other serious objections to the concentration of important French forces along the Belgian frontier.   Such a concentration would inevitably have lent colour to the German contention that France herself had no intention of observing her obligations under the Treaty of 1839, and the German invasion of the unfortunate buffer-state, instead of appearing to the world as the ruthless subordination of a solemn covenant to military expediency, would have seemed no more than a justifiable forestalling of similar action on France's part.   Under such circumstances England's active participation might well have become doubtful and Italy's neutrality jeopardized.   It seems probable, too, that France would have lost in great measure the moral sympathy of the neutral world that ultimately played so important a part in enlisting the decisive intervention of the United States and the other nations of the western hemisphere.

Without going to the extreme advocated by Michel, however, it seems difficult to justify the total neglect to provide modern means of defence for the northern regions or the failure to take full advantage of such means as were already available, and in particular the extent to which the fortifications of Maubeuge were permitted to become obsolete and to fall into disrepair.[7]

In justice it must be said that Plan XVII made greater provision for the eventuality of a German invasion through Belgium than any other of the numerous plans that preceded it.   But it did not go far enough, for it assumed that the German advance would be limited to the eastern and southeastern part of Belgium, instead of the much wider movement which Schlieffen envisaged.   In part, this assumption seems to have been based upon a belief, privately entertained in French military circles, that Belgium would acquiesce in the passage of German armies across her territory, provided that their march did not extend east of the Meuse and that they did not attempt active operations on the left bank of the river.[8]   In fact the German Government made no such proposal to Belgium and could not have done so consistently with the Schlieffen Plan.[9]

[7] Joffre was firmly of the opinion that by reason of the great industrial area which extended unbroken to the frontier, Lille could not be successfully defended, and that no attempt should be made to do so ; but French military opinion, though predominately in accord, was not unanimous.   See Gen. Percin's *Lille* (Grasset, Paris, 1919) and Gen. Lebas' *Places fortes et fortifications pendant la guerre de* 1914–1918 (Payot, Paris).

[8] Gen. Lanrezac in *Le Plan de Campagne Français* (Payot, Paris, rev. ed. 1929) dwells upon this point ; see also Gen. Dupont, *op. cit.*

[9] Maurice Paléologue, formerly an official of the French Foreign Office and Ambassador to Russia, in an article *Un Prélude à l'Invasion de Belgique*, Revue des Deux Mondes, October 1, 1932, has alleged that the French Intelligence Service had full information of the Schlieffen Plan as early as 1904, through the betrayal of a high-ranking German officer.   Any information thus obtained, however, does not seem to have been given credence.

The failure of the initial French offensives, ill-conceived and faulty in execution, and the failure of the French High Command to appreciate the scope of Schlieffen's strategy combined to bring about the collapse of Plan XVII within three weeks of the declaration of war.

CHAPTER III

COMPARISONS

A THOROUGH discussion and comparison of the armies that opposed each other in the Campaign of the Marne would require a volume in itself and would lead into technical and controversial fields far beyond the scope of the present work. Nevertheless, before entering upon the narrative of military operations, it seems desirable to review under a few principal headings the composition and condition of the German and Allied armies and some of their salient points of similarity and difference.

MAN-POWER AND EFFECTIVES

IN literature dealing with the war and its origins, statistics and tabulations abound purporting to set forth the relative military power of the belligerent nations. The data thus given is often based upon computations made at different times and for a wide variety of purposes, and not infrequently theoretical estimates have been confounded or combined with realities in such a way as to produce wholly misleading conclusions. It seems profitless for present purposes to attempt to harmonize the welter of conflicting figures under which the facts lie buried, for we are concerned here only with the restricted question of the effective strength of the opposing forces during the Campaign of the Marne.

It seems sufficient to note that in the opening weeks of the war, despite the difference in population between France and Germany and the corresponding discrepancy in their total available man-power, the Allied armies enjoyed a substantial numerical superiority over the German forces employed against them on the western front.

In round numbers, the seven German field armies that participated in the Campaign of the Marne aggregated 1,700,000 men, including cavalry, Ersatz and Landwehr units and supporting and auxiliary troops. The Allied forces arrayed against them consisted of 1,650,000 French, 125,000 British and 175,000 Belgians, or a total of approximately 1,950,000 men. Though the Allies thus had a superiority in numbers amounting to some 250,000 men, the benefits were more apparent than real, for the German army enjoyed a significant advantage over their principal adversary, the French, in the quality of the troops that constituted their first line of defence.

Both in France and in Germany, the armies called into being by the decrees of mobilization of August 1, 1914, comprised three principal component parts, the Active [1] army, the Reserve army and a third category known in France as the Territorial army and in Germany as the Landwehr. Both countries for years before the war had relied upon national conscription, but while in Germany out of each class of young men reaching the military age of 20 only 50% to 55% were accepted for service in the army, the French, applying a less rigid standard of physical fitness and general aptitude, accepted between 78% and 82%. After completing two years of military service, the German soldier remained for the next 5½ years in the Reserve, subject to call for periods of training, and the German Reserve army was thus composed of men between the ages of 22 and 28. The similar period of service in the Reserve army for the French soldier continued for 14 years, so that the French Reserve army included all men who had received military training between the ages of 23 and 37. The German Landwehr included all men who had graduated from the Reserve up to the age of 39, while the corresponding category in France, the Territorial army, embraced all former reservists up to the age of 48.

In consequence, the units of the German army of all three major classifications were composed of men who were younger, more vigorous and more carefully selected than the men of corresponding units in the French army, a factor of by no means negligible importance, but one that seems to be frequently overlooked in estimates of the relative military value of the two armies.[2]

ORGANIZATION OF THE GERMAN ARMY

At the outbreak of the war, approximately 90% of the total strength of the German army was concentrated in the seven field armies on

[1] The term Active is used in preference to Regular in designating troops actually serving with the colours, inasmuch as the French and German armies, unlike the "Regular Armies" of the United States and England, were not composed of professional soldiers.

[2] For figures on effectives of the various armies, see *Fr. O. H.*, Tome I, Vol. 1 ; *Br. O. H.*; the German Official History, *Der Weltkrieg* 1914–1918, Vol. 1 (Mittler, Berlin), hereinafter cited as *G. O. H.*; the Belgian Official History, *L'Action de l'Armée Belge. Période du 31 Juillet au 31 Décembre 1914*, hereinafter cited as *Bel. O. H.* and also the Report of the First Subcommittee of the Parliamentary Committee of Inquiry established by the German National Assembly, August 21, 1919, Addendum II, *Tables of Strength of Military Forces of Allied and Central Powers* by General von Montgelas — English translation in *Official German Documents relating to the World War* (Carnegie Endowment).

the western front, comprising 22 Active army corps, 14 Reserve corps, two Reserve divisions, 4 cavalry corps (10 cavalry divisions), 6 Ersatz divisions and 14 brigades of Landwehr, exclusive of miscellaneous units and auxiliary troops.[3]

The normal German army corps numbered approximately 42,500 men of all ranks, arms and services and consisted of two infantry divisions and corps troops. The latter, at the disposal of the corps commander, consisted of a battalion of Jäger infantry — light infantry generally corresponding to the French Chasseur battalions — detachments of signal, engineer and bridging troops, field hospitals and ambulance sections, and supply and combat trains. In addition, the army corps of the Active army included in their corps troops a regiment of heavy artillery (16 150 mm. howitzers) and an aviation detachment of 12 aeroplanes, with which the Reserve corps were not provided.

The two infantry divisions, which constituted the backbone of both the Active army corps and the Reserve corps, consisted of two brigades each, and each brigade was in turn composed of two infantry regiments (3 battalions) of approximately 3200 officers and men with a machine-gun company of 6 guns for each regiment (section of 2 guns per battalion).

A material difference existed in the artillery complement of the divisions of the Active army corps and of the Reserve corps, for whereas the former were equipped with an artillery brigade of 12 6-gun batteries (54 77 mm. guns and 18 105 mm. light howitzers), the latter had only 6 batteries (36 77 mm. guns) with no artillery of heavy calibre. In addition to engineer and signal detachments and auxiliary troops, a cavalry regiment (4 squadrons) was attached to each infantry division.

The German peace-time army included 217 infantry regiments, a surplus of 17 over the number required to provide each Active army corps with its full complement of 8 regiments, and this surplus was distributed upon mobilization among the Reserve divisions, giving to many, though not all, of them a leaven of Active troops, so that some Reserve divisions included a brigade of Active troops and some others a single regiment. The policy thus adopted notably enhanced the combat value of the Reserve units affected.

In addition to the divisional cavalry, the German armies included also 4 autonomous cavalry corps, two of them of 3 cavalry divisions and two of them of 2 cavalry divisions. Each cavalry division in-

---

[3] The German forces on the Russian front, the VIII Army, comprised 3 Active army corps, 1 Reserve corps, a Reserve division, a Landwehr division, a Cavalry division, and miscellaneous garrison troops of Reserve and Landwehr units. See Appendix II for details of distribution on the western front.

cluded 3 brigades of 2 regiments each and a mounted machine-gun section (6 guns), as well as a group of horse artillery (12 77 mm. guns).   As infantry support, the German cavalry divisions, in contrast to the French, had one to three Jäger infantry battalions permanently attached to them, each with a machine-gun company (6 guns) and a motor transport column.   The total strength of the German cavalry division came to approximately 5200 men.

The 6 Ersatz divisions that took part in the Campaign of the Marne were composed of supernumerary reservists who had not been previously assigned to organized units upon completion of their military service.   In quality and training these units may, therefore, be assimilated to the status of Reserve divisions, though lacking in some cases the full complement of equipment and material.

To protect lines of communication, to guard supply centres and to escort munition and supply trains, each of the seven German armies had one or more brigades of Landwehr, composed of two infantry regiments, a squadron of cavalry and a battery of field artillery (6 77 mm. guns).   The Landwehr units that took an active part in the operations with which we are concerned were drawn in the main from the younger classes of Landwehr, and were thus in age and training the equals or superiors of many of the French reserve units.[4]

ORGANIZATION OF THE FRENCH ARMY

IN its main lines the organization of the French army paralleled that of the German.   Plan XVII provided for the formation of five field armies, but events soon required an increase in this number to seven, so that for the greater part of the campaign nine Allied armies, including the British and the Belgians, opposed the seven German armies.   At the outbreak of hostilities the French mobile forces consisted of 21 army corps, 25 Reserve divisions and 10 cavalry divisions, as well as 4 infantry divisions, an infantry brigade and a cavalry brigade drawn from the North African forces.

During the course of the campaign, the French armies received important reinforcements, replacing losses from the depots and obtaining support from the Reserve divisions and Territorial divisions constituting part of the garrisons of the fortresses in the Army Zone.   The garrisons of Verdun, Maubeuge and of numerous smaller strongholds made important contributions to the French operations.   The German armies, on the other hand, constantly moving farther away from their depots and their base, received no

4 Dealing with the organization of the German Army, see Prof. d'Almeida's *L'Armée Allemande avant et pendant la guerre de* 1914–1918 (Berger-Levrault, Paris, 1919), and Gen. Buat's *L'Armée Allemande pendant la guerre de* 1914–1918 (Chapelot, Paris, 1920).

substantial reinforcements or replacements until after the stabilization of the front at the end of the campaign.

The typical French army corps was slightly smaller than the German, amounting to approximately 40,000 men, but in composition
resembled it closely. Two infantry divisions constituted the principal component part of the French army corps ; but the corps troops
included a brigade of two regiments of Reserve infantry (2 battalions
each), a cavalry regiment (4 squadrons) and a complement of artillery consisting of 12 4-gun batteries (48 75 mm. guns), in addition
to a company of engineers and auxiliary troops. A French corps
commander thus had at his disposal forces considerably more substantial than the commander of a German corps. In the French
army, however, aviation units and all artillery of calibres heavier
than 75 mm. were army troops.

Each French infantry division consisted of two brigades of two
infantry regiments each, in which each regiment comprised 3 battalions with a machine-gun section of 2 guns per battalion. The
divisional artillery consisted of 3 groups of 75 mm. guns (36 guns)
and the divisional cavalry of 1 squadron, instead of the full regiment
allotted to the German infantry divisions.

The Reserve divisions, which were not organized into corps, differed slightly in composition from the divisions of the Active army
due to the fact that the Reserve infantry regiments had only 2 battalions instead of 3, but to make up for this deficiency, each brigade
had 3 regiments instead of 2, so that the total number of battalions
remained the same. Following the same principle that the Germans
employed, the French sought to give cohesion to their Reserve divisions by attaching to each Reserve brigade a battalion of Chasseurs
from the Active army.

In theory, the Territorial divisions corresponded in organization
to Reserve divisions, but in practice they lacked an important part
of their regulation materiel, notably machine-guns and artillery.

Of the 10 French cavalry divisions, only three were segregated into
corps organization at the beginning of the campaign. The remainder operated separately, or were combined into temporary
corps. The French cavalry division consisted of 3 brigades of 2
regiments (4 squadrons) each with a machine-gun section (2 guns)
to each brigade. It was accompanied by a horse-artillery detachment
of two 4-gun batteries (8 75 mm. guns) and an infantry support of a
cyclist detachment (324 men), but had no motor transport. The
strength of a French cavalry division amounted to approximately
4500 men. In numbers, as well as in artillery and effective supporting infantry, it thus fell considerably short of the German cavalry
division.

INFANTRY

BEFORE the war, the training of both French and German infantry tended to emphasize the importance of offensive action and to deprecate anything that might diminish an aggressive attitude. Especially was this true in France, where the extreme doctrine of the *offensive à outrance* led to a disregard of all other considerations, with the result that the German infantry entered the war with a higher degree of tactical versatility and better prepared than their adversaries to deal with the problems of modern armament which neither had fully foreseen. From the outset the Germans displayed an understanding of defensive organization and an appreciation of the value of positions protected by entrenchments and barbed-wire that the French did not equal for many weeks.

Neither in France nor in Germany had the potentialities of the machine-gun been fully recognized despite the lessons of the Manchurian and Balkan campaigns, and both armies, as well as the British and Belgians, were initially limited to a section of two guns for each infantry battalion. On both sides, the presence of enemy machine-guns constituted a frequently employed explanation of the failure of an infantry unit to advance or to attain its objectives, but it does not seem that in fact either side enjoyed any marked superiority in these weapons at the beginning of the campaign, though the Germans excelled their opponents in their tactical use.

CAVALRY [5]

TRAINED and equipped for dismounted fighting, liberally endowed with supporting infantry with trucks to transport them, and with light artillery half again as numerous as the French, the German cavalry operated effectively and in realistic fashion ; but the doctrine of the offensive again contributed to the notably unsatisfactory performance of the French cavalry during the Campaign of the Marne. Adhering to the romantic tradition of an earlier day, with a faith in the efficacy of the *arme blanche* befitting the descendants of Murat and Lasalle, the French found themselves unable to cope with the more practical, if less picturesque, methods of their opponents. The German cavalry had no interest in charges or in sabre duels, and hastened to take refuge behind its infantry support, never far away,

[5] An authoritative account of the operations of the German cavalry is given by Gen. von Poseck, Chief of Staff of the German 1st Cavalry Corps (Von Richthofen), in *Die Deutsche Kavallerie in Belgien und Frankreich* 1914 (Mittler, Berlin, 1921). For an account of the French cavalry, see Capt. F. Gazin's *La Cavalerie Française dans la Guerre Mondiale* (Payot, Paris, 1930) and Col. Boucherie's *Historique du Corps de Cavalerie Sordet* (Lavauzelle, Paris, 1924). See also for a general discussion of the role of cavalry Gen. Brandt's *Moderne Kavallerie* (Mittler, Berlin, 1931).

armed with machine-guns and entrenched behind barbed-wire. The French troopers, equipped only with a single-action, short-range carbine of an antiquated 1890 model, with only 48 rounds of ammunition and no bayonet,[6] had no chance of engaging their enemy on equal terms and could only retire as best they might, with the hope of later catching some isolated mounted patrol off its guard.

From the very early days of the campaign, a chronic state of exhaustion rendered the French cavalry corps that operated on the left wing of the Allied line all but useless. While this may undoubtedly be attributed in large part to the difficulty and variety of the missions assigned it by the High Command, the result seems to have been due as well to the fact that the French cavalryman's qualities as a horse-master by no means equalled the grace and skill with which, in general, he handled his mount. Instead of dismounting at every opportunity to ease his horse of its burden, many instances are of record where French cavalry units remained in the saddle for hours at a time while halted or advancing along crowded roads at a snail's pace. The unnecessary fatigue thus imposed both on men and animals contributed materially to the inability of Sordet's Corps to play a more useful part.

ARTILLERY

THE most notable difference between the French and German armies appeared in their artillery. In the heavier calibres the Germans held an overwhelming superiority, though it has perhaps been over-emphasized in accounting for the results of the early battles.

The heavy artillery complement of each German infantry division of the Active army consisted of 3 6-gun batteries of 105 mm. light howitzers (18 guns), range 6000 metres, and in addition each Active army corps had 16 heavy 150 mm. howitzers, range 8000 metres. The various armies were further provided with a complement, altered from time to time, of 210 mm. mortars and of guns of 100 mm., 130 mm. and 150 mm., with ranges varying from 9000 to 14,000 metres. The aggregate of German heavy artillery, so distributed, may be approximately stated as 3500 pieces, including 1500 light 105 mm. howitzers, 1000 heavy 150 mm. howitzers and 1000 mortars and guns of assorted calibres and ranges.

To oppose this formidable mass, the French had only a total of some 300 heavy pieces, including 104 Rimhailho 155 mm. guns, range 6000 metres, 96 short 120 mm. guns, range 5000 metres, and 100 long 120 mm. guns (1878 model), range 9000 metres. Although

---

[6] In the earlier stages of trench warfare, it was not uncommon for French cavalrymen, utilized dismounted as infantry, to take their lances with them into the trenches in lieu of bayonets.

before the war arrangements had been made to equip the French army with 105 mm. guns, these were still in process of manufacture at the outbreak of hostilities and did not appear on the front until the end of September 1914.

Though the German advantage in heavy artillery speaks for itself and undoubtedly exerted a powerful influence, the French enjoyed a marked, if not wholly equivalent, superiority in light artillery, for the French 75's out-numbered the corresponding German 77's and out-ranked them both in range and effectiveness.

Each French army corps was equipped with 120 75 mm. guns, apportioned 9 4-gun batteries (36 guns) to each of the two divisions and 12 4-gun batteries (48 guns) as corps artillery, while the German corps of the Active army had only 108 77 mm. guns, divided into 9 6-gun batteries (54 guns) for each of their two divisions, and the German Reserve corps had only a total of 72 guns, 6 batteries per division ; with no corps artillery.

Though in the early stages of the war the French appear rarely to have taken advantage of the extreme range of their 75, its carrying power was nevertheless substantially greater than that of the German 77, 6700 metres against 5300 metres for shrapnel and 8500 metres against 8000 metres for high-explosive. It had the further advantage of greater precision and rapidity of fire, and its lower wheel base made it both steadier and less visible to hostile observation.

The higher effectiveness of the 75 was derived in great measure, too, from the heavier charge carried by its shells.   The total weight of the French projectile was 5.2 kilograms with a charge weighing .65 kgms., while the total weight of the German 77 projectile was 6.8 kgms. with a charge of only .16 kgms. The percentage of effectiveness of the 75 thus became 13% as against 2.5% for the 77.   The same superiority in munitions also existed for the French artillery of heavier calibres as against corresponding German guns, and this fact to some slight degree served to offset the latter's numerical superiority.

In the use of artillery, the French suffered at first by the application of their exaggerated notion of the doctrine of the offensive.   The *Regulations for the Conduct of Major Units,* issued in 1913, declared in pontifical fashion, "Artillery no longer prepares attacks, it supports them," and defined the support of infantry attacks as the major function of artillery in modern war.   During the opening weeks of the war, the orthodox objectives for the fire of the French guns became the enemy batteries, which it may be remarked, so far as the German heavy artillery was concerned, were usually out of range, and the enemy infantry whenever the latter fell under direct observation ; but little attention was deemed necessary to indirect fire or to destructive fire designed to demolish defensive organizations or to effect breaches in the barbed-wire barriers that so often confronted the French infantry. The fallacy soon became apparent. It was, indeed, a far cry from the theory of these early days to the prolonged intensive bombardments which preceded the great offensives of the period of stabilization.

In contrast it was the German method from the beginning to open an engagement with an intensive fire, directed not only against the enemy artillery and infantry lines, but against all defensive works, whether apparently occupied or not, and also against all probable points of concentration or centres of resistance to the rear. The prodigality of expenditure of munitions in the execution of such bombardments, which smothered a wide zone under concentrated shell-fire, amazed and impressed the more frugal French artillery officers.

In general, it may be said that so far as its physical means and the limitations of its tactical theory permitted, the French artillery more than held its own against the German, but in certain respects it suffered from notable deficiencies. One of these lay in the liaison, or lack of it, between the artillery and the infantry.

"It would have been better," General Gascouin,[1] a distinguished French artillery officer has written, "to have had fewer orations on the hearts of the infantry and the artillery beating as one, and to have been equipped instead with a few thousand more yards of telephone wire."

THE BELGIAN ARMY

THE Belgian army requires little comment. At the outbreak of the war, it was in the midst of a reorganization authorized by the Government in 1912 which had not been fully completed, and the mobile army, comprising 6 infantry divisions and a cavalry division, numbered only 117,000 men, instead of the 150,000 called for by the tables of organization. In general the Belgian soldier entered upon the campaign insufficiently trained, inadequately equipped and above all so under-officered that it was the rule rather than the exception to find an infantry company with only one commissioned officer. It is no more than natural that the Belgian army, though it defended itself gallantly behind the fortifications of Liége and Namur, should have proved no match for its formidable foe in the open field, and the Belgian commanders were the first to recognize its short-comings. Politics and dissensions in the General Staff augmented the difficulties

[1] Gen. Gascouin's *L'Evolution de l'Artillerie pendant la Guerre* (Flammarion, Paris, 1920) is one of the best comparative studies of the artilleries of the opposing armies. See also Gen. Herr's *L'Artillerie* (Berger-Levrault, Paris, 1924) and Gen. Gabriel Rouquerol's *Le Canon Artisan de la Victoire* (Berger-Levrault, Paris, 1921).

that confronted King Albert, Commander in Chief in fact as well as in name, and it was not until the Yser that the army was able to give the true measure of its worth.[8]

THE BRITISH ARMY

THE British Expeditionary Force, though amounting in numbers to less than 3 % of the total forces engaged in the Campaign of the Marne, was called upon to play a part of an importance far beyond its numerical strength.

Though it included a substantial number of reservists, Sir John French's Army was composed entirely of units of the regular army, commanded by professional officers. In organization, it differed somewhat from the other armies on the western front.   In the infantry, the battalion rather than the regiment constituted the tactical unit. Four battalions of approximately 1000 men each formed a brigade, and there were three brigades to each infantry division.   The artillery of the British infantry division included 4 brigades of 3 6-gun batteries each, three of them equipped with 18-pounder Q.F. guns (54 guns) and one of them with 4.5 inch howitzers (18 howitzers). The British divisional artillery was thus substantially equivalent to that of the German divisions of the Active army, amounting to 72 pieces, 18 of them of medium heavy calibre.   The total strength of the original five infantry divisions that composed the British Expeditionary Force amounted to approximately 18,000 officers and men each.

Although only a single squadron of cavalry was allotted to each infantry division, Sir John French's command received a more generous proportion of independent cavalry than any other force of corresponding strength on either side, for it had a reinforced cavalry division of 5 brigades of 3 regiments (3 squadrons) each, a total force of some 14,000 men, including supporting artillery and auxiliary troops.   Unlike the French and German cavalry divisions, the British had no permanent infantry units corresponding to the Jäger battalions or cyclist detachments attached to their cavalry division, but on the other hand, the British cavalry division had a more liberal quota both of machine-guns and artillery.   Each regiment had two machine-guns, a total of 30 for the division, as against 6 for the French and German cavalry divisions, a materially larger proportion even with due allowance for the larger size of the British cavalry division. As supporting artillery, the British cavalry division had two brigades

[8] On the character and organization of the Belgian army, see *Bel. O. H.*; also Gen. Galet's *Sa Majesté Albert I devant l'invasion Allemande* (Plon, Paris, 1931) and Gen. de Sellier de Moranville's *Contribution à l'Histoire de la Guerre Mondiale* (Goemaere, Brussels, 1933).

of horse-artillery, each composed of 2 6-gun batteries, or a total of 24 13-pounder Q.F. guns.

In general, in the words of the British Official History, "in every respect the Expeditionary Force of 1914 was incomparably the best trained, the best organized and best equipped British Army that ever went forth to war. Except in the matter of co-operation between aeroplanes and artillery and use of machine-guns, its training would stand comparison in all respects with that of the Germans."

Yet despite the high standard of quality and training that marked the British officers in the lower echelons of command, the British High Command fell far short of the French and German General Staffs both in experience and professional skill. The British General Staff had come into being only six years before the war, at the time of Lord Haldane's reorganization of the army in 1908, and it was neither organized nor prepared to direct the conduct of a war on the continental scale. Prior to the outbreak of hostilities only summary and inadequate attention had been paid to the study of the probable zone of action of the British army in France, despite the understandings that had been reached and the close relations that had been established with the French General Staff. Presumably for fear of wounding tender susceptibilities, the study of German military organization and methods was even specifically forbidden at war games, staff tours and intelligence classes which would have provided the best opportunities for such instruction.

Confronted at last with a trial of strength on a scale which Kitchener and Haig alone among great military leaders seem to have at once appreciated, the British General Staff found that much had been left undone, and that methods which had become matters of routine in the highly specialized General Staffs of France and Germany had to be improvised in the face of the enemy and established by a costly system of trial and error.   In the light of its back-ground, it seems hardly surprising that in the early weeks of the war the British High Command proved less than adequate in the performance of the difficult task that lay before it.

THE HIGH COMMANDS

In the little city of Vitry-le-François, on the upper waters of the Marne, Joffre established the General Headquarters of the French armies, almost in the centre of the zone of concentration.   There he assembled his staff of 96 officers, organized with an eye to maximum mobility in anticipation of a short and active campaign, with little relation to the complex and cumbersome organization that the French High Command became in later years.   Among the French Commander in Chief's principal collaborators, six require especial mention : Belin, the Chief of Staff, or to give him his French title the Major General ; Berthelot, the Aide-Major General in charge of operations, who with Joffre and De Castelnau had taken a major part in the conception and preparation of Plan XVII ; Pellé, the second Aide-Major General, who had formerly served under Joffre in Madagascar, later as Military Attaché in Berlin and finally as Lyautey's Chief of Staff in Morocco ; Pont, Chief of the Operations Section, and Gamelin, Chief of Joffre's Military Cabinet.

Hardly less important were Dupont, Chief of the Intelligence Section, and a group of officers of the Operations Section, among them Alexandre, Bel and Maurin, who served as liaison officers between G.H.Q. and the various Army Headquarters. The system of "vertical liaison" employed by the French High Command, that is, of sending relatively junior officers to lesser headquarters to represent the Commander in Chief, possessed the great advantage of enabling Joffre to remain in constant and intimate contact with his various armies and their commanders ; but it also had disadvantages so serious that the German High Command preferred not to adopt it, for it subjected the army commanders to a supervision so rigid as to limit their initiative and frequently placed them in the anomalous position of appearing to be subordinate to a Major or Lieutenant-Colonel from G.H.Q. Though in the early weeks of open warfare the merits of this system probably outweighed its defects, the officers of Joffre's Operations Section quickly suffered the fate usual to General Staff officers, the cordial dislike of their comrades of the line who bestowed upon them the collective soubriquet of Young Turks. Singly and together, they became targets for political sniping at the hands of those not bold enough to try conclusions with their chief, and pressure exerted by a Deputy or a political personage, often incited by some officer relieved of his command as a result of an unfavourable report, compelled one after another to leave G.H.Q. for service at the front.

In spite of the caustic criticism levelled against the so-called Young Turks, both during the war and since, almost without exception when they left the General Staff they more than justified the high regard in which Joffre held them. Berthelot acquitted himself brilliantly commanding successively a division, an army corps and finally an army. Pellé commanded first a division and later an army corps, and at the close of the war received the important mission of supervising the organization of the Czecho-Slovakian army. Gamelin, after commanding first a brigade and then a division, became after the war Chief of a Military Mission to Brazil, the commander of troops in Syria and today occupies the post of Chief of Staff of the French army, as successor to Weygand and Foch. Bel, who as Chief

of the Personnel Bureau bore much of the odium of Joffre's manifold changes in the High Command and who received the sinister
nickname of Fouquier-Tinville, had come to be regarded as the
apotheosis of the staff officer, inseparably, almost comically, wedded
to his reports and paper-work ; but he fell in Italy while gallantly
directing the attack of a group of battalions of Chasseurs. The
careers of these officers, who exerted wide influence in the early days
of the war, were paralleled in less conspicuous instances too numerous to mention, and many of the most illustrious names in the
French army of the post-war era appeared earlier on the roster of
Joffre's staff.

While the French High Command exercised a constant and direct
supervision over developments along the front, the German General
Staff, despite its great reputation, maintained little practical control
over operations after the completion of concentration. Partly this
was due to a conscious effort to follow the method that Von Moltke
the elder had successfully applied in the War of 1870 ; but partly,
too, it was due to inadequate communications and to the location of
the seat of chief command too far from the scene of action. Until
August 17th, that is, until the German armies had started on their
march through Belgium and after the French offensive in Lorraine
had already been in progress for three days, Von Moltke and his staff
remained in Berlin. On the 17th, he moved to Coblenz, and on the
30th, to Luxembourg after German troops had penetrated far into
French territory. Thus, while Joffre's Headquarters were situated
comparatively close to the line of fire, Von Moltke stayed more than
200 kilometres from the region where the fate of his armies hung in
the balance.

Various explanations have been offered for the remote location of
the German General Headquarters, among them Von Moltke's desire
to remain in constant contact with the Emperor and his fear that
the sovereign's personal safety might be endangered on French
soil. A contributing factor was doubtless a desire to keep the High
Command in a situation where it could view operations as a whole,
in proper perspective, free from the confusing influences necessarily
present close to the battle-front ; but whatever the cause or combination of causes, the location of German General Headquarters need
not necessarily have adversely affected the campaign, if a complete
and efficient system of communications had been provided.

In view of the meticulous precision with which so many details of
German war-plans were settled, it seems surprising that no such system of communications had been devised. For the most part, and
notably during the critical days of the Battle of the Marne, no direct
communication existed between Von Moltke's Headquarters and the

three German right wing armies, or between these armies themselves. No timely effort seems to have been made to take advantage of the net-work of French civilian telephone lines, or to adapt or reconstruct them for military use. The only means of direct communication between the various western Army Headquarters and G.H.Q. was by radio, then still in a state of mechanical imperfection which rendered it always subject to climatic conditions and to interception or interference by the enemy. With no system of liaison officers and with such imperfect means of communication, the German High Command not infrequently remained for twenty-four hours or even longer with no news at all from one or another of the armies, generally at the very moment when the most important developments were taking place. This situation constituted a basic source of weakness in the German method of command, and furnishes the explanation of much of the weakness and indecision attributed to Von Moltke and his advisers.[9]

In organization the German High Command corresponded closely to the French. With the Chief of Staff exercising the functions of Commander in Chief, nominally the Emperor, the duties of second in command fell to the Quartermaster-General who performed duties analogous to those of the French Major General. During the Campaign of the Marne, Von Moltke's Quartermaster-General, Von Stein, was far from exercising the influence that later fell to Ludendorff when he assumed the post under Hindenburg, and Von Stein seems to have concerned himself mainly with matters of administrative detail.

At Von Moltke's Headquarters, as at Joffre's, a group of officers of relatively junior rank played dominant parts, chief among them two Lieutenant-Colonels, Tappen, Chief of the Operations Section, and Hentsch, Chief of the Intelligence Section. Both enjoyed the confidence of the Chief of Staff to a high degree and were consulted on matters of important policy, often without regard to the limitations of their particular fields. Hardly less influential were Colonel Fumatti, Chief of Von Moltke's Military Cabinet, Colonel von Dommes, Chief of the Political Section, Colonel Gröner, Director of Railways and finally Major Nicolai who, by reason of his control of Secret Service and espionage activities, came to be regarded in Allied countries as a particularly sinister figure.

Though the distinction has little practical significance so far as the events with which we are dealing is concerned, the German High Command, the *Oberste Heeresleitung,* which exercised dominion

---

[9] An important discussion of the German system of communications particularly in the right wing armies is Col. Jochim's *Die Operationen und rückwartigen Verbindungen der deutschen I Armee in der Marneschlachi,* 1914 (Mittler, Berlin, 1934).

over the operations of the armies on all fronts must be distinguished from the larger entity, the Great General Headquarters, the *Grosses Haupt-Quartier,* of which it was a part and which embraced the Emperor's personal headquarters and included political and naval, as well as military, sections.

A distinctive feature of the German method of command of the field armies that seems worthy of especial note was the predominant part played by the Army Chiefs of Staff. Following the Prussian tradition that originated with Blücher and Gneisenau, the German army conferred an authority upon the Chief of Staff that far exceeded anything enjoyed by Chiefs of Staff in the Allied armies, and in more than one instance during the Marne campaign important decisions, fraught with strategic consequences, were taken by German Chiefs of Staff independently of their superiors and without consulting them.

It is impossible within short compass to attempt an intelligent comparative criticism of the merits and defects of the two great military organizations that opposed one another in the opening act of the colossal drama of the World War. The events must speak for themselves and furnish their own interpretation.[10]

[10] Out of the mass of literature produced by military writers, biographers and journalists, dealing with the High Commands, it is possible to call attention only to a few of the most significant. On the German side, in addition to works already cited, there should be mentioned : Gen. Tappen's *Bis zur Marne* 1914 (Stalling, Oldenburg, 1920), Gen. von Stein's *Erlebnisse und Betrachtungen aus der Zeit des Weltkrieges* (Barth, Leipzig, 1919), Gen. Gröner's *Der Feldherr wider Willen* (Mittler, Berlin, 1930), Gen. Baumgarten Crusius' *Deutsche Heerfuhrung im Marnefeldzug* 1914 (Scherl, Berlin, 1921) and Lieut.-Col. Koeltz, of the French army's *Le G. Q. G. Allemand et la Bataille de la Marne* (Payot, Paris, 1931) largely drawn from German official sources. A work critical of the German High Command and its plans is Col. Immanuel's *Siege und Niederlage im Weltkriege* (Mittler, Berlin, 1919). On the French side, important primary sources are Joffre's *Mémoires* (Plon, Paris, 1932) and Commandant Muller's *Joffre et la Marne* (Crès, Paris, 1931).

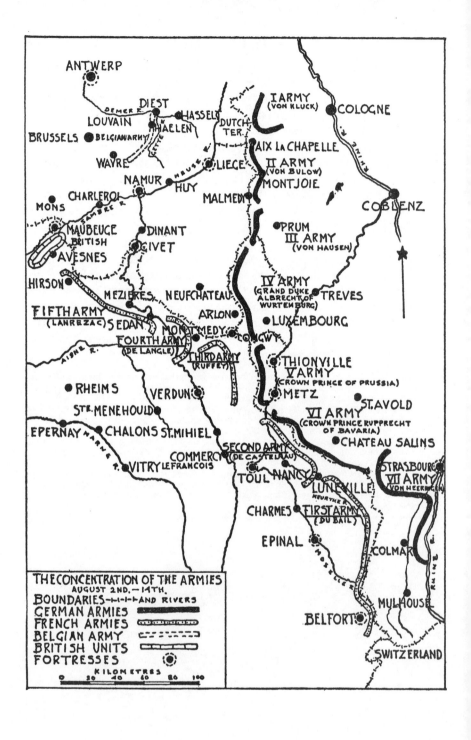

ANTWERP

DIEST
LOUVAIN HASSELT
BRUSSELS HAELEN DUTCH TER.
BELGIAN ARMY
DEMER R.
WAYRE
AIX La CHAPELLE
LIEGE
WAVRE
NAMUR HUY
MALMEDY MONTJOIE
CHARLEROI
MONS SAMBRE R.
MAUBEUGE DINANT PRUM
BRITISH GIVET III ARMY
AVESNES (VON HAUSEN)
HIRSON IV ARMY
MEZIERES NEUFCHATEAU (GRAND DUKE ALBRECHT OF TREVES
WURTEMBURG)
ARLON LUXEMBOURG
SEDAN
FOURTH ARMY MONTMEDY LONGWY
(DE LANGLE) AISNE R. THIRD ARMY THIONVILLE
(RUFFEY) V ARMY
(CROWN PRINCE OF PRUSSIA)
RHEIMS VERDUN METZ
STE.MENEHOULD ST.AVOLD
EPERNAY CHALONS ST.MIHIEL VI ARMY
(CROWN PRINCE RUPPRECHT
OF BAVARIA)
COMMERCY CHATEAU SALINS
VITRY LE FRANCOIS SECOND ARMY
(DE CASTELNAU)
TOUL NANCY STRASBOURG
CHARMES FIRST ARMY VII ARMY
(DU BAIL) (VON HEERINGEN)

COLOGNE

COBLENZ

I ARMY
(VON KLUCK)

II ARMY
(VON BULOW)

FIFTH ARMY
(LANREZAC)

LUNEVILLE
MEURTHE R.

EPINAL

COLMAR

MULHOUSE

BELFORT

SWITZERLAND

THE CONCENTRATION OF THE ARMIES
AUGUST 2ND.—14TH.
BOUNDARIES AND RIVERS
GERMAN ARMIES
FRENCH ARMIES
BELGIAN ARMY
BRITISH UNITS
FORTRESSES
KILOMETRES
0 20 40 60 80 100

CHAPTER IV

THE PRELUDE TO ARMAGEDDON

THE chain of political events from the assassination of the Austrian Archduke Franz Ferdinand and his morganatic wife at Sarajevo on June 28, 1914, to the outbreak of the war has so many times been the subject of hour to hour accounts by apologists of all the nations concerned, that it requires no detailed recapitulation.

From June 28th to July 23rd the world remained in doubt as to what political importance, if any, should attach to the murder of the heir to the throne of the Austro-Hungarian Empire ; but the Austrian note to Serbia ended the suspense and gave the impetus that plunged the world into the abyss of war. Couched in the language of an ultimatum, it required Serbia in effect to surrender sovereign prerogatives and to accept conditions inconsistent with the status of an independent state. Within forty-eight hours, the brief period allowed, the Serbian Government delivered its reply, unexpectedly conciliatory in tone, yet short of an unconditional acceptance of the Austrian terms. A cursory examination sufficed for the Austrian Minister to pronounce it unsatisfactory and to demand his passports. Three days later, on July 28, 1914, Austria-Hungary declared war on Serbia.

In the succeeding days, while a flow of notes and dispatches between the various chancelleries led each nation hourly nearer to the brink of the catastrophe, active military preparations proceeded throughout Europe. Leaves were cancelled, officers recalled to their stations and preliminary orders issued, increasing daily in stringency and extent, designed to forestall a sudden, unannounced outbreak of hostilities.

Fearful that Germany might gain an irretrievable advantage, and acting upon Joffre's urgent solicitation, the French Government on July 31st ordered the covering forces provided for under the concentration plan to take their preliminary positions, but in recognition of the importance of avoiding any incident that might precipitate hostilities, French troops were forbidden "on any pretext" to cross a line established approximately ten kilometres [1] from the German frontier.

---

[1] Certain of the villages that marked the line of the so-called Ten Kilometre Zone were in fact not more than four or five kilometres from the frontier.

The same day, as the French telegraph wires carried the message that set five army corps in motion towards the border, Germany delivered an ultimatum to Russia demanding immediate demobilization, and in the afternoon an impressive scene of military pageantry took place in Berlin.   Before the statue of Frederick the Great, in the centre of Unter den Linden, a detachment of Prussian Grenadiers, troops of the Imperial Guard, stood stiffly at attention, while a prolonged ruffle of drums silenced an awed throng that overflowed the famous avenue and its approaches.   In a voice resounding harshly through the expectant stillness, the commanding officer read a proclamation that by All Highest command, in the name of His Imperial and Royal Majesty, a *Kriegesgefahrzustand,* a State of Danger of War, existed throughout the Mark of Brandenburg, and decreed the subordination of all civil authority to the military power.   As the troops wheeled rapidly away to regain their quarters, a wild tumult of enthusiasm swept the crowd that gradually swelled in thousands of throats into the thunderous peals of *Deutschland über Alles.*

This scene, simultaneously enacted in all the military districts of the German Empire, was translated into the frigid amenity required by diplomatic etiquette, when Baron von Schön, the Emperor's Ambassador at Paris, called at the Quai d'Orsay, where Viviani, the French Premier and Foreign Minister, received him.   Von Schön formally informed the French Government of the steps that his own government had taken, and at the same time requested a statement of France's intentions in the event of war between Germany and Russia. Lacking information as to the immediate situation, Viviani sought to temporize.

"Let us hope that extreme decisions may become unnecessary," he said to Von Schön, "and in any case, allow me to consider your question with the advice of my colleagues."

With polite expressions of mutual hope that a solution might be found, the German Ambassador and the French Premier parted. By avoiding a direct answer to the diplomat's inquiry, Viviani had relieved him of the necessity of delivering an important part of his message, for in the event that France had expressed her intention of remaining neutral, the German Ambassador had been instructed to demand that, as a guaranty of neutrality, France should surrender the vital fortresses of Toul and Verdun to Germany for the duration of the latter's impending war with Russia.   Even had France been disposed to repudiate the obligations of her Russian alliance, she could not have done otherwise than reject so extreme a requirement.   War between France and Germany had become inevitable.

The following day both nations issued formal decrees of general mobilization, and millions of men laid down their normal tasks to assume the unaccustomed duties of soldiers. Convinced that war could no longer be averted, Von Moltke subordinated every considera- tion to military advantage, moving his covering forces close to the frontier and at numerous points authorizing scouting patrols to cross it. More alert to the importance of securing the favourable opinion of neutral nations, and in particular of doing nothing that might alienate British support, the French adopted a contrary policy, rigidly forbidding military forces to cross the international boundary. Though general mobilization led to a removal of the restrictive zone originally imposed, Joffre firmly warned all local commanders against crossing the frontier, even if attacked.

"If there are to be incidents," Joffre wrote, "they must originate and develop only on French soil."

All eyes were turned towards England, and in the determination of her policy Belgium proved the decisive factor. Following the decision Count von Schlieffen had taken long years before, Germany had already resolved upon an invasion of Belgium in the event of war, and as early as July 29th, the German Foreign Office had des- patched to Brussels, by special messenger, a sealed envelope containing an ultimatum, based on a memorandum prepared by Von Moltke on the 26th, to be delivered to the Belgian Government should occasion require. When on August 1st the British Government addressed substantially identical inquiries to France and Germany, her co- guarantors of Belgian neutrality under the Treaty of 1839, the French response was prompt and satisfactory : France would observe her treaty responsibility ; but with the sealed envelope lying in the safe of the German Legation in the Belgian capital and the General Staff's plans laid to the last detail, the German Government could only re- turn an evasive answer which was in effect no answer at all.

The evening of August 2nd brought a final disclosure of Germany's attitude, for on telegraphic instructions from Berlin, the seals on the envelope were broken and the contents delivered to Davignon, the Belgian Minister of Foreign Affairs. It was a demand that Belgium acquiesce in the movement of the German armies across her territory, alleging in explanation "definite information that French forces are about to march on the Meuse by way of Givet and Namur." The alternative plainly stated was war.

In a document of noble dignity King Albert's Government cate- gorically rejected the German ultimatum.

Until Germany's position with regard to Belgium stood revealed, British opinion had been far from unanimous as to the attitude that England should adopt in the European crisis. Whatever the views of Sir Edward Grey and certain of his colleagues as to their obligations to France and Russia and the most expedient channel into which to direct their country's foreign policy, the resignations of Morley and Burns afford ample evidence of the divided counsel that beset Asquith's Cabinet.   When, however, it became apparent that Germany proposed to disregard the Treaty of 1839 and to march across Belgium in defiance of the agreement she had signed, British sentiment crystallized into almost universal popular support of the ultimatum that Sir Edward Grey addressed to the German Government, demanding the withdrawal of the latter's ultimatum to Belgium before midnight [2] of August 4th.

While England's decision was hanging in the balance, events on the continent had moved rapidly towards a climax.   From Rome came the announcement that in view of Austria's aggressive attitude towards Serbia, Italy felt herself released from her obligations under the Triple Alliance and would remain neutral.   The German General Staff received the news with relative indifference, for it had already discounted the likelihood of Italian aid ; but it was particularly welcome to Joffre, for it enabled him to withdraw troops otherwise immobilized along the Alps for more important duty.   Following the language of her pronouncement at the outbreak of the Franco-Prussian War, Switzerland declared that she would also remain neutral, though mobilizing to protect the integrity of her territory, and a declaration of similar tenor came from Holland.

On the afternoon of August 3rd, with the mobilization in full swing, Joffre met three of his army commanders, Dubail of the First Army, De Langle of the Fourth and Lanrezac of the Fifth at the Ministry of War in the Rue St. Dominique in Paris.   Each had received in February the portion of Plan XVII relating to the forces under his own command and there was little to add at the moment, for war had not yet been declared and the mobilization would not be completed for another eleven days.   The meeting was a brief and simple one, unadorned by speeches or fine phrases, the captain calling his team together for a word of encouragement before taking the field, and when it broke up, the three generals, each responsible for the fate of an army, set out for their respective posts.

At six o'clock the same evening a German aviator dropped three bombs near the railway station at Lunéville.   Forty-five minutes later the German Ambassador called once more on Viviani to inform him that by reason of acts of aggression committed by France against Germany, the Imperial German Government "considers itself as be-

---

[2] Midnight German time or 11 P.M. British and French time. Hereafter, for the sake of convenience and uniformity, British and French time will be used, unless otherwise stated.

ing in a state of war with France as a result of the acts of the latter power."

On the morning of August 4th, the French War Minister officially notified Joffre that war had been declared.   In the meanwhile, in London, the British Government awaited an answer to Grey's ultimatum, the last tenuous hope for peace.   At the War Office and the Admiralty the day passed in feverish preparations, while the Foreign Office kept an anxious vigil ; but no word came.   The evening dragged on, while noisy crowds milled through the streets, and at last, as Big Ben boomed out the fateful hour of eleven, a message from the Admiralty directed the British fleet, already mobilized by Churchill's foresight, to commence hostilities against Germany. The following morning Joffre formally assumed command of the armies of the French Republic.[3]

[3] For a complete and impartial account of events leading up to the outbreak of the war, see Professor Sidney Fay's scholarly work *Origins of the World War* (Macmillan, New York, 1928), which contains an elaborate documentation of official sources and other material.   See also the British official narrative, *The Outbreak of the War* 1914–1918 (H. M. Stationery Office, London) by Professor Sir Charles Osman, and *Les Causes de la guerre mondiale* (Hartmann, Paris, 1933) by Professor Camille Bloch.

CHAPTER V

THE CONTEMPTIBLES

WITH the declaration of war an accomplished fact, the extent of England's part still remained open for decision. As early as 1906, a foundation had been laid for British participation in military operations on the continent when the British War Office and the French General Staff entered into direct relations for the first time during the international crisis that culminated in the Conference of Algeciras. Two years later, in January 1908, a definite understanding was reached for the eventual co-operation of a British army, and thereafter informal correspondence and unofficial conferences between high-ranking officers, conducted with greatest circumspection, supplemented and amplified the agreements already tentatively arrived at. When the crisis of Agadir again threatened the peace of Europe, the British War Office sent Sir Henry Wilson, then an untitled Colonel and Director of Military Operations, to Paris to confer with General Dubail representing the French General Staff.

The meeting of these two men, both destined to play leading roles in the coming conflict, established definitely the part that Great Britain would take, in case, as then seemed momentarily possible, political developments put an end to the armed truce of forty years standing between France and Germany.

It was first declared — the minutes of this conference of July 20, 1911, stated — that the conference entered upon, having no official character, could not bind the British or the French Governments in any respect, and that the sole purpose of the conference was to study certain fundamental questions and to consider indispensable preparatory measures.

Yet despite the guarded language of this preamble, it was agreed that in the event of a common war against Germany, a British Expeditionary Force of six infantry divisions and one cavalry division should land in France and should take its place on the left of the French concentration, and the agreement so reached was confirmed by subsequent negotiations through the succeeding years.

When the war-clouds gathered in 1914, the understanding fostered by Wilson became a source of deep concern to British political leaders,

44

and though Asquith assured the House of Commons that England was not committed by any secret understanding, grave doubts subsisted in the minds of Morley and others as to whether the negotiations had not created at least a moral obligation that was tantamount to a military alliance.

Almost simultaneously with the news that England was at war with Germany came the announcement of Lord Kitchener's appointment to the post of Secretary of State for War, then temporarily vacant. His designation to fill this post of pre-eminent importance in the War Cabinet caused general satisfaction throughout the Empire, for he was recognized, next to the venerable Lord Roberts, as Britain's foremost soldier and he enjoyed to an equal degree the respect and confidence of both political parties. During long years spent in Egypt, South Africa and India, Kitchener had contributed more, perhaps, than any one man towards establishing and moulding the modern British Empire, and his experience had accustomed him to view problems in large terms, in terms of peoples and of nations, in which purely military operations assumed a place of relatively secondary importance. Almost alone among responsible leaders, he recognized from the outset the magnitude of the conflict upon which England had embarked, and the supreme military effort that would be required to bring it to a victorious conclusion.

"The British Empire must participate in the land war on the greatest scale," he told the Cabinet soon after his appointment. "In no other way can victory be won." [1]

He had no faith in the doctrine, popular in high military circles, that the war would end after a short and violent campaign. Some years before the war, Count von Schlieffen, high-priest of the Prussian military caste, had published an article purporting to demonstrate on economic grounds that a war between first-class European powers could not possibly continue for more than a few months,[2] and this view, widely accepted, serves to explain in large measure the strategy of the early weeks of the war, and the feverish anxiety with which both sides sought to gain the initiative by offensive action.

But though Schlieffen's thesis became orthodox to a large majority of those in high authority, not only in Germany, but in France and England as well, Kitchener did not agree. The war, he thought, would last at least three years ; a prediction received at first with respectful incredulity by officers of the British General Staff, and later with consternation, as they found their chief calmly basing his plans upon this hypothesis.

In the afternoon of August 5th, the principal leaders charged with

[1] Winston Churchill, *The World Crisis*, Vol. I (Scribners, New York, 1923), p. 304.
[2] *Der Krieg in der gegenwart*, (Deutsche Revue, 1909).

direct responsibility for England's prosecution of the war assembled
for a momentous conference at the Prime Minister's residence in
Downing Street.   Asquith was there, with Grey, the Foreign Secretary, and Haldane, who as Secretary of State for War had been largely
responsible for the reorganization of the British army.   Churchill
and Prince Louis of Battenburg represented the navy.   Kitchener,
who was formally to assume his official duties the following day, attended with his former chief, Lord Roberts, alert and active despite
his eighty-two years.   Among officers high in British military counsels came Sir John French and Sir Ian Hamilton, Haig, Grierson,
Douglas, Murray, Wilson and others of lesser note.   It was a notable
gathering, assembled to decide the fundamental question of British
participation in military operations.   The discussion was long, ram-
bling and distinguished by a lack of precise information.

"An historic meeting of men mostly entirely ignorant of their subject," Wilson called it.[3]   Nevertheless, in true British fashion, a sound
and far-reaching decision emerged from the seeming confusion — the
determination to redeem Wilson's pledges to the French by sending
an Expeditionary Force to cooperate with the French armies.   The
time of its departure, its area of concentration upon arrival and its
exact composition were left unsettled, but the principle was established, and at the conclusion of the meeting, England stood committed, beyond the naval action that many had thought might be
sufficient, to take the field upon the continent against the German
armies.

The solution of the subsidiary questions left unanswered became
Kitchener's first responsibility upon assuming office.   In the years
before the war, England had turned a deaf ear to Lord Roberts'
warnings and had remained true to her traditional policy of relying
upon the mighty British navy for her first line of defence.   The
British army of 1914 consisted wholly of professional soldiers, re-
cruited from volunteers, and was no larger than absolutely necessary
for the protection of the British Isles, the defence of the Empire's far-
flung naval bases and the policing of its colonial possessions.   In
England itself, there were only six divisions of regular troops, reinforced by fourteen divisions of "Territorials,"[4] but the latter were
militia, only partially trained and equipped, in no condition for
immediate active service.

Immediate measures had been taken to increase Great Britain's
land forces.   On August 5th, the Regular Army, Reserves and Territorials had been mobilized, and the same day Parliament had au-

[3] *Diary of Field Marshal Sir Henry Wilson,* edited by Gen. Sir C. E. Callwell
(Scribners, New York, 1927).
[4] Not to be confused with the French Territorials. The British Territorials were
generally analogous to the National Guard in the United States.

thorized an increase of 500,000 men in the regular forces. Two divisions had been ordered home from India, and the garrisons at Malta and elsewhere had been recalled to England ; but some time would necessarily elapse before these steps could become effective, and in the meanwhile, the necessity of sending troops to France arose in pressing fashion. The possibility of a German invasion, or at least of a demonstration in force against the British coast, could not be ignored, nor would it do to strip the country immediately of all its trained soldiers, for Kitchener realized the vital necessity of providing a nucleus for the great armies that would be required in the future. With these considerations in mind, the Secretary of State for War decided to send to France initially a force of four infantry divisions and one infantry brigade and a cavalry division, with appurtenant services, with the understanding that another division would follow shortly and further reinforcements as soon as the condition of the new levies permitted. Pending receipt of direct word from the French Commander in Chief as to his wishes and intentions, the date of departure of the British Expeditionary Force and its zone of con-centration in France were left undecided.

Sir John French had already been selected to command the British forces in France. He was a cavalry officer who had won distinction in the South African War under Roberts and Kitchener, had later held the important Aldershot Command and had also served as Chief of the Imperial General Staff. With him went Sir Archibald Murray, as Chief of Staff, and Sir Henry Wilson, as Deputy Chief of Staff. The two corps of French's army were entrusted respectively to Sir Douglas Haig and Sir James Grierson, while the command of the cavalry division fell to Allenby. To organize the service of supply, French had Sir William Robertson as his Quartermaster-General.[5] The Army itself aggregated approximately 100,000 men, with some 200 guns, and included many of the most famous units of the British army, bearing on their battle-flags the historic names of Waterloo, the battles of the Peninsular, of the Crimea and of many lesser fields.

The arrival of Colonel Huguet, a French artillery officer who had formerly served as Military Attaché in London, brought to a head the all-important question of the time of the British army's departure and its destination in France. These matters formed the subject of a second conference, held at the War Office on August 12th, attended by the principal British commanders. Huguet, speaking on behalf of the French High Command, urged that the British army should embark without delay and should concentrate in the area centred

[5] On the organization and functioning of the British supply service during the open-ing campaign, see Field Marshal Sir William Robertson's *From Private to Field Marshal* (Houghton, Mifflin, Boston, 1921).

around Le Cateau, in the region of the fortress of Maubeuge. This represented, in substance, the understanding reached before the war, and received the enthusiastic support of Wilson and French.

Guided by instinct rather than by information, Kitchener demurred. His long career as a colonial administrator had afforded him little time to study the strategy of a possible European war, and like Joffre, he found himself at a disadvantage in discussing strategic considerations with officers who had devoted years of study to them ; but he remained unconvinced of the validity of the French doctrine of the offensive, and had little faith that it would produce the prompt and decisive victory claimed for it. Nor could he see any justification for the confident belief of the French General Staff that the Germans would not attempt any serious offensive action west of the Meuse River. On the contrary, he anticipated a sweeping invasion of Belgium by the German right wing armies, and he feared that if the British forces assembled around Le Cateau, they would soon find themselves in the forefront of the main German attack, instead of in a relatively quiet area where they could complete their preparations and become acclimatized to unfamiliar conditions, free from enemy interference. He accordingly proposed that Amiens, rather than Le Cateau, should become the centre of the British zone of concentration.

But though he found support from Sir Douglas Haig, who urged that any landing in France be deferred until the campaign had begun and an opportunity afforded to judge of the most effective direction for British co-operation, Kitchener reluctantly yielded at last before the argument that any delay would create distrust in the minds of the French and upset their plan of campaign. It was decided that Sir John French's Army should embark forthwith, to take its place on the left of the French line, with Headquarters at Le Cateau. The events of the succeeding weeks amply proved the justice of Kitchener's fears, and the superiority of his judgment over those whose views he permitted to persuade him.

Two days later, on August 14th, Sir John French broke up his Headquarters at the Hotel Metropole in London, and embarking at Dover with his personal staff, crossed the Channel on H.M.'s Cruiser Sentinel to Boulogne to assume command of his Army in the field. Before his departure he received lengthy secret instructions from the Secretary of State for War [6] which included in particular two cautions.

It must be recognized from the outset that the numerical strength of the British Force and its contingent reinforcement is strictly limited, and

[6] See Appendix III.

with this consideration kept steadily in view, it will be obvious that the greatest care must be exercised towards a minimum of loss and wastage.

Further on, he impressed French with the necessity of maintaining his independence and of avoiding French domination.

I wish you distinctly to understand that your command is an entirely independent one, and that you will in no case come in any sense under the orders of any Allied General.

These instructions could hardly have failed to exert a strong influence on the British Commander in Chief ; but while the French have freely attributed to them the explanation of the extreme circumspection with which British operations were conducted, particularly after the Battle of Le Cateau, it may be suspected rather that they afforded French a convenient explanation for his failure to fall in with Joffre's plans — a failure that ultimately necessitated Kitchener's personal intervention to set right.

Sir John French's landing at Boulogne on August 14th, marked the beginning of England's active military participation in the war. For the first time in a century, British troops stood on the soil of Europe, facing a common foe as the comrades-in-arms of their traditional enemy.[7]

[7] Many British statesmen and soldiers have written memoirs that deal, at least in part, with the period prior to the embarkation of the British Expeditionary Force. Among the most important are : Viscount French, Sir Henry Wilson and Winston Churchill, *op. cit.* ; Viscount Haldane's *Autobiography* (Doubleday Doran, New York, 1929) ; Earl Grey's *Twenty-five Years* 1892–1916 ; and dealing with the subject from the French view-point, Gen. Huguet's *L'Intervention Militaire Britannique en* 1914 (Berger-Levrault, Paris, 1928). A work deserving especial mention is Gen. C. R. Ballard's *Kitchener* (Dodd, Mead, New York, 1930). Written with an understanding humour, refreshing in a military writer, Gen. Ballard's work is more illuminating, though less complete, than Sir George Arthur's solemn "official" biography in 3 volumes, *The Life of Lord Kitchener* (Macmillan, New York, 1920). See also. Gen. Charteris' biography, *Field Marshal Earl Haig* (Scribners, New York, 1929).

CHAPTER VI

LIEGE

WHILE in England statesmen and soldiers planned for the participation of the British Expeditionary Force, and in France the cumbersome machinery of mobilization was gradually bringing the French armies into being, Belgium had already come to grips with the enemy.

It was seven o'clock in the evening of August 2nd, when Davignon, the Belgian Minister of Foreign Affairs, received from the German Minister the ultimatum that brought Belgium to the greatest crisis of her history. Two hours later, in the Royal Palace at Brussels a council assembled, where the King, the members of the civil Government and the principal officers of the General Staff met to determine their country's policy.[1]

The Belgian sovereign's oath to the Constitution includes a pledge to defend the integrity of the nation's territory, and Albert of Belgium — who had received with a rare burst of profanity a reminder from the German Emperor that he was a member of a German royal house — was resolved to carry out his oath to the letter. It took only a short time to decide upon the tenor of the reply to Germany's ultimatum, but the military questions that the decision almost inevitably involved proved more difficult of solution.

Politics had been rife in Belgium's military affairs, so that despite her exposed situation and the virtual certainty that in case of a general conflict she would be caught between the upper and the nether millstone, no well-ordered plan of action had been settled upon to meet the contingency of a violation of Belgian neutrality.[2]

The principal question was the area to be selected for the concentration of the Belgian army. King Albert favoured assembling all available forces along the Meuse River, from Liége through Huy to

[1] See article by Baron de Bassompierre *La nuit du 2 au 3 août 1914 au Ministère des Affaires Étrangères en Belgique ;* Revue des Deux Mondes, February 15, 1915.
[2] Basing their assertions on the so-called "Brussels Documents," published in Nordeutsche Allgemeine Zeitung, Oct.–Dec. 1914, (Eng. trans. Times Documentary History of the War, Vol. II, Diplomatic Part 2, Pgs. 314 et seq.), German apologists have insisted that a pre-concerted plan existed between Belgium, England and France for combined military action. See, for example, Karl Hosse's *Die englischen-belgischen Aufmarschpläne gegen Deutschland vor dem Weltkrieg* (Liepzig, 1930). This has been strenuously denied in Allied countries, and in fact there seems little credible evidence to sustain the German contention.

Namur, taking advantage of the great natural barrier. Despite its lack of training and inadequate equipment, the Belgian army, consisting of six infantry divisions and a cavalry division, thus supported on either flank by the fortifications of Liége and Namur, would have constituted a formidable force, difficult to dislodge. It was a bold plan, and one that, if adopted, might well have altered profoundly the course of subsequent operations by disrupting the German plans at the outset. Such was the view of General von Kluck, Commander of the German I Army, writing after the war : [3]

Events would have shaped very differently had the Belgian army succeeded in offering, or even had it attempted to offer, an energetic resistance to the advance of the I and II Armies with its whole force, basing its operations on Liége, Huy and Namur, and preventing the bursting of the line of forts ; a most serious loss of time would thereby have been imposed upon the German flank armies.

It seems doubtful how strongly this point was stressed at the council of August 2nd, for no formal minutes were kept, and the recollection of those present differs materially as to what was said, but it is certain that the more prudent counsels of the Belgian Chief of Staff, General de Selliers de Moranville prevailed. Unwilling to venture Belgium's entire mobile army at one stroke against so formidable an antagonist, at the risk, in case of defeat, of rendering retreat to the fortifications of Antwerp impossible, De Moranville urged instead the concentration of the main body of the army behind the River Gette, a small stream further to the west, mid-way between the Meuse and Brussels. There, he suggested, the Belgians could await the coming of French and British reinforcements with an opportunity to organize their forces in relative tranquillity and with a reasonable hope that the fortresses of Liége and Namur might retard the invaders long enough to permit the timely arrival of Allied aid.[4]

In this view, King Albert reluctantly acquiesced, insisting however, that the garrison of Liége should be strengthened by one division and one brigade from the mobile army and that Namur should likewise receive the support of another division.

The determination thus reached condemned Liége to bear the

---

[3] *Der Marsch auf Paris und die Marneschlacht* 1914 (Mittler, Berlin, 1920).
[4] The accounts of General de Moranville and of General de Ryckel, Deputy Chief of Staff, as to what occurred at the council of August 2nd are irreconcilably divergent. Both were present and one can only conclude that one or the other has suffered from a severe lapse of memory. It is perhaps significant that General Galet in his book, with a foreword by King Albert, accepts De Ryckel's version. At the time Galet, then a Captain, was not present, but he was King Albert's personal military secretary. See Gen. de Ryckel's *Mémoires* (Chapelot, Paris, 1920) ; Galet, *op. cit.* ; De Selliers de Moranville, *op. cit.* and *Les inexactitudes des Mémoires du Général de Ryckel*, Mercure de France, Paris, 1921.

first brunt of the German attack alone, without the support of a field army.   Only a frail hope remained that Germany's ultimatum might be a colossal feint, designed to deceive her principal enemies as to her real plans, while the main attack developed further to the east as it had in 1870.   This hope vanished when in the morning of August 3rd the advance-guard of Von der Marwitz' cavalry crossed the frontier at Gemmenich.   By the afternoon of the 4th, every road leading from the east seemed choked with grey-clad legions, and the Belgian frontier pickets, after a perfunctory exchange of shots, could only scurry back to the protecting lines of Liége to report that the German invasion had begun.

Situated in the northeastern corner of Belgium, the fortress city of Liége, with a population of 160,000, stands some thirty kilometres from the German frontier to the east and fifteen kilometres from the Dutch frontier to the north.   The Meuse, flowing northwest, divides the town itself.   The defences constructed between 1888 and 1892 by the Belgian military engineer, General Brialmont, consisted in August 1914 of twelve forts, placed at regular intervals, six of them on the right or east bank of the river, and six on the left bank.[5]   One fort on the right bank and an antiquated citadel, used as a storehouse, constituted the inner defences.   With some 400 guns of varied calibres, a majority of them sheltered beneath reinforced concrete, built to withstand the bombardment of 210 mm. guns, Liége was considered a modern fortress of exceptional strength.

The fortress and its garrison, consisting of approximately 40,000 men, including mobile troops, had been placed under the orders of General Leman, who performed the dual functions of commander of the 3rd Division and Governor of Liége.   An officer of engineers, he had served for twenty-five years on the staff of the Belgian War College, where he had acquired a high reputation.   Only a few months before, despite his own doubts as to his qualifications for active command, Leman had been transferred from his academic duties and appointed to the post that of all others carried the highest measure of responsibility at the outbreak of the war.   Events soon amply justified the choice.

From the German point of view, the reduction of Liége had become essential, as a result of Von Moltke's determination to respect the neutrality of Holland, for the Belgian fortress stood squarely in the path of the projected movement of the German right wing armies, and the guns of its forts dominated the roads over which the German I and II Armies were obliged to pass.   Before the German plan

[5] On the right bank: the Forts of Barchon, D'Evégnée, Fléron, Chaudfontaine, D'Embourg and Boncelles.   On the left bank: Pontisse, Liers, Lantin, Loncin, Hollogne and Flémalle.

of operations could develop in orderly fashion, therefore, the obstacle of Liége had to be overcome, and it was desirable that this should be accomplished, if possible, before the important bridges across the Meuse could be destroyed and railway communication with the interior of Belgium severed. It was even more important that the result should be achieved while the German armies were still in process of concentration, so that as soon as the concentration had been completed, their advance could begin without delay.

Before the war, the German General Staff, under the direction of Ludendorff, then Chief of the Operations Section, had laid elaborate plans for a sudden and violent attack upon the fortress in what it was hoped would prove to be overwhelming force. Von Moltke had assigned to the task six brigades of infantry, drawn from the Active army corps of the I and II Armies, comprising 13 infantry regiments and 5 Jäger battalions, the 2nd Cavalry Corps (Von der Marwitz) of 3 cavalry divisions and two batteries of 210 mm. mortars, the whole under the command of General von Emmich, commander of the 10th Army Corps. General von Bülow, who commanded the II Army, exercised general supervision over the operation which the High Command hoped and expected could be brought to a successful conclusion within forty-eight hours.

During the day of August 4th, while the British Government still awaited final word of Germany's intentions, Von Emmich's forces were already pouring across the frontier, dispersing and driving before them the Belgian cavalry and cyclist detachments sent to observe and impede their progress. On the morning of the 5th, Captain Brinckman, German Military Attaché at Brussels, presented himself at Leman's Headquarters in Von Emmich's name to demand the surrender of the fortress.

The day before Leman had received his orders, written in the King's own hand :

I charge you to hold to the end with your division the position which you have been entrusted to defend.

Leman's rejection of the summons to surrender was therefore prompt and categorical, and within an hour, the German bombardment opened, smothering the works of the eastern forts with clouds of black smoke from high-explosive shells and sweeping the approaches to the city with shrapnel. In the late afternoon and during the night, Von Emmich's infantry advanced to the assault in five columns, two from the north, one from the east and two from the south. Leman had thrown up hasty entrenchments in the intervals between the forts, manning them with mobile troops at his disposal, and behind these the Belgians fought with desperate energy, driving back the charging columns under withering rifle and machine-gun fire and holding to their positions at many points in bloody hand-to-hand fighting. When the morning of the 6th broke, the Germans had made little progress, and the Belgian lines remained substantially intact.

At his Headquarters in distant Hanover, Von Bülow received word that the first assault had failed before the obstinate resistance of "fanatical inhabitants" who had barred every avenue of approach and had caused serious losses among the assailants. Resolved to make short work of this unexpected opposition, the German Army Commander dispatched reinforcements, ordering the bombardment to be continued without interruption and the attack to be renewed at nightfall.

To the north, through the narrow corridor that separates Liége from the Dutch frontier, elements of Von der Marwitz' cavalry had already crossed the Meuse, running the gauntlet of the Belgian guns, to bring the forts on the left bank under direct attack. Though Leman's communications with Belgian Headquarters at Louvain remained unbroken for the moment, he foresaw that this move presaged the encirclement of the fortress and the isolation of its garrison. In the course of twenty-four hours, the Belgians had identified units of five German army corps, from prisoners taken and dead left on the field. It seemed obvious, therefore, that the defenders of Liége were confronted by forces of overwhelming strength. The attack was no mere diversion, but a determined effort to gain possession of the fortress that would be pressed to a conclusion, and Leman entertained no illusions as to the ultimate outcome. The first night attack had already tried the strength of the Belgian troops to the limit, and the extension of the German zone of attack had required a corresponding attentuation of the defenders' lines, until at some points they had become reduced to a mere cordon of infantry.

By personal experience, the Belgian commander had been made aware of the fragile nature of his defences, for in the early morning hours of the 6th, just before dawn, his Headquarters in the Rue Sainte-Foi, on the eastern outskirts of the city, had been attacked by a venturesome raiding party that had slipped through the lines. Alarmed by shouts and shots in the street, Leman and his staff had seized their side-arms and rushed to the aid of the Headquarters platoon, struggling in the darkness with grey-clad figures that swarmed about the house. The raiders had fled, leaving a score of dead and wounded behind them, but the lesson was obvious, and its implication of weakness could not be ignored.

Determined to hold out to the last extremity, Leman nevertheless realized that in the end the garrison must succumb before the weight of numbers.   Though the troops of the 3rd Division and the 15th Brigade might contribute materially to prolonging the resistance, they represented a substantial fraction of his country's campaign army and their loss would be a severe blow.   Faced with these considerations, Leman withdrew the mobile troops from their positions during the afternoon of August 6th and sent them, depleted by losses and weary from thirty-six hours of continuous fighting, to join the main body of the Belgian army along the Gette.   Thenceforth, the resistance of Liége depended upon the individual powers of the forts, each of which was left to its own resources with no direct communication with the others.

With the coming of darkness, the German assaults began again. The night before, in the vicinity of the Fort of Fléron, the German central column advancing from the east had effected a breach in the Belgian positions, but had suffered too heavily to exploit its success. With the defending lines between the forts now held only by isolated detachments, the 14th Brigade that formed this column pushed forward to the outskirts of the city.   The brigade acted temporarily under the orders of General Ludendorff, then Quartermaster-General of the II Army,[6] who had been attached to Von Emmich's force by the Army Commander to observe the progress of the attack, and the development of the plans that he himself had devised.   Upon the death of the Brigade Commander, Ludendorff, with Von Emmich's approval, had taken over command of the brigade.   Leading his men boldly forward, Ludendorff first seized the ancient Fort of Chartreuse and after a brief pause turned his attention to the near-by Citadel. Rushing ahead of his troops, accompanied only by a single staff officer, he stood before the closed main gate, hammering upon it with the hilt of his sword.   It is interesting to speculate what the effect of a well-aimed shot at that moment might have been upon the future course of the war, but no shot was fired.   Instead, the gates were opened, and a few score badly frightened Belgian reservists surrendered without resistance.   Ludendorff's example of determination and personal courage won him the decoration *Pour le Mérite,* the highest military order of the German Empire, and contributed materially to his promotion hardly a fortnight later, when he was designated as Von Hindenburg's Chief of Staff on the Russian front.

Though Von Emmich followed Ludendorff and his brigade into the city, and German troops occupied it throughout the day of August

---

[6] As a punishment, it is said, for an insistence embarrassing to the Minister of War in demanding additional appropriations for the army, Ludendorff had been relieved of his post on the General Staff and sent to command a brigade at Strasbourg, in 1912.   Upon the outbreak of the war, his out-standing ability and long staff experience caused his transfer again to staff duty with Von Bülow's Army.

7th, engaging in frequent skirmishes through the streets and across the bridges of the Meuse with Belgian patrols, only fragmentary reports reached the II Army at Hanover and Von Moltke's Headquarters at Berlin. The first authentic news to relieve the suspense came towards the close of the day in the form of a private telegram from Von Emmich to his wife, which Von Bülow's Headquarters intercepted. The information it contained was meagre, "Hurrah, at Liége," was all it said, but two hours later more formal word arrived from the II Army's liaison officer.

General von Emmich entered Liége on August 7th at 7:45 A.M. The Governor in flight. The Bishop a prisoner. Liége evacuated by Belgian troops. Citadel of Liége occupied by our troops. As yet not known which forts have been taken.

Despite the element of doubt suggested in the last sentence, the German High Command accepted the message as an announcement that the struggle was over, and the communiqué from Berlin proclaimed the capture of the fortress. The press hailed the victory, and throughout Germany the public received the news with high satisfaction. Under the impression that the principal barrier to the advance of his Army had been removed, Von Bülow entrained his Headquarters on the night of August 7th, for Montjoie in the zone of concentration.

Disillusion awaited the German Army Commander the following morning when he reached the railway station of Aix-la-Chapelle. There, Ludendorff met him with a personal report on the progress of operations. The facts set forth in the telegraphic report the previous night had been strictly accurate, but the whole story had not been told. The city itself was, indeed, in German hands but the ring of forts remained unbroken. The Belgian tricolor still snapped defiantly above the Fort of Loncin whither Leman had moved his Headquarters. What was worse, the guns of the forts which commanded every road leading to the city were maintaining so accurate a fire and so vigilant a watch, that Von Emmich and the brigade that Ludendorff had led into the city had been cut off from the rest of the besieging forces, whose attacks had failed. For the moment at least, communication with Von Emmich had become impossible.

While the German people rejoiced and Von Moltke's Headquarters blandly issued orders upon the assumption that Liége had fallen, Von Bülow suffered agonies of apprehension. The prestige of the German army and his own career depended upon the fate of the brigade imprisoned in Liége and upon his ability to make good the victory that had already been announced. Twenty-four hours passed without change in the situation, while every effort to reach Von Emmich failed. Seriously alarmed by the possibility that the Belgians, perhaps with French aid, had recaptured the city and had taken Von Emmich and his men prisoners, Von Bülow determined to end the suspense at all costs. On the morning of the 9th, he deputed his senior Corps Commander, General von Einem, to take all elements of the 7th, 9th and 10th Army Corps not already engaged to clarify the situation.

During the day Von Einem succeeded in establishing telephonic communication with the city, and before night brought welcome news to the Army Commander that the German troops were safe. In the early hours of August 10th, Von Emmich himself at last effected a breach in the wall of steel that had held him prisoner, and brought about his own release by the capture of the Fort of Barchon. The next night, another fort, D'Evégnée, fell into German hands.

The guns of Barchon and D'Evégnée, in the northeast sector of the defences on the right bank of the Meuse, had dominated the German lines of communication, and their capture opened the way at last for the arrival of heavy siege artillery. At six o'clock in the evening of August 12th, German 420 mm. guns, the heaviest artillery ever used in modern warfare, opened fire. It was the beginning of the end, for the forts had not been built to withstand calibres heavier than 210. mm. For hour after hour, an unrelenting bombardment continued, pulverizing the powerful concrete foundations of the forts, burying the defenders under masses of debris, destroying the nerves of the survivors with shattering explosions and suffocating them with nauseous fumes. On the 13th, Pontisse that commanded the passages of the Meuse north of the city succumbed, as well as Chaudfontaine and D'Embourg in the southeastern sector. The next day Liers, and Fléron were taken. With the right bank of the Meuse thus cleared, orders for the advance of the German armies were issued.

As Von Kluck's Army and the elements of Von Bülow's Army not engaged in the siege began their march, the attack on the left-bank forts of Liége continued with unabated vigour. On the 15th, Lantin and Boncelles fell, and in the late afternoon, a direct hit from a 280 mm. shell struck the powder magazine of Loncin. Out of the tons of wreckage that overwhelmed three-quarters of the garrison, General Leman was rescued, unconscious, but alive. Before noon on the 16th, the Forts of Flémalle and Hollogne, the last of the circle had ceased firing, and the capture of Liége, announced nine days before by the German Government, had become an accomplished fact.

As a tribute to the gallantry of the Belgian defence, Von Emmich,

who had met Leman at peace-time manoeuvres, visited the wounded
Belgian Commander and extended him every courtesy due a gallant
adversary ; while Von Bülow gave him permission to send a letter
to King Albert, before his departure for Germany as a prisoner of
war.

"I am certain of having sustained the honour of our arms," Leman
wrote. "I have surrendered neither the fortress nor the forts."

In truth, as a feat of arms, the defence of Liége deserves a high
place in military annals.

To the Germans it came as a bitter disappointment. Instead of
a quick, smashing attack lasting forty-eight hours, the reduction of
the Belgian fortress had required a continuous battle and siege of
more than eleven days and an expenditure of men and munitions
beyond all expectations. Despite carefully laid plans, a notable
failure of co-ordination had characterized the operation, and an almost total lack of liaison between the attacking troops and their
directing staffs. In certain instances German units opened fire on
one another in the darkness and confusion, and the losses sustained
by the infantry before the heavy artillery came into action were out
of all proportion to any results achieved.

The actual delay in the development of German plans occasioned
by the resistance of Liége will probably always remain in doubt.
German commentators generally slide over the question, while Von
Bülow, Von Kluck, and Von Kuhl, without saying so in so many
words, indicate that it had no effect. Allied opinions differ widely.
The French General J. Rouquerol, adopting the Belgian point of
view, has estimated the delay at some ten days,[7] the British Official
History places it more conservatively at "about four or five days,"
while General Dupont, Chief of the French Intelligence Service
at the time, insists that it did not delay the German advance at all.
Only upon the supposition — at best a doubtful one — that if Liége
had fallen at the first onslaught, the German armies would immediately have advanced and completed their concentration in hostile territory, does it seem possible to justify a delay of as long as
four days. In Germany, as in France, the first day of mobilization
was August 2nd, and whatever advantage may have been gained by
preparatory measures, there seems no question that the German
right wing armies could not in any case have completed their concentration before the 13th. Certainly, though they might have advanced as far as the left bank of the Meuse, it can hardly be supposed that they would have undertaken a further march which might

[7] Gen. J. Rouquerol, *Charleroi* (Payot, Paris, 1932), pg. 71 ; Gen. Dupont, *op. cit.*
Gen. Normand estimates the delay as "at least two days" ; *Défense de Liége, Namur,
Anvers en 1914* (Fournier, Paris, 1923), pg. 59.

have brought them into conflict with substantial Allied forces before
their own effectives were complete. It seems fair to say, therefore,
that the defence of Liége did not retard the march of the main body
of the German right wing armies into Belgium by more than forty-
eight hours — though as General Dupont has pointed out, this by
no means lessens the credit due the defenders of Liége for their
heroic resistance.

The check sustained, and particularly the ineptitude of the early
attacks was a severe blow to the pride of the German army. The
mortification and chagrin in high military circles over the failure
of their carefully drilled war-machine to function more smoothly
in its first test became an open secret.

"I expected as much," the Emperor remarked bitterly to Von
Moltke on learning of the first German reverses before Liége, "and
your invasion of Belgium has brought England in against us."

Nevertheless, at a heavy price, the obstacle of Liége had been removed, and the path of the German right wing armies lay open before them.[8]

---

[8] In addition to official sources, and authorities already cited, see Field Marshal von
Bülow's *Mein Bericht zur Marneschlacht* (Scherl, Berlin, 1919) and Gen. Schruyver's
La Bataille de Liége.

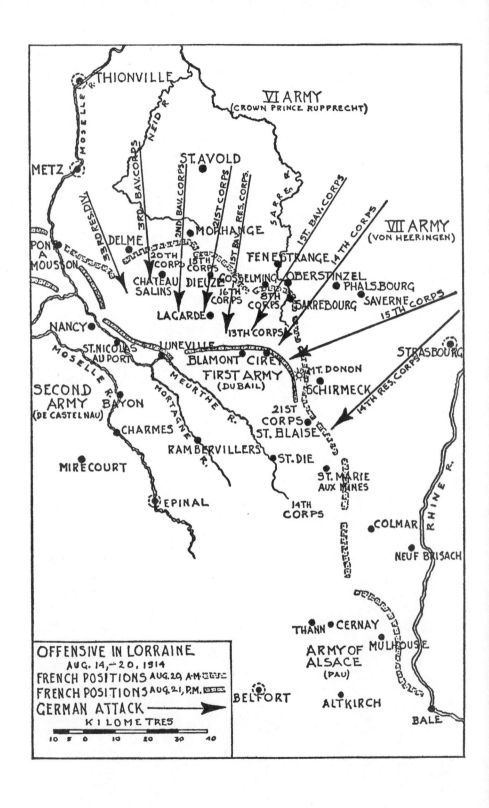

OFFENSIVE IN LORRAINE
AUG. 14,–20, 1914
FRENCH POSITIONS AUG. 20, A.M.
FRENCH POSITIONS AUG. 21, P.M.
GERMAN ATTACK ——————▶
KILOMETRES
10 5 0   10   20   30   40

CHAPTER VII

THE OFFENSIVE IN LORRAINE

WHILE the German guns pounded at the forts of Liége in the prelude to the Schlieffen Plan, the mobilization and concentration of the French armies proceeded with a speed and an absence of friction that attested the competence with which Belin had worked out the administrative detail of Plan XVII, and Joffre made ready to open the French campaign with a great offensive in Lorraine.

Though no major operations marked the first eleven days of hostilities, the opposing armies did not remain wholly inactive. On August 7th, a fraction of Dubail's First Army, the 7th Army Corps (Bonneau), reinforced by a brigade from the Belfort garrison and supported by the 8th Cavalry Division, entered southern Alsace and the following afternoon marched into the little Alsatian city of Mulhouse amid the wild enthusiasm of the French element of the population. The military advantage that Joffre sought by the occupation of Upper Alsace and the seizure of the Rhine bridges was the protection of the right flank of the French First Army during its advance, but this objective seems to have been secondary to a desire to achieve a political *coup de théâtre* to capture the imagination of the French people and to stir their enthusiasm.

In such an operation, vigorous leadership, and above all speed, were essential, for success depended upon the ability of the French to attain their objectives and to consolidate their positions before the enemy could organize his resistance ; but the command of the expedition fell to an officer who had little faith in the enterprise, General Bonneau, commander of the 7th Army Corps, whose chief claim to distinction rested upon a stinging public rebuke he had once administered at general manoeuvres to a Division Commander named Foch. With his untried forces extended over a wide front in semi-hostile country, and handicapped by an almost complete break-down in his service of supply, Bonneau's advance was slow and halting, with frequent trivial delays. When he arrived in Mulhouse, his troops were already weary and somewhat disorganized, though they had encountered insignificant opposition during their two-days' march, and the commander of the German VII Army, Von Heeringen, at his Headquarters at Strasbourg, had had no difficulty in obtaining information as to the numbers and dispositions of the French forces or in guessing their intentions.

On the morning of August 9th, elements of the German 14th and 15th Army Corps opened a vigorous attack against the French detachment occupying Cernay and, debouching from the Forest of Harth, soon extended their efforts eastward to the outskirts of Mulhouse. Though not greatly outnumbered, the French infantry made a poor showing. Local commanders, holding isolated positions along the broad front, were left to their own devices to solve their problems and extricate themselves as best they could, without information as to the positions of adjacent units and without orders from their superiors. Encouraged by their initial success, the Germans pressed their advantage, driving Bonneau's command before them. By nightfall the French had abandoned Mulhouse and two days later, Bonneau wound up in the positions from which he had started, under the sheltering guns of the fortress of Belfort.

The unfortunate outcome of Bonneau's adventure in Alsace led Joffre to make the first major readjustment in his forces. News of the first German attacks which had started in the early morning of August 9th, had not reached Dubail, the Army Commander, at his Headquarters at Epinal until late afternoon, and it seemed evident that the distance was too great for the First Army effectively to direct active operations. Accordingly, the First Army was subdivided and an independent army formed, designated as the Army of Alsace, which included not only the forces that Bonneau had led, but also the group of three Reserve divisions concentrated at Vesoul, the 44th Division from the Army of the Alps, which had been dissolved upon Italy's declaration of neutrality, and a group of five battalions of Chasseurs, furnished by the First Army. This force, with a strength approximately equivalent to three army corps, Joffre placed under the command of General Pau, who had been called out of retirement upon the outbreak of hostilities, but had not yet received an active assignment.[1]

French disappointment over the reverse in Alsace was tempered somewhat by a minor victory won at Mangiennes on August 10th, where a reconnaissance by the German 6th Cavalry Division of the Crown Prince's Army was repulsed with heavy loss, leaving a battery of artillery and a number of prisoners in French hands. The

[1] *La Place de Belfort* (Berger-Levrault, Paris, 1919) by Gen. Thevenet, Governor of the fortress, gives an interesting and authoritative account of the first French invasion of Alsace and of the subsequent operations of the Army of Alsace. The 57th Reserve Division of the Belfort garrison co-operated in these operations.

following day, however, at La Garde on the front of De Castelnau's Army, an over-sanguine effort by the French 2nd Cavalry Division to improve its positions resulted less fortunately, and the Bavarians of Crown Prince Rupprecht's Army drove the French back, taking 2500 prisoners, 8 guns and a battle-flag.

Apart from the abortive invasion of Alsace and the haphazard engagements at Mangiennes and La Garde, no encounters worthy of mention occurred during the period of concentration. On August 13th, the assembly of the French armies was complete, and the campaign began the next day.

In the preamble to Plan XVII, Joffre had expressed his intention of opening the campaign with two major offensive actions,[2] but apart from this general statement no plan of operations had been committed to paper. On August 8th, however, the French Commander in Chief issued his General Instructions No. 1,[3] which constitutes the complement to Plan XVII and the key to French strategy during the first phase of the Campaign of the Marne, the series of great battles known collectively as the Battle of the Frontiers.

Based on two assumptions — both of them erroneous — that the German forces before the French First and Second Armies did not exceed six army corps, and that the principal group of German armies was concentrated in the region of Thionville and Metz, these Instructions wholly ignored the possibility that the enemy might march west through Belgium, beyond the Meuse River. They illustrate strikingly the fundamental weakness of the French High Command at the outbreak of the war, which persisted until after the Battle of the Frontiers, a complete misconception of its adversary's dispositions and intentions which affords the underlying explanation of the outcome of the early battles so disastrous to the Allies.

As Plan XVII had foreshadowed, Joffre's orders envisaged two general offensive movements, the first to be executed by Dubail's First Army (including the Army of Alsace) and by De Castelnau's Second Army, and the second, later, by the Third, Fourth and Fifth Armies against what Joffre then supposed to be the main body of the enemy forces.

In the opening offensive, the four army corps of Dubail's First Army were to form the spear-head of the French attack, striking north across the frontier of Lorraine with the city of Sarrebourg as their initial objective, to drive the German forces assembled there eastward into Lower Alsace in the region of Strasbourg. Dubail's

[2] See pg. 17.
[3] See Appendix IV.

western flank was to be protected by the simultaneous advance of three corps of De Castelnau's Second Army towards Dieuze and Château Salins, while his eastern flank was covered by the north-ward movement of the Army of Alsace. To parry a possible counter-stroke, which Joffre feared might debouch from the region of Metz, two army corps and the group of Reserve divisions attached to the Second Army were to remain in the region of Nancy.

Such was the general scheme, when on August 13th, the French Commander in Chief issued his final orders to set in motion the following day the general offensive in which nearly a third of the effective strength of the French armies participated and which culminated in the Battles of Sarrebourg and Morhange, the first general engagements of the war.

"I count on you absolutely for the success of this operation," Joffre wrote Dubail. "It must succeed and you must devote all your energy to it."

The two men chosen to lead the initial French advance presented a vivid contrast in personality. One of them, De Castelnau, com-mander of the Second Army, had served at Joffre's insistence as Major General during the period of preparation of Plan XVII and had shared with Joffre and Berthelot the major responsibility for its conception. Upon Pau's retirement at the end of 1913, he had succeeded to the command of the Second Army, the largest on the front, embracing in its area the great city of Nancy and the fortress of Toul. A cultured gentleman of ancient lineage, De Castelnau had become personally identified with factions of "the Right" sus-pected of royalist proclivities, and this fact, together with his devout Catholicism, had attracted the hostility of the more radical elements both in the army and in political circles, among them Clemenceau, who ridiculed his small physique and dapper appearance with the nickname of "Monk in Boots."

De Castelnau's modulated courtesy of manner contrasted strongly with the sharp-tongued vigour of his colleague Dubail. Before the war, Dubail had ranked high in the French army and had served for many years as a member of the Superior War Council, conduct-ing in 1911, as Chief of Staff, delicate negotiations with the British. Blunt to the point of brutality, caustic, critical and sparing of praise, Dubail was hardly a popular chief, and his frequent, unheralded appearances at lower headquarters, and even in the front lines, came to be regarded as a scourge.

"Don't be afraid to make staff officers walk," he told his Corps Commanders. "They're only too glad to do it. It's a pleasure for those youngsters to walk around under fire."

But if to his subordinates, Dubail seemed a harsh chief, he was no less unsparing of himself, and Joffre relied heavily, with justice, on his indefatigable energy.[4]

The plans of the French High Command fell almost exactly into the pattern that Count von Schlieffen had anticipated ten years before, and the Germans prepared to meet Joffre's offensive in the classic manner of the pre-war *kriegspiel*.

From the little town of St. Avold, some forty kilometres east of Metz, Rupprecht, Crown Prince of Bavaria, directed the concentration of the German VI Army that stood directly in the path of Dubail and De Castelnau. The tradition which required German royal personages to take the field in person had placed Prince Rupprecht, at the age of forty-seven, in command of an army. "A soldier from a sense of duty," Ludendorff wrote of him, adding, "His inclinations were not in the least military." [5]

To make up for what must have seemed a deplorable weakness in the scion of a reigning house, the German General Staff had provided the VI Army with a Chief of Staff who was one of the strongest and most ambitious leaders in the German military system, Krafft von Dellmensingen. Throughout the campaign, he ruled his princely chief with an iron hand, and freely used his position as representative of the House of Wittelsbach, second only to the Hohenzollerns, to impose his will even upon the Prussianized High Command.

Five army corps comprised Prince Rupprecht's Army, four of them Bavarians, and the fifth, the 21st, Prussians. In accordance with Schlieffen's prescriptions, which Von Moltke had adopted, the Bavarian Army prepared to fight a defensive battle in positions extending from the Nied River on the west to the Sarre, and thence along the heights north and east of Sarrebourg to Phalsbourg and Saverne, on terrain every foot of which had been reconnoitred and studied long before the war. Along the frontier, elements of the 21st Army Corps (Fritz von Below) and of the 1st Bavarian Corps (Von Xylander), supported by the three cavalry divisions of the 3rd Cavalry Corps (Von Frommel), covered the German concentration and maintained contact with the advance guards of the French First and Second Armies, on occasion pushing their reconnaissances boldly into French territory as far south as the Meurthe.

Farther to the east, another German army, the VII, commanded by the former Prussian Minister of War, Von Heeringen, assembled for the protection of Alsace. It was three army corps strong, rein-

---

[4] A biographical article on De Castelnau by Commandant Giraud appears in the *Revue des Deux Mondes* of August 1921. Dubail's own memoirs, *Quatre Années de Commandement* (Fournier, Paris, 1922) are more revealing of the character of the commander of the French First Army than any biography could be, and constitute also a source of cardinal importance for any study of the operations in Lorraine.

[5] Ludendorff, *Meine Kriegserinnerungen* 1914–1918 (Mittler, Berlin, 1919).

forced by a Reserve division from the Strasbourg garrison and two brigades of Landwehr.

To secure unity of strategic action, after Von Heeringen had repelled the French advance on Mulhouse, Von Moltke on August 10th placed both left wing armies under the orders of the commander of the VI Army, an embryo of the later device of the Group of Armies, so that during the subsequent battles in Lorraine, the VI and VII Armies acted nominally under the command of Crown Prince Rupprecht, but actually under the energetic direction of Von Dellmensingen.

On the morning of August 14th, the French advance began in conformity with Joffre's plan, and seven army corps of the French First and Second Armies marched towards the frontier.[6] The reorganization of forces in Alsace, made necessary by Bonneau's reverse, delayed the start of Pau's Army of Alsace, so that Dubail was forced to use his right corps, the 14th, to cover his flank towards the east, a serious dissipation of strength that proved costly.

Along the whole front, the Germans fell back as Von Moltke intended they should, relying mainly on artillery fire to hinder and delay the French advance, but the day did not pass without sharp fighting at several points.   At Blamont and Cirey, Dubail's infantry impetuously sought to drive Von Xylander's Bavarians from positions which they were preparing to evacuate but had no intention of being driven out of, and suffered in consequence costly temporary checks. Near Saint-Blaise in a combat that lasted for the better part of the day, the French 21st Corps converted the retirement of a detachment of German Landwehr and reservists into a rout, seizing 12 cannon, 8 machine-guns and more than 500 prisoners.   At Niargoutte Farm, a point that had been bitterly contested, victorious French Chasseurs unearthed a German battle-flag, buried beneath a pile of straw and abandoned by the defenders in their flight.

On the whole, the offensive seemed to have opened auspiciously for the French, and the following morning the main body of the

---

[6] Order of Battle from east to west :
French : First Army (Dubail) : 14th Corps (Pouradier-Duteil), 21st Corps (Legrand-Girarde), 13th Corps (Alix), 8th Corps (De Castelli), Temporary Cavalry Corps, 2nd, 6th and 10th Cavalry Divisions (Conneau).
Second Army (De Castelnau) : 16th Corps (Taverna), 15th Corps (Espinasse), 20th Corps and 68th Reserve Division (Foch). Two Corps of the Second Army, the 9th (Dubois) and 18th (De Mas Latrie) and the 59th and 70th Reserve Divisions did not participate in the offensive advance.
German : VII Army (Von Heeringen) : 14th Reserve Corps (Von Schubert), 15th Corps (Von Deimling), 14th Corps (Von Hoiningen).
VI Army (Prince Rupprecht) : 1st Bav. Corps (Von Xylander), 1st Bav. Reserve Corps (Von Fasbender), 21st Corps (Von Below), 2nd Bav. Corps (Von Martini), 3rd Bav. Corps (Von Gebsattel), 3rd Cavalry Corps (Von Frommel), 33rd Reserve Division. The VI Army was reinforced on August 18th by 4 Ersatz Divisions and the VII by 2 Ersatz Divisions.

two armies crossed the frontier. While regimental bands played the *Marseillaise,* the men joyously overturned the striped posts that marked the boundary, and the officers ceremoniously received welcoming delegations of the civilian population, who had occasion, a few days later, to repent their premature enthusiasm.

For four days, the French pursued their advance slowly and methodically, their progress punctuated by frequent vigorous actions against German rear-guards, and their columns harassed by long-range fire of heavy artillery. On the 17th, Foch led the 20th Corps into Château Salins, and the next day the 15th Corps occupied Dieuze, while De Maud'huy's 16th Division, on the left of Dubail's Army, marched into Sarrebourg which the enemy had voluntarily evacuated. On the evening of the 19th, the French 20th Corps on De Castelnau's left faced the heights of Morhange, in sight of the red-roofed barracks in the town, but on its right the 15th and 16th Corps had met sterner opposition and had not made such satisfactory progress, holding positions materially to the rear. In Dubail's Army, the 8th Corps (De Castelli) on the left held Sarrebourg, but had not been able to advance beyond it, with the 13th Corps (Alix) and the 21st Corps (Legrand-Girarde) on its right, the latter occupying the strong position of Mt. Donon. On Dubail's right, the 14th Corps (Pouradier-Duteil), guarding the Army flank, stretched out along a front of almost fifty kilometres facing eastwards on the heights of the Vosges. Though its positions were naturally strong and adapted to an effective defence, the absence of reserves made it vulnerable to attack in force.

Only the advance of Pau's Army of Alsace could effectively cover Dubail's right flank, but the commander of the Army of Alsace, determined to avoid a repetition of Bonneau's unfortunate experience, was proceeding with the greatest circumspection, and although opposed only by Landwehr and Reserve units, it was not until the afternoon of August 19th, that troops of the French 7th Corps again entered Mulhouse from which they had been driven ten days before. The Army of Alsace was still a long way from furnishing the First Army with the measure of support that it required, and Dubail awaited Pau's aid in vain.

In the meantime, as the French cautiously advanced, the German High Command prepared its counter-stroke. When news of De Castelnau's advance had reached Von Moltke in Berlin, he had briefly entertained the notion of diverting the German Crown Prince's V Army from its original mission as a pivot for the right wing manoeuvre of the Schlieffen Plan and hurling it against the left flank of the French Second Army. Such an attack, emanating from Metz, was the very manoeuvre that Joffre had feared and an-

ticipated ; but Von Moltke concluded it required too great altera-
tions in the preconceived plan of operations and abandoned the idea,
limiting himself to placing a Reserve division, the 33rd from the
garrison of Metz, at the disposal of the Bavarian Crown Prince, and
further reinforcing him with six Ersatz divisions, which Schlieffen
had originally planned to assemble behind the offensive right wing
armies.   To assure a numerical superiority in the approaching test,
Rupprecht, at Von Dellmensingen's instigation, summoned Von
Heeringen's three army corps from the Alsatian front, placing them
on the left of the VI Army, opposite Dubail's right and subordinating the 1st Bavarian Reserve Corps, on the left of his own VI Army,
to Von Heeringen's command.   To permit the VII Army to gain the
positions assigned it with its full strength, the Bavarian Crown Prince
deferred until the 20th the counter-offensive which he had originally
planned for the 19th.

    Joffre, Dubail and De Castelnau, all three, were aware of the
German strategy, for the resistance to their advance had become
progressively more obstinate and many signs indicated that the
French First and Second Armies were approaching the enemy's main
line of resistance from which a counter-offensive would probably
be launched.   But the French commanders, underestimating both
the numbers and the fighting power of their adversary, relied on
their ability to meet and break the shock when it came.   Nearly
a hundred years before Napoleon had written :

    "Never do what the enemy wants for the very reason that he wants
it ; avoid a battle-ground that he has reconnoitred and studied, and
with even more reason ground that he has fortified and where he is
entrenched."

    It remained for the vanquished of Jena to prove the validity of
the great Emperor's maxim against his own countrymen on August
20th, 1914.

    The struggle waged that day by the French First and Second
Armies against the German VI and VII Armies was in reality two
separate battles, although strategically a unit, for no effective contact existed between De Castelnau and Dubail, and the German onslaught quickly broke what little liaison there was.

    For the First Army, it was Dubail's plan to anticipate the Ger-
man attack with an attack of his own, executed by the 15th Division
of the 8th Corps (De Castelli) on his left wing, while the remainder
of the Army remained on the defensive.   It was Dubail's purpose
to seize the bridges of the Sarre, northwest of Sarrebourg, between
that city and Fenestrange, opening a passage for the Cavalry Corps
by which it could reach the rear of the German positions and roll
up the enemy line towards the east against Phalsbourg and Saverne.

To carry out the designs of the French Army Commander, the 15th Division, theretofore in Army Reserve, had to execute a night march of fifteen kilometres to be followed immediately by an attack over unknown ground against the bridges of Oberstinzel and Gosselming. The attack was set for 3 A.M., an hour before dawn, but unforeseen delays prevented the division's arrival until nearly an hour later. By that time the sky had begun to lighten and the full advantage of surprise had been lost ; nevertheless the French infantry attacked, carrying the village of Gosselming by a furious attack at the point of the bayonet and swiftly moving to consolidate its gain by the capture of Saint-Jean-de-Bassel, a scant kilometre to the north. Here, however, greater difficulty appeared, for the German defenders, of the 1st Bavarian Reserve Division, now fully aroused, met every movement with a furious fire from machine-guns that studded the wooded hills between the two towns, while from the right bank of the Sarre, artillery shelled the attackers' flank and rear without mercy.

The other brigade of the 15th Division, which had been assigned the capture of the bridges of Oberstinzel, fared no better. As they emerged from the woods on the left bank of the river, the French found the enemy alert and waiting at the approaches to the town, and every attempt to force a crossing broke down before well-directed fire.

By seven in the morning the attack of the French 15th Division had collapsed ; a German counter-attack had recaptured Gosselming ; the French with depleted ranks had returned to their starting positions and the cavalry had had no opportunity to advance. For the next two hours, the Germans showed little inclination to press their advantage against the 15th Division, beyond maintaining a lively artillery bombardment, but as the Corps Commander, De Castelli, hastened to reorganize his forces for a renewal of the attacks, the enemy fire suddenly redoubled in intensity and extended along the whole front of the French First Army. Eager to try conclusions at last with the antagonist before whom they had retreated for the better part of a week, five German army corps moved forward.

The full fury of the attack fell on the French left, where neither of the divisions of the French 8th Corps had effectively organized defensive positions. Ill-prepared to meet an assault that exceeded in ferocity anything they had yet experienced, the French fell back as one position after another became untenable, each wave of the German onslaught being preceded by an intensive fire from heavy artillery which the French 75's of shorter range were unable to reach. Around Sarrebourg, De Maud'huy's Division clung tenaciously to its positions, but yielded ground yard by yard, until it became evident that without reinforcements it could not hold the city ; but no reserves were available.

Compelled at last, to his bitter disappointment, to order his command to fall back to the heights south of the city, De Maud'huy did so only after a final gesture of defiance. While the Bavarians engaged the French through the streets, De Maud'huy stood with his staff at the southern outlet of the city, and there, heedless of gusts of shrapnel that swept the road, passed the retreating infantry in review, while the massed bands of the division played the stirring *Marche Lorraine*.

Though the loss of Sarrebourg gave a sharp set-back to Dubail's ambitious plans, the French First Army was still far from decisive defeat. The losses of the 8th Corps had indeed been exceptionally severe, but it had retreated in good order without loss of cohesion, and the other three corps of Dubail's Army, though compelled to face attacks hardly less violent, had succeeded in holding their main positions and at nightfall were still exchanging blow for blow with the issue undecided.[7]

Dubail had already issued orders to his army to stand its ground and continue the battle the following day, when alarming news arrived that caused him drastically to alter his plans. Throughout the day, he had heard little of the fate of De Castelnau's Army beyond the fact that it was heavily engaged and that all was not well. A telephone message from Joffre's Headquarters brought the first authentic word that the French Second Army had suffered severe defeat. The 15th and 16th Corps on the left of the First Army were in full retreat, in a state of disorganization bordering on rout ; only the 20th Corps commanded by Foch had withstood the shock and was covering the retirement of the Second Army ; liaison between the two armies had become completely severed.

In fact, De Castelnau's Army had narrowly avoided complete disaster. At daybreak a violent bombardment fell on its whole front, and soon after, under cover of an early morning mist, Prince Rupprecht's infantry struck the French lines with a violence that took the defenders off their guard. On the Army left, the 39th Division of Foch's Corps was hurled back in a few minutes to the edge of the woods north of Château Salins, and the 11th Division, on the corps right, was similarly swept from its front-line positions. Farther to the right the situation of the 15th and 16th Corps, which had been

7 Two works of especial interest on the Battle of Sarrebourg and the operations of the First French Army generally are *Le 8ie Corps en Lorraine* (Berger-Levrault, Paris, 1925), by Gen. de Castelli, and *Opérations du 21ie Corps d'Armée* (Plon, Paris, 1922) by Gen. Legrand-Girarde. Both corps commanders were relieved of their commands soon after the Battle of the Marne, however, and their views of the High Command are not unnaturally somewhat coloured by this fact.

severely tried the previous day, became rapidly perilous, as the Bavarians swept around the Army's right flank, cutting off all connection with the First Army.

At 7:15, barely two hours after the battle had started, De Castelnau ordered Taverna of the 16th Corps to fall back, and at the same time directed the 15th Corps to counter-attack in the hope that this might stabilize the situation. It soon became evident that this hope was illusory, for with its last reserves engaged, the 15th Corps was itself rapidly falling back and was in no condition to carry out the Army Commander's order.

Only the front of the 20th Corps remained relatively stable. After their initial retreat, both divisions had succeeded in standing their ground, but the Germans now pressed around Foch's western flank, striking at the 68th Reserve Division that guarded his line of communications. The partial withdrawal of the 16th Corps, executed in the face of a hotly pursuing enemy, failed to produce any improvement in the general situation, for the 15th Corps had been unable to counter-attack, and the enemy, with ever-increasing confidence, had renewed his efforts on the right, driving a constantly deepening wedge between the 16th Corps and the First Army. Shortly after ten o'clock, De Castelnau, facing imminent disaster, issued his first order for the general retreat of the army.

This order, welcomed with relief by the shattered remnants of the 15th and 16th Corps, was received with genuine disappointment in the 11th Division of the 20th, which despite its dangerously exposed position had its lines substantially intact for more than five hours in the face of repeated assaults. Gradually the fury of the German drives had diminished, until at the very moment when the order to retreat arrived, the troops had gained the impression that victory was at hand. Until he received a formal order from Foch, General Balfourier, the Division Commander, declined to relinquish his positions.[8]

It is one thing to order a retreat, but quite another to break away from the clutches of an eager and triumphant enemy. So De Castelnau found on the 20th of August. Again and again tempestuous assaults hurled elements of the 15th and 16th Corps from positions where their officers were desperately attempting to organize a stand and to restore some semblance of cohesion. Guns and materiel of all kinds were abandoned, and at every moment, at some point or another, it seemed that the last vestige of order would vanish and the retreat of the Second Army would become a precipitate

---

[8] For accounts of the operations of the French 20th Corps at Morhange, see Gen. Colin's *La Division de Fer* (Payot, Paris, 1929), a history of the 11th Division, and Commandant Lefranc's *Le 20ᵗᵉ Corps à Morhange*, Revue Militaire Française, October, 1930.

flight.   At six in the evening, as the German attacks slackened with the coming of night, De Castelnau despaired of arresting the retreat or of reorganizing his forces in time to make effective resistance to renewed assaults next day.   With a heavy heart he ordered his army to break away under the cloak of darkness, and by a forced march to regain the positions around Nancy from which it had started on August 13th.

On the morning of August 21st, the French Second Army had abandoned all its gains and had broken contact with the enemy ; but it had also left its pursuers more than twenty kilometres behind, and had reached a point of relative safety where the work of rehabilitation could begin.   On the right, Dubail had conformed to his neighbour's movement.   With its western flank left in the air by the Second Army's retreat, the First Army had had no choice but to break off its battle and retreat.   Two days later it too had reached positions behind the Meurthe from which it had started on its ill-starred offensive.

With his left wing firmly anchored to the strong fortified positions known as the Grand Couronné de Nancy, De Castelnau reorganized his army for a defensive stand.   Of the two corps of the Second Army that had not taken part in the advance, one, the 18th (De Mas Latrie) , had already left to reinforce Lanrezac's Fifth Army and the other, the 9th (Dubois), had partly gone to the Fourth Army, but of the latter one division [9] still remained, which, with two Reserve divisions of Leon Durand's group constituted a force that furnished a rallying point for the shaken Second Army.   In the first confusion, De Castelnau had contemplated the necessity of a further retreat behind the Moselle and the abandonment of Nancy, but Joffre firmly insisted that he hold his positions, at least for the moment, and Rupprecht of Bavaria had not pressed his pursuit. Morhange and Sarrebourg had not left the German VI and VII Armies unscathed, and they marched slowly, pausing to cross the frontier with appropriate military ceremony.   For three days both French armies enjoyed relative tranquillity, and for the first time the French soldier demonstrated the recuperative powers that so often astonished his adversaries.

By nightfall of the 23rd, great progress had been made in repairing the damage the First and Second Armies had suffered and De Castelnau and Dubail looked confidently to the future.   There was no more talk of further retreat.   The next day marked the beginning of a new phase in the operations in Lorraine and a new series

[9] The 18th Division, which remained as a part of De Castelnau's Army until it was sent to reinforce Foch's Army during the Battle of the Marne. Humbert's Moroccan Division replaced it in the 9th Corps.

of bloody battles for the protection of Nancy and the defence of the Trouée de Charmes that exerted an influence on the outcome of the Campaign of the Marne hardly less important, though indirect, than the more celebrated conflicts farther to the west.

The French offensive in Lorraine, the first fruits of Plan XVII, thus developed and ended as Count von Schlieffen had expected. By faithful application of methods developed in manoeuvres before the war, the Germans had drawn their adversaries against positions organized in advance, and at a psychological moment of their own choice had counter-attacked to the complete discomfiture of the invaders. The success of the VI and VII Armies fulfilled Von Moltke's most ardent hopes, and flamboyant accounts of victory relayed by Von Dellmensingen nourished the elation of the German High Command. The French right wing armies had been decisively beaten and were in disorganized flight ; such was the tenor of the news that reached Coblenz. Earnestly Prince Rupprecht's Chief of Staff pled for permission to follow up the victory that seemed to him so close at hand. A vigorous drive, he was convinced, would complete the destruction of the French eastern armies, already on the verge of disintegration, striking them back across the Moselle, between Toul and Epinal, overwhelming Nancy, driving one fraction southeast against the Swiss border and turning the flank of the main group of enemy forces to the west.

It was a tempting prospect to Von Moltke, an opportunity to duplicate in the east the enveloping manoeuvre that Schlieffen had prescribed for the right wing armies. Before the eager importunities of the VI Army, Von Moltke yielded.

"Strike and God be with you !" Von Stein, the Quartermaster-General told Von Dellmensingen, though he was not willing affirmatively to order the offensive.

So Sarrebourg and Morhange brought about a major modification in the German plan of operations. The primarily defensive mission of the left wing armies, which would have permitted them to become a reservoir of reinforcements for the decisive right wing was forgotten, and instead their role became an offensive one. In place of the simple enveloping operation by one wing designed by his predecessor, Von Moltke became committed to an effort at encirclement by both wings, the "pincers of Cannae." From August 25th to September 7th, the two German left wing armies dashed themselves against the French defences in the very region against which Schlieffen had warned, while in the meantime Joffre drew from the defending forces the strength of more than four army corps to build up his opposition to the advance of the German right wing.

Thus, in his first major independent decision, Von Moltke undermined the foundations of the German plan of campaign, and prepared the way for his own downfall, and the Battles of Sarrebourg and Morhange — despite their outcome and hardly in the way Joffre had intended — inured to the benefit of France.[10]

[10] In addition to official and other sources already cited, the following are important references bearing on the operations in Lorraine : the Bavarian Official History (Bayerisches Kriegsachiv), *Die Schlacht in Lothringen* (Schick, Munich, 1929), Crown Prince Rupprecht's War-diary, *Mein Kriegstagebuch* (Deutscher National Verlag, Munich, 1928), Gen. von Dellmensingen's *Die Führung des Kronprinzen Rupprecht von Bayern,* Marshal Foch's *Mémoires,* Vol. I (Plon, Paris, 1931) and a monograph based on the French and German Official Histories, *La Bataille des Frontières* (Berger-Levrault, Paris, 1932) by Col. Valarché. See also Lieut.-Col. Koeltz's articles *La Bataille de Lorraine,* Revue de Paris, September and October 1923 ; Commandant de Mierry's *Le Commandement allemand pendant les opérations d'Alsace-Lorraine* Revue de France, May 15, 1922, and Gen. de Mondésir's *Souvenirs et pages de guerre* (Berger-Levrault, Paris, 1934).

CHAPTER VIII

THE OFFENSIVE IN THE ARDENNES

WITH the march of the First and Second Armies into Lorraine started under conditions apparently satisfactory, Joffre turned his principal attention to preparing the second major offensive contemplated by Plan XVII and by his Instructions of August 8th, the offensive north of the line Verdun-Metz. As originally projected, this movement was to constitute the principal effort of the French armies, with the object of driving northward the enemy forces congregating in the Grand Duchy of Luxembourg and in the fortified region of Thionville. Assuming its success and that of the operations of the two armies farther to the east, the way would lie open for an investment of Metz.

Joffre's plans initially contemplated the participation of the Third, Fourth and Fifth Armies, the whole of the French left wing, in this manoeuvre, but disquieting developments to the north, the first hint of the true character of the German strategy, caused him to alter his arrangements. Even before the outbreak of hostilities, Lanrezac, commander of the Fifth Army on the extreme left of the French line, feared that the German right wing armies might cross the Meuse in force and by extending their movement to the west attempt to envelop his flank. In a letter delivered on July 31st he had communicated his fears to Joffre in somewhat tentative fashion. This communication, as Lanrezac wrote after the war, he had written with the greatest care in the hope that it might provoke a general discussion of the role of the Fifth Army ; but to his chagrin it remained unanswered. For better or worse, the French High Command had decided that there was nothing to fear from such a movement as Lanrezac suggested ; the possibility had been considered and rejected as too remote to warrant any alteration in the plans already settled. On the eve of the declaration of war the moment for theoretical discussion of strategic considerations had passed. Though time proved Joffre's forecast of the enemy's action to be erroneous, it seems hardly astonishing that Lanrezac should have received no reply to his letter, and in view of its equivocal phrasing, the importance later attached to it by Lanrezac's admirers seems unjustified.[1]

As the days passed, however, the conviction grew in Lanrezac's mind that the manoeuvre of the German right wing would extend beyond the flank of his own army, and that only by shifting the Fifth Army's area of concentration farther to the northwest could this danger be averted or minimized. The power of the German assault against Liége, coupled with an estimate of the French Intelligence Service that the northern group of German armies might include eight army corps and four cavalry divisions, tended to confirm his view, and Joffre so far yielded to his subordinate's importunities as to authorize the 1st Corps (Franchet d'Esperey), on the left of the Fifth Army, to move west of the Meuse and to take up the guard of the bridges between Givet and the Belgian fortress of Namur. But the French Commander in Chief could not wholly reconcile himself to depriving his major offensive of the powerful aid of the Fifth Army, and when, on August 14th, Lanrezac went personally to Vitry-le-François to urge his point of view on the High Command, Joffre, Belin and Berthelot successively assured him that the enemy had prepared no attack on the left bank of the Meuse and that his fears for the safety of his army's flank were groundless.

The events of the next day, August 15th, however, seemed to substantiate Lanrezac's apprehensions and brought about Joffre's conversion. German cavalry, the Guards Division of Von Richthofen's[2] 1st Cavalry Corps, supported by five Jäger infantry battalions and three groups of field artillery, arriving on the Meuse midway between Givet and Namur after a forced march, launched a powerful attack upon the important bridges at Dinant. Though Franchet d'Esperey's 1st Corps eventually drove back the attackers, the French received a sharp lesson in minor tactics at a cost of nearly 1100 casualties,[3] which caused genuine alarm at Vitry-le-François where it was accepted as a warning of the enemy's intent to cross the Meuse north of Givet. Combined with news received the same day that the Belgians had evacuated Huy, further to the north, before enemy forces estimated at 10,000 men, the affair at Dinant confirmed Lanrezac's predictions, and Joffre promptly ordered the Fifth Army to move towards the northwest, into the right angle formed by the junction of the Sambre and Meuse Rivers at Namur.

[1] For text of Lanrezac's letter, see *Fr. O. H.*, Annex to Vol. 1, Doc. No. 19. See also Lanrezac, *op. cit.*
[2] General Baron von Richthofen, commander of the German 1st Cavalry Corps, was the father of the celebrated and gallant German Ace who caused havoc to Allied aviation later in the war.
[3] Lieut-Col. Larcher's monograph, *Le 1er Corps à Dinant, Charleroi, Guise* (Berger-Levrault, Paris, 1932) gives a detailed account of the German attack on Dinant and its consequences.

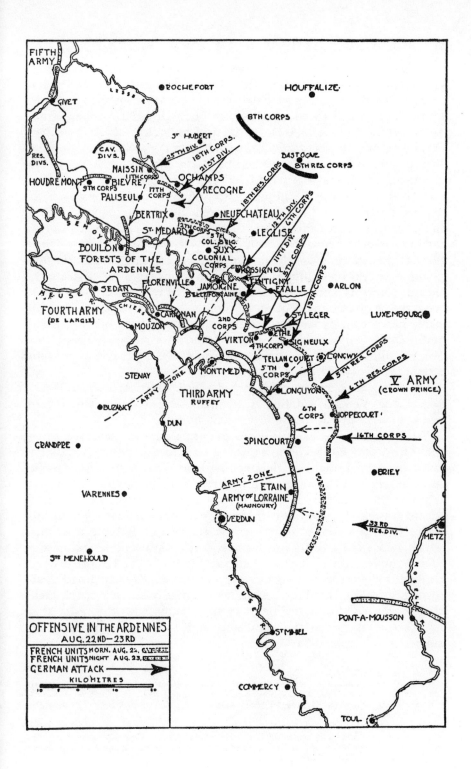

FIFTH
ARMY

ROCHEFORT

HOUFFALIZE

GIVET

LESSE

8TH CORPS

ST HUBERT

BASTOGNE
8TH RES. CORPS

CAV.
DIVS.

25TH DIV.

18TH CORPS.

21ST DIV.

RES.
DIVS.

MAISSIN
11TH CORPS

HOUDREMONT
9TH CORPS
BIEVRE

OCHAMPS
RECOGNE

18TH RES. CORPS

PALISEUL
11TH
CORPS

BERTRIX
NEUFCHATEAU

12TH DIV.
4TH CORPS

SEMOY
ST MEDARD
12TH CORPS

LECLISE

11TH DIV.
5TH CORPS

BOUILON
SUXY
COL. BRIG.

5TH
COLONIAL
CORPS

FORESTS OF THE
ARDENNES
FLORENVILLE
JAMOIGNE
TINTIGNY

ROSSIGNOL

13TH CORPS

ARLON

MEUSE R.
SEDAN
BELLEFONTAINE
ETALLE

FOURTH ARMY
(DE LANGLE)

CHIERS R.
CARIGNAN
MOUZON

2ND
CORPS

ST LEGER

LUXEMBOURG

VIRTON
ETHE

4TH CORPS
SIG NEULX

STENAY
ARMY ZONE
MONTMEDY

TELLAN COURT
5TH
CORPS

LONGWY
5TH RES. CORPS

6TH RES. CORPS

V ARMY
(CROWN PRINCE)

BUZANCY

DUN

THIRD ARMY
RUFFEY

LONGUYON

6TH
CORPS

JOPPECOURT

GRANDPRE

SPINCOURT

16TH CORPS

BRIEY

VARENNES

ARMY ZONE
ETAIN

ARMY OF LORRAINE
(MAUNOURY)

33RD
RES. DIV.

STE MENEHOULD

VERDUN

METZ

MOSELLE R.

MEUSE R.

PONT-A-MOUSSON

OFFENSIVE IN THE ARDENNES
AUG. 22ND—23RD

FRENCH UNITS MORN. AUG. 22,
FRENCH UNITS NIGHT AUG. 23,
GERMAN ATTACK
KILOMETRES
10   5   0   10   20

ST MIHIEL

COMMERCY

TOUL

This order,[4] the first affirmative step taken by the French High Command to counteract the right wing manoeuvre of the Schlieffen Plan, reduced the forces available for the offensive in the Ardennes by the strength of three army corps ; but in partial compensation, Joffre ordered Lanrezac to leave behind him the 11th Army Corps (Eydoux), two Reserve divisions and a cavalry division, and he further sent to De Castelnau's Second Army for the 9th Army Corps (Dubois), which had been held in reserve at the beginning of the offensive in Lorraine.   The necessities of the Second Army after its defeat at Morhange, however, prevented the complete execution of the Commander in Chief's intentions with respect to the 9th Corps, for only one division, the 17th, joined De Langle's Fourth Army, the other remaining to aid in the defence of Nancy ; but the opportune arrival of Humbert's Moroccan Division from Africa gave the 9th Corps its conventional complement of two infantry divisions. As a result of these and other reinforcements, De Langle's Fourth Army had grown by August 20th from a reserve army of three corps and a cavalry division to a formidable force of six army corps, two Reserve divisions and two cavalry divisions, the latter combined into a temporary cavalry corps.

On the right of the Fourth Army, Ruffey's Third Army with Headquarters at Verdun, totalled three army corps, one of which had three infantry divisions, and a cavalry division.

While the duty of executing the offensive advance devolved upon the Third and Fourth Armies, there remained a possibility that a German counter-offensive, debouching from Metz across the Moselle into the plain of the Woevre, might reach the flank and rear of the Third Army.   It was the same danger that had existed in the case of De Castelnau's offensive in Lorraine, and to guard against it, Joffre formed a new army composed entirely of Reserve divisions, which he designated on August 21st as the Army of Lorraine and placed under the orders of General Maunoury.[5]   Unfortunately, through some error in staff-work, never satisfactorily explained, Ruffey commanding the Third Army was not fully advised of the creation of the Army of Lorraine or of its mission, with the result that in subsequent operations confusion and lack of co-operation resulted.[6]

---

[4] See Appendix VI, (1).

[5] The Army of Lorraine included: the 3rd Group of Reserve divisions (Paul Durand) formerly part of the Third Army, comprising the 54th, 55th and 56th Reserve Divisions, the 65th, 67th and 75th Reserve Divisions and the garrison of Verdun, including the 72nd Reserve Division.

[6] In *La Bataille de la Frontière-Briey* (Bossard, Paris, 1920) M. Fernand Engerand, Deputy of Calvados and Reporter of the Briey Parliamentary Commission of 1919, has dealt fully with the formation of the Army of Lorraine and the resulting misunderstanding between Ruffey and Maunoury.

With the right flank of his offensive group thus covered, the French Commander in Chief fixed the towns of Arlon and Neufchâteau in Belgian Luxembourg as the intitial objectives of the Third and Fourth Armies. A broad belt of heavily wooded country, the forests of the Ardennes, separated the French forces from these objectives. It is not accidental that from the earliest times invaders of France have scrupulously avoided this region, whenever possible, for it is a wholly unpromising field for military operations. Devoid of industrial development, and in the main unsuited to agriculture, the Ardennes have remained for centuries covered by a succession of tangled woods, "a great forest of small trees," cut at frequent intervals by small streams flowing into the Meuse or into one of its two major tributaries, the Semoy or the Chiers. A lack of main highways accentuates the difficulty of transporting and supplying troops.

Joffre had no expectation of giving battle in the forests themselves, for a firm conviction existed at French General Headquarters that no important enemy forces held the immediate front of the Third and Fourth Armies, and that the forests which separated them from their first objectives would be found to be occupied, if at all, only by fragile screens of cavalry that could readily be driven back or dispersed.

"No serious opposition need be anticipated on the day of August 22nd," such was the substance of the official view of the French High Command transmitted to De Langle and Ruffey as they made ready to start their march towards the northeast.

On August 16th, the Intelligence Section of Joffre's staff had estimated the German forces opposed to the Third and Fourth Armies at six army corps and three cavalry divisions.[7] When, therefore, the French Commander in Chief set his forces in motion with a strength of eight army corps and three cavalry divisions,[8] he did so in the confident belief that he had secured a definite numerical advantage for the forthcoming operations. For the second time the French High Command was embarking upon a major offensive with a profound misconception of its opponents' strength, for the realities were quite different from what Joffre supposed.

[7] See Appendix V (1).
[8] Order of Battle from east to west :
French : Third Army (Ruffey) : 7th Cavalry Division, 6th Corps (Sarrail), 5th Corps (Brochin), 4th Corps (Boelle) ; *Fourth Army* (De Langle) ; 2nd Corps (Gérard), Colonial Corps (Lefévre), 12th Corps (Roques), 17th Corps (Poline), 11th Corps (Eydoux), Temporary Cavalry Corps (Abonneau), comprising 9th and 4th Cavalry Divisions. The 9th Corps (Dubois) and the 60th and 52nd Reserve Divisions on the left wing of the French Fourth Army did not participate in the initial advance.
German : V Army (German Crown Prince) : 16th Corps (Von Mudra), 6th Reserve Corps (Von Gossler), 5th Reserve Corps (Von Gündell), 13th Corps (Von Fabeck), 5th Corps (Von Strantz) ; *IV Army* (Duke of Wurtemburg) : 6th Corps (Von Pritzelwitz), 18th Reserve Corps (Von Steuben), 18th Corps (Von Schenck), 8th Reserve Corps (Von Egloffstein), 8th Corps (Von Tschepe und Weidenbach).

Between the northern boundary of the Grand Duchy of Luxembourg and the forts of Metz, two German armies had assembled, the centre group of the Schlieffen Plan, the IV under Duke Albrecht, heir to the throne of Wurtemburg, and the V commanded by the German Crown Prince. Together they comprised no less than ten army corps and two cavalry divisions, supported by six brigades of Landwehr, exclusive of the garrison troops of Metz. The superiority in numbers thus rested on the German side by a substantial margin.

Those two German armies formed the pivot of the encircling manoeuvre of the German offensive right wing, the hub of the wheel, of which Von Hausen's and Von Bülow's Armies were the spoke and Von Kluck's the outer rim. After the fall of the last of the forts of Liége, they had started their forward movement on August 18th like their northern neighbours, but their speed had been necessarily regulated by the progress of the forces on their right, and their marches on the succeeding days had been relatively short compared to the strides taken by Von Bülow and Von Kluck. At nightfall on August 21st, as the French Third and Fourth Armies prepared to start their march towards the northeast, across the forests of the Ardennes, the German IV and V Armies faced generally southwest, on the opposite side of the forests. A head-on collision became the inevitable consequence.

On the night of August 21st the general situation was not favourable to the Allies. In Lorraine, the French First and Second Armies were still reeling from the blows they had received the day before at Sarrebourg and Morhange ; Liége and Brussels had fallen, and the Belgian army had fallen back to the shelter of Antwerp ; the outposts of Lanrezac's Fifth Army were already engaged against Von Bülow on the Sambre, with Von Hausen rapidly approaching from the east ; Namur was invested, and Von Kluck and the British were marching from opposite directions towards Mons. Nevertheless Joffre adhered resolutely to his plan, and issued his orders for the offensive of the French Third and Fourth Armies to begin the following morning.

"The enemy will be attacked wherever encountered." This was the key-note of the orders that Joffre sent to his centre armies, the epitome of the philosophy that still dominated the French High Command.

Until the late afternoon of the 21st, the German IV and V Armies had no expectation of being called upon to fight a general engagement the following day. The Duke of Wurtemburg and the German Crown Prince had both expected to remain in their positions or at most to make short moves forward on the 22nd ; but despite all efforts at secrecy, the movements of De Langle's and Ruffey's forces and their preparations had not escaped the notice of German cavalry and aviation, and the reports that reached Army Headquarters led the German commanders to revise their plans. Without prescribing a definitely offensive advance, the Duke of Wurtemburg ordered the German IV Army to make ready for battle, and the German Crown Prince took a bolder part. Spurred, perhaps, by news of Rupprecht of Bavaria's victory in Lorraine, he appealed to Von Moltke for authority to begin a general offensive movement, but when this was denied, succeeded in obtaining permission for a limited advance, which he represented as designed to improve his Army's liaison with the fortified position of Thionville. The approval thus received, the Crown Prince and his Chief of Staff, General von Knobelsdorff,[9] forthwith expanded into general orders for the forward movement of the whole V Army, with its main body moving southwest, directly into the line of advance of Ruffey's Third French Army.

In the early hours of August 22nd, on opposite sides of the wooded defiles of the Ardennes, two French and two German armies began their forward movements, the former towards the northeast, the latter towards the southwest. French writers have habitually referred to the battle fought that day and the day following, under the collective name of the Battle of the Ardennes, while the Germans have generally divided it into two parts, separately designated as the Battle of Longwy and the Battle of Neufchâteau. Neither nomenclature seems wholly satisfactory, for it was in fact not one battle, nor even two, but a series of engagements, fought simultaneously by army corps, divisions, brigades and even battalions, for the most part independently of any central control and independently of the conduct of adjacent units. The character of the terrain rendered liaison between forces fighting almost side by side difficult, if not impossible, and prevented from the outset any continued direction of operations from Army, or even from Corps, Headquarters.

Throughout the two-day battle the advantage rested with the Germans, not alone by reason of their numerical superiority, for their preponderance in this respect was not so great that a skilful and determined adversary might not have overcome it, but by reason of their appreciation of the realities of the strategic and tactical situation. Though the German Crown Prince and the Duke of Wurtemburg were by no means fully informed of the strength and dispositions of their enemy, they nevertheless entertained no illusions as to the character of the opposition they were likely to encounter and

[9] As in the case of Rupprecht of Bavaria, the German High Command had assigned professional soldiers of high repute to the German Crown Prince and the Duke of Wurtemburg as Chiefs of Staff ; General Schmitt von Knobelsdorff for the V Army and General von Lüttwitz for the IV.

marched towards the battlefield ready to meet a powerful and aggressive adversary of at least equal strength.   In the preceding days the forests of the Ardennes had been patrolled and explored by the two divisions of the German 4th Cavalry Corps (Von Hollen), and German troopers stood ready to guide and support the main bodies as they approached from the rear.   The French, on the other hand, had arrived in the vicinity only the day before — in some instances during the night of the 21st — insufficiently informed of the character of the ground, inadequately supplied with maps,[10] and thanks to the over-optimism of the High Command, with only the most meagre information as to the enemy before them.

It was Joffre's general plan that five army corps of the Fourth Army should undertake the principal offensive action, crossing the belt of forest during the day of the 22nd and reaching the line Maissin-Ochamps-Neufchâteau by nightfall, while the Third Army on its right, marching on Arlon, had the primarily defensive mission of protecting the right flank of the attacking group.

The French dispositions in execution of this plan have been likened to a flight of steps, descending to the right, each step represented by an army corps with its principal front to the north.[11] Theoretically intended to permit each corps to face either to the north or to the east, as occasion might require, this arrangement actually made the security of the right flank of each corps dependent upon the successful advance of its right-hand neighbour.   The failure of any one corps to progress, not only exposed the flank of the adjacent corps to the left to an attack from the east, but also created a grave risk that the whole structure might collapse, like a row of nine-pins.   This was precisely what happened almost immediately.

The point of weakness that frustrated Joffre's plan developed on the front of the 5th Army Corps (Brochin) in the centre of Ruffey's Third Army.   In the late afternoon and evening of August 21st, a heavy rain had fallen, changing during the night to a dense mist, that hung over the ground and covered the wooded zone between the opposing armies with a shroud of grey.   Through the chill darkness of the early morning hours, the infantry of the German 5th Corps (Von Strantz) and of the 13th Corps (Von Fabeck), the right wing of the Crown Prince's Army, marched from Etalle and St. Leger through the forest. Dawn had not yet broken when cavalry scouts, preceding the advance-guards, fell back with word that they

[10] Officers of certain units of the 4th Army Corps (Boelle) of the French Third Army, for example, were provided with complete sets of large-scale military maps of the Rhineland, but of Belgian Luxembourg had only tourist road-maps or in some cases maps torn out of railway time-tables.
[11] Col. Valarché, *La Bataille des Frontières* (Berger-Levrault, Paris, 1932), pg. 136.

had reached the immediate vicinity of the French lines at Virton, Ethe and Signeulx. Awaiting daylight before launching their attack, the Germans halted under cover of the edge of the woods and entrenched.

The French started their movement in the opposite direction several hours later than their opponents, and it was already light when the heads of their columns entered the woods where the Germans were waiting in improvised positions. Wholly unprepared to find an enemy before them in force, the infantry of Brochin's 5th French Corps stumbled in the fog against the positions of Von Fabeck's 13th German Corps, as it was preparing to attack on its own account. For nearly two hours, the line of battle swayed back and forth, as both sides struggled blindly, helpless to distinguish friend or foe. Then the fog lifted, disclosing the French artillery emplacements in unprotected positions close behind the infantry lines. A prompt bombardment fell upon the French guns, while at the same time, the German infantry advanced to the attack. Suddenly deprived of their artillery support, panic seized the French infantry, and the confusion augmented as time went on, until the whole 5th Corps was retreating on Tellancourt, heedless of the efforts of its officers, leaving a yawning gap in the centre of Ruffey's Army.

The collapse of the French 5th Corps left the two corps on either side of it condemned to fight a defensive battle for their own safety, and before eleven o'clock in the morning all hope of offensive action by the French Third Army had vanished. The best that it could expect was to stand its ground against the German onslaught that had developed along its whole front.

On the Third Army's right, Sarrail's 6th Corps [12] gave a good account of itself, despite the initial confusion caused by the 5th Corps' retreat ; but though it succeeded in driving back the German 6th Reserve Corps (Von Gossler), it was halted and forced to give ground in turn by the 5th Reserve Corps (Von Gündell) advancing from the region of Longwy. Sarrail's right division, the 42nd, valiantly held its positions throughout the morning against the leading division of Von Mudra's 16th Corps, but the arrival of the second German division in the afternoon threatened the French 6th Corps' right flank and compelled its retirement.

On the left of the Third Army, the French 5th Corps' defection produced more serious consequences, and the fallacy of the "flight-of-steps" dispositions became apparent. With its right flank uncovered, the French 4th Corps (Boelle) became engaged at Virton

[12] This Corps had three, instead of the usual two, infantry divisions, the 12th, 40th and 42nd Divisions.

and Ethe against Von Strantz's 5th Corps, soon aided by some elements of Von Fabeck's 13th Corps not committed to the pursuit of the retreating French centre. In a violent struggle, two French divisions fought throughout the day, less than five kilometres apart but with no contact between them, holding their ground, but unable to progress.[13]

As a result, Gérard's 2nd Corps, on the extreme right of De Langle's Fourth Army, found itself likewise held up. Unwilling to advance with his flank unprotected, Gérard made no serious effort to move on Tintigny, but halted on the outskirts of Bellefontaine while he delivered an attack towards the east in an effort to aid the 4th Corps on his right.[14] Though Gérard's action brought precious aid to Boelle's hard-pressed command, it wrought disastrous effects upon the fortunes of the Colonial Corps on his left.

To the Colonial Corps, De Langle had assigned the capture of Neufchâteau, the Army's principal objective. It was a *corps d'elite* composed in large part of professional soldiers, veterans of countless expeditions and campaigns in Africa and Indo-China. The crosses of the Legion of Honour that decorated the standards of its regiments represented, not relics of the glory of some remote era, but recognition of achievements within the memory of the men who marched beneath them. With orders to attack the enemy wherever encountered and with information, furthermore, that it had no serious forces before it, such a corps could not hesitate or display undue solicitude for the safety of its flank.

Without waiting for news of the 2nd Corps on its right, the Colonial Corps pushed towards its objective in two columns, one on the left consisting of a mixed brigade, through the Forest of Chiny by way of Suxy, and one on the right, the 3rd Colonial Division, through the adjacent Forest of Neufchâteau by way of Rossignol. The two routes of march were separated by a broad area of tangled woods that made liaison between the two columns impossible, but both roads eventually came out on the outskirts of Neufchâteau, where both forces were expected to join hands for the final attainment of their objective, the capture of Neufchâteau, which the High Command anticipated would be occupied only by enemy patrols or advance detachments.

As the left-hand column marched through the woods, evidence accumulated of the immediate proximity of the enemy. From

[13] In two monographs, *Ethe* (Berger-Levrault, Paris, 1927) and *Virton* (Berger-Levrault, Paris, 1926), Col. Grasset, who served as a company commander at Ethe, has given a meticulously detailed account of the operations of the French 4th Army Corps on August 22nd.

[14] Though the 87th Brigade of the French 4th Division fought bravely, it received little support. See Gen. Cordonnier's article, *A la droite de la 4e Armée le 22 août 1914*, Revue Militaire Français.

thickets by the road-side, Uhlans suddenly appeared, emptying their carbines at close range, only to jump in their saddles and gallop away, and more than once bold German troopers dashed at full speed across the road, with hoarse shouts of derision — a meaningless gesture of defiance, but unsettling nevertheless to troops advancing to their first contact with the enemy. Overhead a German aeroplane, the black crosses on its wings plainly visible, hovered above the column and followed its progress. Yet despite these ominous signs, the Colonial Brigade reached the northern edge of the forest without serious interference ; but there its progress halted, for it found Neufchâteau and the vicinity, not held by outposts or mere covering detachments, but by the main body of the German 18th Reserve Corps (Von Steuben), marching westward towards Bertrix. It was a unit of Hessians and men from the Rhine Provinces, strengthened by the incorporation of an infantry regiment of the Active army, but the German reservists, though brave and eager, lacked the solidity of the hardened French Colonials. Though outnumbered more than two to one,[15] the French held off their assailants in desperate combat until sundown, inflicting devastating losses, while Goullet, the Brigade Commander, hung on grimly to his positions awaiting the arrival of the right-hand column of the Colonial Corps ; but no word came either from Army or Corps Headquarters, and no news of the fate of the other column, many hours over-due. Realizing the superiority of the enemy and the danger of envelopment that beset him, Goullet at last broke off the unequal struggle, and as darkness set in, the 5th Colonial Brigade fell back, unmolested by the enemy, along the road it had come, until it reached the positions south of the River Semoy from which it had confidently set out in the morning.

In the meanwhile, at Rossignol, north of the Semoy, and around St. Vincent, south of the river, an epic struggle was in progress, in which disaster — the worst suffered by the French during the Campaign of the Marne — overtook the 3rd Colonial Division which constituted the right-hand column of the Colonial Corps. Hardly had the leading brigade of the division entered the woods north of Rossignol, before it ran headlong against the main body of the German 12th Division, of Von Pritzelwitz' 6th Army Corps, advancing from the opposite direction towards Rossignol. Believing at

[15] At Neufchâteau, the French 5th Colonial Brigade was composed of 6 infantry battalions (6000 men), a troop of cavalry, a company of engineers and 3 batteries of artillery (12 75 mm. guns). It was opposed from the north, by 6 battalions of the German 41st Reserve Brigade (21st Reserve Division), a squadron of cavalry, a battalion of engineers and 3 batteries of artillery (18 77 mm. guns), and from the east, by 6 battalions of the German 50th Reserve Brigade (25th Reserve Division), the 7th Reserve Dragoons, and 6 batteries of artillery (36 77 mm. guns). The German 49th Reserve Brigade remained in reserve.

first that only isolated elements of cavalry stood before them, five French infantry battalions, packed one behind the other on a front of barely six hundred yards, launched a series of furious frontal attacks, charging desperately with fixed bayonets through the thickets in the face of a murderous fire. In fact, their adversaries comprised nine infantry battalions, three squadrons of dismounted cavalry and a company of engineers, methodically deployed on a wide front that extended far beyond both French flanks. Only one outcome was possible, and at last the French, baffled and disorganized by losses, especially heavy in officers,[16] fell back on Rossignol to stand their ground there, until the second brigade of the division could come to their assistance.

The help they looked for never arrived, for the failure of the French 2nd Corps (Gérard) to advance had not only laid bare the flank of the Colonial Corps, but had liberated a German brigade [17] which had promptly opened an attack from the east, towards St. Vincent, against the flank of the French Colonial Division, and had compelled the Colonials' second brigade to turn aside from its march towards Rossignol in order to meet the new menace from an unexpected direction.

The River Semoy, that divided the two brigades, each heavily engaged with no liaison between them, is a narrow stream, no more than fifteen or twenty yards wide, but deep and difficult to ford, with low-lying, marshy banks, that render crossing impossible for artillery or wagons, except by a single stone bridge at Breuvanne, two kilometres south of Rossignol. A German bombardment, falling on this bridge with furious intensity, rendered it impassable and proved the decisive point in the battle, for thenceforth the 3rd Colonial Division was cut in two, with the retreat of the brigade in Rossignol cut off and no possibility of aid reaching it.

The French brigade at St. Vincent, though hard-pressed, managed to hold its own and to give as good as it received, but the name of Rossignol evokes memories of Thermopylae and Roncesvalles, of the Alamo and the Little Big Horn. Hopelessly outnumbered and completely surrounded, the Colonials fought with the valour of desperation, and at last, as darkness fell, with all hope gone, buried their regimental colours in the shell-swept ground, as the final grey assaulting wave swept over the flaming ruins of the little Belgian village. By nightfall the 3rd Colonial Division had virtually ceased to exist as a fighting unit, with more than 11,000 men killed, wounded and prisoners, including the Division Commander and

[16] In the first hour of fighting in the forest, a single burst from a German machine-gun struck down three French battalion commanders as they conferred by the road-side.
[17] The 22nd Brigade of the 11th Division of the German 6th Army Corps (Von Pritzelwitz).

one Brigade Commander killed, the other Brigade Commander lying helplessly wounded in Rossignol, a prisoner of war, and with
practically the whole of the divisional artillery in the enemy's hands.
Only a few isolated groups of the brigade north of the Semoy groped
their way through the night, among patrolling detachments of
jubilant Germans, to regain the French lines south of the river.

Though Gérard's failure to advance with his 2nd Corps contributed heavily to the catastrophe that befell the Colonial Corps, it
was not the sole cause, for throughout the day, at Jamoigne, a scant
five kilometres away, the 2nd Colonial Division remained unengaged
in Army Reserve.   In the absence of instructions from the Army
Commander, General Lefévre, commander of the Colonial Corps,
dared not send his second division into action, and the permission
for which he appealed in the early afternoon did not arrive from
Army Headquarters until after dark.   The vigorous intervention
of a fresh division, either to aid the 5th Brigade near Neufchâteau,
or the 3rd Division at Rossignol, might well have turned the tide
and reversed the tactical situation.   In like case, at Marengo, Desaix
had advanced without orders towards the sound of the guns, arriving in time to turn apparent defeat into one of the greatest of
Napoleon's victories.   But if Lefévre was no Bonaparte, Leblois,
the commander of the 2nd Colonial Division,[18] was no Desaix, and
though he ventured to send forward one battalion to create a diversion, it was not enough, and the reinforcements so near at hand,
which might have spelled salvation, remained idle for lack of orders.[19]

The defeat of the Colonial Corps and its failure to make the
advance expected of it, produced immediate repercussions upon the
three left corps of De Langle's Army.   On the immediate left of the
Colonial Corps, Roques, the commander of the 12th Corps, followed
the example set by Gérard, and perceiving after the check of Goullet's Brigade before Neufchâteau that the flank of his own Corps
might be jeopardized, halted its advance after an initial success near
St. Médard,[20] although the way then lay open before him as far as
Recogne.   Just as Gérard's concern for his own security had contributed to the Colonial Corps' disaster, Roques' failure to progress
led to like results in the 17th Corps (Poline) on his left.   The

[18] When Leblois, an officer high in favour with radical political groups, was removed
from his command, some months later for incapacity, Clemenceau came vigorously to
his defence.   By refusing to alter his decision, Joffre earned the implacable hostility
of Clemenceau and his adherents, that contributed largely to his own later downfall.

[19] An interesting parallel might be drawn between the conduct of Leblois' Division
and that of Major Reno's detachment in Custer's battle against the Sioux at the Little
Big Horn.

[20] Against the 43rd Brigade of the 21st Reserve Division of the German 18th Reserve
Corps (Von Steuben), the same corps whose other brigades were engaged against the
French Colonials near Neufchâteau.

latter corps, after crossing the forests without difficulty during the morning, reached the open country beyond and arrived in mid-afternoon before the town of Ochamps, its objective for the day, which it found occupied by the enemy with strong defensive organizations. An attempt to carry the village by a brusque assault broke down before obstinate resistance, and while a new effort was in course of preparation under the personal direction of the Corps Commander, a sudden German counter-attack, debouching from the east, fell upon the lines of communication of the French 17th Corps. In the Forest of Luchy, a long train of wagons and artillery choked the road, awaiting the fall of Ochamps before resuming its northward movement. Against this column, inadequately guarded and helpless in the thick woods, elements of the 21st Division of the German 18th Corps (Von Schenck) delivered their blow. Utterly surprised by this attack from the direction in which they believed themselves covered by the 12th Corps, the French offered only a perfunctory resistance and broke away in confusion. Of the artillery immobilized along the road, one group managed to make its escape, but the remainder, unable to deploy in the wooded tangle, fell helplessly into the enemy's hands without firing a shot. The contagion of panic spread rapidly, until the whole corps had become involved in precipitate flight which continued in disorder until late at night and could not be arrested until the corps had reached positions far to the rear of its starting point.

The retreat of the 17th Corps, which left a breach in the front of the French Fourth Army similar to the one caused in the front of the Third Army by the retreat of the 5th Corps earlier in the day, resulted in checking the advance of the French 11th Corps (Eydoux), on the left of De Langle's attacking group, which had reached Maissin and after a bitter struggle had dislodged the 25th German Division on the right of Von Schenck's 18th Corps. Learning that the 17th Corps had fallen back, Eydoux, commander of the 11th Corps, adopted the part of prudence and evacuated Maissin, withdrawing to the more readily defensible heights to the south of it.

In summary, the day of August 22nd had proved a costly one for the French Fourth Army. By pursuing a policy of caution, two corps, the 2nd and the 12th, had remained virtually intact, but neither of them had attained its objectives and in each case its caution had been attended with disastrous results, for the Colonial Corps on the left of the 2nd had suffered severe reverses at Rossignol and Neufchâteau, and the 17th Corps on the left of the 12th had been punished no less severely. Of the two, the Colonial Corps was in somewhat better posture, for though one division had been virtually destroyed, the other had remained unaffected, while in the

17th Corps, both divisions had become equally involved in the general disorder.   Only the 11th Corps on the Army left had carried out the mission assigned to it.

In the Duke of Wurtemburg's Army, only three out of five army corps had been engaged, for neither the 8th Corps (Von Tschepe und Weidenbach) nor the 8th Reserve Corps (Von Egloffstein) reached the field before nightfall.   On the German left, the 6th Corps (Von Pritzelwitz) had paid dearly for its victory at Rossignol, where the French Colonials had exacted heavy toll, and the 18th Reserve Corps (Von Steuben) had suffered in even greater measure at the hands of the Colonial Brigade at Neufchâteau.   But if honour is to be accorded to Goullet's French Brigade, no less a tribute is due to Von Schenck's 18th Corps, one of whose divisions, the 21st, routed the French 17th Corps single-handed, while the other, the 25th, fought the French 11th Corps to a stand-still.

At his Headquarters at Stenay, De Langle remained throughout the day powerless to intervene in the battle and receiving only fragmentary and belated news.   It was late at night before he could render Joffre a coherent report of what had occurred.

All corps engaged today.   On the whole results hardly satisfactory. Serious reverses in the region of Tintigny (Rossignol) and Ochamps. Successes before St. Médard and Maissin cannot be maintained.   Have given orders to hold the front Houdremont-Bieuvre-Paliseul-Bertrix-Straimont-Jamoigne-Meix-devant-Virton.

From the Third Army Headquarters, Commandant Bel reported :

On the whole the Army occupies the front on which it was engaged this morning from Virton to Joppécourt. . . General Ruffey estimates that he has before him the 16th, 8th and part of the 13th German Army Corps, and the equivalent of one brigade from Thionville.

Even after a day of battle, the underestimate of enemy strength persisted, for Ruffey had before him, not three army corps, but five, and De Langle, though he had met only three corps on the 22nd, had two fresh corps to deal with, that had just arrived.   But despite the meagre results obtained, and the pessimistic reports from his Army Commanders, Joffre was not yet willing to give up.

Information collected, taken as a whole, shows only approximately three Army Corps before your front.   Consequently you must resume your offensive as soon as possible.

This message De Langle received from Joffre early in the morning of the 23rd, and like a good soldier he attempted to conform to the views of his superiors ; but it was a hopeless effort and at the close of the day of the 23rd, the French Fourth Army held positions substantially farther to the rear.

Worn out by three days of continuous marching and fighting, shaken by the losses they had sustained, every corps of the French Fourth Army required an opportunity to rest and reorganize in positions of greater security, and to this end, with Joffre's approval, shortly after midnight on August 24th, De Langle ordered the retreat of his Army behind the protection of the Meuse River.

Like the offensive in Lorraine, the second great French effort in the Ardennes ended in complete failure. Though on August 24th and 25th, Ruffey's Third Army and Maunoury's Army of Lorraine made a sporadic effort to resume the offensive and achieved some measure of tactical success against the German Crown Prince's Army in the region of Etain, there were no reinforcements available to mount a serious effort under the threatening shadow of the forts of Metz, and Maunoury's seven Reserve divisions were plainly unequal to the task. In the meantime, too, the Battles on the Sambre and at Mons had been fought and lost and the Allied left wing armies were in full retreat. On the 26th, upon Joffre's orders, Maunoury broke off his effort to redeem the defeat of the 22nd, and the brief career of the Army of Lorraine came to an end the following day, with the transfer of two of its divisions, the 55th and 56th Reserve Divisions, and of the Army Commander himself to form the nucleus of the new Sixth Army assembling around Amiens.

From the Headquarters of the German IV and V Armies reports of "complete victory" went to Von Moltke's Headquarters at Coblenz, with vivid word-pictures of triumphant German troops driving a confused and shattered enemy before them in utter rout. In point of fact, though the Germans had obtained an undeniable advantage, the margin had been a narrow one and both the Crown Prince and the Duke of Wurtemburg had paid a heavy price to win it. Had Gerard, Roques and Leblois displayed a little more boldness and a little higher appreciation of the part they were required to play in the strategic whole, or had Von Schenck, on the German side, shown a little less determination, the result might well have been wholly different. As it was, the French Third and Fourth Armies, though defeated, remained unbroken, still able and willing to fight, and the paean of victory complacently accepted at face value at German General Headquarters proved premature.

The close of the battle in the Ardennes marked the end of the strategy of Plan XVII. Coupled with Lanrezac's defeat on the Sambre and the British retreat from Mons, it led to the beginning

of a new manoeuvre that opened with the general retreat of the
Allied armies and ended at the Marne.[21]

[21] In addition to official sources and authorities already cited, see : Crown Prince
Wilhelm of Germany, *Meine Erinnerungen aus Deutschlands Heldenkampf* (Mittler,
Berlin, 1923), Gen. von Gossler, *Erinnerungen an den grossen Krieg* (Breslau, 1919) ;
Gen. von Moser, *Feldzugaufzeichnungen 1914–1918* (Belserche, Stuttgart, 1920). Deal-
ing with the operations of the French Colonial Corps, see two monographs by Col.
Grasset, *Neufchâteau* (Berger-Levrault, Paris, 1930) and *Rossignol-St. Vincent* (Berger-
Levrault, Paris, 1932), and an article by Lieut.-Col. Pugens, *Rossignol ;* Revue Militaire
Française, March–April, 1930. A brief discussion of the role of the French 6th Corps
appears in Col. Herbillon's biography of Sarrail's Chief of Staff, *Le Général Alfred
Micheler* (Plon, Paris, 1934), and in *La 56 ie Division au feu* (Berger-Levrault, Paris, 1919),
Gen. de Dartein has written of the operations of the Army of Lorraine.

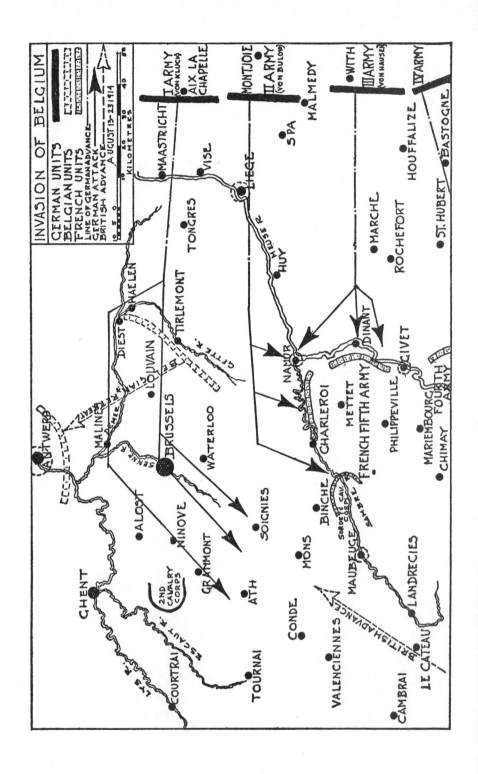

CHAPTER IX

BELGIUM INVADED

WHEN the last of the forts of Liége fell into Von Emmich's hands on August 16th, the preparations for the German conquest of Belgium, begun many years before by Count von Schlieffen, had been completed. Though Von Moltke's modifications of the Schlieffen Plan had somewhat weakened the three German right wing armies, they remained, nevertheless, far more powerful than the Allied forces concentrated to oppose them. Along the frontier of Belgium, from Aix-la-Chapelle to the northern boundary of the Grand Duchy of Luxembourg, sixteen German army corps and two corps of cavalry were assembled, picked troops, three-quarters of them Prussians, the flower of the Empire's military power.

While the command of the more easterly armies had been confided to royal personages, prompted needless to say by competent Chiefs of Staff, the leadership of the all-important right wing rested in the hands of professional soldiers of highest repute. Von Kluck commanded the I Army, on the extreme right of the line, Von Bülow the II, and Von Hausen the III.

Of the three, Von Bülow enjoyed the highest measure of consideration in official circles, a consideration attested by the presence in his Army of the famous Prussian Corps of the Imperial Guard. Descendant of an ancient family of the Prussian nobility, an elder brother of the former Chancellor of the Empire, Von Bülow's background and connections had furthered a brilliant career in the army. To a marked degree, he possessed the confidence of the Emperor and of his superiors, and as early as 1906 he had even been mentioned as a possible successor to Schlieffen as Chief of the General Staff.

Von Kluck offered a striking contrast to Von Bülow. His father had been a government architect of a modest Westphalian family with no pretentions to aristocracy, and he had risen in the army by his own efforts. In the wars against Austria in 1866 and against France in 1870, he had won distinction on the field of battle and in time of peace had obtained rapid promotion through successive grades. A major in 1887, he was a Division Commander by 1902, and in 1909 had received a hereditary title of nobility. Unlike Von

Bülow, his career up to the outbreak of the war had been based almost entirely upon service with troops with little or no staff duty. It is perhaps not unnatural that Von Kluck, the self-made man, and Von Bülow, the product of the officer class, should have viewed each other with mutual suspicion and dislike.

From the point of view of the Prussian military caste, the third member of the group, Von Hausen, was also an outsider. A Saxon by birth and formerly Saxon Minister of War, Von Hausen deeply resented the Prussian domination of the German army, a domination which Von Bülow seemed to personify. On his part, Von Bülow appears to have held Von Hausen in something akin to contempt, arrogantly infringing upon the latter's authority whenever occasion seemed to require and in one instance, in the midst of the Battle of the Marne, issuing orders direct to elements of the III Army without the formality of consulting or even informing Von Hausen.

That all three were men of patriotic devotion, each eminent in his profession, seems beyond question, but there existed among them from the beginning the germs of discord that grew and developed in the heat of battle, until at the moment of crisis, when co-operation and understanding were most needed, there appeared instead jealousy and distrust.

On August 13th, when the fall of the Fort of Pontisse and the evident effects of the bombardment of the heavy German siege artillery made it obvious that the capture of Liége would be no more than a matter of hours, or at most of a few days, Von Kluck's I Army started its long march, passing in three columns through the narrow, cobbled streets of the ancient city of Aix-la-Chapelle on its way to the Belgian frontier. Two days later, on the evening of the 15th, the main body of its advance corps had reached the left bank of the Meuse, west of Liége.

Belgium's repeated appeals for assistance to the Allied guarantors of her neutrality had called forth moving assurances of sympathy, but had remained unproductive of tangible results, and only the Belgian army, hardly more than 100,000 strong, assembled behind the Gctte, stood in the path of the German advance that became daily more threatening. The state of this army as a fighting force left much to be desired, for it was composed for the most part of partially trained reservists wholly lacking in the rigid discipline that so notably characterized its adversaries. The forces commanded by King Albert were manifestly ill-qualified to meet the finest troops of the most powerful army of Europe, and it was advisedly that in a report to his Government on August 14th, the King referred to the troops under his command as "militia."

The firm conviction of the French High Command that no important German forces would cross the Meuse, and indeed that the composition of the German army would not permit of such an operation, led Joffre firmly to refuse to modify his preconceived plans by sending any troops to the aid of the Belgian army. At Lanrezac's suggestion, he did indeed authorize Franchet d'Esperey's 1st Corps to take over the protection of the Meuse bridges between Givet and Namur, and he furthermore directed Sordet's Cavalry Corps to move into southern Belgium,[1] to ascertain the character of German concentrations to the east, with instructions — more misleading perhaps to the Belgian inhabitants than to the enemy — "to spread the report that the whole French Army is following," but such limited assistance afforded little practical comfort to the Belgians along the Gette.

On various occasions, German cavalry raids tested the main Belgian positions, more to feel out the temper of the opposition than to obtain any definite strategic advantage. Notably, on August 12th, at the little village of Haelen on the Gette, elements of the German 2nd Cavalry Corps (Von der Marwitz), with supporting detachments of Jäger infantry and artillery, fell upon the Belgian Cavalry Division on the extreme left of King Albert's Army in an effort to secure possession of the bridge-head. From dawn until sunset the Belgians withstood a series of attacks, and though the Germans succeeded in obtaining control of the village and the bridge, the opportune arrival of a Belgian infantry brigade prevented the invaders from making further gains. The next day as the Belgian commander, General de Witte, prepared a counter-attack, the Germans withdrew, leaving the Belgians masters of the field.

The stubborn defence of Liége and the ferocity of the Belgian resistance at Haelen and other points did not fail to impress the German commanders with a new respect and to compel caution, despite the low esteem in which the German High Command had held the Belgian army before the war. With a general engagement against the whole of the Belgian forces in prospect, it was not until August 17th, after the last of the Liége forts had fallen and the fortress remained completely in Von Bülow's hands, that Von Moltke issued his orders for the German right wing armies to advance.

The orders by which the German Chief of Staff set in motion the principal manoeuvre of the Schlieffen Plan directed the I, II and III Armies to begin their march on August 18th and assigned to the I and II Armies the objective of cutting off from Antwerp the Belgian

[1] From August 6th to 15th Sordet's Cavalry scoured southeastern Belgium and even ventured northward as far as the outposts of the German forces besieging Liége, vainly endeavouring to gain contact with the German cavalry. The results achieved by this expedition and the meagre information it obtained fell far short of expectations.

forces concentrated along the Gette, while the III Army marched directly west towards Namur. Following the precedent he had already set by placing Von Heeringen's VII Army under the orders of Rupprecht of Bavaria, Von Moltke sought to obtain like unity of direction in his two right wing armies by subordinating Von Kluck to the orders of Von Bülow.

A difference of opinion, the first of many, promptly arose between the two Army Commanders, for in planning the combined operation against the Belgian forces, Von Bülow demanded that a flank attack be executed from the north by the 2nd Corps (Von Linsingen) of Von Kluck's Army and adhered to his determination, issuing orders overruling his colleague's objections that such a move was unnecessary, would impose needless fatigue and would waste valuable time. On the morning of August 18th, three corps of the German I Army and three corps of the II Army moved towards the Gette, while Von Linsingen's 2nd Corps marched towards positions north of Diest, where it could strike against the Belgian left flank as Von Bülow desired.

The German commanders fully expected a pitched battle against the main body of the Belgian army, but this was precisely what King Albert was determined to avoid. Early in the morning of the 18th, reports began to arrive at his Headquarters at Louvain, bringing cumulative warning of the enemy's approach in overwhelming force. Convinced of the futility of attempting to stand his ground against an army greatly superior both in numbers and quality to his own, the Belgian King ordered a general retreat, and the withdrawal of his Army behind the fortifications of Antwerp. The decision called forth an energetic protest from the Chief of the French Military Mission, Colonel Aldebert, who still clung tenaciously, in the face of all contrary evidence, to the official French theory that the Germans would not advance in force beyond the Meuse. King Albert replied somewhat sharply, adhering to his decision, and the French Government, alarmed by the incident and fully appreciating the importance of cordial relations with Belgium, promptly transferred the over-zealous Colonel to other duties.

In the main the Belgians carried out their retirement without serious difficulty, though on the Belgian left, near Tirlemont, the 1st Division became heavily engaged against fractions of Von Kluck's 9th Army Corps (Von Quast) and sustained important losses.[2] Two days later, on August 20th, the entire Belgian mobile army, except for the division left at Namur, was installed in the En-

---

[2] Though little notice has been given in most historical works to the engagement at Tirlemont, the Belgian 1st Division's casualties there aggregated 1630 officers and men, substantially the same as the losses sustained by the whole British Army at Mons.

trenched Camp of Antwerp, somewhat the worse for vigorous skirmishes at many points, but substantially intact.

The wisdom of King Albert's decision can hardly now be questioned. For the Belgian Army to have joined battle against six or perhaps seven German army corps would have been nothing less than suicidal and would have coincided fully with the plans of the German High Command. To be sure, the retreat involved the abandonment of Brussels, but that was a matter of moral importance only, for the national capital had no military value. By his timely withdrawal King Albert not only prevented the enemy from attaining the principal objective that Von Moltke had fixed for the German I and II Armies, to cut the Belgian forces off from Antwerp, but he also compelled Von Kluck to detach from his Army one army corps, the 3rd Reserve Corps (Von Beseler), to cover Antwerp and thereby brought about a substantial reduction in the strength of the German right wing before the campaign had fairly opened. Thereafter the Belgian Army remained a constant source of danger to the invaders' lines of communication ; but except for two sorties from Antwerp, one on August 25th and the other on September 9th, during the Battle of the Marne, its main body played no further part in the campaign.

Whether, as some French writers have suggested, it would have been preferable for King Albert's Army to have retreated southwest, so as to fall in line with the British and extend the Allied left wing towards the west, seems at least open to debate. It is doubtful whether the Belgian Army, as then constituted, could have brought support commensurate with the accompanying disadvantage of strengthening the German right wing by the two army corps, which Von Moltke was in fact compelled to use to cover Antwerp.[3]

During the days that followed the Belgian retreat, Von Bülow's II Army, pivoting around Namur, turned southwards towards the Sambre to meet the French forces concentrating along the river, while Von Kluck marched west on the heels of the retreating Belgians. On August 20th, the German 4th Army Corps (Von Arnim) entered Brussels, parading through the Belgian capital with an impressive display of strength and passing in review before its commander. The same night new orders arrived from Von Moltke, directing the siege of Namur to begin at once and indicating a combined attack by the II and III Armies against the French forces assembled west of Namur. These forces, which were in fact Lanrezac's Fifth Army, the German Chief of Staff prescribed in

---

[3] In defence of the Belgian retreat and the direction taken, see the Belgian Chief of Staff, Gen. de Selliers de Moranville's *Pourquoi l'Armée Belge s'est-elle retirée sur la position fortifiée d'Anvers le 18 août 1914* (Dewit, Brussels, 1922). Expressing the French view-point, see Gen. Mangin's *Comment Finit La Guerre* (Plon, Paris, 1920).

general terms should be attacked simultaneously by Von Bülow's II Army from the north and by Von Hausen's III Army from the east. The details Von Moltke left for determination by agreement between the Army Commanders concerned.

With Von Moltke's orders, came an information bulletin issued from General Headquarters, estimating the French forces south of the Sambre at between seven and eight army corps ;[4] but more important than this slight exaggeration of the enemy strength before Von Bülow's Army, was the fact that Von Moltke's Headquarters apparently had no accurate information with respect to the British forces that had landed at Le Havre ten days before.

We must count on the British landing at Boulogne and on their being used in the vicinity of Lille. It is the view here that no important debarkations have so far taken place.

In fact, the concentration of Sir John French's Army, 100,000 strong, had all but been completed around Le Cateau, and it was preparing to start its northward march towards Mons.

The news so received from Von Moltke became the contributing cause of a new dissension that arose between Von Bülow and Von Kluck, for it indicated that while Von Bülow's Army might have to deal with very substantial forces south of the Sambre, there seemed little likelihood of Von Kluck meeting serious opposition. On August 21st, as the advance-guards of the II Army came into contact with Lanrezac's outposts on the banks of the Sambre, Von Bülow became not unnaturally preoccupied with the tactical situation of his own command to the exclusion of the strategic position of the German right wing as a whole, and despite vigorous objections from Von Kluck and from the latter's Chief of Staff, Von Kuhl, ordered the I Army which was still subordinate to him, to change its line of march from southwest to due south, so as to bring its front into alignment with that of the II Army on the latter's right, and to assure the security of its flank.

Bearing in mind the strategic mission of the I Army under the Schlieffen Plan, it was Von Kluck's view that he should rather continue his march in a southwesterly direction, so as to insure the ability of his own Army to reach a position outside the Allied left flank from which it could eventually execute the enveloping move-ment contemplated by the general plan, and which would bring it into the region of Lille, where Von Moltke had warned that British forces might be expected to appear. Before Von Bülow's imperative

4 In fact, Lanrezac's Fifth Army comprised forces approximately equivalent to 6½ army corps — 10 Active divisions, 3 Reserve divisions and 3 cavalry divisions.

orders, however, Von Kluck had no choice but to yield. It was an important decision and one of the most unfortunate for the Germans in the course of the campaign. Had Von Kluck been permitted to carry out his own plan, his march would have brought him outside the western flank of the British Army and wholly changed the character of the Battle of Mons, greatly to Von Kluck's advantage. Instead, the change of direction prescribed by Von Bülow brought the German I Army into headlong collision with the British Army at Mons, and the indecisive character of the action fought there may undoubtedly be ascribed, in part at least, to this fact.

At the same time that the main body of the German II Army marched southwards towards the Sambre, Von Bülow turned his attention to the Belgian fortress of Namur as Von Moltke had directed. Though Namur did not have the same importance as Liége in the development of the German plan of operations, it constituted an obstacle far from negligible, and its reduction became essential for the future security of both the II and III Armies. The capture of Namur therefore became the joint task of the two armies, under Von Bülow's supervision as the Army Commander nearest to the scene of action. Von Bülow formed for the purpose a separate Army Detachment composed of the Reserve Corps of the Guard (Von Gallwitz) from his own Army and the 11th Army Corps (Von Plüstow) from Von Hausen's Army, supported by one division of the 7th Reserve Corps (Von Zwehl) and by the siege artillery that had been used at Liége, the whole under the command of General von Gallwitz. The Belgian garrison, reinforced by the 4th Division, aggregated some 35,000 men under the command of General Michel, behind fortifications hardly less formidable than those of Liége. On August 19th, the withdrawal of King Albert's Army to Antwerp had severed its communications with the fortress and had left Michel and his men to their own resources, except for such aid as they could secure from the near-by French Fifth Army.[5]

In the siege of Namur, the Germans profited by the experience gained at Liége. There was no need for a brutal onslaught, and no particular haste. Von Gallwitz set up the heavy artillery brought from Liége and gave it full opportunity to break down the defences of the forts before serious infantry attacks were attempted. The fortifications of Namur, like those of Liége, had been constructed to withstand the shock of 210 mm. guns, but they could not long withstand the bombardment from the 305 mm. and 420 mm. cannon

---

[5] The assistance that Namur actually received from the French Fifth Army was limited to three infantry battalions, a regiment of Mangin's Brigade, sent rather to give moral support than to provide the garrison with any serious reinforcement.

brought to bear against them.   On the morning of August 21st, the German fire opened and by evening of the 23rd, the defences were in ruins.

Despite King Albert's orders : "Resist to the last," Michel perceived that to hold his positions longer with his mobile troops could result only in their capture and could not long postpone the inevitable end.   With the survivors of the 4th Division he made his escape in the evening of August 23rd, retreating southwards behind the lines of the French Fifth Army.[6]   For forty-eight hours more, the forts of Namur maintained a gallant but futile resistance, until the last of them succumbed on August 25th after they had been completely demolished by heavy artillery fire ; but to all practical purposes, the siege of the fortress which had begun on the 21st ended two days later.[7]

On the night of August 22nd, the invasion of Belgium, so far as it was accomplished during the Campaign of the Marne, was all but complete.   Von Kluck, following Von Bülow's directions, had turned his Army south after leaving Brussels and was approaching Mons.   Von Bülow himself had reached the Sambre west of Namur and was already engaged against Lanrezac south of the river.   Von Hausen was marching westward, aiming at the line of the Meuse in the vicinity of Givet, to strike the eastern flank of the French forces between the Sambre and the Meuse.   The right wing German armies had disposed of the Belgians as active antagonists, and stood ready for the crucial conflict against their principal enemies.   It was the eve of the Battle of Mons and of the decisive day on the Sambre, the final act in the drama of the Battle of the Frontiers.[8]

[6] The Belgian 4th Division was transported to Havre and thence taken by sea to Ostende, where it arrived on August 27th, ultimately rejoining the main body of the Belgian army in Antwerp.

[7] On the siege of Namur, see Gen. Normand, *op. cit.* The Belgian losses amounted to approximately 15,000 men of whom 10,000 were of the 4th Division.

[8] In addition to official sources, authorities of primary importance on the operations of the German right wing armies during their invasion of Belgium and throughout the remainder of the campaign are the works of Von Kluck and Von Bülow, already cited, Gen. von Hausen's *Erinnerungen an den Marnefeldzug* (Köhler, Leipzig, 1919) and Gen. von Kuhl's *Der Marnefeldzug* 1914 (Mittler, Berlin, 1921).

CHAPTER X

THE BATTLE OF THE SAMBRE

THREE orders, issued from Joffre's Headquarters on August 15th, 18th and 21st respectively,[1] defined the role of the Allied left wing as envisaged by the French High Command, as the significance of the manoeuvre of the right wing German armies became increasingly clear. The first directed the movement of Lanrezac's Fifth Army into the region between the Sambre and the Meuse as a precautionary measure, induced mainly by the German attack against Dinant, without any commitment as to the army's future course of action. The second, three days later, contemplated two possibilities, an offensive to the north in case it appeared that the German right wing was crossing in force to the left bank of the Meuse or in the alternative an offensive to the east, linked with the offensive of the French Third and Fourth Armies, in the event that the main body of the German right wing turned south along the right bank of the Meuse. The last order, on the late afternoon of the 21st, recognized that the first eventuality had materialized and definitely directed Lanrezac's Army in co-operation with the British to take the northern enemy group as its objective. By the time the latter instructions reached the Headquarters of the Fifth Army, the Battle of the Sambre had already become engaged.

After a five-day march of something over 100 kilometres, slow but painful in the intense midsummer heat, the advance-guards of the French Fifth Army reached the banks of the Sambre on the afternoon of August 20th, halting there to await further orders. A perplexing dilemma confronted the Army Commander : whether to cross the river immediately and occupy the heights along the northern bank, or to wait south of the river for the advance of the British on his left and of De Langle's offensive which was about to open in the Ardennes, on his right.

Both courses seemed open to serious objection. Although the first alternative seemed the more consonant with the offensive intentions of the High Command, it involved the risk of engaging the Fifth Army alone, with the river at its back, against an enemy of

[1] See Appendix VI.

unknown and possibly superior strength.   On the other hand, the second alternative presented the possibility that the enemy might arrive and occupy the dominating heights north of the river, and so greatly increase the difficulty of a crossing when the moment for taking the offensive finally arrived.

Between Charleroi and Namur, the valley of the Sambre is a thickly populated section; a succession of small industrial towns, in which factories, warehouses and dwellings stand in close juxta-position along both banks of the river, intersected by narrow, cob-bled streets.   This region, known as the Borinage, which extends for several hundred yards back of the stream, both to the north and south, offers obvious difficulties from a military point of view. Though readily adaptable to defence by small groups of infantry and machine-gunners, its numerous walls and houses render it particu-larly unfavourable for the effective use of light artillery; an area wholly unsuited to manoeuvering, and one to be avoided in a gen-eral engagement intended to produce decisive results.

The unfavourable nature of the terrain in the Borinage led Lanrezac to reject all thought of risking a battle in the valley of the Sambre itself, and to conclude that if the French Fifth Army re-mained south of the river, it must fall back to defend a line of heights that parallel the Sambre several kilometres to the south.

The problem Lanrezac was called upon to solve was one that had recurred innumerable times in the war-games and map-exercises that he had directed and criticized as a professor at the French War College; but compelled to take a decision himself, with the fate of an army possibly at stake, he could not make up his mind.   For forty-eight hours he waited, in the meanwhile leaving his Corps Commanders wholly in the dark as to the course their chief proposed to adopt and obliging them to use their own initiative in taking tactical dispositions which obviously depended upon whether the army was to push across the river at once or was to wait defensively south of it, pending a concerted advance with the British.

Though Lanrezac has stated that he reached his decision in the evening of August 20th and caused orders to be drafted directing the army to take up defensive positions south of the river, with the bridges held only by outposts to repel incursions of cavalry patrols, some doubt seems to have lingered in his mind for at 12:30 P.M. on the 21st, he applied to Joffre for instructions.   But his effort to shift the responsibility to higher authority did not succeed, for the same evening the "buck" came back, in accordance with the im-mutable law of the army.

"I leave it entirely to you to judge the opportune moment for starting your offensive movement," Joffre replied.

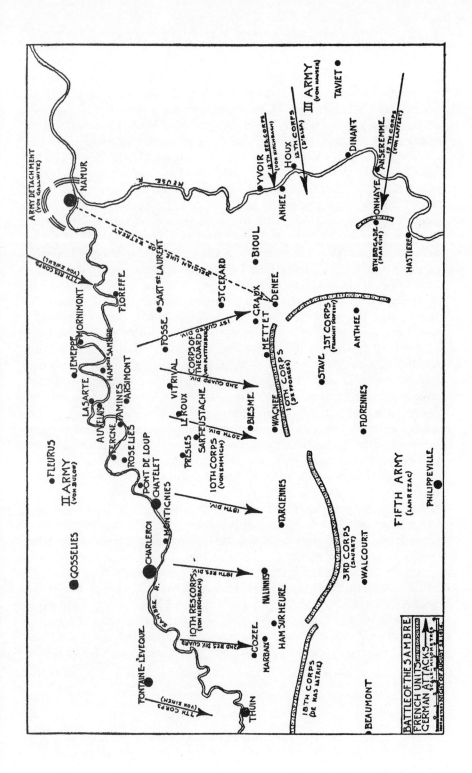

BATTLE OF THE SAMBRE
FRENCH UNITS ▭▭▭▭▭
GERMAN ATTACKS ▬▬▬▶
SITUATION NIGHT OF AUGUST 21ST 1914

Though Lanrezac himself has stated that he issued orders at 8 A.M. on August 21st, fixing his Army's main line of resistance along the heights south of the Sambre, the French official records contain no evidence of the issuance or receipt of such orders until 4 P.M., and such a course would seem inconsistent with Lanrezac's communication to the Commander in Chief mentioned above.

When at last, at a conference of Corps Chiefs of Staff held at Army Headquarters at Chimay in mid-afternoon of August 21st, Lanrezac communicated his intentions to his subordinates, it was too late, for Von Bülow's advance-guards had reached the Sambre and a bitter struggle for the possession of the bridges was already in progress, in the very region of the Borinage that the Army Commander had wisely determined to avoid. The difficulties and ultimate defeat of the French Fifth Army may be laid in no small measure to this indecision of its commander at the very outset of the battle.[2]

As the German II Army was approaching the Sambre from the north, Von Bülow at first proposed to push boldly across the river; but Von Moltke's orders of the 20th and the information bulletin accompanying them led him to alter his determination and to communicate with Von Hausen with a view to obtaining a combined attack of the II and III Armies from the north and east. When Von Hausen informed him that the III Army would not be able to open its bombardment of the French positions along the Meuse before evening of the 21st at the earliest, Von Bülow resolved to postpone any attempt at crossing the Sambre until he could feel assured of Von Hausen's support.

"The II Army will not attack today," he radioed Von Hausen at 9 o'clock on the morning of the 21st. "The Guard and the 10th Corps will only advance as far as the Sambre."

Summoning his Corps Commanders, Von Plettenberg of the Guard and Von Emmich of the 10th Corps, he gave them verbal orders to the same effect.

Along the south bank of the Sambre, opposite the line of march of the German Guard and 10th Corps, advance detachments of the French 10th and 3rd Army Corps held the bridges from Floreffe to Charleroi. The troops along the river-bank had received no instructions as to what to do in case the enemy appeared, but they knew that in order to carry out the offensive intentions of the Commander

---

[2] Confirming Lanrezac's statement, Gen. J. Rouquerol states that he knows in irrefutable evidence — which, however, he does not specify — that orders were dispatched from Army Headquarters in the morning of August 21st, *Charleroi* (Payot, Paris, 1932), pg. 115. He admits, however, that a search of the official records reveals no trace of such an order and other authoritative writers categorically affirm that no orders were issued or received until afternoon, after the battle had already started. See Col. Lucas *Le 10ⁱᵉ Corps à la Bataille de Charleroi* (Lavauzelle, Paris, 1930); Col. Valarché, *Le Combat d'Arsimont* (Berger-Levrault, Paris, 1926), and Lieut.-Col. Larcher, *op. cit.*

in Chief they would eventually have to cross the river and, logically enough, they determined that, if attacked, they would resolutely defend the bridges they had been sent to guard.

In the afternoon and night of the 20th, German cavalry and cyclist patrols in increasing numbers north of the river heralded the approach of Von Bülow's Army. Throngs of terror-stricken Belgians, fleeing southwards with their belongings packed in carts or trundled in wheelbarrows, brought confirmation of the advance of enemy columns. At the little town of Auvelais, particularly, the situation seemed alarming to the French captain in command, for the bridges for which he was responsible constituted one of the key-positions of the French line of outposts and the heights of La Sarte, rising abruptly on the opposite shore, dominated Auvelais completely. From the railway station, he telephoned Battalion Headquarters at Arsimont, two kilometres away.

"My positions are all in a hollow," he told his Battalion Commander. "My men will be shot down as if they were at the bottom of a well. I request authority to cross to the opposite shore and organize the heights of La Sarte."

"It's impossible to give you that authority," the Battalion Commander replied. "We have strict orders not to cross the Sambre."

"Then let me fall back to the higher ground behind Auvelais."

"You can't do that either," the Battalion Commander answered. "Our orders are to hold the bridges, not to abandon them."

He finally disposed of his subordinate's importunities by sending another company to Auvelais in reinforcement. Thus, on a lesser scale, the same problem that troubled the Army Commander also confronted the junior officers responsible for the defence of the Sambre, but their situation admitted of no temporizing, for they knew what the Army Commander did not yet realize, that the enemy was at hand.

It was almost noon on August 21st when the main body of the 2nd Division of the German Guard reached the north bank of the Sambre and halted, awaiting orders, while its commander, General von Winckler, personally reconnoitred the French positions from the northern heights. What he saw of the defences did not impress him, and he hastened to send word to Von Plettenberg, his Corps Commander, that an opportunity seemed at hand to effect a crossing cheaply. Remembering the instructions he had received from Von Bülow earlier in the day, Von Plettenberg was at first inclined to demur, but Ludendorff happened to be at the Headquarters of the Corps of the Guard and heard Von Winckler's message. On the Quartermaster-General's assurance that he would explain matters satisfactorily to the Army Commander, Von Plettenberg yielded to

Von Winckler's appeal and authorized the 2nd Division of the Guard to attack the Sambre bridges at Auvelais and Jemeppe and to cross the river, if it could.

From the heights of La Sarte, the German artillery opened its bombardment against Auvelais, but the defenders of the bridges remained doggedly at their posts, sweeping the southern face of the heights on the opposite shore with a continuous fire and frustrating every effort of the enemy infantry to reach the river-bank.

For a few moments the French fire slackened, then halted altogether, as the officer directing it observed through his field-glasses a procession emerging from the church of La Sarte, priests in full vestments followed by a train of choir-boys, walking in solemn cadence down the slope towards the river. As the procession reached a stone wall over-looking the stream, however, its character suddenly changed. Casting aside their religious garb, its members produced rifles, hitherto concealed beneath, and opened fire from the shelter of the wall. The success of this *ruse de guerre,* which had temporarily converted the Prussian Guard into choir-boys, did not materially alter the situation, and two hours after the combat had started, General Bonnier, the French Division Commander, hopefully reported that, though seriously attacked, his men still held their ground.

The mission of the French infantry company sent to Auvelais the night before had been "to guard the bridge." In fact, it found not one bridge, but eight, and it is perhaps not surprising that one of them should have been overlooked ; but the oversight proved costly, for it did not escape the vigilance of a German patrol, creeping cautiously along the bank in search of a safe passage. Between Auvelais and Tamines to the west, a railway viaduct had been left unguarded ; the defenders of each town apparently believing that it lay within the other's sector. A detachment of German infantry and machine-gunners swept across it, and more soon followed, taking the French defenders of Auvelais under their fire from the west and southwest. Faced with encirclement, retreat became the only course open to the French. Abandoning their dead and wounded, they fell back across the fields with the Germans in hot pursuit as far as Arsimont, where they halted and re-formed their lines under a steady bombardment from the German guns north of the Sambre. A battalion in reserve launched a furious counter-attack that checked, but could not drive back, the pursuing enemy. Just at nightfall, a second attack, by a whole regiment this time, still without benefit of artillery support, met no better fate. Darkness found the German Guard firmly installed in the northern half of Arsimont, with the bridges of Auvelais in their possession.

Elsewhere along the Sambre, at Tamines, Ham, Jemeppe and Mornimont, in more favourable terrain, French detachments had successfully defended the bridges committed to their charge, but the loss of the bridge-head at Auvelais rendered their positions so pre-carious that Defforges, commander of the French 10th Corps, felt compelled to order their retreat. Farther to the west, on the front of the French 3rd Corps (Sauret), events had followed much the same course. At almost the same time that Von Winckler had opened his attack against Auvelais, the German 10th Corps reached the Sambre between Tamines and Pont-de-Loup. Mindful of Von Bülow's orders, Von Emmich halted its advance and even refused Von Winckler's request to assist the attack on Auvelais by a simul-taneous assault against Tamines. But at Tergné, the advance-guard of the German 19th Division found another unguarded bridge that offered a prospect too inviting to resist. With the somewhat re-luctant consent of the Corps Commander, an infantry regiment boldly crossed, and to consolidate its gain pushed forward to the town of Roselies from which it drove the French defenders in sharp hand-to-hand fighting. It was a repetition of the Guard's exploit at Auvelais. During the night, the 5th Division of the French 3rd Corps attempted to retrieve its loss by a night attack against Roselies, but the effort completely broke down, with shattering loss to the two battalions engaged.

So in the afternoon of August 21st, contrary to the intentions of the commanders of both armies, a bloody struggle took place in the Borinage. As a result of the day, the German II Army had forced the passages of the Sambre and had established a solid foothold on the southern bank.

At his Headquarters at Chimay, thirty kilometres from the line of fire, Lanrezac received little news of developments on his Army's front, and apparently attached little importance to such information as did come to him, for he sent Joffre a report on the day's operations that was brief and misleadingly reassuring :

Nothing new on the front of the Fifth Army except an outpost engage-ment on the front of the 10th Corps at the bridge of Arsimont-Tamines.

There was no mention of Auvelais or Roselies, or of the attempts made at other points, and no indication that the "outpost engage-ment" in question had given the Germans command of the line of the Sambre.

During the night Lanrezac received complete reports from his Corps Commanders.

"The 19th Division has abandoned the Sambre bridges by my

order," was the nucleus of Defforges' report for the 10th Corps. "It is my intention to renew the battle at dawn, and in co-operation with the 3rd Army Corps, to attack the enemy and drive him back across the Sambre."

From Sauret of the 3rd Corps came the added news of the failure of the 5th Division's night attack against Roselies.

The reports that came in to Army Headquarters could have left no doubt in Lanrezac's mind that his principal lieutenants proposed to exert their full strength to recover the Sambre bridges, and to commit themselves to a policy directly contrary to the spirit of his orders of the afternoon. A counter-attack by the 3rd and 10th Corps could only mean a continuance of the battle in the Borinage with the objective of recovering possession of the very bridges that Lanrezac had already ordered should be abandoned upon the appearance of the enemy in force. It was the negation of the Army Commander's expressed intention of giving battle along defensive positions on the heights south of the river ; nevertheless, though Lanrezac was apprised of his Corps Commanders' intentions before midnight and there was still time to intervene, no word, either of approval or dissent, came from Army Headquarters, and the attack of the two French army corps was permitted to proceed without interference or suggestion.

On the German side, despite the day's successful outcome, the Corps Commanders were somewhat uneasy, for they had disregarded their orders and felt none too sure that their initiative would find approval. Indeed, when he first learned that the Guard and the 10th Corps had crossed the Sambre, Von Bülow felt inclined to order their immediate retirement north of the river, but detailed reports of the action convinced him that such a move was unnecessary, and his orders for the day of August 22nd directed the army corps to hold and consolidate their positions, but not to advance. To Von Hausen he dispatched a radio :

The attack of the II Army beyond the Sambre will open on the morning of the 23rd, left wing on Jemeppe-Mettet.

Shortly after daybreak, while a thick mist, rising from the river, blanketed the valley of the Sambre, the French opened their counter-attack against the German forces holding Roselies and Arsimont. Before Arsimont, the French infantry made a gallant show, advancing across the Belgian beet-fields with colours unfurled and bugles sounding the shrill notes of the "Charge." As the bayoneted ranks drew near to the German lines, their officers in the lead, rifles and machine-guns poured forth a rapid-fire of death from behind walls and hummocks and from the windows of houses. Before it the attack wilted. Running, stumbling, crawling, the French sought cover and safety as best they could, and the attack ended leaving the German Guard undisputed masters of the field.

Heedless of the lesson they might have learned the day before, the French infantry had derived no benefit from the presence in the immediate vicinity of two artillery regiments (72 75 mm. guns) and had attacked wholly without artillery preparation or support. In the haste in which orders had been prepared during the night, no pains had been taken to secure co-ordinated action between infantry and artillery, and the gunners had been left with no precise information as to the objectives of the infantry, the time of the attack or the role the artillery was expected to play.[3]

Hardly had the French attack against Arsimont ceased, when an order from Corps Headquarters directed the German troops holding Arsimont to fall back to Auvelais. In vain General von Gontard, the German Brigade Commander, protested that such a retreat was both unnecessary and unwelcome. He had no choice but to obey, but once at Auvelais new orders arrived to re-occupy the positions so valiantly defended and so reluctantly abandoned, and the Guard retraced its steps. The manoeuvre had been unobserved and unmolested by the French, but for several hours the ground so hotly contested during the early morning remained unoccupied by either side ; an episode that offers an illustration of the misunderstandings and confusion, so frequent even in modern warfare, that occasionally determine the fate of battles.

West of Arsimont the attack of the French 3rd Corps had likewise failed. To meet its advance Von Emmich had launched a vigorous counter-offensive by his whole corps, pushing resolutely across the plateau south of the Sambre and driving the French before him, in bold disregard of Von Bülow's orders to remain along the river-bank. Fortunately, perhaps, for the commander of the 10th Corps, the German Army Commander had changed his mind again. Aviation reports received in the early morning convinced him that, after all, the French forces south of the Sambre were not so formidable as Von Moltke's information seemed to indicate, and he determined to drive his Army forward, regardless of what he had told Von Hausen, and to reach the line Binche-Mettet at the close of the day.

He had little difficulty in accomplishing his purpose. By nightfall on August 22nd, the French Fifth Army had fallen back to

---

[3] The engagement at Arsimont affords one of the most striking and tragic examples of the inadequacy of the blindly offensive tactics adopted by the French at the outset of the campaign. Against the 4th German Guards Brigade and one regiment of the 3rd Brigade, two regiments of the French 19th Division, one of the 20th and one of the 37th were engaged.

defensive positions as its commander had intended, but it had done so under pressure from the enemy at the price of staggering losses, and in the end held a line considerably south of the one originally designated by Lanrezac.   Only in the vicinity of Thuin, where the 18th Corps (De Mas Latrie) had moved up to prolong the front of the Fifth Army to the west, did the French still maintain a foothold on the Sambre ; but the presence of the 18th Corps brought Lanrezac no additional numerical advantage, for during the afternoon, Von Bülow's 10th Reserve Corps (Von Kirchbach) had also reached the Sambre and taking advantage of unguarded bridges at Montignies and Hameau, had driven a brigade of the French 6th Division out of Charleroi and Marchienne-au-Pont.

On the extreme left of the French line, in the vicinity of Fontaine l'Evêque and Binche, two divisions of the German 7th Corps (Von Einem) had been encountered, one by a brigade of the French 3rd Corps detached as infantry support for Sordet's Cavalry Corps, and the other by a British cavalry brigade, conducting a reconnaissance before Sir John French's front.   In each case, the combats resulted in the retreat of the Allied forces before the advancing Germans. Sordet's Cavalry, which had hitherto operated north of the Sambre, covering Lanrezac's left wing and protecting the area into which the British Army was marching, was compelled to seek refuge behind the river.

"By reason of the fatigue of men and horses, it will be difficult for me to carry out the mission assigned to me for tomorrow," Sordet reported to Lanrezac that night.   In fact, from the opening days of the campaign, the Cavalry Corps had been constantly on the move and had literally worn itself out in profitless exertion.   Its presence had become a liability, and it was in no condition to perform any useful service during the Battle of the Sambre.

At 10:30 P.M., Lanrezac rendered his report for the day to Joffre :

Violent attack on the front Namur-Charleroi.   The 10th Corps compelled to withdraw to the front Biesmes-St. Gérard, which will oblige the northernmost elements of the 1st Corps to withdraw in turn and to abandon the defence of the Meuse below Yvoir (i.e. between Yvoir and Namur).

10th Corps severely tried.   General Boë (20th Division) seriously wounded.   Large number of officers casualties.

3rd Corps had its 5th Division heavily engaged before Chatelet.[4]

18th Corps intact.

The Cavalry Corps, extremely fatigued, has been obliged to withdraw

[4] Actually one brigade of the 38th Division had also been heavily engaged, as well as both brigades of the 6th Division, one at Charleroi and one at Fontaine l'Evêque, so that there remained in the 3rd Corps only one brigade of the 38th Division which had not been involved in serious fighting.

under cover of an infantry brigade that supported it and which is occupying the vicinity of Thuin.   The Cavalry Corps will only be able to maintain liaison with the Army W. (British) still in echelon to the rear of the Fifth Army.

Lanrezac

The report seems open to criticism at several points as giving a picture of the situation of the French Fifth Army that is at least incomplete, but the striking inaccuracy of the last sentence seems difficult to understand or explain.   The British Army had moved forward from Le Cateau according to schedule on the 21st, and on the night of the 22nd held a front, running roughly from Condé on the west through Mons to Peissant.   Though a gap of some ten kilometres separated Sir John French's right from Lanrezac's left, the British line centred on Mons was not "in echelon to the rear" of the French Fifth Army, but actually substantially in advance of it. In spite of the tenuous contact between the Headquarters of the two Allied armies, Lanrezac could hardly have been unaware of this fact, for during the afternoon a report from the 18th Corps (De Mas Latrie) had given the British positions with approximate accuracy, and furthermore, at 11 o'clock the same evening, a staff officer from the French Fifth Army had requested the British Commander in Chief to advance next day towards the northeast to attack Von Bülow's western flank.   Such a request would hardly have been made, had Lanrezac not known of the situation of the British Army.

At the end of the second day of battle, the French Fifth Army held a defensive line south of the Sambre, but in a far less favourable situation than Lanrezac had expected.   Two army corps had been engaged for the better part of thirty-six hours, and though faced by forces substantially inferior in numbers to their own, had had decidedly the worst of it.   The French 3rd and 10th Army Corps, each of them three divisions strong,[5] had been driven from their positions along the Sambre and forced to fall back nearly ten kilometres south of it by three German divisions, two of the 10th Corps and one of the Guard.[6]   Such was the net result of the opening phase of the Battle of the Sambre.

By no means the least important of the unfortunate consequences of the battle in the Borinage was the necessity of weakening the security of the Fifth Army's right flank, covered along the Meuse by Franchet d'Esperey's 1st Corps.

"The Fifth Army is obliged to leave an army corps on the Meuse

[5] The 37th and 38th Divisions from the North African Army had been assigned respectively to the 10th and 3rd Army Corps in reinforcement.

[6] Only the 2nd Division of the German Guard was engaged on August 21st and 22nd. The 1st Division, in echelon to the rear covering the II Army's flank towards Namur, did not come into action until the 23rd.

between Givet and Namur as a flank-guard, so long as the Fourth Army has not crossed the Lesse, at least by its advance-guards," Lanrezac had written Joffre at noon on the 21st, and in fact nothing could afford complete protection to the vulnerable right flank of the Fifth Army, except an advance by De Langle's Fourth Army on a wide front. This in turn depended upon the success of the offensive then in progress in the Ardennes.

The reverse sustained by the 10th Corps at Arsimont gave rise to some doubt as to whether it could sustain further onslaughts, and led Lanrezac, in order to insure its stability, to direct Franchet d'Esperey to move the main body of his two divisions into the area between Sart St. Laurent and St. Gérard, facing north and northwest, so that they could participate in the battle against Von Bülow and solidly sustain the 10th Corps' right wing. Along the Meuse they were to be replaced by the 51st Reserve Division of Valabrégue's Group, which Lanrezac had originally intended should reinforce the 1st Corps.[7]

Though rendered somewhat uneasy by increasing evidences of enemy activity east of the Meuse, that heralded the approach of Von Hausen's Army, Franchet d'Esperey was eager to take an active part in the battle and readily complied with the Army Commander's orders. As elements of the 51st Reserve Division arrived during the evening, they took over the positions held by units of the 1st Corps, until by morning of the 23rd, a complete change of front had been accomplished, and the main body of the 1st Corps had wheeled into position on the right of Defforges' 10th Corps. In place of the 1st Corps, the 51st Reserve Division held a front along the Meuse of nearly twenty kilometres, between Givet and Anhée,[8] with the result that the eastern front of the Fifth Army, so sedulously guarded by two divisions of the Active army while the enemy was still remote, was entrusted to a single Reserve division at the very moment of gravest danger, when Von Hausen's attack from the east, which Lanrezac had long foreseen and feared, was about to materialize.

In defence of the action of the Army Commander, it has been said that he hoped that the action of the Fourth Army might avert the danger and compel Von Hausen to turn away from his flank ; but though he repeatedly urged speed upon the High Command, Lanrezac seems to have had little faith in the operation that Joffre had planned for the Third and Fourth Armies.

[7] Of the three Reserve divisions of Valabrégue's group, one, the 51st, had been ordered on the 18th to march eastward to reinforce the 1st Corps along the Meuse, while the other two remained at Vervins until the 20th, when Lanrezac ordered them to march northward to the region of Avesnes, behind his left wing. They arrived in proximity to the front on August 23rd but took no material part in the battle.

[8] One battalion of Mangin's Brigade of the 1st Corps held the line of the river between Anhée and Rivière.

"If you go into that death-trap of the Ardennes, you will never come out," he is reported to have remarked to one of De Langle's officers.[9] The word that he received from De Langle himself during the night of the 22nd could have brought him little encouragement.

The left corps of the Fourth Army (11th Corps) tonight has its main body around Paliseul. Serious engagements along the whole front of the Fourth Army, and to the right of the latter, along the front of the Third Army.

A message from Joffre, somewhat more reassuring in tone, reached Lanrezac the next morning.

The Fourth Army has been engaged since yesterday afternoon under favourable conditions on the general front Paliseul-Bertrix-Straimont-Tintigny-Meix-devant-Virton.

Though the outcome of the fighting on August 22nd at Neufchâteau, Rossignol and Virton hardly justified the phrase "under favourable conditions," it seems unlikely that Lanrezac could have been seriously deceived, for the front specified was substantially the one that he himself had designated in his letter to Joffre of July 31st as the starting point of the offensive, in which it was then expected that the Fifth Army would take part, and he must have been aware that a considerable further advance was necessary before the action of the Fourth Army could prove of any practical benefit to the Fifth. In any case, the message had no practical effect upon his action, for his dispositions for a change of front by the 1st Army Corps had already been taken before Joffre's telegram arrived.

Contrary to all expectations, August 23rd opened in relative calm along the northern front of the French Fifth Army. The morning was well advanced before the German bombardment opened against the positions of the French 18th Corps (De Mas Latrie), entrenched between Thuin and Ham-sur-Heure, which had arrived late in the afternoon of the 21st and had not so far seriously participated in the fighting. At 10 o'clock, the two divisions of the German 10th Reserve Corps (Von Kirchbach) advanced against the French lines, one of them, the 19th Reserve Division, taking as its objective the positions held by the extreme left of Sauret's 3rd Corps around Nalines, and the other, the 2nd Reserve Division of the Guard, directing its assault against Marbaix and Gozée, both held by the 36th Division of the French 18th Corps.

At Nalines, the French 12th Brigade resisted with desperate

9 Gen. J. Rouquerol, *op. cit.*, pg. 110.

energy, beating off repeated attacks and counter-attacking furiously until at four o'clock in the afternoon, the German 19th Reserve Division reported that it was no longer in condition to pursue its attacks. To the west, the little village of Gozée became the scene of an epic struggle, changing hands three times in the course of the day, and remaining in the possession of the Germans at the cost of disproportionate losses.[10]   On this part of the field, the French returned every blow with interest, and at nightfall Count von Kirchbach, commander of the 10th Reserve Corps, sent Von Bülow a report that was frankly pessimistic :

In case the enemy renews his attacks, the sector held by this Army Corps is too extended to assure its defence with the means we have at our disposal.

Nevertheless the fighting around Marbaix had had unfortunate repercussions on the adjoining front of the French 3rd Corps.   In the course of one of the attacks, a French infantry battalion on the extreme right of the 18th Corps had been compelled to fall back to avoid being cut off by the enemy advance.   In the process of retirement, a German detachment succeeded in slipping around its flank to the east and in opening fire against the rear of the French 12th Brigade that had so obstinately defended Nalines.   The unexpected attack produced a sudden panic, and the French infantry retreated in disorder, followed successively by other units of the 6th Division and finally by the 5th Division further to the right.   Fortunately for the French, the German 19th Reserve Division was itself too exhausted to profit by the opportunity thus unexpectedly presented and did not press the pursuit ; but for a time confusion reigned throughout the French 3rd Army Corps.   To make matters worse, at the critical moment, the Corps Commander was nowhere to be found, and the task of restoring order fell to the commander of the Corps Artillery, General Gabriel Rouquerol.   The break was checked before it could develop into the rout that had threatened, but the French had relinquished their main positions and had fallen back nearly five kilometres before the retreat could be halted.

Towards the eastern end of the northern front, matters developed somewhat more favourably for the French.   The German 10th Corps and the Guard, both of which had suffered hardly less than their adversaries in the two preceding days, moved forward with great circumspection, and for two hours, between ten o'clock and noon, no infantry attacks developed while shells of all calibres beat upon

[10] In the capture of Gozée, the 2nd Reserve Division of the German Guard lost 79 officers and approximately 1700 men.

the lines of the French 10th Corps. The lighter French artillery, doggedly refusing to be silenced, replied vigorously, and shortly after noon, as the divisions of the German Guard seemed about to launch their expected assault, Franchet d'Esperey's 1st Corps made ready to fall on their flank from the east. Giving up for the moment all thought of pursuing their intended attack towards the south, the Guard turned instead to face the unexpected apparition that threatened its left.

With all dispositions taken and the French 1st Corps already in movement, an unparalleled opportunity seemed to lie open for the French to score a brilliant tactical success, when news arrived that compelled a sudden halt and change of plans.

Since early morning, Von Hausen's Army had been battering at the positions of the 51st Reserve Division along the Meuse, and though repulsed between Houx and Dinant, the Germans had at last gained a foothold on the west bank in the vicinity of Hastière, driving the French reservists before them as far as Onhaye, two kilometres west of Dinant. Boutegourd, commander of the 51st Reserve Division, sent an urgent appeal for aid to Franchet d'Esperey, reporting that one of his brigades, "crushed by artillery fire, with heavy losses," had been compelled to retreat in disorder.

The long expected attack from Von Hausen's Army had at last reached the point of imminent danger, and the flank and rear of the French Fifth Army stood in gravest peril.

The news reached the commander of the French 1st Corps at the very moment that his divisions were moving forward to attack the flank of the German Guard, and one of them, the 2nd, had already established contact with the enemy. Without waiting for word from the Army Commander, Franchet d'Esperey broke off his attack and ordered his Corps to retrace the path it had taken the night before. Among the officers with him at the time, Franchet d'Esperey saw Mangin, an old comrade of colonial days, whose brigade, reduced to two battalions, was waiting in reserve.

"General, the enemy has crossed the Meuse behind our right," the Corps Commander said. "The Reserve Division is giving ground. The situation must be re-established. Go immediately and take your two battalions.   I will follow as fast as I can with the main body of the corps."

How, an hour later, Mangin with his two battalions and a cavalry regiment, picked up along the way, arrived before Onhaye ; how, with Boutegourd, he reorganized the shattered units of the 51st Reserve Division ; and how, at last, with all the savage energy that made him famous, he led a bayonet charge that swept the Germans out of Onhaye, constitutes one of the most colourful and dramatic episodes of the early days of the war.[11]   When at nightfall, the little village that commanded the approaches to Dinant and Hastière was again in French hands, Mangin was eager to push forward to the Meuse, but the capture of Onhaye had temporarily at least restored the equilibrium.   Franchet d'Esperey, who had arrived on the scene, was well content with the results already achieved, and was unwilling to hazard a night attack against forces which he knew might well prove superior to his own.

Though the prompt intervention of the 1st Corps had averted the immediate danger from the east, the situation of the French Fifth Army as a whole was far from satisfactory to its commander on the evening of August 23rd.

On the left, the 18th Corps had given a good account of itself and had taken a heavy toll from the German 10th Reserve Corps that had opposed it in the fighting around Gozée and Marbaix.   Nevertheless, largely by reason of the retreat of the 3rd Corps on its right, it had finally given ground, and its commander took a gloomy view.

"The 18th Corps can still defend itself, but is incapable of attacking," General de Mas Latrie summarized the situation to Lanrezac.

With more justification, Sauret's report on the 3rd Corps was no less pessimistic.

"My troops are very tired.   I shall need a day to restore order in my units," he said.

Though the 10th Corps had lost the villages of Wagnée and Graux in the late afternoon, it had on the whole successfully stood its ground ; but all three of its divisions had been put to severe tests and had undergone heavy losses, and it could not be relied on too far.

On the Army right, the 1st Corps was again facing east, but it no longer had the advantage of the river as a barrier before it, for Von Hausen's Saxons had gained footholds at numerous points and firmly held both Dinant and Hastière.   Though the enemy had not yet effected a crossing in force, matters would certainly become more serious the following day, and Lanrezac had abandoned all hope of any aid from the Fourth Army.

To the west, around Mons, Von Kluck's Army had fallen on the British — in whom Lanrezac had little confidence — and from Namur a dispatch received in the afternoon announced the evacuation of the Belgian fortress by its mobile garrison, which was retreating be-

---

[11] In *Des Hommes et des Faits* (Plon, Paris, 1923) Gen. Mangin has given his own account of the recapture of Onhaye.   See also Lieut.-Col. Larcher, *Le 1ier Corps à Dinant, Charleroi, Guise* (Berger-Levrault, Paris, 1932).

hind the lines of the French 1st Corps, congesting the roads and impeding the movements of Franchet d'Esperey's troops.   It seemed merely a matter of hours before Von Bülow and Von Hausen would be substantially strengthened either by support from Von Kluck's Army, or from Von Gallwitz' forces besieging Namur, or both.

In the light of these considerations, the risk of destruction seemed overwhelming, and Lanrezac courageously took the most difficult decision given to a professional soldier.   At eleven o'clock in the evening he ordered the retreat of his Army, conveying the news to Joffre half an hour later in a brief message :

The 3rd Army Corps, attacked at 4 P.M., failed to hold its ground and retreated on Walcourt.   Enemy is threatening my right on the Meuse ; a detachment of infantry having crossed by a ford north Hastière, has succeeded in occupying Onhaye.   Givet is threatened, Namur taken.   In view of this situation and the delay of the Fourth Army, I have decided to withdraw the Army tomorrow on the front Beaumont-Givet.

Before daylight on August 24th, the retreat of the French Fifth Army began, and early the same day, Joffre ratified Lanrezac's decision.

In the German camp, Von Bülow and Von Hausen were hardly more satisfied than Lanrezac with the day's result.   The former had expected a substantial advance towards the south, but had met instead an obstinate resistance, and on his right, the 10th Reserve Corps had suffered a marked check.   At last convinced that Von Moltke had been right, and that the whole French Fifth Army stood before him south of the Sambre, Von Bülow addressed urgent appeals both to Von Kluck and Von Hausen to aid him by converging from either side against the enemy's flanks, while he renewed the attack from the north the following day.   The message reached Von Kluck too late for any action, but it had an unfortunate effect on Von Hausen's plans.

The Saxon Army Commander had originally hoped that his whole Army could reach the west bank of the Meuse by nightfall, but the destruction of the bridges and the stiff opposition of the French 51st Reserve Division had prevented the attainment of this objective.   Only advance infantry detachments, without artillery or wagon trains, had succeeded in crossing.   Nevertheless, Von Hausen intended to continue his efforts the following day, and with the passages of the river at last in his control, anticipated better success. With a just appreciation of the strategic situation, the commander of the German III Army intended to direct his main effort towards the southwest in the direction of Givet, so as to reach the rear of the French forces facing Von Bülow, and this intention had been approved by Von Moltke ; but hardly had orders been issued, when a staff officer from the II Army arrived at Von Hausen's Headquarters at Taviet, bearing a pressing request from Von Bülow for an attack by the III Army in a due westerly direction.

Reluctantly Von Hausen yielded, and shortly after 5 o'clock in the morning altered his orders so as to orient his attack to the west in the direction of Mettet, instead of towards the southwest, as he had previously planned.   It was a decision of cardinal importance, for by acceding to Von Bülow's importunities, Von Hausen sacrificed the chance that lay before him to convert the Battle of the Sambre into a strategic as well as a tactical victory, and to encompass the destruction of Lanrezac's Army.

When the German attack opened a few hours later, the II Army advancing from the north and the III from the east, only rear-guards opposed them, for the French, retreating towards the southwest, had already escaped.   In his anxiety to assure his own progress and the tactical security of his own Army, Von Bülow had lost sight of the larger objectives that lay almost within his grasp, for had Von Hausen adhered to his original design, it would have been difficult, if not impossible, for the French Fifth Army to have got away, at least without fighting a second battle more difficult than the first.

It was a strategical error of the first magnitude, for which Von Bülow must bear the primary responsibility, that put beyond the reach of the German right wing armies the decisive victory they so eagerly sought.[12]

---

[12] The Battle of the Sambre, generally called by French writers the Battle of Charleroi and by German writers the Battle of Namur, has given rise to much controversy in France, and much that has been written on the subject is frankly partisan and polemic in character.   In addition to source material already cited, the following seem especially worthy of note : Gabriel Hanotaux, *L'Enigme de Charleroi* (L'Edition Française Illustrée, Paris, 1917) ; Prof. Jules Isaac, *Joffre et Lanrezac* (Chiron, Paris, 1922) ; Fernand Engerand, *Le Secret de la Frontière*, 1815–1871–1914. *Charleroi* (Bossard, Paris, 1918).

CHAPTER XI

MONS

IN THE week following his arrival in France, Sir John French lost no time preparing his command for its part in the campaign. Delaying in Paris only long enough for a visit of ceremony to President Poincaré, he proceeded on August 16th to Vitry-le-François for his first meeting with the French Commander in Chief, to learn at first hand of the military situation. It was the day after the affair at Dinant, and Joffre had just issued orders to Lanrezac to begin his march towards the northwest, to meet what still seemed no more than a possibility, that the German right wing armies might extend their action to the left bank of the Meuse. Thus, even before he joined his Army, the British Commander in Chief received a hint that the earlier forecasts of the French Staff might prove incorrect, and that he might be required to take an active part in the Allied line of battle much sooner than he had expected ; but it was a cloud scarcely larger than a man's hand, and Sir John French found an atmosphere of general confidence at French General Headquarters.

Operations in Lorraine were developing favourably ; the frontier had been crossed by two armies, and Joffre had just received the first enemy flag taken in battle.[1] Genuine cordiality seems to have marked the first meeting between the two Commanders in Chief. Each gained a favourable impression of the other, and they parted filled with mutual respect and good hope for the future.

On his way to Le Cateau, where he was to set up his Headquarters, French stopped at Rethel to call on Lanrezac of whom Joffre had spoken in glowing terms. It was a gesture of friendliness, highly significant in an officer so punctilious in matters of military etiquette as Sir John French ; but the interview proved a disappointment. A pessimism reigned at the Headquarters of the French Fifth Army that contrasted strangely with the cheerful attitude of Joffre's officers.

"So you have come at last," General Hély d'Oissel, the Army Chief of Staff, remarked gloomily to Colonel Huguet, as they ushered the

---

[1] See pg. 66.

British Commander in Chief into Lanrezac's presence. "It is high time. If we are beaten, we shall owe it to you."

Lanrezac opened the interview with an eager inquiry as to when the British would be ready to move forward, and showed visible disappointment when French replied that it would not be before August 24th, and that he should even like another week to allow his men to become acclimatized before sending them into action. Lanrezac then suggested that French should combine Allenby's Cavalry with Sordet's Cavalry Corps, but mindful of Kitchener's instructions French was determined to keep his independence and firmly declined.

Lanrezac detailed the situation north of Namur and mentioned the report that the Germans had reached the Meuse near Huy.

"What are they doing there?" French asked, interrupting his French colleague's voluble explanation. "What are they likely to do ? Why are they crossing the river ?"

"Pourquoi sont-ils là? Mais pour pêcher dans la rivière," [2] Lanrezac replied drily.

"What does he say ?" the British Commander in Chief asked sharply, turning to Sir Henry Wilson, who was acting as interpreter.

"That they are going to cross the river, sir," Wilson answered. The British Commander in Chief, who was not wholly ignorant of French, accepted this tactful translation without comment, but soon after took his leave with a distinctly unfavourable impression of the Commander of the French Fifth Army.

"He was a big man with a loud voice," French wrote in later years, describing the interview, "and his manner did not strike me as being very courteous."

Subsequent developments did not improve matters. Lanrezac did not see fit to return the British Field Marshal's call ; an omission justifiable perhaps, in the circumstances, but which confirmed French's impression of bad manners, and intensified the personal coolness between the two commanders. At the very time the British Army was completing its concentration, the French 18th Corps (De Mas Latrie) was detraining in the adjacent area to take up its position on the left of Lanrezac's Army. A series of minor misunderstandings ensued over the use of terminal facilities, routes of march and the like, insignificant in themselves, but which required many explanations and prolonged petty negotiations between weary staff-officers, speaking different languages and still not fully familiar with their duties. Irritation on both sides inevitably resulted, which it does not seem that either French or Lanrezac took any pains to dissi-

[2] "Why are they there ? Why to fish in the river."

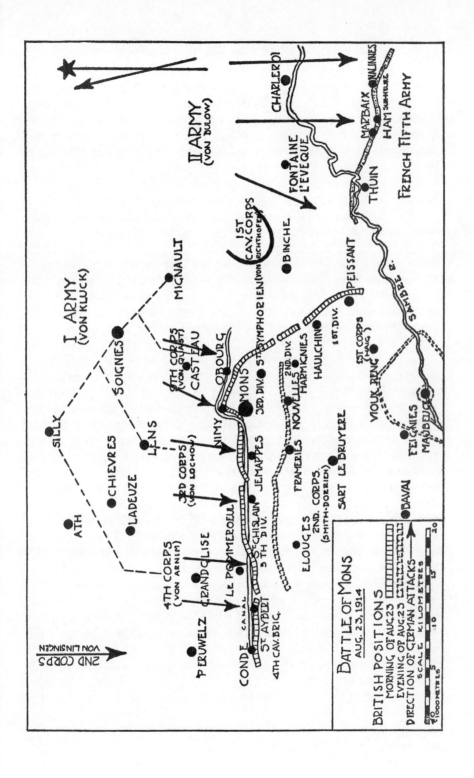

BATTLE OF MONS
AUG. 23, 1914

BRITISH POSITIONS
MORNING OF AUG.23
EVENING OF AUG.23
DIRECTION OF GERMAN ATTACKS →
SCALE KILOMETRES
1000 METR.0.5 5   10   15   20

pate. Out of such minor friction there soon grew up, behind a barrier of icy politeness, an atmosphere of mutual suspicion and dislike, that jeopardized the effective co-operation of the two armies.

The sudden death of Sir James Grierson left a vacancy in the command of the British 2nd Corps, and French importuned Kitchener by telegram and letter to designate General Plumer in Grierson's place.

"I very much hope you will send me Plumer," the British Commander in Chief wrote. "Please do as I ask in this matter ?"

Kitchener ignored the request, and on August 21st, Sir Horace Smith-Dorrien arrived at Le Cateau to take command of the 2nd Corps. He was a good soldier, who had served with French in South Africa and had made a fine record there as a Brigadier, but he was not the man French had asked for. It is difficult to say what weight, if any, this incident may have had in the severe judgement that the British Commander in Chief passed in later years upon the operations of the 2nd Corps and its commander.[3]

In his Special Orders No. 15 of August 21st,[4] Joffre requested the British Army to move north in the general direction of Soignies, to take the offensive in co-operation with the French Fifth Army against the German forces operating to the north. Such were Sir John French's intentions as his Army started from its area of concentration to take up its position west of Lanrezac's line, already established along the Sambre. The night of August 22nd found the British 2nd Corps (Smith-Dorrien) facing north along the canal between Condé and Mons, with the 1st Corps (Haig) on its right, facing northeast, between Mons and Peissant. On the outskirts of Binche, the 5th Cavalry Brigade guarded the right flank of the army and maintained a precarious liaison with Sordet's Cavalry, until the latter was forced to retreat behind the Sambre. The other four brigades of Allenby's Cavalry Division were grouped around Condé and to the east of it, on the left of Smith-Dorrien's Corps.

During the days of August 21st and 22nd, a multiplicity of signs pointed to the presence of the enemy in force before the British front. Near Casteau, on the road from Soignies to Mons, a squadron of the 2nd Cavalry Brigade met a detachment of the German 9th Cavalry Division in the first British engagement of the war, and soon after, near Binche, the Scots Greys encountered a mixed detachment of the German 7th Corps (Von Einem). Both skirmishes broke off inconclusively with minor casualties on either side, but

---

[3] It may be noted that in May, 1915, when Smith-Dorrien for reasons that seem obscure resigned command of the British Second Army, Plumer who at the time was commanding the 5th Army Corps succeeded him.

[4] See Appendix VI (3).

sufficed to serve notice of the enemy's presence. Aviation reports indicated strong German columns filling the roads leading from Brussels to the French frontier, and in particular brought word of infantry marching along the road from Brussels through Ninove to Grammont which, if true, indicated a movement that might lead the enemy outside the British left flank. Under the optimistic influence of Sir Henry Wilson, French was at first inclined to attach little importance to these reports, but when the British liaison officer [5] with the French Fifth Army brought discouraging news of the situation of Lanrezac's command, telling of its engagement in the valley of the Sambre and its retreat to the heights south of the river, the British Commander in Chief began seriously to question the feasibility of Joffre's plan for a combined offensive towards the north.

The sum total of the information received up to the evening of August 22nd persuaded Sir John French that he would not be able to reach Soignies, the objective set by Joffre, without opposition from the enemy, and that the part of prudence required him to defer any definitely offensive move, until the character of such opposition had become more clearly defined. He, therefore, declined to accede to a suggestion from Lanrezac that the British Army should wheel to the right the following day and attack the western flank of the German forces along the Sambre; but agreed to hold his positions, covering Lanrezac's left flank, for another twenty-four hours pending developments.

In the meanwhile, Von Kluck's Army approached Mons from the north. By evening of the 22nd, the three army corps in the van had reached the general front Silly-Soignies-Mignault, some fifteen kilometres north and northeast of the British positions. After a vain appeal to Von Moltke, the German I Army was in the process of complying with Von Bülow's orders and altering its course towards the south, instead of continuing towards the southwest as its commander had desired.[6]

Like Sir John French, Von Kluck had received reports of the cavalry engagement near Casteau, and had learned from other sources of the presence of British troops before his front; but only two days before, G.H.Q. had assured him that no important British forces had so far landed, and he was far from suspecting the immediate appearance of the main body of the British Army. Accordingly, his orders for August 23rd prescribed merely a continuance of the march southward, with no expectation of a general engagement.

[5] Lieutenant, now Brigadier General, Spears, whose book, *Liaison* 1914 (Doubleday, Doran, New York, 1931) is an authority of primary importance on the relations between the French Fifth Army and the British.

[6] See pg. 98.

In Mons and the surrounding villages, the morning of Sunday, August 23rd, opened in undisturbed tranquillity, with only the rumble of Von Bülow's guns to the east to break the Sabbath calm. The church-bells called to mass, and the inhabitants thronged the streets, watching the British troops with a friendly curiosity, seemingly oblivious of the significance of their presence or of the imminence of danger. At Sars-la-Bruyère, the Headquarters of the 2nd Corps, French met Smith-Dorrien, Haig and Allenby early in the morning and reviewed the situation. All expressed confidence in their ability to hold their ground, if attacked, and the British Commander in Chief left for Valenciennes to supervise the detraining of the newly arrived 19th Brigade [7] on the left of his line. Before he returned, the battle had started.

Between nine and ten o'clock in the morning, the advance-guards of the German 18th Division of Von Quast's 9th Corps appeared before the British line between Nimy and Obourg, where it formed a salient, following the canal north of Mons. From emplacements on high ground to the north, the German artillery opened a vigorous bombardment, and after a brief interval the infantry advanced to the attack in mass formation.

It was a far cry from fighting Boer Commandoes to opposing the Imperial German Army of 1914, but the British had not wholly forgotten the lessons they had learned in South Africa thirteen years before, and in particular the value and importance of well-directed, concentrated rifle fire. Again and again, the field-grey waves swept forward, only to waver, break and fall back before a fire of such rapidity and intensity as to convince the German commanders that they were confronted by a concentration of machine-guns. Nevertheless, heedless of losses, they continued their efforts and extended their attacks around the whole front of the Mons salient, as fresh units arrived, while shell and shrapnel beat mercilessly upon the British battalions.

Smith-Dorrien had foreseen that the positions of the salient might prove too vulnerable to be defended against a prolonged attack, and he had reconnoitred and prepared new positions south of Mons. To these positions, the British forces in the salient began to fall back early in the afternoon under the pressure of both divisions of the German 9th Corps. The fighting continued long after dark, but before midnight the British were entrenched on a new line, between Nouvelles and Framerie, some five kilometres south of Mons.

Farther to the west, along the canal between Mons and Condé, the German I Army met with even less success. Two hours after the at-

---

[7] Formed from battalions originally assigned to guard lines of communication.

tack against the Mons salient had started, the German 3rd Corps (Von Lochow) came into action, concentrating its efforts on the British positions around Jemappes and in the vicinity of St. Ghislain.[8]

Contrary to their custom elsewhere on the front, the Germans began their attacks with no more than a perfunctory artillery bombardment, perhaps under the impression that only weak detachments opposed them, and perhaps, too, under the influence of the psychology engendered by the Emperor's reference to England's "contemptible little army." In any case it proved a costly error, for again British rifles took a deadly toll among the clumsy massed formations of the German infantry,[9] and though after an afternoon of strenuous fighting, the Germans succeeded in clearing the British from the north bank of the canal, they found it impossible to open a passage across it. The evacuation of the salient compelled the abandonment of Jemappes, but between St. Ghislain and Condé the canal remained the British main line of resistance at nightfall.

On the whole, the result of the day was inconclusive. Smith-Dorrien's 2nd Corps, though compelled to withdraw from the Mons salient, had in general stood its ground successfully against the attacks of two German Corps,[10] and Haig's 1st Corps on the British right, though subjected to a severe artillery bombardment, had not been in action. Exhausted by their efforts and by the losses they had sustained, the Germans made little effort to cross the canal in pursuit of their adversaries, and were content to watch the British draw off, only sending out patrolling detachments after dark. Though often set down as a British defeat, the Battle of Mons was not so considered in the British Army at the time. On the contrary, the men took up their positions for the night with a gratified sense of a good day's work accomplished. Nor did the British Commander in Chief consider his Army as beaten.

"I will stand the attack on the ground now occupied by the troops. You will therefore strengthen your position by every possible means during the night," French told Smith-Dorrien at 8:40 P.M.; while Von Kluck issued orders for a renewal of the battle at dawn.

During the day of August 23rd, no news had come to the British

---

[8] Three books by officers of different regiments of the German 3rd Corps give vivid accounts of its operations at Mons, *Vormarsch* (Grethlein, Leipzig) by Walter Bloem, *Die Sturmer von Douaumont* (Scherl, Berlin) by Von Brandis, and *Unter Emmich vor Lüttich. Unter Kluck vor Paris* (Bahn, Schwerin) by H. Huebner.

[9] For example, the 12th Brandenburg Grenadiers of the German 5th Division lost 25 officers and more than 500 men.

[10] The 4th Corps (Von Arnim) on Von Kluck's right did not arrive until late afternoon, and except for some attacks in the vicinity of Pommeroeul, which were not seriously pressed, took no part in the battle.

Commander in Chief of the progress of the battle that the French Fifth Army was waging on his right. Events had proved the wisdom of Sir John French's refusal to comply with Lanrezac's request of the evening before, for if he had attempted to execute the desired attack towards the east, Von Kluck's blow would inevitably have fallen upon the British Army in full movement, with results that could hardly have failed to prove disastrous ; but as soon as Lanrezac learned that he could not expect immediate assistance against Von Bülow, he seems to have lost all interest in the fate of the British Army. He ignored French's request that he use the two Reserve divisions behind his left wing to establish liaison between the Allied Armies and made no effort to keep French informed of his own movements or intentions.

The failure to secure better co-ordination between the French Fifth Army and the British seems difficult to understand, in view of the express injunctions of the French Commander in Chief, and particularly in view of Lanrezac's statement to Joffre of the 21st, in which he assigned the desirability of concerted action as one of the principal reasons for postponing a crossing of the Sambre. It is a fact, however, that during the crucial day of August 23rd, no communications of any importance passed between the Headquarters of the French Fifth Army and those of Sir John French, and that a gap of some twelve kilometres existed between the British right and the French left, which Lanrezac made no serious effort to close.

The official explanation, that the French Fifth Army did not have adequate means at its disposal to maintain contact with its Allies, seems unconvincing when it is recalled that only one of the two divisions of Lanrezac's left corps, the 18th, held front-line positions, and that two Reserve divisions remained behind the left of the French line and took no part in the action.

The fact seems to be, as Lanrezac himself has indicated in his memoirs,[11] that for reasons of his own, he did not wish to establish close contact with Sir John French's Army ; partly, no doubt, because, lacking confidence in the British and their commander, he did not wish to become too closely identified with the operations of a foreign army, which he could not control and which might compromise the safety of his own command.

It is hard to predict the military consequences that might have attended the establishment of a united front between Lanrezac's Army and the British, and so have joined the battle against Von Bülow with the battle against Von Kluck. To Lanrezac, the risk of misunderstanding at a critical moment must have seemed to outweigh the benefits of concerted action, but it is certain that unfor-

11 See Lanrezac, *op. cit.*, pg. 325.

tunate consequences resulted from his attitude. In the minds of Sir John French and his officers, it gave rise to the impression that they had been badly "let down" in a moment of deadly need, by the allies they had come to help and from whom they had expected the fullest measure of loyal support. The atmosphere thus created endured throughout the campaign, complicating immeasurably the task of the French High Command and contributing in no small degree, as well, to Lanrezac's own downfall.

When at last word came to Sir John French of the situation of the French Fifth Army, it was a report from the British liaison officer of Lanrezac's decision to retreat and the reasons that motivated it: the fall of Namur, the passage of the Meuse by Von Hausen's Army, Von Bülow's advance and the failure of De Langle's offensive in the Ardennes. Joffre's Headquarters had already given warning that the British might expect an attack by at least three German army corps and two cavalry divisions. Convinced of the futility of attempting to stand his ground single-handed in his advanced positions, the British Commander in Chief reversed his earlier decision and ordered his Army to fall back. Before daybreak on August 24th, the British retreat from Mons began.[12]

[12] On the Battle of Mons, in addition to references already given, see Von Kluck, Von Kuhl, French and Huguet, *op. cit.*, and Gen. Sir Horace Smith Dorrien's *Memories of Forty-eight Years Service* (Murray, London, 1925).

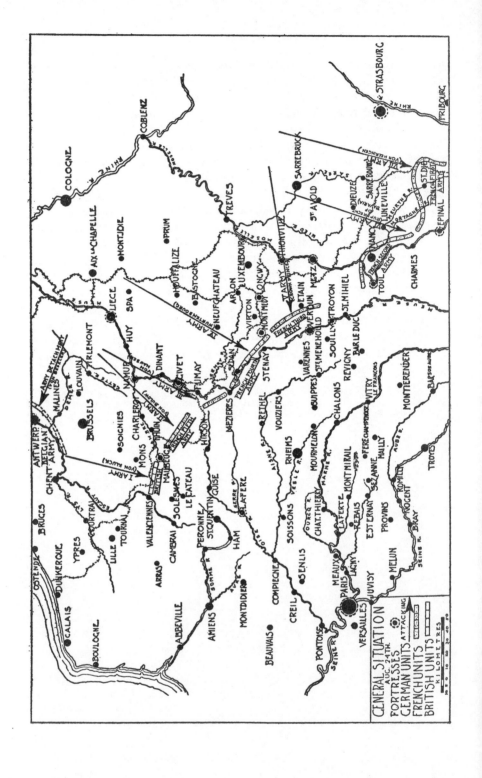

GENERAL SITUATION
AUG. 24TH
FORTRESSES
GERMAN UNITS ATTACKING
FRENCH UNITS
BRITISH UNITS
KILOMETRES

CHAPTER XII

THE GENESIS OF THE MARNE

THE DAY of August 23rd, 1914, saw the collapse of De Langle's offensive in the Ardennes, the defeat of Lanrezac's Fifth Army south of the Sambre, the start of the British retreat from Mons and the fall of the Belgian fortress of Namur. These events brought to a close the first phase of the Campaign of the Marne and marked the final break-down of the French strategy based on Plan XVII Four days of fighting, from August 20th to 23rd, had decided the result of the Battle of the Frontiers and had laid France open to the invader.

From the Sambre to the Vosges, the Allied armies had been defeated and were in retreat before a victorious enemy. For the moment, at least, the initiative had definitely passed to the Germans. Rarely in history has a Commander in Chief confronted a problem more difficult than the one Joffre faced on the morning of August 24th. His plan of operations, to which he had resolutely adhered since the outbreak of hostilities, had resulted in complete failure. A new one had to be improvised and put into effect under the most difficult conditions.

At Vitry-le-François, a profound depression had supplanted the gay confidence that had reigned only a few days before. On the verge of despair, the young officers of G.H.Q., bred in the offensive school, saw the Commander in Chief prepare a manoeuvre that their oracles had unhesitatingly pronounced impossible — a general retreat in the face of the enemy.

Only Joffre and Berthelot maintained an unruffled calm and an apparently imperturbable faith in ultimate victory. This faith the moral qualities demonstrated by the Allied armies in the Battle of the Frontiers seemed to justify. The reverses of the French armies, the retreat of the Belgians to Antwerp and of the British from Mons had, indeed, been tactical failures, but they had been far from decisive defeats. In each case, they had left the armies concerned intact for future operations. In spite of faulty leadership, and a discouraging realization that the enemy was equipped with weapons which they had not the means or the skill to combat, French, British and Belgian troops alike had become imbued with a conviction that the German armies were not the pattern of invincibility they had represented themselves to be. This conviction gave rise to a confidence that on another day, under more favourable circumstances, the result might be altogether different.

In short, though beaten at every point, the morale of the Allied armies remained high and their determination unimpaired. With a sure judgement, the more remarkable in one of his prosaic temperament, Joffre realized this imponderable advantage and appraised it at its true worth.

In the formulation of a new plan, the necessity of a regrouping of forces presented itself in imperative fashion. Lanrezac's Army and the British had proved themselves plainly insufficient to cope with the unexpected strength of the German right wing, and it became essential, therefore, to provide reinforcements on the Allied left that would suffice to parry the German effort at envelopment, which had at last become clearly defined. Two alternative methods suggested themselves by which this result might be accomplished. The first, strongly advocated by Berthelot, involved the formation of a new army behind the Allied left wing, with the ultimate purpose of attacking the German extreme right wing army from east to west, to separate it from its neighbours by driving it to the west or northwest. If successful, this plan would have served to foil the drive against the Allied left flank envisaged by the Schlieffen Plan, but it offered serious objections, for it presupposed the ability of Lanrezac's Army and the British to delay the enemy advance long enough to permit the formation of a new army behind them, and further assumed the ability of the new army, once organized, to defeat Von Kluck. In the event of failure the encircling movement that seemed the German objective would become an accomplished fact.

Joffre, therefore, rejected Berthelot's advice and pinned his faith instead to a second alternative, the formation of a new army sufficiently far to the west to place it on the outside of the German right flank and enable it eventually to strike from west to east against the enemy outer flank.

This conception, which constituted, in effect, the second French plan of operations, Joffre embodied in General Instructions No. 2,[1] issued to his armies in the evening of August 25th. Three paragraphs give the substance of Joffre's intentions :

1. Having been unable to carry out the offensive manoeuvre originally planned, future operations will be conducted in such a way as to re-

[1] See Appendix VII.

construct on our left a force capable of resuming the offensive by a combination of the Fourth and Fifth Armies, the British Army and new forces drawn from the east, while the other armies hold the enemy in check for such time as may be necessary.

2. Each of the Third, Fourth and Fifth Armies, during its retreat, will take account of the movement of the neighbouring armies, with which they must remain in liaison. The movement will be covered by rearguards left at favourable points in such fashion as to utilize all obstacles to halt the enemy's march, or at any rate, to delay it, by short and violent counter-attacks in which artillery will be the principal element employed.

* * *

6. Before Amiens, between Domart-en-Ponthieu and Corbie, or behind the Somme between Picquigny and Villers-Bretonneux, a new group of forces will be constituted by elements transported by rail (7th Corps, four Reserve divisions and perhaps another Active army corps) between August 27th and September 2nd.

This group will be ready to take the offensive in the general direction of St. Pol-Arras or of Arras-Bapaume.

The instructions so issued by the French Commander in Chief on August 25th, contained the strategic basis upon which the Battle of the Marne was fought. By reason of a combination of circumstances, Von Kluck's unexpectedly rapid advance and the British defeat at Le Cateau, Joffre's plan for an offensive launched from the region of Amiens proved impossible of execution as originally conceived, and the Allied counter-offensive actually took place, not on September 2nd, but four days later and on positions considerably farther to the south than the French Commander in Chief originally expected, but the relative situations and missions of the various armies remained substantially unaltered when the decisive battle began on September 6th. It was the new group, referred to in Paragraph 6, later designated as the Sixth Army, that executed the stroke against Von Kluck's outer flank that Joffre had planned.

When Joffre's orders reached the French armies on August 26th, the general situation seemed by no means promising. Only in Alsace had matters taken a favourable turn. There, after a slow, methodical campaign, Pau had succeeded in recovering the ground that the French had so hastily seized and as quickly lost at the outbreak of hostilities; but the strip of Alsace in French hands held no more than a sentimental value, and it was no time for sentiment at Joffre's Headquarters. Pau's Army, small though it was, constituted the principal reservoir from which Joffre could draw the additional forces so sorely needed on his left wing, and no alternative offered but to relinquish the ground won and to withdraw the

Army of Alsace to defensive positions that could be held by reduced forces.   In the stunning news of general defeat, the second evacuation of Mulhouse passed almost unnoticed.

In Lorraine, between the Meurthe and the Moselle, and on the Grand Couronné de Nancy, De Castelnau and Dubail, somewhat recovered from the effects of Morhange and Sarrebourg, were reacting to new onslaughts from Crown Prince Rupprecht's victorious Bavarians with a vigorous counter-offensive, that gave Joffre his only ray of encouragement.

Although east of Verdun, the Third Army and the Army of Lorraine still maintained an offensive posture, the attack around Etain, started on the 25th by Maunoury's Reserve divisions, could not greatly affect the general strategical situation in the absence of reserves to exploit their success, and Joffre needed two divisions from the Army of Lorraine and the services of the Army Commander himself in the formation of the new Sixth Army.

To the left of the Third Army, De Langle had fallen back behind the protection of the Meuse.   The fighting in the Ardennes had taxed the Duke of Wurtemburg's Army hardly less than it had the French, and the German IV Army had followed its retreating adversary warily, making no serious attempt to cross the Meuse until the 26th.   Then, though the German 8th Corps (Von Tschepe und Weidenbach) gained a foothold on the left bank when the French 60th Reserve Division gave ground around Domchéry, De Langle forthwith replied with a series of furious counter-attacks that checked every effort to extend the gain, and forced the German Army Commander to appeal for aid to his neighbour, Von Hausen. But De Langle, like the other French commanders, was fighting on the defensive, and though confident that he could hold his ground, was in no position to regain the initiative he had lost.

The French Fifth Army, after the Battle of the Sambre, had dextrously extricated itself from its difficult position, thanks in no small degree to Von Bülow's influence in persuading Von Hausen to direct his Army's advance towards the west rather than the southwest.   In the days that followed, Lanrezac retreated rapidly to the south, leaving the fortress of Maubeuge to its fate, and maintaining contact with Von Bülow's pursuing Army only by a series of delaying rear-guard actions.

Thus, in the interval between the close of the Battle of the Frontiers and August 26th, the French armies fought defensively, each seeking its own safety, until Joffre's General Instructions No. 2 provided a co-ordinated plan that established their common aim. Though it could not be carried out in its entirety, it remained the basis of the Allied strategy throughout the remainder of the campaign, and constituted in its essentials, the foundation of the victory of the Marne.[2]

[2] Joffre's *Mémoires* (Plon, Paris, 1932) discuss fully the preparation of General Instructions No. 2 and the reasons that motivated them.

CHAPTER XIII

AT COBLENZ

ON AUGUST 17th, Von Moltke advanced the field Headquarters of the Great General Staff from Berlin to Coblenz, and there the Emperor also moved his personal Headquarters, emulating the example of his grandfather. Together the titular Commander in Chief and his Chief of Staff received the reports of victory, as day by day they flowed in, in a crescendo of exultation. Thousands of prisoners and scores of cannon taken, cities captured, fortresses stormed, the enemy in precipitate flight ; so the word came, the news so eagerly awaited and only too gladly received. Memories revived of the early weeks of the War of 1870, that saw the pathetic collapse of the ill-led armies of the Second Empire, and visions dawned of a new Sedan within the grasp of the victorious German armies.

From Rupprecht of Bavaria came the story of how the French had plunged headlong into the net spread before them in Lorraine, just as Schlieffen had expected they would, only to be hurled back discomfited from the heights of Morhange and Sarrebourg. The royal princes commanding the centre armies brought a like offering of victory, two French armies crushed and in disorderly retreat. Finally, before the mighty right wing, the Belgians, the French and at last the British had been put to flight ; Liége and Namur had fallen ; Antwerp and Maubeuge had been completely invested. From August 20th to 26th, the reports of the German Army Commanders became a continuous song of triumph, with scarcely a discordant note, picturing the Allied forces, beaten strategically and tactically, fleeing in all but helpless disorganization.

Although the situation on the western front seemed wholly favourable, things had not gone so well in the east. Two Russian armies, acting with unlooked-for vigour, had crossed the frontier of East Prussia, menacing Von Prittwitz' VIII Army by the weight of numbers. When, on the 21st, word came that a further retreat was projected, opening German territory still further to invasion, the position seemed critical, and Von Moltke acted promptly. Von Hindenburg, with Ludendorff as his Chief of Staff, replaced Von Prittwitz and hastened eastward to set matters right.

To reinforce the forces fighting the Russians, as soon as French resistance in the west had been definitely broken, constituted an integral part of the Schlieffen Plan. The news that he received from every hand, convinced Von Moltke that the moment had come even sooner than he had anticipated, and he determined to strengthen Von Hindenburg's hand with forces withdrawn from the western front. General Tappen, then Chief of the Operations Section at German G.H.Q., has explained the mental attitude underlying this determination :

The wholly favourable news that came to us each day and which continued to arrive on the 25th, combined with the great victory obtained by the VI and VII Armies in Lorraine, gave rise to the conviction at G.H.Q. that the great decisive battle on the western front had been fought to our advantage. Believing in this "decisive victory" the Chief of Staff decided, in spite of objections presented to him, to send reinforcements to the eastern front. He believed that the moment had come when, having won a decisive victory in the west, substantial forces might be diverted to the east, in conformity with the general plan of operations, to seek an equally decisive result there.[1]

Though in a memorandum written in 1915, Von Moltke himself has denied that he over-estimated the extent of the victory in the west, and has alleged that it was rather the precarious situation in the east that motivated his action,[2] the fact remains that on August 25th, a decision fraught with momentous consequences was taken.

Von Moltke's plans originally called for the withdrawal of six army corps from the western front, two of them from the left wing group of armies, two from the centre and two from the right, but they met with serious objections. An energetic protest from Von Dellmensingen caused action to be suspended, so far as the VI and VII Armies were concerned, pending the outcome of the new offensive battle developing in Lorraine, and finally only one cavalry division [3] was withdrawn from Crown Prince Rupprecht's group. The 5th Army Corps (Von Strantz), of the German Crown Prince's Army, left the front and made its way to Metz, ready to entrain for the east, and the withdrawal of the 6th Army Corps (Von Pritzelwitz) from the IV Army was also prepared; but nothing came of these measures, for the two centre armies soon found themselves so heavily engaged in forcing the passages of the Meuse that Von Moltke agreed they could not safely be deprived of any strength.

[1] Tappen, *Bis zur Marne* 1914 (Stalling, Oldenburg, 1920).
[2] Von Moltke, *op. cit.*
[3] The Saxon cavalry division. It seems strange that this division should have been attached to the 3rd Cavalry Corps (Von Frommel) while Von Hausen's Saxon Army remained wholly without independent cavalry units throughout the campaign.

Only on the right wing did Von Moltke's determination take effect. There the Army Detachment under Von Gallwitz, which had just successfully concluded the siege of Namur, received orders to proceed to Aix-la-Chapelle and to embark for the Russian front. Thus, the Reserve Corps of the Guard (Von Gallwitz) and the 11th Army Corps (Von Plüstow) did not return to the II and III Armies of which they had originally been a part, but went instead to aid Von Hindenburg and Ludendorff. Ironically enough, these two corps, whose presence at the Marne might well have turned the tide decisively, arrived too late to participate in Von Hindenburg's triumph, for the Battle of Tannenburg had been fought and won before they reached their destination.

The whole burden of Von Moltke's unfortunate decision fell on the three right wing armies, upon whose success the German plan of operations primarily depended.

"It was a mistake, I admit," Von Moltke later wrote, "which we paid for at the Marne."

Though the departure of two army corps for the eastern front constituted the most notable diminution of the strength of the German right wing, it was by no means the only one. The retreat of the Belgians to Antwerp without giving battle had already compelled Von Kluck to sacrifice one of his army corps, the 3rd Reserve Corps (Von Beseler), to the task of covering the great Belgian fortress, and in addition he had left behind one brigade of the 4th Reserve Corps (Von Gronau) as a garrison for Brussels. The French fortress of Maubeuge required Von Bülow to take similar measures, for though it had not been modernized or equipped to the same extent as the French eastern fortresses, with its garrison of some 50,000 men, it could not be overlooked or left behind unguarded, and the mission of its reduction fell to the II Army. To conduct the siege, Von Bülow detached the 7th Reserve Corps (Von Zwehl) and one brigade of the 7th Corps (Von Einem), supported by heavy artillery. Though the French fortress and its garrison finally capitulated on September 8th, after a gallant defence, and its resistance did not materially affect the principal operations of the campaign, it served nevertheless to prevent the besieging forces from taking part in the decisive battle.

The little fort of Charlemont, at Givet, presented Von Hausen with a similar though less formidable problem. Its garrison consisted of only 3500 men, chiefly Territorials, but it rejected a summons to surrender and compelled a full-fledged siege, finally succumbing on August 31st, after its defences had crumbled to ruins under the bombardment of siege artillery transported from Namur.

As a result of the delay before Charlemont, one division [4] of the Saxon 12th Reserve Corps (Von Kirchbach) did not rejoin its command until the night of September 7th, and took part only in the last day of the Battle of the Marne.

So, while Joffre was bending every effort to reinforce the Allied left wing, the three armies on the German right had progressively weakened. Instead of the 16 army corps with which they had entered Belgium, they had left on August 26th only 11. Von Kluck had been reduced from 6 army corps to 5, less one brigade, and Von Bülow from 6 army corps to 4, also less a brigade, while Von Hausen's Army had fallen from 4 army corps to 2½.

With far-sighted wisdom, Schlieffen had originally planned a second echelon to follow the decisive marching wing, to undertake the necessary secondary missions without reducing the power of the main body ; but before the war Von Moltke had suppressed this second echelon and now had no forces available with which to improvise one. Having yielded to the temptation of gathering what he had been led to believe would be an easy victory in Lorraine, he had put it beyond his power to strengthen his right by withdrawals from his left, for as a result of a too-ready acquiescence in Von Dellmensingen's plea, Prince Rupprecht's Armies had become committed prematurely, contrary to Schlieffen's precepts, to a thoroughgoing assault against the French fortified line in the east which could not be broken off without a demoralizing confession of failure.

The consequences of this weakening of the German right wing and of the offensive operations in Lorraine that prevented its reinforcement, did not become immediately apparent, however, and Von Moltke resolved to adhere to his conception of Schlieffen's strategy. To this end, he issued on August 27th, a General Directive [5] to all the German armies on the western front, directing the five right wing and centre armies to continue their offensive march towards the southwest, while the two left wing armies, now also transformed into an offensive group, continued their attacks against the line of the Moselle

"His Majesty orders," Von Moltke's instructions ran, in the traditional form of such documents, "that the German armies advance in the direction of Paris."

To each army he assigned a specific line of march. The I was to proceed towards the lower Seine, southwest of Paris, the II towards Paris itself, the III towards Château Thierry, east of Paris, the IV towards Epernay, still farther to the east, and the V, after crossing the

---

[4] The 24th Reserve Division.
[5] See Appendix VIII.

Meuse near Dun, north of Verdun, towards the Marne between Châlons and Vitry-le-François. The VI Army, with the VII still subordinate to it, was first to parry any French counter-attack in Lorraine or Alsace, or in case of a French retreat was to force its way across the Moselle, between Toul and Epinal, advancing in the general direction of Neufchâteau.

"It is urgently desirable," von Moltke wrote in the concluding paragraph, "that the armies move forward rapidly, so as not to allow the French time to re-form and organize new resistance."

Von Moltke's General Directive further distorted the Schlieffen Plan, expanding its scope far beyond the idea of its author, for it imposed upon the five western German armies the execution of a manoeuvre that Schlieffen himself had expected would be carried out by a very much stronger group, reinforced by a powerful second echelon, and in addition, it prescribed offensive operations for the two left wing armies far more ambitious than the mission originally assigned to them by Schlieffen. Only upon the assumption that as a result of the outcome of the Battle of the Frontiers the resistance of the Allied armies had definitely broken down, could the amplitude of Von Moltke's plans find justification.

At the very period when the French High Command, sobered by adversity, had at last achieved a sense of reality, the German High Command dwelt in a paradise of its own imagining.

CHAPTER XIV

LE CATEAU

THE victorious German armies had not passed unscathed through the fiery ordeal of the Battle of the Frontiers ; on the contrary, except for Von Hausen's Saxons who had been engaged for only one day along the Meuse, their losses had been heavy and the troops' endurance had been tried to the utmost. As a consequence their pursuit of the French lacked something in vigour, but against the British, Von Kluck maintained an unrelenting pressure.

In the retreat from Mons, the British Commander in Chief set his course a little west of south. Though tempted to seek shelter in the fortress of Maubeuge, French remembered the fate of Bazaine's Army at Metz and recalled Sir Edward Hamley's comment : "In clinging to Metz he acted like one who, when the ship is foundering, should lay hold of the anchor." Accordingly, he avoided Maubeuge and withdrew instead to the south of it, passing it by on his right flank.

The British retirement was not accomplished without difficulty, and the burden fell principally upon the 2nd Corps, which had already borne the brunt of the fighting at Mons.[1] At Elouges, Audregnies and other points, Smith-Dorrien found himself involved in sharp rear and flank guard actions, while Haig had no trouble in breaking contact before daybreak each morning and in reaching his assigned positions before nightfall, without serious opposition. Convinced that the British had landed at Calais or Boulogne and were based on the Channel Ports, Von Kluck concentrated his efforts on an endeavour to envelop their western flank and to cut what he supposed to be their lines of communication.

In the late afternoon of August 25th, the eve of the Battle of Le Cateau, Haig's 1st Corps arrived without incident at the positions around the southern boundary of the Forest of Mormal that Sir John French had prescribed as the limit of its retreat for the day and entered its billets at Maroilles and in the deserted cavalry barracks at

---

[1] From August 23rd to 25th inclusive the total British casualties amounted to 5149 officers and men, of which 4361 were in the 2nd Corps. The 2nd Corps' casualties in the Battle of Mons itself were 1588.

Landrecies before starting its southward march again at 2 o'clock the following morning.   At dusk a German attack took the British outposts by surprise and soon spread alarm and confusion through the whole corps.   At Landrecies, panic-stricken staff officers made ready to destroy the Corps Headquarters records and worked feverishly erecting barricades to defend the town.

"If we are caught, by God, we'll sell our lives dearly," cried Sir Douglas Haig, shaken for once out of his habitual cold dignity, and he dispatched messages to French at St. Quentin and to Smith-Dorrien, describing the situation as very critical and calling on the 2nd Corps for aid.

Surprise, the uncertainty and confusion of fighting in the dark, and the nervousness engendered by a first encounter with the redoubtable enemy infantry led the British 1st Corps to view the situation with a seriousness wholly unwarranted by the facts, for the Germans had no intention or expectation of giving battle, and the engagements at Landrecies and Maroilles were in fact no more than accidental encounters with venturesome advance-guards.[2]   At Sir John French's Headquarters, however, so great was the consternation caused by Haig's reports, that Sir Archibald Murray, the Chief of Staff, fainted, overcome by his emotion, and long afterwards the impression endured that the 1st Corps had had a very narrow and lucky escape.

As on the preceding two days, however, it had been Smith-Dorrien's 2nd Corps that had passed through the real danger on August 25th. The passage of Sordet's French Cavalry Corps, from east to west across the British line of retreat, had delayed the 2nd Corps' start in the morning, so that it had found itself at grips with the enemy before its march could fairly begin.   The day had passed in a succession of combats, until as night fell the main body of the Corps reached Solesmes, where the 4th Division, newly arrived from England, held the heights to the south, covering Smith-Dorrien's retreat.   Civilian refugees, fleeing by the thousands from the northern villages, choked the main roads converging on the town and mingled inextricably with the British convoys and trains.   A cavalry attack, vigorously led into this congested mass might well have thrown the left wing of the British Army into hopeless disorder and spelled disaster, but the German commanders failed to exploit their opportunity.   Nevertheless, it was late in the evening before the last of the harassed British

[2] For an interesting account of events at Landrecies, see *At G.H.Q.* (Cassell, London, 1931) by Brig.-Gen. J. Charteris, then Chief of Intelligence at British 1st Corps H. Q. The German forces actually engaged were: at Landrecies, the 14th Brigade of the 7th Division of the 4th Army Corps (Von Arnim), and at Maroilles, the 48th Infantry of the 5th Division of the 3rd Army Corps (Von Lochow).   The total British casualties in the two engagements amounted to less than 250.

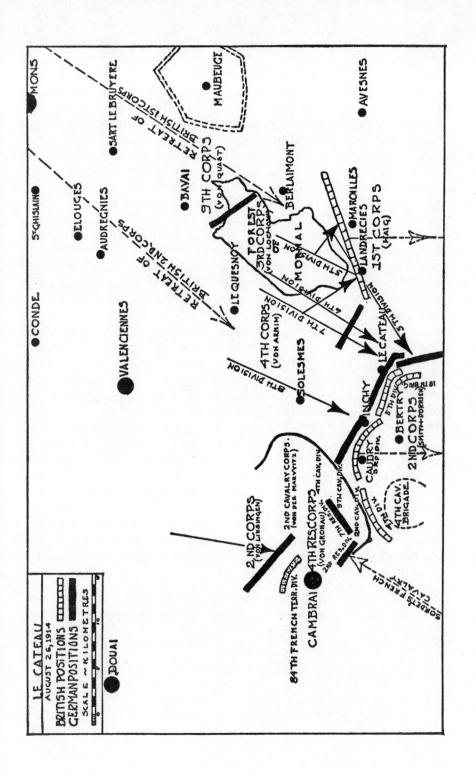

LE CATEAU
AUGUST 26, 1914
BRITISH POSITIONS
GERMAN POSITIONS
SCALE ~ KILOMETRES
0   5   10

MONS
SART LE BRUYÈRE
MAUBEUGE
AVESNES
St GHISLAIN
ELOUGES
AUDREGNIES
BAVAI
9TH CORPS (VON QUAST)
BERLAIMONT
MAROILLES
LANDRECIES
1ST CORPS (HAIG)
RETREAT OF BRITISH 1ST CORPS
CONDE
RETREAT OF BRITISH 2ND CORPS
LE QUESNOY
FOREST OF MORMAL
3RD CORPS (VON LOCHOW)
5TH DIVISION
4TH DIVISION
CAMBRAI
DOUAI
VALENCIENNES
4TH CORPS (VON ARNIM)
7TH DIVISION
SOLESMES
8TH DIVISION
LE CATEAU
5TH DIVISION
INCHY
BERTRY
5TH DIV.
19 TH BRIG.
CAUDRY
3RD DIV.
2ND CORPS (SMITH-DORRIEN)
2ND CORPS (VON LINSINGEN)
2ND CAVALRY CORPS (VON DER MARWITZ)
4TH RES CORPS (VON GRONAU)
2ND RES. DIV.
7TH RES DIV.
4TH CAV. DIV.
9TH CAV. DIV.
2ND CAV. DIV.
4TH CAV. BRIGADE
SORDET'S FRENCH CAVALRY
84TH FRENCH TERR. DIV.

units could pass through Solesmes, and midnight before the 4th Division could relinquish its covering positions and move southward itself.   When at length the 2nd Corps wearily settled down on the line Le Cateau-Inchy-Caudray, only a few hours of darkness remained, and its outposts were still in close contact with the German advance patrols.

French's orders prescribed a continuance of the retreat the following day, and Smith-Dorrien had already issued instructions accordingly when, soon after midnight, Allenby arrived at Corps Headquarters at Bertry to report the immediate proximity of the enemy and his belief that it would be impossible to get away without a fight.   Summoning Hamilton, commander of the 3rd Division, from his Headquarters near by, the British leaders took stock of the situation.   After three days of uninterrupted fighting, the troops who had reached their billets long after dark had come to the point of exhaustion and desperately needed a respite, if only for a few hours. Only by beginning its march before daylight did it seem possible that the 2nd Corps could break away from its adversary without a further engagement ; but the lateness of the hour and the condition of the men made this little short of a physical impossibility.   To attempt the movement after daylight, under the very guns of an alert and active enemy, seemed to court disaster.   Only one chance remained : for the British to stand their ground defensively, in the hope of beating off the enemy, if attacked, and resuming their retirement the next night after dark.

Such was the determination Smith-Dorrien reached after conferring with his subordinates.   It was a courageous decision, for it involved a modification of direct orders received from the Commander in Chief, and Smith-Dorrien was not wholly *persona grata* at French's Headquarters.   Nevertheless, when French received a message, dispatched at 3 A.M., telling of the plan for the 2nd Corps to stand fast at Le Cateau, he replied as follows :

If you can hold your ground, the situation appears likely to improve. The 4th Division must co-operate.   French troops are taking the offensive to the right of the 1st Corps.   Although you are given a free hand as to method, this telegram is not intended to convey the impression that I am not as anxious for you to carry out the retirement, and you must make every effort to do so.

Shortly after six o'clock, Smith-Dorrien again communicated with G.H.Q. by telephone from the railway station, explaining the situation and his decision to Sir Henry Wilson.   He had no difficulty in securing the Deputy Chief of Staff's agreement that the 4th Division should fight with the 2nd Corps and protect its flank.

"Good luck to you," Wilson said, as the conversation ended. "Yours is the first cheerful voice I've heard these three days."

The Battle of Le Cateau, fought by coincidence on the anniversary of Crécy, opened with a German bombardment along the whole front of the British 2nd Corps shortly after six in the morning. Smith-Dorrien's main position faced north, running west from Le Cateau,[3] but Haig's Corps, after remaining all night under arms, began its retreat before daylight, leaving the flank of the 2nd Corps wholly uncovered and compelling Smith-Dorrien to face east, as well as north, towards the heights dominating Le Cateau, where the enemy artillery soon installed itself.

Von Kluck had as yet no very clear conception of the opponent against whom he had fought for the past three days, and seems to have believed that the British front ran from north to south, facing east ; nor did he expect that the British would attempt to give battle around Le Cateau. Accordingly, the orders to the German I Army for the day of August 26th were issued in anticipation of a continued pursuit of a retreating enemy. When it became apparent, however, that the Army Commander had misjudged his adversary's intentions, the German Corps Commanders showed no reluctance to join issue, and the struggle soon raged violently from end to end of the front.

In the centre, the British withstood the initial attacks of Von Arnim's infantry without great difficulty, and a long-range rifle and machine-gun duel soon developed across the Cambrai road with units of the German 4th Army Corps posted to the north. But on the flanks it was another story.

Unlike the previous days, it was the eastern instead of the western flank of the British 2nd Corps that became the critical point of the battle; for Von Lochow's 3rd Corps soon occupied the outskirts of Le Cateau and gradually extended its efforts farther and farther to the south, into the area on the British right, left open by Haig's retreat. With the line of the 19th Brigade, covering the British flank becoming constantly more attenuated in its endeavour to prevent the German attempt at envelopment, Smith-Dorrien threw his only reserve, two infantry battalions, into the battle to save the right of his line from being taken in the rear. But this did not suffice, and soon after noon it became evident that nothing but prompt retirement could save the 19th Brigade and its neighbour the 5th

[3] Order of Battle from east to west : *British 2nd Army Corps* (Smith-Dorrien) : 1st and 3rd Cavalry Brigades, 19th Brigade, 5th Division, 3rd Division, 4th Division, 4th Cavalry Brigade.

German I Army (Von Kluck) : 3rd Army Corps (Von Lochow), 4th Army Corps (Von Arnim), 2nd Cavalry Corps (Von der Marwitz), 4th Reserve Corps (Von Gronau). The German 9th Corps (Von Quast) and 2nd Corps (Von Linsingen) were not engaged in the battle.

Division from encirclement.   At 2 P.M., Sir Charles Fergusson, commander of the 5th Division, ordered a retreat.

It was an operation at once difficult and risky, for many British units were closely locked in almost hand-to-hand combat when the order to fall back reached them.   As a result, when the 5th Division and the 19th Brigade attempted to break away, they could do so only under heavy fire and with great confusion.   Certain units, which apparently never received Fergusson's order, held their positions with the traditional tenacity of British infantry, until ultimately surrounded and captured.   The artillery found itself in a particularly serious plight, for German rifle and machine-gun fire beat upon it from two sides, while shell-fire swept its line of retreat.   Despite heroic efforts, a large proportion of the 5th Division's guns remained in the enemy's hands.   It was fortunate for the British that the necessity of covering the southwestern front of Maubeuge kept the German 9th Corps (Von Quast) from taking part in the battle, and fortunate too, that due perhaps to lack of initiative on the part of local commanders, the German 3rd Corps did not vigorously follow up the success it had obtained.

On the opposite flank, the situation had become hardly less critical for the British.   Von der Marwitz' cavalry divisions, fighting dismounted and strongly supported by artillery, held the British 4th Division under incessant fire and succeeded in dominating Smith-Dorrien's left wing.   On the extreme left, a British brigade [4] was forced back in confusion, and a counter-attack by one of its battalions shattered.   As disorder increased in the British ranks, contact between the various units became momentarily more precarious.   The arrival in the early afternoon of two divisions of Von Gronau's 4th Reserve Corps to reinforce the German cavalry divisions might have led to the collapse of the British left wing but for an opportune diversion in the shape of an attack from the southwest by elements of Sordet's Cavalry Corps.   Compelled to direct their efforts against this new adversary, the Germans relaxed their pressure on the British front, so that the hard-pressed 4th Division could execute without serious difficulty the order for a general retreat that reached it about 5 P.M., though here, as on the right wing, isolated detachments were cut off and surrounded.

Behind Von Kluck's right wing, the German 2nd Corps (Von Linsingen) had been hurrying to join the 4th Reserve Corps in striking the British left ; but it did not arrive in time, for on the outskirts of Cambrai, the unexpected appearance of the 84th French

---

[4] The 12th Brigade of the 4th Division, fighting against the German 2nd Cavalry Division and two Jäger battalions.   For an account of the operations of the German cavalry units, see Gen. von Poseck, *op. cit.*

Territorial Division [5] obliged it to halt.   Though the French Ter-ritorials proved no match for Von Linsingen's ardent youngsters in the engagement that ensued, the delay prevented the German 2nd Corps from arriving before nightfall and saved Smith-Dorrien from dealing with two more divisions on his flank.

At the close of the day, thanks in no small degree to French inter-vention, the British 2nd Corps had been enabled to resume its re-treat.   In the greatest battle fought by a British Army since Water-loo, Smith-Dorrien had stood off forces greatly superior to his own, approximately six divisions against four, but the British losses for the day amounted to more than the aggregate of all losses suffered by the army up to that time.[6]   The disorder and intermingling of units, particularly in the 4th and 5th Divisions, left Smith-Dorrien's command in an extremely vulnerable condition.

Von Kluck, however, had incurred losses hardly less than those of his adversary, and once the combat had been broken off, the Brit-ish 2nd Corps withdrew from the field virtually unmolested. Though active fighting ended some hours before sun-down, the Germans made no serious attempt at pursuit until early the next morning.   By that time contact had become completely severed, and Von Kluck's Headquarters remained in doubt as to the direction the retreating British had taken.   When the German I Army resumed its advance, it took a southwesterly direction, apparently under the continued belief that the British would endeavour to reach their supposed base to the west, whereas in fact the British 2nd Corps marched almost due south towards St. Quentin.   As a result, the day of August 26th ended for some time all contact between the British and Von Kluck's Army, and in the rear-guard actions fought during the following days, elements of Von Bülow's Army became Sir John French's opponents.

Even in the light of all information that has since become avail-able, it remains difficult to say whether Smith-Dorrien's decision to stand his ground at Le Cateau was a wise one.   At first Sir John French seemed enthusiastically to approve his Corps Commander's conduct.

I cannot close the brief account of the glorious stand of the British troops without putting on record my deep appreciation of the valuable

---

[5] Of d'Amade's Group of four Territorial divisions formed on August 16th to protect the northern cities and surrounding country from German raids. See Col. Bujac's *La Belgique envahie* (Fournier, Paris, 1916).

[6] British forces at Waterloo amounted to 31,585 with 8458 casualties. At Le Cateau approximately 40,000 were engaged with 7812 casualties and 38 guns lost; see *Br. O. H.* Sir John French in *1914* states the losses as "at least 14,000 officers and men" and about 80 guns, but offers no authority for this statement, which, however, has been frequently repeated by other writers.

services rendered by General Sir Horace Smith-Dorrien — the British Commander in Chief wrote in his dispatch to Kitchener of September 7, 1914 — I say without hesitation that the saving of the left wing of the Army under my command on the morning of the 26th August could never have been accomplished unless a commander of rare and unusual coolness, intrepidity and determination had been present to personally conduct the operations.

Later, however, in his memoirs written after the war, French virtually withdrew this laudatory statement, and went so far as to deny that he or his Headquarters had ever approved Smith-Dorrien's determination to fight at Le Cateau :

In more than one of the accounts of the retreat from Mons, it is alleged that some tacit consent at least was given by Headquarters at St. Quentin to the decision of the commander of the 2nd Corps. I owe it to the able and devoted officers of my staff to say that there is not a word of truth in this statement.[1]

Despite Von Kluck's failure or inability to pursue, it seems beyond dispute that Le Cateau constituted a British defeat with consequences far more serious than the inconclusive battle at Mons.   The course adopted by Smith-Dorrien brought the 2nd Corps to the very brink of disaster, and only the narrowest of margins saved it from plunging into the abyss.   Yet it cannot be said with any degree of assurance that the same result, and perhaps worse, might not have followed an effort to comply literally with French's orders and to lead exhausted troops from the field in the early morning with the imminent danger of an attack during the retirement.

One thing is certain, that in failing to pursue the British energetically, whatever the reason, Von Kluck lost one of the great opportunities of the campaign to achieve an outstanding and perhaps a decisive victory.

[1] Viscount French, *op. cit.* Cf. pg. 142.

CHAPTER XV

THE COUNTER-STROKE

To MAKE sure that the plan outlined in his General Instruction No. 2 was fully understood and agreed to by the commanders of the Allied left wing forces, Joffre arranged a meeting at British Headquarters in St. Quentin on August 26th to which he summoned both Lanrezac and D'Amade, commander of the group of Territorial divisions operating to the west of the British.

The conference took place while the Battle of Le Cateau was in progress, and its outcome left Joffre very little hope for the success of his new plan. In the billiard-room of the house that Sir John French had made his Headquarters, Joffre listened without comment to the frankly pessimistic statements of his two subordinates as they successively detailed the difficulties of their respective commands, breaking silence only to authorize Lanrezac to orient the retirement of his left wing on La Fère instead of on St. Quentin, in order to avoid confusion with the British. But it was the attitude of the British Commander in Chief that caused Joffre the greatest concern.

The experiences of Mons and during the following days, and increasingly unsatisfactory relations with Lanrezac and the French Fifth Army, had produced a complete change in the attitude of mind of the British High Command. All of the French estimates which had been so confidently accepted had proved erroneous. The Germans had not only crossed the Meuse, contrary to the predictions of the French General Staff, but had done so in such force that the British Army was engaged in a life and death struggle against an overwhelmingly superior enemy. Lanrezac's conduct in leaving the British severely alone to get out of their predicament as best they could had completely destroyed French's confidence in his ally's character and military ability, and the British Commander in Chief had already written Kitchener suggesting the advisability of preparing for the defence of the base at Le Havre.

With no sign of the calm optimism that had impressed Joffre so favourably at Vitry-le-François ten days before, French launched upon an exposition of the difficulties confronting the British Army in which he became openly critical of the conduct of the French Fifth Army.   Wholly preoccupied with the news he had received of Haig's engagements at Landrecies and Maroilles and with the battle then in progress around Le Cateau, where the fate of his 2nd Corps hung in the balance, French had not even seen Joffre's General Instructions of the night before.   When the substance was explained, he raised some objections, but did not press them before the French Commander in Chief's insistence, and expressed a willingness to co-operate within the limits of his ability.   French made no secret, however, of his doubt of his Army's ability to undertake further offensive operations, or even to make a prolonged stand, until it had had an opportunity to rest and reorganize, and Joffre returned to his Headquarters discouraged at the prospect of obtaining effective aid from the British in delaying the advance of the German right wing long enough to permit the formation of a new army around Amiens.

On his arrival at Vitry, more bad news greeted him, a message from Colonel Huguet, Chief of the French Military Mission at British Headquarters, on the outcome of the Battle of Le Cateau.

The battle has been lost by the British Army which seems to have lost all cohesion.   To be reorganized, it will have to have serious protection. Headquarters tonight Noyon.   Further details later.

Though Huguet's pessimism proved somewhat exaggerated, Joffre realized that to preserve any hope of the co-operation essential to the success of the Allied left wing manoeuvre contemplated by his General Instructions No. 2, steps must urgently be taken to relieve the pressure upon Sir John French's Army, at least momentarily.   An offensive by Lanrezac's Army, directed against the enemy forces on the heels of the retreating British, seemed the best means to accomplish the result he sought.

In its retreat from the Sambre the French Fifth Army had reached on August 27th a line running east and west, just south of the Oise River and its tributary the Thon.   Its retirement had been almost due south, while its adversary Von Bülow's Army, had marched towards the southwest, so that only the Guard and the 10th Corps on the left of the German II Army remained in contact with Lanrezac's forces along the Oise, and the other two corps, the 10th Reserve and the 7th Corps with Von Richthofen's cavalry had reached St. Quentin, where they had established contact with the British rear-guards.   It was against the latter two corps that Joffre intended the French Fifth Army to deliver its arresting blow, so as to divert their attention from the British and give Sir John French the respite he needed. The operation required Lanrezac to change the main front of his Army from north to west and to launch his principal attack in the direction of St. Quentin, while a smaller fraction held the enemy in check, facing the Oise in the vicinity of Guise.

To apprise Lanrezac of his intentions and to arrange the details of execution, Joffre sent Lieutenant-Colonel Alexandre of the Operations Section of his staff to the Fifth Army Headquarters at Marle.

From the beginning of the campaign Lanrezac had taken little pains to conceal his low opinion of the strategical ability of the officers at Joffre's Headquarters, many of whom in former years had been his pupils, or to dissimulate his annoyance at the slight consideration paid to his multiple criticisms and observations. Standing before a map, with his glasses hooked over one ear, he was fond of delivering strategical lectures in academic fashion to the officers of his staff, expressing himself with a freedom that, whatever the justification, exceeded the bounds of discretion, and directing caustic comments impartially against the staff officers of Joffre and Sir John French. As might have been foreseen, Lanrezac's remarks did not fail to find their way, doubtless often in embellished form, to the ears of the very officers to whom he referred. Of Joffre's entourage, Lieutenant-Colonel Alexandre, who had more than once acted as the mouthpiece of the French Commander in Chief, had been a particular source of irritation to Lanrezac, and accordingly when Alexandre arrived at Marle on the afternoon of August 27th, bearing verbal instructions from Joffre which required a complete revision of the orders for the following day that had already been sent out to the Corps Commanders, his reception lacked something in cordiality.

A conference ensued at which Alexandre sought to explain the Commander in Chief's wishes to Lanrezac, General Hély d'Oissel, the Chief of Staff, and Commandant Schneider, Chief of the Army's Operations Section. An earnest, plodding soul, deeply conscious of the seriousness of his responsibility, Schneider seemed slow to grasp Joffre's intentions.

"It's quite simple," Alexandre remarked, with a shade of annoyance, laying his hand with fingers extended on the table. "You are now facing north. You are directed to face west, to attack St. Quentin." And he turned his hand sharply at right angles.

Irritated at hearing the difficulties he foresaw thus summarily disposed of, Schneider replied sharply.

"Don't talk nonsense, Colonel."

"Very well, if you don't care to do anything," Alexandre answered, shrugging his shoulders impatiently.

Lanrezac, who had so far listened in silence to this colloquy, now came stoutly to his subordinate's defence, and in no uncertain terms voiced his opinion of the strategy of G.H.Q.

"Before trying to teach me my business, sir," he concluded to the astonished Alexandre, by way of peroration, "go back and tell your little strategists to learn their own."

Without another word Alexandre saluted and left for Vitry-le-François.[1]

Despite his brusque treatment of Joffre's emissary, Lanrezac devoted the evening to preparations for the regrouping of his forces that the Commander in Chief's plans required. The River Oise, which flows from east to west near its source, turns sharply south just west of Guise, forming a right angle within which the Fifth Army was obliged to hold two fronts, one towards the north and one towards the west, in a situation roughly analogous to the position it had previously occupied between the Sambre and the Meuse. As envisaged by Joffre the principal front of the army would be towards the west in the direction of St. Quentin, and here Lanrezac planned to group two army corps, the 3rd and the 18th, for the main attack against the part of Von Bülow's Army that was harassing the British, while the northern front, in the direction of Guise, was to be held defensively by one army corps, the 10th, covering the flank and rear of the main operation. In the centre of the rectangle thus formed, Franchet d'Esperey's 1st Corps was to wait in reserve, ready to participate either to the north or to the west, as occasion might require.

While these dispositions were in process of execution, Joffre arrived at Lanrezac's Headquarters at Marle at 8:30 the following morning. Disturbed by Alexandre's report, the Commander in Chief had resolved to intervene personally to make sure that his instructions were being carried out. Lanrezac received him, and without bothering to explain the preparatory steps already taken, flung himself into a criticism of the wisdom of the move, dilating upon the fatigued condition of his troops, and the probability of an enemy attack from the north while the offensive towards the west was developing. Well aware of the difficulties and dangers involved, but convinced that the condition of the British Army justified the risk, Joffre not unnaturally construed Lanrezac's remarks as an unwillingness to carry out the orders of superior authority, and for one

[1] Two days after this incident, Commandant Schneider was transferred to the staff of his father-in-law, General Maunoury. "His departure," Gen. Spears remarks, *Liaison 1914*, pg. 262, "was an ominous reminder of the fact that it is unwise to quarrel with supreme authority or its representative."

of the few times in the course of the campaign abandoned the calm that so notably characterized him. A violent scene ensued in which Joffre threatened to remove Lanrezac from his command unless he obeyed forthwith without further discussion.[2] Somewhat mollified at last by the Army Commander's assurance that his plans would be executed and were in fact in course of execution, Joffre at last returned to his own Headquarters ; but he was far from satisfied. His confidence in his subordinate, hitherto unlimited, had been shaken, and he must have asked himself whether, after all, there was not some justification for Sir John French's attitude.

"The impression I brought back with me from this visit was so painful," Joffre later wrote, "that when I reached G.H.Q., I decided to return next morning to Lanrezac and supervise his execution of my orders."

During the day of August 28th, the German 10th Corps (Von Emmich) and the Guard (Von Plettenberg) on the left of Von Bülow's Army crossed the Oise between Guise and Marly, overcoming with relative ease the resistance of a brigade of the French 53rd Reserve Division and of elements of the 18th Corps (De Mas Latrie), but the German II Army otherwise displayed little activity before the northern front of Lanrezac's command, and the French were able to take their dispositions for the coming battle without serious hindrance.

To protect the flank of his attacking group and to strengthen the force of its blow, Lanrezac sought the co-operation of the British, and succeeded in obtaining Haig's consent to a limited attack by the British 1st Corps in a northerly direction towards St. Quentin. On learning of the proposed participation of British troops, however, Sir John French firmly over-ruled his Corps Commander, and insisted that the 1st Corps should remain in its positions during the day to obtain the benefit of the opportunity for rest afforded by the French attack. In the face of positive orders from his Commander in Chief, Haig could only inform Lanrezac that he would be unable to cooperate as previously arranged, and the latter, after expressing his vexation in terms more eloquent than wise, issued orders instead to Valabrégue to attack with his two Reserve divisions on the left of the 18th Corps in place of the British.

Before dawn on August 29th, despite the shortness of the time and the manifold technical difficulties of transportation and supply, Lanrezac had completed his arrangements preliminary to carrying

[2] According to Poincaré, *L'Invasion* (Plon, Paris, 1928), pg. 206, Joffre even threatened to have Lanrezac shot. Though both Joffre and Lanrezac mention the incident in their respective memoirs, neither indicates that Joffre went to such an extreme. Poincaré received his account at second-hand from Col. Pénelon, his liaison officer, and probably obtained an exaggerated version.

Joffre's plan into effect, and the French Fifth Army stood ready for the impending battle which was destined to exert a profound influence on the subsequent course of the campaign and to contribute materially to its ultimate outcome.

CHAPTER XVI

GUISE–ST. QUENTIN

THE SECOND pitched battle fought by the French Fifth Army against the German II Army on August 29th and 30th has been called by French writers the Battle of Guise and by the Germans the Battle of St. Quentin, and both sides have vociferously claimed the victory. The explanation lies in the fact that it was actually two separate battles in one of which, along the northern front in the vicinity of Guise, the French gained the upper hand and in the other, on the western front in the neighbourhood of St. Quentin, the incontestable advantage rested with the Germans.

Almost immediately the battle took the strategical form which Lanrezac had predicted rather than the one which Joffre had intended, for before the 3rd and 18th Corps on the French Fifth Army's left had reached the Oise from which they were to launch their attack against St. Quentin, a serious German attack had developed from the north and for the rest of the day it was the northern rather than the western front that became the principal scene of action.

The ease with which the German 10th Corps and the Guard had effected a crossing of the Oise during the afternoon of the 28th, encouraged Von Bülow to believe that he would not encounter serious resistance until he reached the heights of the Aisne, and he issued orders to Von Emmich and Von Plettenberg to continue their march forward during the day of the 29th, fixing Faucouzy, Marfontaine and Parpéville as their objectives, with a view to preparing a converging attack against the position of La Fère — an obsolete fortress which the French in fact had no intention of defending.

Through the thick mist that filled the valley of the Oise, the two German corps began their march towards the south at an early hour. Assuming that they had no enemies in the immediate vicinity, the German commanders did not delay for extensive reconnaissances and took few precautions. Before the front of the 1st Division of the Guard an over-zealous group of telephonists, anxious to install their communications promptly, pushed forward from Gomont with a wagon carrying their apparatus, driving complacently along the road ahead of the infantry points until on the outskirts of the little hamlet of Rue Guthin a sudden volley greeted them out of the fog. The sound of the rifle shots and the appearance of the wagon, a moment or two later, careering wildly back along the road with its driver frantically lashing his terror-stricken horses, gave the German infantry warning of hostile forces and afforded them a chance to deploy in combat formation. Elsewhere, however, at Jonqueuse, Audigny and Colonfay, the German advance detachments, unable to see more than 100 yards before them, ran headlong against the French outposts.

It soon became apparent that the French had no intention of falling back after a mere exchange of shots and that a full-fledged attack would be necessary to reach the objectives that Von Bülow had assigned. As the rising sun gradually dispelled the mist, the four divisions of Von Emmich's and Von Plettenberg's Corps set about their task in earnest, and in the villages of Haution, Le Sourd and Bertaignemont bitter fighting was soon in progress.[1]

By ten o'clock, Defforges of the French 10th Corps had sent Lanrezac an urgent appeal for help :

I am very violently attacked on my whole front. They are getting around my right flank. I will hold at all costs. Give me support as soon as possible on my right and on my left.

To the west of the French 10th Corps, the 3rd Corps (Hache[2]) had been marching towards the Oise to take part in the principal attack against St. Quentin when Von Emmich's attack opened on the flank-guard of the French 5th Division at Jonqueuse and Bertaignemont, and one regiment had already crossed the river at Mont d'Origny ; but Hache, without waiting for orders, halted the movement and faced north, at the same time informing the 18th Corps (De Mas Latrie) that he could not proceed with the attack to the west until the menace against his flank had been disposed of. By a wise precaution the artillery of the 3rd Corps had already taken up positions facing north, in the vicinity of Courjumelles and consequently found itself ready to lend immediate support and to bring the weight of its fire upon Von Emmich's advancing lines.

Until early afternoon the Germans slowly but steadily progressed, pressing the French lines back and carrying one position after an-

---

[1] Order of battle on northern front from east to west :
German II Army (Von Bülow) : Guard (Von Plettenberg), 2nd Division and 1st Division ; 10th Corps (Von Emmich), 20th Division and 19th Division.
French Fifth Army (Lanrezac) : 10th Corps (Defforges) ; 3rd Corps (Hache). In reserve, 1st Corps (Franchet d'Esperey).
[2] On August 28th, on Lanrezac's recommendation, Joffre had relieved Sauret of command of the 3rd Corps and replaced him with Hache, who had formerly commanded the 40th Division of Sarrail's 6th Corps.

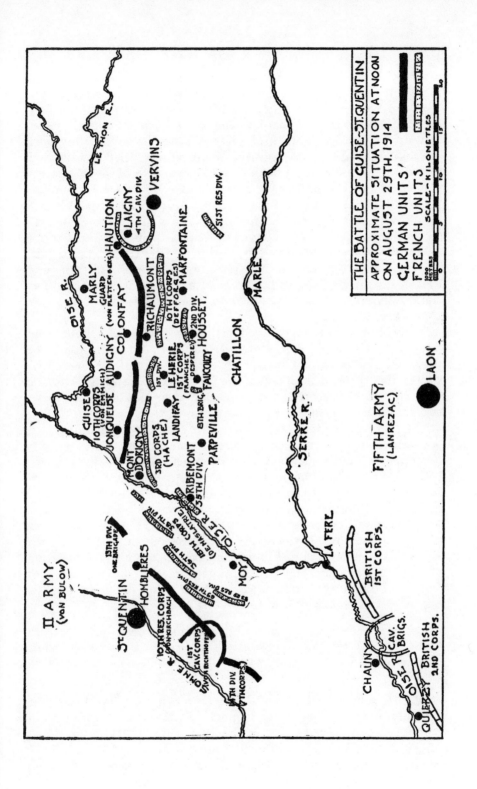

THE BATTLE OF GUISE-ST.QUENTIN

APPROXIMATE SITUATION AT NOON
ON AUGUST 29TH. 1914

GERMAN UNITS
FRENCH UNITS

SCALE-KILOMETRES

II ARMY
(VON BULOW)

ST.QUENTIN
HOMBLIERES

OISE R.
10TH RES. CORPS (VON KIRCHBACH)
1ST CAV. CORPS (VON RICHTHOFEN)
OISE R.
2ND (VIITH CORPS)
5TH DIV.

13TH DIV.
ONE BRIGADE

MON
36TH DIV.
18TH CORPS (DE MAS LATRIE)
33RD RES DIV.
25TH DIV.
OISE R.
35TH DIV.
RIBEMONT

MONT
D'ORIGNY
3RD CORPS
(HACHÉ)
LANDIFAY

OISE R.
GUISE
10TH CORPS
(VON EMMICH)
JONQUEUSE

MARLY
GUARD
(VON PLETTENBERG)
AUDIGNY
COLONFAY
RICHAUMONT

HAUTION
LAIGNY
4TH CAV. DIV.
VERVINS

LE THON R.

1ST DIV.
LE HERIE
1ST CORPS
(FRANCHET
D'ESPEREY)
2ND DIV.
8TH BRIG.
PARPEVILLE
FAUCOUZY
HOUSSET
MARFONTAINE
10TH CORPS
(DEFFORGES)

51ST RES DIV.

CHATILLON

MARLE

SERRE R.

PARPEVILLE

LA FERE

FIFTH ARMY
(LANREZAC)

LAON

MOY

BRITISH
1ST CORPS

CHAUNY
OISE R. CAV. BRIGS.
BRITISH
2ND CORPS

QUIERZY

other by a series of assaults, but they achieved their gains at a heavy price and there were many anxious moments.   The 1st Regiment of the Guard, commanded by Prince Eitel Friederich of Prussia, driving the French out of Colonfay after a stubborn resistance, pushed forward on Richaumont, three kilometres to the south ; but worn out with heat and fatigue and with many officers killed or wounded, the weary troops hesitated before the heights north of the village and seemed inclined to fall back.   As they wavered Prince Eitel forced his way into the front ranks and seizing a drum beat upon it furiously, rallying the men around him.   The sight of the Emperor's second son in the very forefront of the battle-line provided the added stimulus that was needed, and the regiment pressed on to occupy the heights which the French had already abandoned ; but there it halted, for the limit of endurance had been reached, and the men could only make ready to stand their ground and hold their gains, if attacked.

The same situation prevailed generally along the whole front both of the German Guard and the 10th Corps, for after an average progress of some five kilometres the fierce energy of the French resistance had broken the momentum of the attack, and the German commanders became resigned to rest on their positions and to recuperate their strength before attempting further gains.

The German artillery maintained a fire of undiminished intensity, however, and the French commanders, momentarily expecting a renewal of the attacks, viewed the prospect pessimistically, for they too had reached the limit of their strength and doubted their ability for further resistance.   Since early morning both Defforges and Hache had been calling for help, urging the intervention of the 1st Corps, which was waiting in reserve behind their line, but Franchet d'Esperey had been unable to comply in the absence of orders from the Army Commander and had limited his participation to the insertion of one brigade at Le Hérie to fill a gap between the 3rd and 10th Corps.   To his great relief, however, shortly after one o'clock a message from Lanrezac gave him full liberty of action :

At the moment, the primary mission of the Army is to drive back across the Oise the enemy troops that have crossed to the left bank. The 1st Army Corps will be engaged as circumstances best require in liaison with the 3rd and 10th Army Corps.

With the tactical control of the battle on the northern front thus virtually left in his hands, the commander of the 1st Corps did not hesitate, but prepared to enter the line between Hache and Defforges and to launch a combined counter-attack.   With his Headquarters set up in an open field near a railroad crossing on the road to Le Hérie, Franchet d'Esperey, mounted on a chestnut charger, personally directed the advance of his Army Corps under the enemy's fire ; but he was determined not to engage his units piecemeal, and it was nearly six o'clock before his artillery could all be placed in position and his infantry could be massed for the supreme effort.

Rightly sensing that the difficulties of the 3rd and 10th Corps were mainly moral and that in fact they had already fought their opponents to a stand-still, Franchet d'Esperey arranged a spectacular entrance. With fixed bayonets gleaming in the light of the setting sun, the regiments of the French 1st Division marched down the slopes north of Le Hérie with colours flying and with bands playing the *Marseillaise*, while behind them the massed artillery of the whole 1st Army Corps thundered against the enemy's lines. It was a deliberate bit of showmanship and a highly successful one, for it gave new heart to the exhausted troops on either side who had been fighting since early morning. Convinced that victory at last lay within their grasp, the units of the 3rd and 10th Corps, hitherto holding their lines only under the grim exhortations of their officers, spontaneously joined in the advance, and the counter-attack swept forward. It was too late to accomplish any great tangible results, for darkness was already settling down, and though the villages of Bertaignemont and Richaumont were re-taken and the enemy outposts driven back, the German main lines of resistance, firmly held and organized for defence with characteristic thoroughness, were not subjected to a general assault. Nevertheless Franchet d'Esperey's intervention had produced a decisive effect, for in a brief space of time it had altered the whole morale of the army and had created a definite impression of victory. With confidence restored, the three French army corps took up their positions for the night, determined to complete their task of driving the enemy back across the Oise in the morning and confident of their ability to do so.

A corresponding depression pervaded the German side of the battlefield, for the day had turned out contrary to all expectations. Despite prodigious efforts, two army corps had made only a negligible advance and still remained far from the objectives that Von Bülow had intended them to reach. Von Plettenberg in particular had cause for worry, for the responsibility for the German II Army's left flank rested upon the Guard, and the appearance of French cavalry in the vicinity of Laigny [8] during the afternoon had caused him grave alarm and had led him to send back his trains and convoys to the north bank of the Oise. Though Von Bülow's order for the next day required the Guard and the 10th Corps to attack at daybreak, neither Von Emmich nor Von Plettenberg felt any assurance that they would

[8] Advance elements of the French 4th Cavalry Division.

be able to do so, and took their dispositions rather with a view to re-sisting an anticipated attack on the positions they already held.

Von Plettenberg had no rest that night. Long after midnight, when Corps Headquarters had settled down with all reports received and orders issued, he rode out alone across the battlefield, stopping at every dressing-station and eagerly questioning the driver of each passing ambulance — not as the commander of the proud Corps of the Imperial Guard, but as an anxious father, vainly seeking news of his son, a lieutenant in Prince Eitel's regiment who had fallen that day at Colonfay.

In the meanwhile on the western front facing St. Quentin, where Joffre had expected the principal attack to develop, the results had been less favourable to the French. Hache's message telling of the engagement of the 3rd Corps towards the north had caused De Mas Latrie to check his advance, and in the afternoon to fall back before an attack by the German 10th Reserve Corps (Von Kirchbach) supported by Von Richthofen's Cavalry.

Though Von Bülow had commended the 10th Reserve Corps for its rapid march along the west bank of the Oise towards St. Quentin, its exploit also constituted a source of danger, for it resulted in open-ing a breach in the German front between the 10th Reserve Corps and the 10th Corps, east of the Oise, which had not progressed be-yond Mont d'Origny. A determined French advance towards the northwest into this gap might have placed the German II Army in a precarious situation and menaced at once the flanks of the group fighting around St. Quentin and of the other group fighting south of Guise. Von Bülow himself was the first to perceive the danger, for as he reached Hombli ères on his way to St. Quentin in the early morning, the sound of a cannonade to the southwest led him to leave his car and scale the heights northeast of the town from which he could see a thin line of French skirmishers approaching from the southeast. Two infantry companies, hastily assembled by the Army Commander himself, sufficed to arrest the enemy advance. Shortly afterwards, Von Bülow turned aside a brigade of the 13th Division marching from Maubeuge to rejoin its command,[4] the 7th Corps (Von Einem), and obtained the further aid of the artillery of the 9th Corps (Von Quast) of Von Kluck's Army, that had also been covering Maubeuge. The gap was filled and the menace averted.

Fortunately for Von Bülow the French had no Franchet d'Esperey west of the Oise that day, and De Mas Latrie was a commander of a very different stamp. Alarmed at the prospect of joining battle

---

[4] The other brigade of the German 13th Division remained for the remainder of the campaign as a part of Von Zwehl's Army Detachment before Mauheuge.

alone against what he conceived to be very superior forces, and lacking any instructions from Lanrezac applicable to the new situation in which he found himself, the commander of the 18th Corps, though he had three divisions at his disposal,[5] seems to have offered little serious resistance to the German 10th Reserve Corps, and to have hastened his retreat behind the Oise, closely followed by the enemy, while on his left two brigades of Von Einem's 7th Corps took the measure of three brigades of Valabrégue's reservists. Apart from the strategical consequences, which amounted to no less than the abandonment of Joffre's plan of attack, this withdrawal placed the French Fifth Army in a critical tactical position, despite its success to the north, for elements of the 18th Corps fell back into the area immediately behind the front of the 3rd Corps, with the result that in the event either of a retirement by the 3rd Corps or of an advance by the enemy forces opposing the 18th Corps, the northern front of the French Fifth Army might have been thrown into confusion and taken in the rear.

Throughout the day Lanrezac remained at his Headquarters at Laon, thirty kilometres from the firing-line, without direct telephone or telegraph communication with his army corps, too far away to exercise any practical direction over the development of the battle.[6] Early in the morning Joffre had arrived at Laon, ready if necessary to relieve Lanrezac of his command and to replace him by Franchet d'Esperey, but on arrival he had been relieved to find Lanrezac completely master of himself with the situation well in hand. Studiously refraining from interference, Joffre had remained throughout the morning, leaving about noon, while the issue remained in doubt, to visit Sir John French at Compiègne without giving any instructions as to the future conduct of the Fifth Army. When the result of the day became known, and the hazardous situation of the French Fifth Army seemed clear, despite its advantage over Von Bülow's left wing corps, Lanrezac telephoned G.H.Q. seeking further orders in a determined effort to disengage all personal responsibility for the manoeuvre of which he did not even yet approve. Joffre had not returned from Compiègne, and Belin, the Major General, answered the call.

"Must the Fifth Army delay in the region of Guise-St. Quentin at the risk of being captured?" Lanrezac asked abruptly, again a victim of his unlucky faculty of emphasizing the wrong thing at the wrong time.

[5] The 38th Division, which had been part of the 3rd Corps on the Sambre, had been transferred to the 18th Corps.
[6] In contrast to Lanrezac's method of command, Von Bülow and Von Kluck, as well as many of the French Army Commanders, established their posts of command close to the front-line, almost within range of the enemy artillery.

"What do you mean, let your Army be captured?" cried Belin, utterly taken aback. "That would be absurd!"

Lanrezac went on to explain that he had undertaken the offensive upon imperative orders from the Commander in Chief and would not break it off without equally definite instructions. Nevertheless, in view of the likelihood that either Von Kluck or Von Hausen, or possibly both, would soon lend aid to the German II Army, he felt it the part of prudence to continue his retreat.

Belin refused to give orders in Joffre's absence, but the soundness of Lanrezac's views were beyond question, and Joffre promptly ratified his suggestion, but by the manner of his presentation, Lanrezac had once again dramatized his fears and heightened the impression of over-timidity that already existed at G.H.Q.

Though by an unfortunate error Joffre's order to retreat did not reach Lanrezac at Laon until the morning of the 30th, no serious harm was done by the delay. By early afternoon the French Fifth Army, which had renewed the battle at dawn, had drawn off and had again taken up its southward march. Von Bülow's weary troops were glad to see it go and made no attempt to follow.

For the execution of the difficult manoeuvres preparatory to the battle, Lanrezac and his staff deserve full credit, but the Army Commander failed to achieve the full measure of success to which he was entitled, for again, as on the Sambre, he neglected to take advantage until too late of the numerical superiority which he possessed from the outset, engaging Franchet d'Esperey's 1st Corps only after the 3rd and 10th Corps had already worked themselves to exhaustion and leaving Abonneau's Cavalry Division and the 51st Reserve Division virtually idle throughout the day on the Fifth Army's right flank. An effective stroke against the German Guard's left flank was what Von Plettenberg momentarily expected and feared, and the risk to the French of such an operation would have been negligible, for a gap of nearly fifty kilometres separated Von Bülow's left from Von Hausen's right, the latter heavily engaged on its own account against the French 9th Corps (Dubois) near Novion Porcien; but although Lanrezac somewhat tardily recognized the opportunity and ordered the 4th Cavalry Division to advance, nothing came of it, and a golden opportunity to convert a somewhat inconclusive success into a serious defeat for Von Bülow's Army slipped away.

Though in his estimate of the strategical problem confronting the French Fifth Army Lanrezac was right and Joffre was wrong, the Battle of Guise-St. Quentin, which Lanrezac reluctantly fought, accomplished the principal purposes of the French Commander in Chief, for Von Bülow's Army was halted in its tracks for a full thirty-six hours, while the French and the British continued their retreat unmolested.   Neither was seriously engaged again until the Battle of the Marne six days later.   In addition it contributed to a more important, though secondary, result by inducing Von Kluck, far off to the west, to execute a radical change in direction that profoundly modified the German strategy and in the end nullified the Schlieffen Plan.[7]

[7] The works of Von Bülow, Lanrezac and Spears, already mentioned, contain accounts of the Battle of Guise-St. Quentin.   In addition reference should be made to monographs of Gen. G. Rouquerol, *La Bataille de Guise* (Berger-Levrault, Paris), Col. Valarché, *La Bataille de Guise* (Berger-Levrault, Paris, 1928), Lieut.-Col. Koeltz, *La Garde Allemande à la Bataille de Guise* (Lavanzelle, Paris), and Lieut.-Col. Larcher, *op. cit.*

CHAPTER XVII

VON KLUCK CHANGES COURSE

W HEN the German I Army remained masters of the battlefield of Le Cateau on the morning of August 27th, the British had disappeared and Von Kluck had no very clear idea of the direction they had taken. Certain reports indicated that they had retreated southwards towards St. Quentin, but on the other hand it seemed equally probable that they had gone towards the southwest to make another stand along the Somme. The general plan of operations required the German right wing army to march towards the southwest, until the time came for the enveloping turn which was to be the culmination of the Schlieffen Plan, and Von Kluck accordingly turned his Army in the direction of Péronne.

With high satisfaction, the Army Commander and his staff welcomed a message from Von Moltke ending the subordination of the I Army to Von Bülow. For the first time since the opening of the campaign Von Kluck became a free agent, released from the galling restraint of his arrogant colleague, and enjoyed a liberty of which he made full use in the days to come.

With relative ease, the German I Army marched southwest for the next four days, but though the British seemed to have vanished, French troops in ever-increasing numbers appeared in the area of Von Kluck's advance. On the 27th and again on the 28th, Von der Marwitz' cavalry and Von Linsingen's 2nd Corps drove back elements of the French 61st and 62nd Reserve Divisions and of D'Amade's Territorials, and on the 29th, near Proyart, Von Linsingen fought a somewhat more serious engagement against a division of the French 7th Corps (Vautier) which had detrained from Alsace only the night before ; but despite these incidents, Von Kluck attached little importance to the French forces he encountered, rating them as isolated detachments of negligible strength, and he became convinced that the moment was at hand for the turning movement towards the southeast, designed to bring the Schlieffen Plan to consummation. The Headquarters of the I Army summarized the situation on August 28th as follows :

The left wing of the main French forces (i.e. Lanrezac's Fifth Army) is retreating in a southerly and southwesterly direction in front of the victorious II and III Armies. It appears to be of decisive importance to find the flank of this force, whether retreating or in position, force it away from Paris and outflank it. Compared with this new objective, the attempt to force the British away from the coast is of minor importance.[1]

This conception Von Kluck put in the form of a communication to Von Bülow, suggesting that the I Army should turn its march towards Compiègne and Noyon, while the II Army executed a corresponding change from southwest to south to bring its right flank against Quierzy and Chauny ; but Von Kluck's proposal remained unanswered, for in the meanwhile Von Moltke's General Directive of the 27th arrived, which required the I Army to continue its southwesterly march towards the Seine below Paris, and Von Bülow became engaged in the Battle of Guise-St. Quentin.

In the late afternoon of August 30th, however, a radio from the II Army raised the question again in more pressing form :

Enemy defeated today in decisive fashion. Important fractions are retreating on La Fère. To exploit success effectively the conversion of the I Army towards La Fère-Laon around Chauny as a pivot is immediately desirable.

Von Bülow's message obliged Von Kluck to make a decision similar to the one he had faced after Le Cateau : should he continue towards the southwest in accordance with Von Moltke's Directive, or, in the light of the new situation created by the victory claimed by the II Army, should he turn his course in response to Von Bülow's appeal ?

By adopting the former course, he would carry out literally the orders he had received from the High Command and would assure the protection of the right flank of the German armies against enemy forces assembling to the west ; but on the other hand, he had become convinced that the French forces on his right might safely be disregarded and that the British, after Le Cateau where he believed he had encountered their whole army,[2] no longer constituted a serious menace. He had already thought it advisable to turn against the French left flank, and Von Bülow's communication gave added weight to this view.

On the night of August 30th, the German I Army had reached

---

[1] Von Kluck, *op. cit.*

[2] Even after the war, Von Kluck retained the impression that he had dealt at Le Cateau with six British divisions, whereas in fact he had fought only three divisions and one brigade, exclusive of Allenby's three cavalry brigades. See Von Kluck, *op. cit.*

approximately the line of the Avre between Moreuil and Roye. A literal compliance with Von Bülow's suggestion would therefore have required it to make a sharp turn directly towards the east. In case the French retreated rapidly before the II Army, as might be fairly expected, such a manoeuvre did not seem to Von Kluck adequate to accomplish the desired result, for the enemy might escape to the south before the German I Army could reach his flank. Accordingly he modified Von Bülow's proposal by taking instead a southeasterly course, directing his Army against Compiègne and Noyon, as he himself had suggested two days before, and leaving one army corps, the 4th Reserve Corps (Von Gronau), in echelon behind his right wing to cover the army flank towards the west.

Orders in this sense had already been issued when an officer from Von Bülow's Headquarters arrived with the disconcerting news that the II Army would rest on its positions during the day of the 31st. To Von Kluck, who had never doubted that Von Bülow would press his pursuit vigorously, this information brought the dawn of a doubt as to the "decisive" nature of the victory won, but it did not alter his decision. Indeed, it seemed rather to confirm its wisdom, for under the circumstances a continued march towards the southwest while Von Bülow remained stationary would materially have increased the distance that already separated the I Army from the II, and would have subjected the former to the risk of isolation. Even without the measure of support that he had expected from Von Bülow, Von Kluck resolved to press forward, alone if necessary, to strike the flank and rear of the main body of the French armies as they retreated southwards.

For the next six days this remained Von Kluck's primary objective, and his decision, taken as a result of the Battle of Guise-St. Quentin, placed the German I Army on the path that ultimately led it into the area southeast of Paris and permitted the concentration of the French Sixth Army to proceed undisturbed outside the German right flank. Quite unconsciously Von Kluck thus put an end to any possibility of successfully carrying out the outflanking manoeuvre that had been the corner-stone of the Schlieffen Plan.[3]

The situation of the Allied armies seemed, nevertheless, anything but reassuring to Joffre on August 30th. The establishment of the new offensive front from Amiens to Verdun, contemplated by his General Instructions No. 2, had become impossible of realization, as a result of the British defeat at Le Cateau and of Von Kluck's rapid

[3] In studying the strategical role of the German I Army, Gen. von Kuhl's *Der Marnefeldzug 1914*, already cited, will be found of the greatest value and for an understanding of the views and intentions of the High Command of the I Army, it is indispensable. It is an outstanding contribution to the literature of the Marne campaign.

advance which had prevented Maunoury's forces from assembling in the region originally planned. With the menace to the French capital becoming daily more pronounced, the necessity devolved upon Joffre of devising new means to halt the on-rushing tide, and in all the dark hours of the next four years, the flame of the Allied cause never burned lower than in these closing days of August.

CHAPTER XVIII

THE LITTLE RED SCHOOLHOUSE

ON AUGUST 29th Von Moltke moved his Headquarters a second time and the following day established them at Luxembourg where they remained for the rest of the campaign. In a little red-brick schoolhouse, the German Great General Staff crowded its offices into cramped class-rooms where staff-officers, far from their luxurious quarters in Berlin, toiled before plain board tables by the light of candles or at best of kerosene lamps. Out of a somewhat belated regard for the feelings of the population of the little Grand Duchy, Von Moltke wished to avoid exercising the power of requisition that might have procured him more elaborate accommodations, appreciating too, perhaps, the psychological importance of simplicity at Headquarters so remote from the firing-line, while his comrades were enduring dangers and real hardship at the front.

The Russian front no longer caused the Chief of Staff anxiety, for under the leadership of Von Hindenburg and Ludendorff, the German armies had already established the ascendancy that they retained to the end of the war ; but events in the west had not fully corresponded to early hopes and had tempered somewhat the initial mood of extravagant optimism. Though the right wing armies seemed to be pursuing their way in eminently satisfactory fashion, and daily bulletins of victory continued to arrive from Von Bülow and Von Kluck, on the left wing Crown Prince Rupprecht had notably failed to make any substantial progress and his drive, which had started so promisingly, seemed wholly to have lost momentum.[1] Serious difficulties had also attended the centre armies, for instead of pursuing a scattered and disorganized enemy, the German Crown Prince and the Duke of Wurtemburg had found the French solidly established behind the Meuse, defending it tenaciously, and the Duke of Wurtemburg had been compelled to make repeated requests for aid to his neighbour on the west, Von Hausen.

Due to the persistent opposition he had encountered in the region

---

[1] During the period immediately following the Battle of the Frontiers (Aug. 25–28) the German left wing armies were in fact falling back before Dubail's and De Castelnau's counter-offensives. See Chapter XXXVIII.

of Signy l'Abbaye and immediately to the south of it, Von Hausen had not been able fully to respond to his royal colleague's appeals, but on the 30th, in order to assure closer contact with the centre armies, he resolved to direct the future progress of the German III Army towards the south, rather than towards the southwest, and applied to Von Moltke for his approval.

The day before, while the Duke of Wurtemburg was still calling for help, the French Fourth Army opposed to him had relaxed its hold of the line it had so successfully defended and had started to fall back. Actually, De Langle had acted with some reluctance upon Joffre's direct order, but when the Duke of Wurtemburg found that at last he was able to advance, he reported the fact to Von Moltke in such terms as to give the French retreat the aspect of a German victory and to hold out hopes of a great success, if the pursuit could be pressed by the III and IV Armies in a southerly direction.

In the evening of August 30th, therefore, the German High Command had before it four important messages, one from the Duke of Wurtemburg (IV Army) announcing that he had finally overcome French resistance before his front and that the passages of the Meuse lay open, another from Von Hausen (III Army) suggesting that he pursue his march towards the south so as to come into closer liaison with the IV Army on his left, a third from Von Bülow (II Army) announcing a "complete victory" in the region of Guise-St. Quentin, and finally an intercepted message from Von Bülow to Von Kluck [2] suggesting that the I Army should turn towards the east to cut off the retreating French Fifth Army.

The combination convinced Von Moltke of the propriety of modifying the prescriptions of his General Directive of August 27th to conform to the situation as it seemed to be actually developing by changing the direction of the German II, III, IV and V Armies from the southwest to the south, and approving Von Kluck's turn towards the southeast, and he accordingly despatched a radio to Von Hausen :

The intention of the III Army to pursue a southerly direction is approved. The IV Army must co-ordinate its movements with those of the III Army. The left wing of the II Army will take the approximate direction of Rheims.

To the I and II Armies he sent a like message of approbation :

The III Army has converged towards the south against the Aisne, attacking by Rethel-Semuy, and will pursue a southerly direction. The movements undertaken by the I and II Armies conform to the intentions of the High Command.

[2] See pg. 163.

Co-operate with the III Army.   Left wing of the II Army approximate direction Rheims.

Thus Von Moltke modified the strategical conception of his previous directions and constituted the III Army, in the centre, the axis of his manoeuvre.

In the following days, as the progress of the Duke of Wurtemburg and of the German Crown Prince, hitherto so slow and painful, began to accelerate its pace, Von Moltke found new grounds for encouragement and even hoped that his centre armies might achieve decisive victory.

"Today and tomorrow the centre armies are fighting a decisive struggle whose outcome will have incalculable consequences," he wrote his wife, the Countess Elsa, on the 31st.

Accepting at face value the reports that came to him that the French forces before his centre armies were "in flight," Von Moltke never doubted that the result had been obtained by an affirmative victory in combat, and the possibility that the French retirement might constitute a part of a preconceived manoeuvre directed by the French Commander in Chief seems never to have crossed his mind.

"Exploit the victory, in concert with the III and V Armies," he directed the Duke of Wurtemburg in the evening of September 1st. In truth, the great decisive battle in which Von Moltke pictured his III, IV and V Armies as being engaged existed only in the imagination of the German High Command, for slowly and methodically, Sarrail,[3] De Langle and Foch were falling back towards the south and southwest, halting now and again to strike back at their pursuers as Joffre had ordered, only to resume the retreat in accordance with his general plan, but there was no general engagement, and the French made no effort to do more than to check or hinder the German advance as opportunity offered.

During the days of August 31st and September 1st, only the most meagre reports reached Luxembourg from the two German right wing armies.   Preoccupied primarily with his centre and with the possibility of a decisive stroke there, Von Moltke seems to have felt little concern for the fate of his right wing, confident, perhaps, of the capability of its experienced commanders.   The fact that the II Army rested on its positions for thirty-six hours after the Battle of Guise-St. Quentin — an attitude hardly appropriate for an army which had just won the decisive victory Von Bülow claimed — caused him no concern, nor did Von Kluck's failure to deliver the blow

[3] On August 30th, Sarrail had replaced Ruffey in command of the French Third Army. See pg. 190.

against the retreating enemy's flank for which he had changed his course to the southeast. Though reports of secret agents gave abundant notice of French troops assembling in the Entrenched Camp of Paris and of great activity there, under the energetic direction of Galliéni, Von Moltke saw no immediate significance in these facts and did not deem it necessary to pass on the news to Von Kluck.

With his attention still focussed on his centre armies, Von Moltke concluded that the decision would have to be obtained in the area between Paris and Verdun into which the main body of the Allied forces seemed to be retreating. To accomplish the result he sought, he determined to reduce the scope of the enveloping movement originally planned and to abandon all thought of an immediate attack on Paris, instead directing the march of the II, III, IV and V Armies southwards towards the Marne, while the I Army covered their right flank towards Paris and the west. In this operation, his strategical objective became the separation of the main body of the Allied forces from the capital by driving them towards the southeast. If Rupprecht of Bavaria could reasonably soon break through the fortified line to the east, and could cross the Moselle between Toul and Epinal, Joffre's forces would be threatened with envelopment from both flanks.

This determination Von Moltke embodied in a radio dispatched to the right wing armies during the night of September 2nd:

It is the intention of the High Command to drive the French back in a southeasterly direction, cutting them off from Paris. The I Army will follow the II in echelon and will also cover the right flank of the armies.

It was a strategical decision of cardinal importance. Apparently without fully realizing the implication of his action, Von Moltke paved the way for the complete abandonment of the Schlieffen Plan by altering the primary mission of the I Army, hitherto the spearhead of the intended enveloping attack, by converting it into a flank guard. More important still, however, the decision was based upon an assumption that the Allied armies had suffered complete defeat and were retreating as best they could, deprived of all liberty of manoeuvre, wholly failing to take into account the possibility that Joffre had succeeded in regrouping his forces to provide his left wing with the strength it had so notably lacked in the Battle of the Frontiers.

Still ignorant of the existence of Maunoury's Sixth Army, a spirit of intemperate optimism again pervaded the German High Command. On September 1st, the anniversary of Sedan, the Emperor returned in high spirits from a visit to the Crown Prince's Army, and Von Moltke inspected the ruins of the little French fort of Longwy, noting with satisfaction the devastating effects of the German heavy artillery. Von Moltke, Von Stein and Tappen, all three, looked to the future with enthusiastic confidence. Only the Prussian Minister of War, Von Falkenhayn, struck a discordant note. Alone of those in high authority at Luxembourg, he had personally visited the Headquarters of Von Hausen, the Duke of Wurtemburg and the German Crown Prince, and he had returned frankly skeptical.

"It isn't a battle won, it's an orderly retreat," he said. "Show me your trophies and your prisoners."

In fact, the German Army Commanders had little concrete evidence to substantiate their claims of decisive victories ; a few cannon, demolished by lucky hits and abandoned, a few prisoners — deserters, wounded, or footsore stragglers left behind and lost — but no booty that corresponded to what a victorious army might expect to take from a beaten and disorganized foe. The capture of minor French fortresses and their garrisons sufficed to swell the numbers of prisoners and cannon to feed the communiqués issued to press and public, but these achievements had little military significance. Though unheeded, Von Falkenhayn's point was well taken.

CHAPTER XIX

VON KLUCK DISOBEYS

WHILE VON BÜLOW recuperated from the effects of Guise-St. Quentin, then cautiously resumed his advance to invest La Fère, which the French had already abandoned, Von Kluck drove his Army forward with prodigious strides in his effort to strike the flank of the retreating French and British. By the evening of September 2nd, the German I Army was stretched out across the region between the Oise and the Marne with its advance guards at Château Thierry.

In sharp skirmishes near Crépy-en-Valois and Villers-Cotterets on September 1st, contact had been established with British rear-guards, and at Néry, the 4th Cavalry Division of Von der Marwitz' Corps, after a forced march, had come upon the British 1st Cavalry Brigade and had fought a brief but bitter combat in which the German cavalry division lost most of its accompanying artillery. These minor engagements were not what Von Kluck had hoped for, however, and when Sir John French continued his retirement on the 2nd, and crossed the Marne between Lagny and La Ferté-sous-Jouarre, the German Army Commander was obliged to recognize that the British had eluded him and to give up all further thought of reaching their flank ; but he still hoped for better fortune against Lanrezac whose main body had not yet crossed south of the Marne.

Von Bülow's more leisurely pace had brought the II Army midway between the Aisne and the Marne, with its left wing south of the Vesle around Fismes, and its right south and east of Soissons.

A continuation of the respective courses of the German I and II Armies would bring Von Bülow to the Marne between Château Thierry and Epernay, and would bring Von Kluck diagonally across Von Bülow's line of march, south of the river. Assuming that the II Army could keep Lanrezac's attention engaged to the north, Von Kluck hoped to strike his flank and to cut across his rear before the main body of the French Fifth Army could retreat south of the Marne. The result, if accomplished according to Von Kluck's design, meant nothing less than the consummation of the Schlieffen Plan, the enveloping stroke against the enemy's left flank that formed the principal objective of the original German plan of operations.

At his Headquarters in the great Château of Compiègne, Von Kluck received Von Moltke's radio of September 2nd[1] late in the evening. The message created no little confusion of mind in the staff of the I Army. The statement that it was the intention of the High Command to drive the French to the southeast cutting them off from Paris indicated that the views at G.H.Q. conformed to the plans of the Army Commander, but the second sentence, directing the I Army to follow the II in echelon, seemed to Von Kluck wholly inconsistent with the first. As a result of Von Bülow's day of rest on August 31st, the German I Army was in fact a full day's march south of the II, and to follow the II Army in echelon as Von Moltke's orders prescribed, meant that the I Army would have to mark time until the II Army could catch up with it. In the meanwhile, the French would certainly cross the Marne and would reach positions to the south of the river where it would no longer be possible to attain their flank or to drive them towards the southeast as the High Command directed.

Wholly ignorant of Von Moltke's hopes for a decisive victory by the centre armies, and fully believing that the second sentence of the Chief of Staff's message resulted from an inaccurate or incomplete appreciation of the relative positions of the I and II Armies, Von Kluck deliberately determined to ignore it and to continue his drive across the front of the II Army in an effort to strike Lanrezac's flank.

Von Quast's initiative committed the Army Commander further to this course. Encountering French cavalry around Château Thierry, the commander of the German 9th Corps believed that the opportunity he had so eagerly sought lay within his grasp, and on the morning of September 3rd, he boldly pushed across the Marne to press his attack. Faced with the necessity either of recalling his impetuous subordinate or of supporting him, Von Kluck chose the latter alternative, and set his whole Army in motion towards the southeast, crossing the Marne in the wake of the 9th Corps.

Von Kluck was doomed to disappointment, for the French troops that the 9th Corps had met around Château Thierry were not the left wing of Lanrezac's Army as Von Quast had supposed, but elements of a new cavalry corps that Joffre had inserted between the Fifth Army and the British.[2] While Von Quast was engaged at Château Thierry, with Von Kluck pressing at top speed to his support, the main body of Lanrezac's Army had in fact successfully

[1] See pg. 169.
[2] Composed of the 8th Cavalry Division from the Army of Alsace, the 10th Cavalry Division from the Second Army, and the 4th Cavalry Division which was already part of the Fifth Army. The French forces which Von Quast encountered around Château Thierry were elements of the 8th Cavalry Division and a detachment of Territorials guarding the bridges across the Marne.

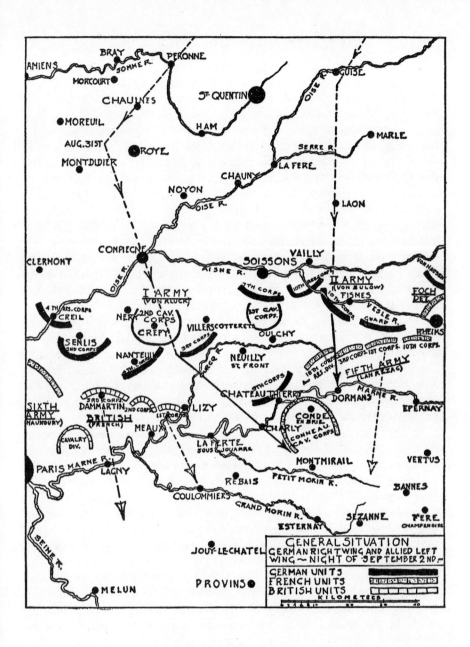

AMIENS
BRAY
SOMMER.
PERONNE
MORCOURT
CHAULNES
ST. QUENTIN
MOREUIL
HAM
MARLE
AUG.31ST
ROYE
SERRE R.
MONTDIDIER
CHAUNY
LA FERE
NOYON
OISE R.
LAON
CLERMONT
COMPIEGNE
VAILLY
SOISSONS
AISNE R.
VON HAUSEN
OISE R.
I ARMY
(VON KLUCK)
7TH CORPS
10TH RESCORPS
II ARMY
(VON BULOW)
10TH CORPS
FISMES
FOCH
DET.
4TH RES. CORPS
CREIL
NERY
2ND CAV.
CORPS
1ST CAV.
CORPS.
VESLE R.
GUARD R.
RHEIMS
SENLIS
2ND CORPS
CREPY
VILLERSCOTTERETS
OULCHY
3RD CORPS
9TH RES.DIV
3RD CORPS. 1ST CORPS. 10TH CORPS.
NANTEUIL
7TH CORPS
3RD CORPS
NEUILLY
ST FRONT
FIFTH ARMY
(LANREZAC)
SIXTH
ARMY
(MAUNOURY)
3RD CORPS
DAMMARTIN
2ND CORPS
1ST CORPS
9TH CORPS
CHATEAUTHIERRY
DORMANS
MARNE R.
EPERNAY
LIZY
CHARLY
CONDE
EN BRIE
BRITISH
(FRENCH)
MEAUX
CONNEAU
CAV. CORPS
CAVALRY
DIV.
LA FERTE
SOUS JOUARRE
MONTMIRAIL
VERTUS
PARIS
MARNE R.
LAGNY
BANNES
REBAIS
PETIT MORIN R.
SEINE R.
COULOMMIERS
GRAND MORIN R.
SEZANNE
FERE
CHAMPENOISE
ESTERNAY
JOUY-LE-CHATEL
MELUN
PROVINS

GENERAL SITUATION
GERMAN RIGHT WING AND ALLIED LEFT
WING ~ NIGHT OF SEPTEMBER 2ND ~
GERMAN UNITS
FRENCH UNITS
BRITISH UNITS
KILOMETRES
5 2 1 6 8 10   20   30   40

crossed the Marne farther to the east, between Dormans and Epernay, and had continued its retreat southwards towards Montmirail to positions which placed it definitely beyond the reach of the blow that Von Kluck had aimed against its flank.

Since turning towards the southeast on August 31st, Von Kluck had become wholly absorbed in the effort to execute what he hoped would prove a decisive stroke, and had given little thought to the defensive mission that also devolved upon the I Army as flank-guard of the German line. Convinced that at Proyart and in the other engagements in the region of Amiens he had finally dispersed the feeble French forces assembling on his outer flank, he had felt that extensive aviation or cavalry reconnaissances were unnecessary and had remained wholly in the dark as to the existence of Maunoury's Sixth French Army which was daily gaining strength. Nor did the proximity of Paris cause him any great concern, for Von Moltke had told him nothing of the activity observed there or of French troop movements reported from east to west. Though he appealed to Von Moltke in somewhat perfunctory fashion for reinforcements to cover his flank, the necessity did not appear so pressing as to require the I Army to delay its march, and by nightfall of September 4th, Von Kluck's three leading army corps had reached the banks of the Petit Morin River, a southern tributary of the Marne, along a line from Montmirail on the east to a point west of Rebais.

In the early days of September communications between the I Army and Luxembourg had become increasingly imperfect, so that it was not uncommon for twenty-four hours and even more to elapse between the sending of a message by Von Kluck and its receipt by Von Moltke. Thus it happened, that although the commander of the I Army despatched three messages during the day of September 3rd relative to his crossing south of the Marne, it was not until the morning of the 4th that Von Moltke learned that Von Kluck had disregarded his order to follow the II Army in echelon, and that the I Army, instead of falling behind the II Army, had actually pushed still further ahead of it. Aware, as Von Kluck was not, of the increasing concentration of enemy troops around the Entrenched Camp of Paris, the news that at last arrived caused the German Chief of Staff grave concern for the security of his armies' flank.

CHAPTER XX

LAST DAYS OF RETREAT

WHEN VON KLUCK changed his direction on August 31st and began his march on Compiègne and Noyon, he relieved the pressure against Maunoury's newly formed Army and permitted it to assemble without further interference, placing thereby in the hands of the French Commander in Chief the instrument he needed for the fulfilment of his designs.

The German I Army's movement did not escape the observation of French cavalry scouts [1] and Maunoury was quick to realize its strategic importance.

"If the situation requires that I intervene tomorrow, September 1st," he telegraphed Joffre, "I will attack in spite of the great fatigue of my troops in the direction of Clermont, towards the northeast."

It was an offer that might sorely have tempted a commander less resolute than Joffre. The tide of invasion was sweeping daily nearer to the capital with a force seemingly irresistible, and the civil Government, on the verge of panic, clamoured for protection. Even in the army, discouragement had almost reached the point of despair, for on top of the disappointment of defeat in the Battle of the Frontiers had come the realization that Joffre's second project for resuming the offensive along the line of the Aisne had also failed. Though the ill-assorted elements of Maunoury's little Army, hastily scratched together and already buffeted in the preceding days, could hardly have been expected to inflict a decisive defeat upon Von Kluck's hardened legions, they might at least have checked their headlong rush towards Paris and have provided a welcome diversion. Not to accept Maunoury's suggestion and deliver the attack he offered to make, required an iron nerve and courage of no common order, but Joffre was determined to play for bigger stakes. His objective was no less than the strategical defeat of all the invading armies, and to attain it, he was prepared to take all incidental risks and to make all necessary sacrifices. Unhesitatingly, he rejected Maunoury's proposal :

[1] Capt. Lepic of the Temporary Cavalry Division, formed from the best units of Sordet's Corps, reported the German movement in the afternoon of August 31st.

You appreciate the situation very clearly, but by reason of the distance that separates you from the Fifth Army your intervention might well be ineffective. We cannot count on a British offensive. Your role consists in covering Paris. Accordingly retreat on the capital and establish contact with the Military Governor.

From the French point of view, it was premature to predicate any action upon Von Kluck's new manoeuvre, for its strategical significance depended upon the German I Army's subsequent course. As viewed by the French High Command, three possible lines of action lay open to Von Kluck on September 1st: (1) he might continue on the course he was then taking, which would bring him ultimately into the region south of the Marne, east and southeast of Paris, (2) he might divert his course so as to attack Paris itself directly from the north, or (3) he might again turn and proceed towards the southwest, which would bring him eventually to the lower Seine, west and southwest of Paris. It became Joffre's task to develop a plan of action that would provide, so far as possible, an effective answer to all three of these contingencies, and at the same time would afford the Allied armies an opportunity to resume the offensive at the opportune moment and to recover the strategical initiative they had lost.

In a new set of orders, General Instructions No. 4,[2] issued on September 1st and supplemented the following day by a confidential explanatory memorandum, Joffre set forth his intentions for the manoeuvre of the Allied armies. These orders prescribed a continuation of the general retreat until the Fifth Army could escape from the danger of envelopment created by Von Kluck's advance towards the southeast, fixing as the extreme limit of the retreat — without, as Joffre specifically stated, implying that the limit need necessarily be reached — the region southeast of Paris, behind the Seine, for the Fifth Army, with Foch's Army Detachment behind the Aube on its right and with the Fourth and Third Armies holding a line curving towards the northeast to a point north of Bar-le-Duc. The British were to retire to the Seine, between Juvisy and Melun, southeast of Paris, while Maunoury's Sixth Army covered Paris itself, with the aid of the garrison and defences of the Entrenched Camp, remaining between Von Kluck's Army and the capital. When the Allied armies reached these positions, or sooner if opportunity offered, they would resume the offensive, strengthened by reinforcements from their depots, on a line that roughly described a vast arc from Paris to Verdun.

The dispositions thus provided for have been subjected to theo-

2 See Appendix IX.

retical criticism [8] mainly on two counts, first that they would uncover Verdun and second, that they left Paris inadequately protected. While both criticisms have some foundation, in the sense that Joffre offered no assurance that either Paris or Verdun would enjoy immunity from attack, there seems no ground to suppose that the French Commander in Chief intended or expected to abandon either one of them. Though by no means impregnable, both Paris and Verdun had ample means at their disposal to withstand a sudden assault, and the general offensive that constituted the basic purpose of Joffre's instructions afforded the best guarantee that they would not be required to sustain a regular siege. There seems no fair ground to doubt the sincerity of Joffre's expressed intention to resume the offensive at the earliest possible moment. The whole tenor of the numerous orders that emanated from his Headquarters between August 31st and September 4th, and all the measures taken to reorganize the Allied forces during that time, combine to show that an immediate resumption of the offensive was the dominating thought in the mind of the French Commander in Chief, and to negative the idea that he had any intention of settling down on a fortified line back of the Seine to await developments.

The dispositions contemplated by Joffre's Instructions of September 1st adequately corresponded to the alternatives actually under consideration by the German High Command.

If the German armies took a generally southwestern course, as Von Moltke had prescribed in his General Directive of August 27th, the British Army from its position south of Paris could readily pivot around the capital to meet Von Kluck face to face, with the support of Sordet's cavalry on its left, while Maunoury, debouching from the Entrenched Camp, could strike Von Kluck on his left flank, driving him towards the west, away from Von Bülow. In the meanwhile, Von Bülow would again face his old antagonist the French Fifth Army. Von Hausen would oppose Foch, and the German IV and V Armies would once more come to grips with the French Third and Fourth Armies. In this hypothesis, the form of the battle would follow the conception, originally put forward by Berthelot,[4] of an Allied offensive from east to west against the German right wing.

If, as actually proved to be the case, Von Kluck continued his march to the southeast, he would still find the British before him, with the French Fifth Army by its side, while Maunoury debouched

[8] See, for example, Gen. Gros, *La Genèse de la Bataille de la Marne* (Payot, Paris, 1919) ; and Lieut.-Col. Grouard, *op. cit.* ; but cf. Gen. Berthaut's *L' "Erreur" de 1914 — Réponse aux critiques* (Von Oest, Paris, 1919).
[4] See pg. 130.

from the Entrenched Camp of Paris towards the east, in this case against the German I Army's right flank.

So long as Maunoury remained in close touch with the Entrenched Camp, as Joffre had instructed him to do, Paris had little to fear from a headlong attack from the north, and indeed, this possibility never seems to have been contemplated by the German High Command, though Joffre had provided against it.

During the first three days of September, the Allied armies retreated in conformity with Joffre's plan, while Maunoury, hanging on Von Kluck's outer flank, remained between the Germany I Army and the French capital. On September 3rd — though the German Army Commander was not aware of it — all chance for the envelopment of the left flank of the French Fifth Army ended, for on that day Lanrezac crossed the Marne and retreated to the south. Thenceforth, protected on its left by the newly arrived cavalry corps and on its right by Foch's Army Detachment, the Fifth Army enjoyed relative security, and the condition precedent for a resumption of the offensive, fixed by Joffre's instructions, had been fulfilled.

While the strategical form of the Allied counter-offensive depended above all on the conduct of Von Kluck's Army, a question even more fundamental concerned the French Commander in Chief, namely, whether the Allied armies would be able to take the offensive at all. The answer to this question rested upon two principal factors, the ability of the French High Command to regroup its forces in time, so as to redeem the errors of the plan of concentration by providing strength sufficient to overcome the evident initial superiority of the German right wing ; second, and even more important, the ability and willingness of the British to cooperate in a general forward movement.

Joffre had no authority to issue orders to Sir John French. He could only suggest and persuade. The confidence of the British Commander in Chief and his staff had been sorely shaken, and the co-ordination essential to common action had suffered correspondingly. The first of a long series of military crises, due to a lack of unity of command, confronted the Allies less than a month after the war had started. It was a situation that Joffre could not manage alone, and it was fortunate for him, and for the solidity of the Entente, that he received powerful aid.

CHAPTER XXI

KITCHENER INTERVENES

To THE neutral world, and above all to the enemy nations, the Entente Powers strove mightily to present their alliance in terms of a combination created for a common cause and united in perfect harmony; but behind a series of profusely congratulatory messages, interchanged at frequent intervals and sedulously publicized, sources of friction existed in the military no less than in the political field which often rendered co-operation impossible and occasionally jeopardized the basic structure. In large measure the differences that arose between the French and the British during the opening weeks of the war may be traced to the temperamental divergences of Sir John French and Lanrezac and to the unfortunate events of August 23rd; but in part they were due as well to conflicting conceptions that prevailed in high military circles in France and England as to the probable duration of the conflict and the role to be played by the British army.

With all the weight of his enormous prestige, Kitchener supported the view that the war would be a long one and would ultimately require the participation of a British army of unprecedented size, and he steadfastly refused to be stampeded by those who sought to have England throw all her military resources into the field immediately, in the hope of producing a speedy decision.[1] Kitchener's policy did not meet with the approval of the French High Command or with that of British officers, who like Sir Henry Wilson, accepted its views as gospel. As early as August 19th, the French Military Attaché complained to Messimy of Kitchener:

I think that if the Secretary of State for War is delaying somewhat the sending of the 4th and 6th Divisions to the continent, it is with the idea of sustaining a prolonged effort. This conception seems to me unfortunate, and I am doing all I can to show the importance and necessity of England's participating in the decisive battles with the maximum forces.

[1] "Taking a complete survey," Winston Churchill writes, *op. cit.*, pg. 304, "I consider now that this prudent withholding from the Army in the field in the face of every appeal and demand of the key-men who alone could make the new armies, was the greatest of the services which Lord Kitchener rendered to the nation at this time, and it was a service which no one of lesser authority than he could have performed."

I cannot conceal the fact, however, that it is difficult to argue these questions with Lord Kitchener ; he is a man of strong will and extremely obstinate.

In exasperation at what he conceived to be his chief's errors, Sir Henry Wilson was more out-spoken.

Kitchener's shadow armies for shadow campaigns, at unknown and distant dates, prevent a lot of good officers, NCO's and men from coming out. It is a scandalous thing. Under no circumstances can these mobs now being raised, without officers and NCO's, without guns, rifles or uniforms, without rifle-ranges or training grounds, without supply or transport services, without morale or tradition, knowledge or experience, under no circumstances could these mobs take the field for two years. Then what is the use of them ? What we want and what we must have is for our little force out here to be kept at full strength with the very best of everything. Nothing else is any good.[2]

A few days later he wrote :

His (Kitchener's) ridiculous and preposterous army of 25 Corps is the laughing stock of every soldier in Europe. It took the Germans forty years of incessant work to make an army of 25 Corps with the aid of conscription. It will take us to all eternity to do the same by voluntary effort.

Kitchener's armies, which became Haig's armies on the Somme and during the two years that followed, far from being a laughing stock, provided their own justification, and no comment is needed on the shallow injustice of Wilson's criticism.[3] Nevertheless, the difference in point of view between England's recognized military leader and the French General Staff created an atmosphere in the summer of 1914 that did not tend to smooth the path of relations between the two Allied armies.

The interview with the French commanders at St. Quentin on August 26th had merely afforded Sir John French an opportunity to voice his irritation and had accomplished little towards establishing a more cordial feeling. Neither the timely aid given to the British 2nd Corps at Le Cateau by Sordet's cavalry, nor a message of flowery eulogy that Joffre sent French at Colonel Huguet's suggestion sufficed to appease him.

Two days later, during the Battle of Guise-St. Quentin — in which, perhaps by way of reprisal for Lanrezac's conduct of the previous

---

[2] Diary of Field Marshal Sir Henry Wilson, Vol. I, pg. 178.
[3] By coincidence, on the date of Kitchener's death, June 5, 1916, the last of the seventy divisions organized in accordance with his program had just embarked for France.

week, French had refused to allow Haig to take part — Joffre again
visited British Headquarters at Compiègne. The second meeting
proved no more productive of results than the earlier one, for French
had become resolved not to take part in any offensive action until
his command had had ample opportunity to rest and refit.

I pointed out to him how important it was for the British Army to keep
in contact with its neighbours on each side, in order to prevent a breach
being opened in the Allied line of battle — Joffre wrote in his memoirs,
describing the interview — My arguments seemed to produce no effect
upon French. Moreover, while I was talking, I distinctly saw his Chief
of Staff, Sir Archibald Murray, pulling the skirt of the Field Marshal's
tunic as if to prevent him from yielding to my insistence. Thus, all I
could obtain from him was the reply : "No, no, my troops need forty-
eight hours of absolute rest. When they have had this, I shall be ready
to participate in anything you want to do, but not any sooner."

Sir John French himself has given a somewhat less pessimistic
picture of his own attitude, in his account of the same conversation.

I assured the French Commander in Chief that no serious gap should
be made in his line by any premature or hasty retirement, but I imperatively demanded the necessary time to refit and obtain reinforcements.

The following day, August 30th, he wrote to Kitchener :

My confidence in the ability of the leaders of the French Army to carry
this campaign to a successful conclusion is fast waning, and this is my
real reason for the decision I have taken to move the British forces so
far back. . . I have been pressed very hard to remain, even in my shattered condition, in the fighting line, but have absolutely refused to do
so, and I hope you will approve of the course I have taken.

Though in fact the British Army had not been in serious contact
with the enemy since August 26th, and was actually nearly two days'
march to the south of the French Fifth Army, the British Commander in Chief seemed determined to continue the retreat in-
definitely. A number of high-ranking British officers, among them
Sir Archibald Murray and Sir Horace Smith-Dorrien, were reported
to advocate a retreat to the base and a re-embarkation for England,
with the idea of landing on the continent again later after the British Army had been thoroughly reconstituted.

Profoundly disturbed at the possibility of a complete withdrawal
of the British Army, as much for its moral effect both on the Allies
and the enemy, as for the military difficulties it would create, Joffre

took the unusual course of appealing through diplomatic channels for the intervention of the Government. A direct appeal from President Poincaré reached Sir John French through the British Ambassador, Sir Francis Bertie, but to this message French replied as he had to Joffre's personal requests, that approximately a week's rest would be required before the British Army would be fit for offensive operations.

"The demand that we should stand and fight was not only urgently repeated, but was actually backed by imperative messages from the French President," French has recorded, adding, "I refused."

The series of letters and telegrams which brought news of Sir John French's intentions alarmed Lord Kitchener no less than Joffre himself. Though skeptical from the outset of the strategical conceptions of the French High Command and particularly of the doctrine of the offensive to which it was wedded, Kitchener clearly perceived the disastrous consequences that might flow from Sir John French's attitude. As a young subaltern, Kitchener had served as a volunteer in the French army for a brief period during the Franco-Prussian War, and he had retained an affection and respect for France, as deep perhaps, if not so articulate, as that of Sir Henry Wilson and other vociferous admirers of the French military school. The idea of seeming to leave his Allies in the lurch, whatever the provocation, seemed to Kitchener abhorrent to the tradition of the British army, and the thought that British troops might be deemed by Allies and enemies alike incapable of withstanding adversity seemed no less repugnant. Aside from sentimental or military aspects, Kitchener further foresaw the profound political consequences, perhaps even the destruction of the Entente, that might attend a defeat suffered by the French armies as a result of a British withdrawal.[4]

On August 31st, he telegraphed French for further information :

I am surprised at your decision to retire behind the Seine. Please let me know, if you can, all your reasons for this move. What will be the effect of this course upon your relations with the French army and on the general military situation ? Will your retirement leave a gap in the French line or cause them discouragement of which the Germans might take advantage to carry out their first program of first crushing the French and then being free to attack Russia ?

A few hours later, after discussing the matter with his colleagues in the Cabinet, he sent a more urgent message.

[4] Winston Churchill, *op. cit.*, pg. 290, has vividly described Kitchener's anxiety during this period : "The apparition of Kitchener *agonistes* in my doorway will remain with me as long as I live. It was like seeing old John Bull on the rack."

The Government are exceedingly anxious lest your force, at this stage of the campaign in particular, should, owing to your proposed retirement so far from the line, not be able to co-operate closely with our Allies and render them continuous support. They expect that you will, as far as possible, conform to the plans of General Joffre for the conduct of the campaign.

French's replies proved anything but reassuring to the Secretary of State for War.

If the French go on with their present tactics, which are practically to fall back right and left of me, usually without notice, and to abandon all idea of offensive operations, of course, then, the gap in the French line will remain and the consequences must be borne by them.

In the early morning of September 1st, French again wired Kitchener :

I hope you understand quite clearly that in its present condition the force under my command is unable to support our Allies effectively, whatever their position may be. It does not seem to be quite realized how shattered two divisions of my small force are, and how necessary it is even for the remainder to rest and refit. As long as we are in close contact with the enemy it is impossible to make things right. I have no definite idea of General Joffre's general plan ; its general result is the advance of the Germans and the retreat of the Allies.

Before this last message was received in London, Kitchener was already on his way to France. At the War Office he had anxiously awaited French's earlier telegrams, taking them down word by word as they were decoded, and their completely pessimistic tone indicated that the British Commander in Chief's morale had become seriously impaired. At one o'clock in the morning of September 1st, Kitchener aroused Sir Edward Grey in his bed-room to inform the Foreign Secretary that with Asquith's approval he was leaving at once for France, and before daybreak a destroyer was taking him across the Channel. He summoned Sir John French to a conference at Paris the same day.

"I deeply resented being called away from my Headquarters at so critical a time," French has written, nevertheless he went and took with him his Chief of Staff and Colonel Huguet. At the British Embassy, Kitchener with Sir Francis Bertie, Viviani and Millerand met French, Murray and Huguet.

During the South African War, French had served under Kitchener's orders and a very real affection and respect had grown up between the two men, but the interview at Paris marked the beginning of a breach that never healed.   Sensitive by nature, with a strong sense of personal dignity, French came to the meeting reluctantly and felt keenly the criticism implied in Kitchener's summons.   Finding Kitchener in the blue, undress uniform of a British Field Marshal, which in fact was the attire he habitually wore, French felt that his former chief was adopting the attitude of a military superior calling a subordinate to account, rather than appearing in his proper role as a member of a civilian Cabinet.   The tone of the discussion became so sharp that Huguet felt discretion required him to withdraw out of ear-shot, and shortly, at Kitchener's request, the two Field Marshals retired to an adjoining room, to continue their talk out of hearing of the French representatives.

No official account remains of this conversation, and Kitchener left no record of it.   As might be expected the version contained in French's memoirs redounds wholly to his own credit ; but whatever French may have said to Kitchener or Kitchener may have said to French, the result is certain.   It was a telegram that Kitchener sent to Asquith in London.

After a discussion with General French and the War Minister here about the situation, there is apparently little more that I can do, so unless I hear from you to the contrary tonight, I will return early to-morrow and let you understand the situation.   General French has not quarrelled with General Joffre, but their work separates them a good deal and it seems difficult to make combined plans.

French's troops are now engaged in the fighting line, where he will remain conforming to the movements of the French Army, though at the same time acting with caution to avoid being in any way unsupported on his flanks.

To French, Kitchener handed a letter, quoting the second paragraph of this communication and adding :

I feel sure that you will agree that the above represents the conclusions we came to ; but in any case, until I can communicate with you further in answer to anything you may wish to tell me, please consider it as an instruction.

By being in the fighting line, you of course understand I mean dispositions of your troops in contact with, though possibly behind the French as they were today ; of course you will judge as regards their position in this respect.

From that time forth, there was no more talk of a British withdrawal from the line, or of a retirement behind the Seine, except as contemplated by Joffre's general plan, and the pace of the British retreat became notably slower.

Another consequence of the Paris meeting was the presentation to Joffre, through Millerand, of a project for an Allied stand along the line of the Marne and northwest of Paris. Sensing perhaps that he might be criticized for lack of aggressiveness, French had drafted this plan and brought it with him to the meeting. It showed evidences of hasty preparation, and from a strategical stand-point had little value, for in substance it amounted to no more than a frontal resistance to the German advance on a position that would have left both Allied wings exposed to envelopment. In any case, it came too late, for Joffre had already sent out his General Instruction No. 4, when the British Commander in Chief's plan reached his Headquarters. Nevertheless, it represented a significant change in French's attitude, and indicated at least that he was once again willing to stand and fight. In a tactful letter, Joffre rejected the suggestion on the ground that the French Fifth Army was not in a position adequately to protect the British flank, and sent French instead a copy of his General Instruction No. 4 and of the supplementary memorandum accompanying it.

In his reply, the British Commander in Chief adopted a tone of cordiality in marked contrast to his attitude of the preceding days.

I felt some considerable hesitation in putting forth my views as to the general trend of the future operations and I am much indebted to you for the kind and friendly support you have accorded to my expression of opinion. I have now received your Instruction No. 4 and your *Note pour les Commandants d'Armée* of September 2nd, and I completely and clearly understand your plans and the part you desire me to take in carrying them out. You may rely on my most cordial co-operation.

Kitchener's visit had borne fruit.

In one respect French obtained a victory that afforded him no little satisfaction. With the concurrence of Sir Francis Bertie, he dissuaded Kitchener from making a personal inspection of the Army in France. In view of the reports that the Government had received of the shattered state of the British forces, it is difficult to discern the impropriety in the Secretary of State for War's desire to confirm the situation at first hand ; but French believed that for him to do so would be derogatory to his own prestige as Commander in Chief, and the British Ambassador agreed that it would diminish French's standing in the eyes of the Allies. In the face of energetic objection, Kitchener yielded and abandoned the project. With the main purpose of his visit accomplished, the Secretary of State for War returned to London, while Sir John French, after a late dinner at the Ritz, rejoined his retreating Army.

Following Kitchener's departure, French's relations with Joffre immediately and manifestly improved, and his dealings with the Secretary of State for War were marked with outward signs of cordiality, but the sting of Kitchener's intervention remained, and the British Commander in Chief professed himself unable to understand its necessity.   A week later, on September 6th, as the Battle of the Marne was opening, he found time to write Churchill :

I can't understand what brought Kitchener to Paris.   I am writing to you as one of my greatest friends and I know you'll let me write freely and privately.   His visit was really most unfortunate.   He took me away from the front to visit him in Paris on a very critical day, when I should have been directing the operation most carefully and I tell you between ourselves *strictly* that when I returned to my Headquarters I found a very critical situation existing (8 P.M.!) and authoritative orders and directions badly needed.   It was the day when the Guards and a Cavalry Brigade were so heavily engaged.[5]

Despite the opinion thus expressed, Kitchener's intervention in the Campaign of the Marne was an episode of high importance to the Allied cause, more important than seems generally realized. In the Battle of the Marne, the British Army was called upon to play a part of primary strategic importance that became an essential factor in the Allied victory.   That it was present at all was due in great measure to Kitchener's far-sighted appreciation of the general situation, to his willingness to take upon himself the heavy burden of over-ruling the commander in the field, and to his ability to impose his will.   The result of his visit to Paris on September 1st constitutes by no means the least part of the great debt the Allied nations owe to Kitchener's memory.[6]

[5] In fact, on September 1st, the British were engaged only in local rear-guard actions (see pg. 171) which were relatively insignificant and hardly seem to have required the presence of the Commander in Chief.   The most important of these, the cavalry engagement at Néry, was over by 8:45 A.M., before French left for Paris ; the action of the British 5th Division at Crépy-en-Valois ended at noon ; and the fighting in which the Guards were engaged around Villers-Cotterets only lasted until 6 P.M. (See *Br. O. H.* ; also Gen. Ballard, *op. cit.*, pg. 244).   The comment of the British Commander in Chief, while significant as indicative of his frame of mind, hardly seems warranted by the facts.

[6] For accounts of the interview at Paris, see French and Huguet, *op. cit.*, and Lord Bertie's *Diary* 1914–1919 (Doran, New York, 1924) ; see also Sir George Arthur and Gen. Ballard, *op. cit.*

CHAPTER XXII

JOFFRE PREPARES FOR BATTLE

THE INITIAL reverses suffered by all the Allied armies imposed on the French Commander in Chief the monumental task of devising the strategical bases for future operations, of supervising the retirement of his armies, of regrouping his forces and of reorganizing the high command to remedy weaknesses disclosed in the opening engagements ; all this quite apart from his relations with the British and from his dealings with the civil government and political forces in the rear.

With energy the more remarkable for its absence of nervous waste, Joffre set to work. The ascendancy that in the end he achieved over the imagination of his soldiers and over the people of France arose by no means solely from the fact that he commanded the French armies at the Battle of the Marne. It derived also from the presence in the man himself of qualities that constitute the strength, and at times the weakness, of the French peasant ; qualities readily recognizable to the ordinary Frenchman, which command his confidence.

The traditional maxim of the French farmer, speaking of his hands, formed an integral part of Joffre's creed :

"Il ne suffit pas de leurs z'y dire, il faut encore leurs z'y faire faire ; — It's not enough to tell 'em to do it, you've got to make 'em do it too."

Though on occasion the application of this homely saying gave rise to bitter complaint that G.H.Q. sought to regulate matters of detail beyond its province, it was never more usefully applied than during the period preliminary to the Battle of the Marne.

In contrast to Von Moltke, who emerged from the monastic seclusion of his remote Headquarters only for one brief visit to the Crown Prince's Army, Joffre displayed the greatest activity, going almost daily to the various armies to draw his conclusions from personal observation. On the 26th he met French, Lanrezac and D'Amade at St. Quentin ; on the 28th he visited Lanrezac at Marle and returned the following day to Laon, stopping en route to see

French at Compiègne and to talk with Sir Henry Wilson at Rheims ; on the 30th he went to Varennes, the Headquarters of the Third Army, and saw De Langle at Monthois ; on the 3rd, he went again to the Headquarters of the Fifth Army, at Sézanne this time, and on the 5th he met Sir John French at Melun.   So it went, while in the meanwhile at his own Headquarters he received a succession of visitors : Foch, Maunoury, Millerand and Messimy, among others, with each of whom he discussed the general situation and the particular role each was required to play.   Despite his ponderous physique and apparently phlegmatic temperament, never has a Commander in Chief shown greater personal activity or maintained more intimate contact with his subordinates.

Well aware of the susceptibility of his countrymen to extremes of optimism and despair, Joffre maintained everywhere an Olympian calm, and in the most agonizing moments his demeanour of unshakeable confidence, whatever the realities, steadied and strengthened the resolution of all who came in contact with him.

Up every morning at five, in bed at eleven at night, Joffre adhered unfalteringly to a régime of Spartan simplicity and regularity that made confusion impossible and panic incongruous at his Headquarters.

"In spite of the series of disquieting news that had been arriving particularly since the 20th," Foch has written, describing his visit to G.H.Q. on the 28th, "at the seat of chief command one saw no trace of agitation, still less of panic.   Order, coolness, decision ruled in absolute fashion."

Once it became evident that the forces provided by the French plan of concentration were numerically inadequate to meet the armies massed on the German right, Joffre lost no time.   At 11:30, on the night of August 23rd, came the news of Lanrezac's retreat ; at 7 next morning the wires flashed an order to Pau in Alsace to prepare the embarkation of the 7th Corps (Vautier) towards the northwest.   In less than a week, two armies ceased to exist and two new ones came into being.   The Army of Lorraine — originally formed to protect the flank of the Third Army against an attack from Metz — had no further reason for existence after the offensive in the Ardennes had broken down, and its commander and two of its Reserve divisions forthwith left for Amiens to join the new Sixth Army. Similarly the operations of Pau's Army of Alsace, which were linked to the offensive of Dubail's First Army, could have no strategical future after Dubail had retreated from Sarrebourg, and the 7th Corps immediately set out for the Sixth Army, again vesting control of the forces in Alsace in the First Army, and leaving the officers and men of Pau's Headquarters available for other duty.

De Langle's Fourth Army, powerfully constituted for the major offensive in the Ardennes, with six army corps spread out over a wide front, became too unwieldy for effective management in retreat under one command, and was divided by separating its left wing into an autonomous army detachment under Foch. On the eve of the Marne, Foch's Army Detachment became the Ninth Army, occupying the centre of the Allied line, between the Fifth Army and the Fourth Army, during the historic struggle before the Marshes of St. Gond.

During the period between the close of the Battle of the Frontiers and the beginning of the Battle of the Marne, the strength of the five German armies operating against the main body of the Allied forces had been diminished to the extent of 3 army corps (6 divisions) and 1 brigade ; [1] but except for the transfer of the 6th Army Corps (Von Pritzelwitz) from the IV to the V Army, their relative positions and order of battle remained unchanged and they received no material reinforcements from the rear.

In contrast Joffre made widespread changes in the French order of battle and levied on his two eastern armies, although they were almost continuously engaged against Rupprecht of Bavaria, for 9 infantry divisions and 2 cavalry divisions, all for the benefit of the Allied left wing.

In spite of the errors of the French plan of concentration and the manifold difficulties of a two weeks' retreat, the French Commander in Chief succeeded in altering the centre of gravity of his dispositions so as to achieve at last a substantial numerical superiority at the western extremity of the front which he had come to recognize as the decisive point.   On August 23rd, during the Battles of the Sambre and of Mons, the German I, II and II Armies had aggregated $24\frac{1}{2}$ infantry divisions and 5 cavalry divisions, exclusive of the $2\frac{1}{2}$ army corps (5 divisions) besieging Namur, and on the same day the French Fifth Army and the British totalled $17\frac{1}{2}$ infantry divisions and 4 cavalry divisions.[2]   At the Marne, two weeks later, the same three German armies comprised only $23\frac{1}{2}$ infantry divisions and 5 cavalry divisions and were confronted not only by the French Fifth Army and the British, but by the French Sixth, Ninth and part of the Fourth Armies as well, amounting in all to 41 infantry divisions and $8\frac{1}{2}$ cavalry divisions.   Moreover, Joffre provided, as the German High Command did not, for the reinforcement of his troops by reservists called up from the depots, so that in the French units losses in men and material had in large measure been made good before the Battle of the Marne opened.

---

[1] Exclusive of the 3rd Reserve Corps detached to cover Antwerp.
[2] Forces available, on or near the battle-front.

The regrouping of the Allied armies thus accomplished by the foresight and energy of the French Commander in Chief must be recognized as one of the primary causes for the situation of strategical advantage in which the Allies were placed on September 6th, and the transportation and supply of these troops, under the most trying conditions, justly ranks as one of the outstanding achievements of its kind in military history.   General Laffont de Ladebat, Director of the Services of the Rear on Joffre's staff, and Lieutenant-Colonel Ragueneau, Director of Railways, deserve high rank among those who made possible the Allied victory of the Marne.[3]

Concurrently with the regrouping of his forces, Joffre made drastic changes in the higher commands.   With unyielding resolution, he eliminated officers, whatever their seniority, who seemed unequal to the duties assigned to them.   Between the opening of hostilities and September 6th, two army commanders, seven corps commanders and a host of commanders of divisions and brigades found themselves, in the conventional formula, "placed at the disposal of the Minister of War." [4]   Though Joffre declined to accept Messimy's extreme view, that in accordance with French Revolutionary practice all officers removed from their commands should forthwith be tried by court-martial, and if found to have done less than their full duty, should be shot or publicly disgraced, he was inexorable in what he conceived to be the interests of highest efficiency. Once convinced that an officer was unfitted for the task he was called upon to perform, whatever the reason, neither the ties of comradeship nor the pressure of political influence could move him. Occasionally — as in the case of General Grossetti, who was relieved as Chief of Staff of the Third Army and assigned a division — officers of recognized ability were transferred to other active assignments more suited to their capabilities ; for some, posts were found in the various services of the rear, outside the Army Zone, whence a few later returned to the front ; but many of the officers summarily removed by Joffre spent the remainder of the war in enforced idleness, hoping against hope for another chance.   There can be no doubt that in some cases injustice was done and the country deprived of the services of able and devoted soldiers, for battle is a rough trial, in which the scales of justice are not too nicely balanced.

The most conspicuous examples of Joffre's action were Ruffey and Lanrezac, respectively commanders of the Third and Fifth Armies.

[3] For detailed statement of Orders of Battle and comparative effectives at the Marne, see Appendix X.

[4] In his memoirs Joffre states that during this period he removed fifty general officers, including two army commanders, ten corps commanders and thirty-eight division commanders. These figures are somewhat deceptive, however, as they include officers promoted to the command of higher units, as well as those relieved for incompetence or other causes.

Of the removal of Ruffey, whom Joffre replaced on August 30th with Sarrail, little has been said or written. The cause Joffre assigned was nervous fatigue, brought on by the hard engagements of the Third Army, which had thrown Ruffey into conflict with his colleagues and subordinates and had impaired his judgement to a point where it had become no longer safe to leave him in command. Whether or not he acquiesced in Joffre's view, Ruffey received his fate in soldierly silence, and apparently without personal rancour, for he dined at Joffre's table on the night of his removal. Nor does it appear that thereafter by political intrigue or by the intercession of powerful friends he sought a reversal of the judgement.

In striking contrast was Lanrezac's conduct. Though apparently accepting the decision at the time it was made, and preserving a decorous silence until the end of the war, he devoted the rest of his life to an effort at his own rehabilitation — a task that his son has piously continued — and became the centre of a series of violent attacks against his former Commander in Chief on every conceivable ground, to none of which Joffre, from his retirement, ever replied.

Before the war, Lanrezac had enjoyed a wide reputation as one of the most brilliant and promising of French general officers. In 1906, when Joffre commanded the 6th Division, Lanrezac had served under him as a colonel and had then won the confidence and esteem of the future Commander in Chief. Eight years later, upon Galliéni's retirement, Joffre designated Lanrezac to replace him as commander of the Fifth Army and presented him to President Poincaré as "a future Commander in Chief."

During his career before the war, Lanrezac had seen relatively little service with troops. His reputation had been won as a professor in the French War College, where his intelligence, his keen critical faculty and his lucid analyses of technical problems commanded the admiration of officers who studied under him. But with the declaration of war, the time for theoretical discussion had passed and the qualities essential for a teacher no longer sufficed. The time had come for men who would act promptly and boldly, and the ability to do so became the sole criterion of success. This Lanrezac seems to have been unable to understand. To the end he maintained the mentality of a schoolmaster, studying, dissecting and criticizing the orders he received, commenting bitterly the while to his subordinates on the folly of higher authority. His experience in the class-room had accustomed him to speak with pontifical authority, and it irked and chagrined him beyond endurance to find that former pupils, now officers on Joffre's staff, ignored or brushed aside his observations. Endowed with the gift of Cassandra, a most dangerous quality for a soldier, he exercised his powers in season and out, prophesying calamity and suffering the unpopularity that is the usual fate of such prophets.

The very real dangers and difficulties that confronted him became magnified in his mind to unsurmountable proportions, and he complained in all sincerity at what he deemed the lack of vision and shallow optimism of Joffre and his officers. In battle, though reaching sound decisions based on a true appreciation of the strategic situation, he seemed unable to translate his conclusions promptly into action, and neither on the Sambre nor at Guise-St. Quentin did he exercise effective control over the development of operations or the conduct of the troops under his command.

Convinced, as his memoirs amply testify, of the enemy's superiority both in the theory and practice of war, the fact seems to be that Lanrezac lacked confidence in himself, in his superiors and what is more serious, in the men under his orders : the faith in victory, so characteristic of Foch, that is the basic quality of successful military leadership in time of war.

So great was Joffre's regard for Lanrezac that it may be doubted whether the latter would have been actually relieved of his command, despite his failure to fulfil expectations, had it not been for the unfortunate relations that developed between Lanrezac and the British Commander in Chief ; but on the threshold of a great battle, where co-operation had become of vital importance, the cumulative result of minor frictions had frustrated the earnest efforts of diplomatic officers on both sides. Though outward forms of military courtesy had been observed, inner harmony had become impossible between the two Army Commanders who were unluckily compelled to remain in closest liaison.

Determined not to lose the benefit of Sir John French's change in attitude, Joffre drove on September 3rd to the Headquarters of the Fifth Army at Sézanne, and there, in a brief but painful interview, informed Lanrezac of his decision and turned the command of the Fifth Army over to Franchet d'Esperey. He lost no time in informing French of the change he had made.

"Inform Marshal French," he telegraphed Huguet, "that General Franchet d'Esperey has been placed in command of the Fifth Army."

In his own hand he added two sentences to the formal dispatch prepared for his signature :

"He has orders to act in close and cordial relations with the Field Marshal. . I base great hopes on this understanding."

Though it could hardly be supposed that Sir John French would have been guilty of the impropriety of interfering in the organization of the French army by suggesting Lanrezac's removal, Joffre could hardly help but be aware that a change of leadership in the

Fifth Army would not displease the British Commander in Chief, and the words so added to the message of notification offer revealing evidence of one of the primary motives underlying Joffre's action.

Mindful of Joffre's injunction, Franchet d'Esperey's first care was to set about repairing the misunderstandings that had arisen during his predecessor's tenure of command, and to this end he arranged for a meeting with Sir John French the very next afternoon, September 4th, at Bray-sur-Seine. This meeting, intended primarily as a gesture of cordiality, played a part of wholly unexpected importance in the developments of the next few days.

Joffre's selection of Franchet d'Esperey to succeed Lanrezac was typical of the nature of the changes he made throughout the army, for the new Army Commander was essentially a fighting general. A veteran of many years in the colonies, with a career of action analogous to Joffre's, his energy as well as his brusqueness of manner had already become a byword, and his attitude and mental outlook represented the antithesis of his more scholarly predecessor. An order once given by Franchet d'Esperey admitted of no discussion, still less of criticism. A few minutes after Joffre's departure from Sézanne, while Franchet d'Esperey sat at his table familiarizing himself with his new responsibilities, a telephone call arrived from the 18th Corps. It was the Corps Commander, General de Mas Latrie, weakened by dysentry, discouraged, pessimistic for the future, explaining at length to the Chief of Staff the difficulties in the way of an Army order just received, the fatigue of the troops, their demoralization, the physical obstacles, the menace of the enemy. Becoming impatient at the length of the conversation, the new Army Commander interrupted.

"What is it ?" he asked.

"It's General de Mas Latrie, General," replied Hély d'Oissel, "reporting on the difficulties he finds in carrying out the orders he has received."

"Let me speak to him," said Franchet d'Esperey, taking the receiver himself. "Hello, hello, this is Franchet d'Esperey speaking. Within the last few minutes I've assumed command of the Army."

Then, without pausing to allow De Mas Latrie to recover from his astonishment, he went on.

"You've received an order. It must be carried out. From now on the word is : march or croak." And he hung up.

Thus, in brutal fashion, Franchet d'Esperey took hold of his task, conscious that the imminence of battle made it imperative to remedy without delay the demoralization that had begun to infect the Fifth Army. With surprising rapidity he brought about a change of attitude on the part of his subordinates and the troops under their command. Extensive changes in the higher grades contributed to the result. At the head of the 18th Corps, which so far had failed to respond to expectations, De Maud'huy, whose handling of the 16th Division in Lorraine had marked him for promotion, replaced De Mas Latrie. In the 3rd Corps, Hache, another fighting general, had already relieved Sauret, and its two divisions, the 5th and 6th, had respectively been placed under the orders of Mangin and Pétain, former brigade commanders. Deligny, from the 2nd Division, took command of Franchet d'Esperey's 1st Corps. These and other changes soon found their reflection in a new spirit that permeated all ranks, and the French Fifth Army advanced to battle on the morning of September 6th, a fighting force that no longer corresponded to the exultant descriptions of Von Bülow or to the discouraged account of its former commander.

It could hardly be expected that the many changes which Joffre made could be effected without much bitterness and many heartaches that gave rise to fierce criticism. It has been pointed out that in a majority of cases, the officers relieved owed their original appointment to Joffre, and from this fact it has been deduced that his judgement of men was faulty. The first and most obvious answer to such criticism lies in the different standards necessarily applicable in peace and in war. Many officers, like Lanrezac, with distinguished peace-time records, proved deficient through no fault of their own in qualities of leadership, when they were compelled to make and execute rapid decisions under the strain of battle with the lives of men at stake.

Almost without exception, in making changes, Joffre followed the recommendations of the immediate superiors of the officers concerned, the army or corps commanders as the case might be, though he recognized and accepted his own ultimate responsibility. What the French Commander in Chief sought above all at the critical stage of the Campaign of the Marne were energetic leaders, men of action— men who would fight. His ability to select them is evidenced most impressively by the names of those he chose. Foch and Franchet d'Esperey, who both attained the dignity of Marshals of France after Joffre himself had passed into retirement, received the command of armies ; Pétain, Mangin and Guillaumat, all brigade commanders when the war broke out, had their divisions before the Marne. Fayolle, Maistre, Humbert, De Maud'huy, Weygand and many others who led the French armies to final victory, owed their initial preferment to Joffre's discernment in the opening weeks of the campaign.

Two factors played parts of cardinal importance in the French Commander in Chief's preparations for the great counter-offensive which he foresaw and desired : the transfer of forces from east to west to give the Allies the advantage of numbers before the German right wing armies, and to enable them to seize once more the strategical initiative they had lost, and the changes in the High Command, to strengthen the morale and the combatant value of the units affected, and to establish the aggressive attitude that would make it possible to turn the tide.

CHAPTER XXIII

THE DEFENCE OF PARIS

THOUGH the military history of Paris began in the early centuries of the Christian era, when the galleys of Norse raiders plied the waters of the Seine and the walls of the fortified city offered refuge to the harassed inhabitants of the countryside, and throughout the succeeding centuries the protection of the capital became one of the basic aims of French military policy,[1] the defence of the city and the modernization of its fortifications had received scant attention in the years immediately preceding the outbreak of the war. An industrial centre of first importance, Paris had become the terminal for the great railways of the north and east and the heart of a web of other lines extending to every part of France, so that from a strictly military stand-point the main consequence of its loss would have been the dislocation of the field armies' lines of communication and services of supply.

The moral effect, however, of the entry of enemy troops into Paris would have been incalculable, for the words of Vauban : "Paris is as necessary to the existence of France as the heart is to the existence of man," remained as true in 1914, as the day they were written. For five centuries, the principal events in the growth of the French nation had occurred within its ancient walls. The stately towers of Nôtre Dame, linking across the centuries the religion of past and present ; the Sorbonne, where the flame of learning had burned undimmed since the Dark Ages ; the Invalides, sheltering beneath its gilded dome the relics of unforgotten military glory ; even the tinselled gaiety of Montmartre and the more spontaneous life of the Latin Quarter, all represented to the French people the embodiment of cultural, religious and historical values, whose possession constituted a priceless heritage and whose loss could only mean utter disaster and defeat. In a sense and to a degree difficult for a foreigner to comprehend, Paris is in truth the heart of France.

In the fall of 1913, the Military Governor of Paris, General Michel

[1] In 1689 the great French military engineer Vauban wrote a treatise *L'Importance dont Paris est à la France et le Soin qu'on doit prendre de sa Conservation ;* published in 1821.

— the same whom Messimy had unceremoniously removed as Joffre's predecessor in 1911 — had put into effect a comprehensive plan for the defence of the capital and its conversion into an Entrenched Camp upon the outbreak of hostilities. The plan involved the preparation for defence of the 14 forts that had withstood the siege of 1870 and of the outer ring of 25 forts, completed between 1880 and 1890.[2] The area around Paris was divided into a series of fortified zones at a distance of 15 to 20 kilometres from the city itself, with an advanced line of defence extending over a front of approximately 160 kilometres, three times the perimeter of 1870. Its organization required the preparation of extensive trench-lines protected by barbed-wire entanglements and the construction of more than 70 centres of resistance and artillery emplacements at selected points, as well as two new forts. It was an elaborate plan, carefully worked out, and though upon completion the Entrenched Camp would hardly have been relatively any stronger than it was in 1870, the existence of such a plan, the credit for which belongs to Michel, gave the defenders of 1914 a great advantage over their predecessors of the Franco-Prussian War.

During the first three weeks of hostilities, neither Michel, Messimy nor anyone else in high authority seemed greatly concerned with the possibility that Paris might become involved in active operations, still less the corner-stone of the first line of defence, and for reasons which in justice it must be said were not wholly within Michel's control, the work of preparation proceeded at a leisurely pace.

With a realization of the true import of defeat in the Battle of the Frontiers, however, something like panic overwhelmed the Government. For a time there was even talk of abandoning all efforts to defend the capital, but bolder counsels prevailed. Determined, if necessary, to resort to the most desperate measures, Messimy turned to Galliéni for aid, and the veteran of Madagascar who had thus far taken no part in military activities, except for one brief visit to Joffre's Headquarters, readily accepted the appointment which the Minister of War tendered him.

The change in command occurred on August 26th, at a moment of political crisis, when Messimy himself was about to give place to Millerand as Minister of War. Summoning Galliéni and Michel to his office in the War Ministry, Messimy informed the latter that he had been relieved of his command. Surprised and indignant at such summary action, Michel at first refused to surrender his authority and demanded an immediate court-martial. Blazing with

2 Work on these fortifications was Joffre's first assignment to duty as a subaltern of engineers after the Franco-Prussian War.

anger and threatening Michel with arrest and imprisonment, Messimy left the room, but the opportune arrival of the Premier, the suave Viviani, saved the situation.   Under his mollifying influence, Michel acquiesced in the decision, and as a patriotic soldier requested and received a subordinate post under his successor, the command of the southern sector of the Entrenched Camp.[3]

Admirably fitted for his task, both by temperament and experience, Galliéni set feverishly to work to make up for lost time, and pushed the preparation of Michel's plan with unremitting zeal as the enemy lines drew nearer to Paris day by day.   To the government and to Joffre, Galliéni lost no opportunity of pointing out the insufficiency of the means of defence at his disposal.   On August 25th, Messimy had already sent the following order to the Commander in Chief :

If victory does not crown our arms, and if our armies are forced to retreat, an army of three army corps as a minimum must be sent to the Entrenched Camp of Paris to assure its protection.   Receipt of this order will be acknowledged.

This order, personally delivered by an officer of the Minister of War's staff, caused consternation at Joffre's Headquarters.   The day of its arrival, August 25th, was a particularly critical one for all the armies.   A literal compliance would have required the withdrawal of three army corps from the front, an operation impossible of execution without gravely disrupting the military plans of the Commander in Chief and compromising the security of the armies as well.   While Joffre fully concurred in Galliéni's view that only a powerful field army could adequately assure the safety of the capital, he appreciated also the political significance of such an order, issued "for the record" by an out-going minister, and with sound good sense interpreted it to mean, not that the front should be weakened by the immediate withdrawal of three army corps, but that measures should be taken to insure the availability of such forces, if and when the proximity of the enemy endangered the city.

Ever mindful of the great responsibility resting upon him, and prompted too, perhaps, by a not unnatural desire to exercise a military command commensurate with his reputation, Galliéni insisted almost daily to Joffre upon the need for the troops contemplated by Messimy's order, and did not hesitate to carry his importunities into political quarters, appearing on the 30th before the full Council of

[3] For an account of Michel's removal and Galliéni's appointment see article by Messimy, *Comment j'ai nommé Galliéni*, Revue de Paris, Sept. 15, 1921. See also Michel's and Messimy's testimony before the Briey Parliamentary Commission of 1919.

Ministers to urge his views ;[4] but the French Commander in Chief, never losing sight of the great military objective he had set, refused to be diverted from it, even for the greater security of the capital itself, and it was not until September 1st, with the arrival of Maunoury's Army on the outskirts of the Entrenched Camp, that Galliéni received the mobile forces he so urgently demanded.

On August 30th, the same day on which Galliéni appeared before the Council of Ministers, the Government reached the decision to remove the seat of civil authority to Bordeaux. Two days later, at Joffre's request, Paris became a part of the Army Zone, a step which strengthened the hand of the Military Governor by giving him control over various services theretofore directed by civilian ministries, but which also, somewhat to Galliéni's distaste, constituted him Joffre's direct military subordinate.

The garrison of Paris, at the time Galliéni assumed command, consisted of 4 Territorial divisions and 1 Territorial brigade, each division with a complement of two squadrons of cavalry ; a cavalry brigade of ten squadrons and six groups of field artillery (72 75mm. guns), in addition to the artillery assigned to the defence of the forts and fortified positions. In the next four days, the garrison received substantial reinforcements,[5] including a brigade of marines which the Government, remembering the troublous days of the Commune, had brought in to aid the police in repressing civil disorder. This force Galliéni succeeded in wresting from the unwilling hands of the Prefect of Police and in adding to the garrison. Except for the North African division, and the marines, however, the quality of the units entrusted with the direct defence of the capital left much to be desired. Insufficiently trained, inadequately officered and equipped, they could hardly expect to put up a first-rate resistance, unaided, against a determined thrust by Von Kluck's Army. The return to the garrison of the 61st and 62nd Reserve Division of Ebener's Group added but little to the resources of the Military Governor, for these divisions, during a brief experience in the north as a part of D'Amade's command, had been roughly handled by Von Kluck's Army and had returned to Paris much the worse for wear.

On September 1st, Joffre subordinated the Sixth Army to the orders of the Military Governor of Paris, at the same time that he took the capital under his own command. Maunoury's Army was

---

[4] A vivid account of Galliéni's appearance before the Council of Ministers appears in Poincaré, *L'Invasion*, pgs. 213–214.

[5] The 92nd Territorial Division, the 45th Algerian Division, a Brigade of Spahi Cavalry, the 61st and 62nd Reserve Divisions, two detachments of 400 artillerymen each from Boulogne and another detachment of 1650 naval gunners, with artillery and munitions to man the defences of the Entrenched Camp, as well as a brigade of marines.

hardly the powerful field army that Galliéni had so insistently urged, either in numbers or in quality, but it consisted nevertheless of a force of some 60,000 men, to be reinforced within a few days by the 4th Army Corps, already en route from the Third Army, and its performance along the Ourcq a few days later hardly justified the low estimate that Galliéni at first formed of its morale and fighting capacity.

In all, on the eve of the Battle of the Marne, the forces under Galliéni's command, the so-called Armies of Paris, included 5 Active divisions, 5 Reserve divisions, 5½ Territorial divisions and 4 cavalry divisions, including Sordet's Corps. Though it must be conceded that the combat value of these troops hardly equalled that of Von Kluck's Army, nevertheless, when it is remembered that the total strength of the German I Army amounted only to 10 infantry divisions, two of them Reserve divisions, and 3 cavalry divisions, it is apparent that the security of the French capital had not been wholly neglected.

On September 2nd, while Maunoury and Galliéni devoted their whole efforts to preparing for the imminent conflict and Von Kluck drew hourly nearer to Paris, the Government took its departure for Bordeaux. In order that there might be no misunderstanding, Galliéni requested definite instructions from Millerand, as the latter was about to leave.

"Paris must be defended to the last extremity," said the Minister of War.

"You realize, Mr. Minister, what that means. It involves very serious action, destruction, ruins. I may have to blow up historical monuments, the bridges — the bridge of the Concorde for example."

"To the last extremity," Millerand repeated, and took his departure.

With the control of the whole destiny of the capital in civil as well as military affairs in his hands, Galliéni posted his famous proclamation the next morning in all the public places of the city :

Army of Paris.
Citizens of Paris.

The members of the Government of the Republic have left Paris to give a new impetus to the national defence.

I have been entrusted with the duty of defending Paris against the invader.

This duty I shall carry out to the last extremity.

Galliéni

Paris, September 3, 1914.

Military Governor of Paris,
Commanding the Army of Paris.

The resolute tone of this proclamation electrified the nation, instilling new hope and awakening new confidence. Throughout France,

Galliéni's ringing phrases served at once to arouse a realization of
the deadly peril in which the capital stood and to dispel the doubt
and uncertainty of the last days.   Paris was threatened with disaster,
of that there could be no doubt, but no less surely, it would be
valiantly defended.   The words *"jusqu'au bout,"* used by Galliéni
are hardly susceptible of translation in their full significance.   Only
in the original do they retain their connotation of determination
never to surrender that linked them throughout the remainder of
the war in the minds of the people with an unalterable will to conquer.

Galliéni determined, if necessity arose, to leave the enemy no more
than a shell of a city.   With Hirschauer, his Chief of Engineers, he
mapped out a program of ruthless destruction to include every
building or edifice that might prove of military value to the enemy.
The bridges of the Seine without exception were doomed ; the Eiffel
Tower was to become a mass of twisted wreckage.   Military expediency alone controlled and every consideration of sentiment fell
before it.   With the flight of the Government and Galliéni's proclamation, the true situation could no longer be minimized or dis-
guised, and preparations hitherto deferred for fear of causing undue
alarm now proceeded without concealment.   The Governor's confidence in the populace proved not to be misplaced, for though thousands left the city, packing the south-bound trains,[6] there were no
disorders.   Catching the spirit of its resolute defender, the population of Paris grimly awaited the future.

Preparing a great city to withstand a besieging army presents
problems of overwhelming magnitude and complexity.[7]   Though
Michel's plan of defence had established the tactical dispositions of
the defending forces beyond the possibility of important alteration,
little had been done or could be done before the outbreak of hostilities towards its execution, for it necessarily involved the demoli-
tion of buildings and other structures, the cutting of trees to provide
adequate fields of fire and extensive encroachments of like character
upon private property.   The actual construction of the defences
envisaged by the plan required the immediate provision of vast
quantities of building material, thousands of tons of concrete, thousands of feet of lumber, millions of yards of barbed-wire, tools and
machinery of all sorts, and above all labour.   The few companies
of engineers attached to the garrison hardly sufficed for more than
foremen to supervise the work, and to use the Territorial infantry

[6] The Military Governor encouraged the departure of all inhabitants who had the
means and who could not contribute to the defence.
[7] An admirable account of the measures taken for the defence of Paris is contained
in *Paris en état de défense* (Payot, Paris, 1927) by General Hirschauer, then Chief of
Engineers of the Military Government, in collaboration with his assistant, General Klein.

meant sacrificing much-needed military instruction. Civilian la-
bourers were needed, thousands of them, who had to be enlisted
without crippling essential industries already handicapped by the
general mobilization, and who had to be fed, lodged and paid.[8]   As
each fortification neared completion, its prescribed armament had to
be set in place, stocks of munitions provided, its garrison installed
and communications established.   Reserve depots of munitions had
to be placed at accessible points to serve the 2924 guns of assorted
calibres [9] that constituted the armament of the Entrenched Camp.
Deficits in machine-guns, rifles and other equipment had to be supplied, and extensive additions made to the telephone and telegraph
systems.

For the necessities of the civilian population as well as of the garrison, in case of siege, great stocks of food-stuffs and other supplies
had to be accumulated, and at the same time arrangements completed
for the evacuation of all railway material, rolling stock, machinery
and other equipment that might be of service to the enemy — all
without unnecessarily or prematurely disrupting the city's normal
industrial life.

A vigilant guard had to be maintained, to cover all means of access
to the capital against sudden raids by enemy cavalry or armoured cars,
and preparations had to be made promptly to render the roads impassable upon the approach of the enemy by erecting barricades,
felling trees or tearing up stretches of pavement.   The possible destruction of more than eighty bridges across the Seine, the Oise and
the Marne had to be provided for, many of them railway bridges
and most of them of heavy construction, with due precautions to see
that no action should be taken except upon the order of competent
authority given under actual necessity.

The responsibility for the whole rested upon the Military Governor and his staff who were obliged to carry out their task with the
greatest possible rapidity, but at the same time to strike a nice balance between military necessity and too great an interference with
the normal life of the citizens which might precipitate a general
panic and lead to the riots and civil disturbances that the police
feared.

Though work on the defences had hardly reached a point satisfactory to the Military Governor, the advance of the German I Army
by the night of September 2nd made an attack the next day seem by
no means a remote possibility, and Galliéni ordered the entire gar-

[8] Paul Boncour, a former Minister of Labour, serving as a lieutenant on Galliéni's
staff, successfully arranged for the employment of a large part of the civilian labour
required.
[9] The armament of the Entrenched Camp on August 26th which was somewhat increased later by the arrival of naval guns and heavy artillery from Boulogne.

rison to its combat positions at dawn on the 3rd. The expected attack did not materialize, but the afternoon brought portentous news. Aviators from the Entrenched Camp observed Von Kluck's columns, stretching over sixteen kilometres, marching towards Château Thierry and the Marne, away from Paris. The British aviation reported like observations, and in the evening Maunoury's cavalry confirmed them.

Though the southeasterly direction of Von Kluck's march had been known to the French High Command since its inception on August 31st, it had hitherto been too early to predict the enemy's intentions with any certainty. When, however, the Germany I Army continued on the same line into the area east of Paris, ignoring the capital, a new situation immediately arose of which Galliéni was quick to perceive the strategic significance. If Von Kluck kept on his way across the Marne, a stroke towards the east against his flank might well prove decisive. It was the very opportunity that Joffre had been waiting for, but the chance might be a fleeting one, and there was not a moment to be lost. By every available means, the intentions of the enemy for the following day must be ascertained at daybreak, so that the advantage should not be lost. Impatiently awaiting the moment that might bring him confirmation of his hopes, the Military Governor of Paris passed a sleepless night.[10]

10 The *Mémoires du Général Galliéni*, posthumously published (Payot, Paris, 1920), give a detailed story of the preparation of the French capital for defence and of the part played in the Battle of the Marne by the Military Governor, as he himself visualized it. See also *Le Rôle du Gouvernement Militaire de Paris* (Berger-Levrault, Paris, 1920) by Gen. Clergerie, Galliéni's Chief of Staff, and *Les Carnets de Galliéni*, edited by his son, (Michel, Paris, 1932).

CHAPTER XXIV

THE SCHLIEFFEN PLAN DISCARDED

WHOLLY oblivious of the eager interest with which Galliéni observed his movements, Von Kluck resumed his march on the morning of September 4th, following his 9th Corps (Von Quast) southeast towards Montmirail. Still intent on reaching the flank of the French Fifth Army, the German Army Commander gave little thought to the possibility of danger lurking in the region of Paris, but at Luxembourg a vague uneasiness had gradually replaced the optimism of the previous days.

Even a comforting report from Von Bülow on the evening of the 3rd, that he had crossed the Marne on the heels of the French who were retreating in a state of complete dissolution, did not suffice to allay the German Chief of Staff's anxiety that something he did not understand was going on behind the Allied front. For several days Von Moltke had known that the major part of Pau's Army had left Alsace for an unknown destination, and on the evening of the 2nd Von Hausen had reported important troop movements along the railway lines running to the west. On the morning of the 4th the Duke of Wurtemburg sent word of similar activity on the line between Châlons and Vitry-le-François, and in the afternoon Rupprecht of Bavaria added the news that two army corps had withdrawn in a westerly direction from the front of his army group. These reports from the front, taken in conjunction with reports from secret agents of great activity around Paris, caused Von Moltke the gravest concern. It seemed wholly logical that Joffre would make every effort to strengthen his left wing, and though the daily victory bulletins of the German Army Commanders depicted the French as retreating precipitately beyond all possibility of planned manoeuvre, Von Falkenhayn — the only man at G.H.Q. competent to speak from personal observation — outspokenly expressed his belief that they had, to say the least, adopted an over-sanguine view.

The ever-increasing length of relatively unprotected lines of communication gave further cause for anxiety. British forces of undetermined strength were reported to have landed at Ostende, and disquieting rumors reached Luxembourg that they constituted the forerunners of 80,000 Russians being transported by sea from Archangel.[1] A determined sortie of the Belgian army from Antwerp remained an ever-present possibility, and it further seemed likely that some of the forces moving from east to west behind the Allied front might be assembling near Lille.

Yet despite his growing fears for the safety of the right flank and communications of the German armies, Von Moltke conveyed no hint of danger to Von Kluck. The omission seems unaccountable. but it may be assumed that Von Moltke supposed that on receipt of the radio orders of September 2nd, Von Kluck would halt his advance north of the Marne and fall in behind the II Army in echelon. If Von Kluck had obeyed those orders, the danger, from Paris at least, would have been averted.

For nearly forty-eight hours Von Moltke remained helplessly in his Headquarters in Luxembourg in complete ignorance whether his orders to the I Army had been received, still less whether they had been obeyed, and it was not until mid-afternoon of September 4th that two dispatches, sent by Von Kluck respectively 28 and 20 hours before, informed the High Command that the injunction to follow the II Army in echelon had not been obeyed and that the I Army was pressing forward as fast as it could south of the Marne.

Increasingly convinced that the right flank of the German armies stood in real jeopardy from an attack debouching from the Entrenched Camp of Paris, and that the withdrawals observed all along the French eastern front could only mean that Joffre had such a manoeuvre in mind, Von Moltke decided to take prompt and drastic action.

It had become evident that the main bodies of the French armies were retreating southwards towards the Seine, probably to take refuge behind the barrier of the river, and it was equally apparent that Von Kluck's Army was insufficient to provide an adequate flank-guard along the whole northern and eastern fronts of the Entrenched Camp of Paris between the Seine and the Oise. Von Moltke therefore decided to convert both the I and II Armies into a flank-guard, assigning to the II Army the sector between the Seine and the Marne and to the I Army the sector between the Marne and the Oise, while the centre and left armies pressed forward to achieve the decisive victory of which he did not yet despair.

It was a complete abandonment of the Schlieffen Plan. All thought of an envelopment of the Allied left wing was discarded.

[1] Von Moltke's fears in this regard were illusory. In fact 3 battalions of British marines landed at Ostende on the 27th and 28th of August but re-embarked on the 31st. The report of Russian forces was apparently the repercussion at German G.H.Q. of rumours current in England at about the same time, possibly initiated by the British Intelligence for enemy consumption.

Instead, the decision would be sought by a converging attack against the French fortified region to the east, the VI and VII Armies driving towards the southwest to break the line of the Moselle between Toul and Epinal, while the IV and V Armies, turning towards the southeast, struck at the French forces between Verdun and Vitry-le-François.   In the centre, the III Army marching south on Troyes would drive a wedge through the middle of the French line, ready to turn east or west as occasion might require.

The two right wing armies, on whose action Schlieffen had based his strategical conception, resigned the initiative to the enemy, mounting guard over Paris and the forces which the French Commander in Chief had assembled there, until the other armies could get the upper hand over the French eastern armies which Von Moltke believed had been substantially weakened by Joffre's withdrawals.

During the evening of September 4th, Von Moltke announced his new plan to the armies concerned by radio, while Tappen drafted a lengthy General Directive which he presented to the Chief of Staff for signature the following morning.[2]

Von Moltke's General Directive of September 5th involved only a change in direction from the south to the southeast for the IV and V Armies ; for the III Army it meant no more than a continuation of its march due south ; for Von Bülow's II Army, though the plan radically altered its strategic role, no tactical difficulties seemed to arise, for it was simply required to wheel towards the west in the region between the Marne and the Seine, pivoting on its right wing, until it reached its assigned position facing Paris ; but for Von Kluck, Von Moltke's orders meant the complete abandonment of all the efforts of the past ten days and required the I Army to retrace its steps, giving up the ground it had won at the cost of painful marches and hard fighting against the enemy's rear-guards, and a return to the area between the Marne and the Oise.

The radio message which the Chief of Staff had signed at about 6:30 P.M. did not reach the commander of the I Army until 7 o'clock next morning.

The I and II Armies will remain facing the eastern front of Paris. The I Army between the Oise and the Marne, holding the passages of the Marne west of Château Thierry; the II Army between the Marne and the Seine, holding the passages of the Seine between Nogent and Méry inclusive.   The III Army will march on Troyes.

Von Moltke

With uncomprehending amazement, Von Kluck received the laconic dispatch which could mean only one thing — that the Schlieffen Plan had failed.   For reasons as yet obscure, the envelop-

2 See Appendix XI.

ing manoeuvre of the German right wing armies had been abandoned in favour of a new strategical conception the exact nature of which was not indicated.

Von Kluck knew little of the situation on the fronts of the other armies, and he had accepted at their face value the daily communiqués of victory issued from G.H.Q. which led logically to the conclusion that the defeat of the French had been so complete and their retreat so disorganized as to preclude any possibility of a regrouping of their forces.   Moreover, he had no inkling of the existence of Maunoury's Army, of Galliéni's activity in the Entrenched Camp or of the intentions of the French High Command.   Engrossed in the offensive aspects of his Army's mission, he had neglected what seem in retrospect rudimentary precautions, for he caused no serious aerial reconnaissances to be made of the region of Paris nor did he send out his cavalry to test the strength of enemy forces around the Entrenched Camp, using his aviation instead to locate the retreating French and British columns and employing Von der Marwitz' divisions to pursue and harass them.

Even Von Moltke's radio did not convince Von Kluck of the error of his course or of the necessity of complying immediately with the wishes of the High Command.   His army corps were already on the march when the message arrived on the morning of September 5th, and he determined to allow them to continue to their assigned objectives for the day, believing that if the enemy could be forced to continue his retreat behind the Seine, the movement prescribed by the High Command would become easier of execution, and hoping that it might not become necessary to execute it at all.[8]

The arrival in the late afternoon of Lieutenant-Colonel Hentsch at the Headquarters of the I Army at Rebais brought enlightenment as to the true state of affairs.   Von Moltke's General Directive and Hentsch's verbal explanation revealed to Von Kluck for the first time that things had not gone so well as they had been represented. As Von Moltke stated in so many words, the enveloping manoeuvre of the right wing armies had become impossible of execution.   The Battle of the Frontiers had not sufficed to break the cohesion of the Allied armies and their retreat had been rapid and methodical. The German I Army, despite the dynamic energy of its commander, had not succeeded in turning Joffre's flank, but on the contrary, stood in grave danger of being outflanked itself, while the main body of the enemy, still undefeated, had withdrawn to the south.   The armies attacking the line of the Moselle had so far failed to progress,

---

[8] For an interesting commentary on the strategical aspects of the German right wing, see Col. Valarché's *Cannes et la Marche de Von Kluck sur Paris* (Berger-Levrault, Paris, 1929).   See also Gen. Camon's *L'effondrement du plan allemand en septembre 1914* (Berger-Levrault, Paris, 1925).

and the French had been able to withdraw important forces from their front and to transfer them from east to west, so that every day's advance increased Von Kluck's danger and the likelihood of a blow from the west by French troops concentrated around Paris, on his flank.

In the face of these considerations, as Hentsch explained them, Von Kluck could only recognize the imperative necessity of carrying out the dispositions indicated by the Chief of Staff, and with Hentsch, Von Kuhl and Von Grautoff, his Chief of Operations, he planned the details of the proposed retirement of the I Army north-ward into the region between the Marne and the Oise.

On the night of September 5th, the positions of the German I Army formed a rough semicircle extending from Esternay (9th Corps) west to Sancy (3rd Corps), curving thence northwest to Choisy (4th Corps) and Coulommiers (2nd Corps), with the 4th Reserve Corps still above the Marne north of Meaux.

Though the German High Command was at last alert to the danger of the very manoeuvre that Joffre intended and was taking measures to parry it, there was no suspicion either at Luxembourg or at Rebais that an Allied counter-stroke was imminent. On the contrary, it seemed that there would be plenty of time to carry out the change of positions prescribed by Von Moltke's General Directive.

"The manoeuvre must be carried out calmly and in orderly fashion," Hentsch told Von Kluck. "There is no need for haste."

It was accordingly decided to devote two days to the gradual withdrawal of the four army corps of the I Army north of the Marne. On the 6th, the 2nd Corps (Von Linsingen) would re-cross the Marne northeast of Meaux, the 4th Corps (Von Arnim) would march north as far as Doue in the direction of La Ferté-sous-Jouarre, the 3rd Corps (Von Lochow) would move to La Ferté Gaucher, while the 9th Corps (Von Quast), to gain a breathing spell after its strenuous exertions of the preceding days, would remain on its positions. On the 7th, another series of marches would complete the I Army's retirement north of the Marne to the same general situation it had held on the night of September 2nd, with its corps holding the same relative positions facing Paris, the 4th Reserve Corps on the Army right, the 2nd, 4th and 3rd Corps in the centre, and the 9th Corps on the left, nearest the Marne. In the meanwhile, Von Bülow's II Army would have swung around on the left of the I Army, facing the eastern front of the Entrenched Camp of Paris, with its right wing on the Marne and its left wing on the Seine.

Hardly had this plan been embodied into orders issued to the army corps, when unsettling news arrived from the 4th Reserve Corps which had been left north of the Marne with one division of Von der Marwitz' cavalry. The Corps Commander, General von Gronau, reported that in the region northeast of Paris the French were moving in force towards the Ourcq and had been attacked by the 4th Reserve Corps. The engagement had lasted from noon until dark, and though Von Gronau had gained some advantage, he had not obtained a decisive result and expected a renewal of the combat in the morning. The French strength was still undetermined. Reinforcements were urgently requested and pending their arrival, Von Gronau was falling back behind the Thérouanne, a small tributary of the Marne, to avoid having his flank turned from the north.

This intelligence, though disquieting, did not seem of vital moment to Von Kluck. The 4th Reserve Corps was confronted, it seemed, with a sortie of the kind foreseen by Von Moltke's General Directive which the right wing armies were instructed to resist offensively. Nevertheless, the appeal for aid could not be ignored, and the Army Commander resolved to accelerate the movement already planned for the 2nd Corps towards the north. Accordingly, instead of waiting until next day, Von Linsingen's men were aroused in their billets at midnight and put on the march towards the Marne.

Though reluctantly compelled to acquiesce in the abandonment of the Schlieffen Plan, Von Kluck remained fully convinced that Joffre's forces had never fully recovered from their early reverses and were incapable of any immediate concerted offensive effort. It was a conviction he shared with Von Bülow and other German Army Commanders, and with the Chief of Staff as well.

Shortly before the war, Conrad von Hötzendorff, the Austrian Chief of Staff, had asked Von Moltke when he estimated a decision could be obtained on the western front, and the latter had replied, "on the 36th to 40th day of mobilization." [4] It was a very accurate forecast, for September 6th was the 36th day of mobilization. If Von Moltke had forgotten his prophecy when he issued his orders for the regrouping of the right wing German armies on September 5th, he received a sharp reminder of it the next morning, when from Paris to Verdun, the guns of the Allied armies roared forth Joffre's answer to the invader's challenge.

[4] Conrad von Hötzendorff, *Aus meiner Dienstzeit* (Rikola, Vienna, 1923).

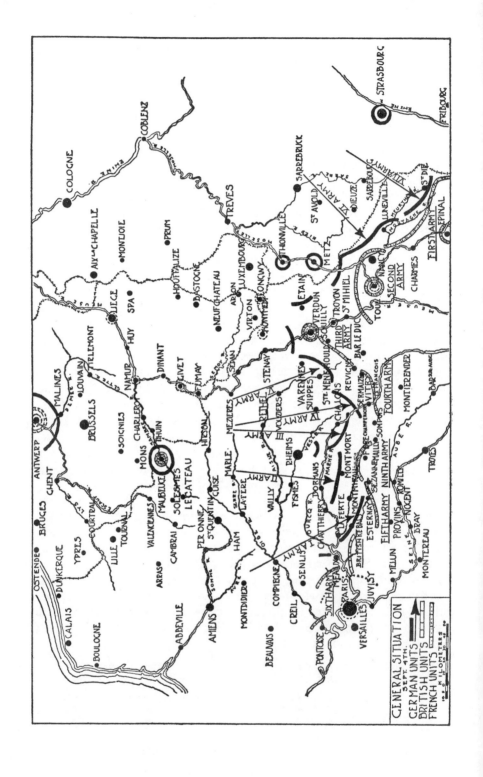

GENERAL SITUATION
SEPT. 4TH.
GERMAN UNITS
BRITISH UNITS
FRENCH UNITS

CHAPTER XXV

THE CRITICAL DAY

ALONG the fighting line from the Entrenched Camp of Paris to the wooded heights of the Meuse, little of note occurred on Friday, September 4th. Of such a day, later in the war, it might have been written that all had been quiet on the western front; but it was nevertheless the critical day of the Campaign of the Marne, for at Luxembourg, as we have already seen, Von Moltke had determined to abandon the redoubtable Schlieffen Plan and to substitute for it a new strategical conception of his own devising, while at Bar-sur-Aube, where Joffre had transferred his Headquarters,[1] decisions no less momentous were in the making.

It was not yet nine o'clock in the morning when French aviators and cavalry scouts brought the Military Governor of Paris word that the German I Army was continuing its march east of Paris, disregarding the Entrenched Camp and leaving its right flank hourly more vulnerable to attack. Without delay Galliéni sent Maunoury a preliminary order instructing him to prepare to move his Army eastward against the enemy flank, and Clergerie, Galliéni's Chief of Staff, communicated the situation by telephone to Joffre's Headquarters.

With no less interest than Galliéni, Joffre had been following Von Kluck's progress, for like Galliéni, he realized that the moment might be at hand to launch the great offensive, provided only Von Kluck continued his course far enough to give Maunoury a fair target at which to strike. During the night of September 3rd, the French Commander in Chief had written both Galliéni and French, advising the former that Maunoury's Army might be required at any time to advance in the general direction of Meaux, and suggesting to the latter that in such event the British should also advance towards the east, resting their left on the Marne, protected by the Army of Paris. Neither letter gave precisions as to the form such movements should take, for at the time of writing Joffre was await-

---

[1] On September 1st, French General Headquarters were moved from Vitry-le-François to Bar-sur-Aube, some 55 kilometres south, and again on September 5th 30 kilometres farther south to Châtillon-sur-Seine.

ing further news of Von Kluck's advance, but both disclose that fundamentally the manoeuvre contemplated by Joffre was identical with that envisaged by his subordinate, and though Galliéni had not yet received Joffre's communication, his preliminary order to Maunoury wholly coincided with the Commander in Chief's ideas.

At Bar-sur-Aube, on the morning of September 4th, a lively discussion had opened among the officers of Joffre's staff. Assuming that Von Kluck continued his southeastward march, leaving the Entrenched Camp of Paris on his flank, what action should be taken ?

Joffre's advisers divided into two camps. Gamelin and others believed that Maunoury and the British should strike the German flank without delay, for no one could tell when Von Kluck might realize his danger and change his course. Berthelot, on the other hand, favoured waiting another twenty-four hours to allow Von Kluck to penetrate more deeply into the pocket formed by the Allied line, and then to strike not from the west, as Gamelin and Galliéni thought, but towards the northwest along the front of the Ninth and Fourth Armies. It was basically the same conception that Berthelot had advocated ever since the close of the Battle of the Frontiers, a blow from east to west, rather than from west to east, and the suggested delay had the merit of permitting the arrival of three army corps, the 4th, 15th and 21st, to participate in the opening stages of the counter-offensive that all agreed was imminent.

Joffre listened silently to the argument, without expressing his own views, until at 9:45 Clergerie's telephone call to Colonel Pellé put an end to further speculation. Von Kluck was still marching towards the southeast, ignoring the Entrenched Camp, and Galliéni had suggested moving Maunoury's Army towards the east in conjunction with the British. The problem had ceased to be an academic one, for the hypothetical assumption had been realized and a decision was required.

From the necessarily limited perspective of only one army, with the security of the capital uppermost in his mind, Galliéni had been confronted with a relatively simple problem, but Joffre was obliged to take a broader view, and elements essential to a final determination remained in doubt. The Commander in Chief's objective was not to relieve the momentary peril of the Entrenched Camp of Paris, or even to deliver an arresting blow against Von Kluck ; but to defeat the main body of all the German armies and to roll back the whole tide of invasion. To accomplish this end, nothing short of a combined general offensive by all the Allied armies would suffice. The wisdom of an immediate attack, to which Galliéni had already whole-heartedly committed himself, depended on the measure of support that the neighbouring armies could afford, and the concurrence of Sir John French, Franchet d'Esperey and Foch were indispensable.

To Foch's Headquarters, Joffre sent an officer of his Operations Section, Lieutenant-Colonel Paquette, to explain the situation and to find out the extent to which the commander of the Ninth Army felt he could co-operate. To Franchet d'Esperey, Joffre telegraphed :

Circumstances are such that it may be advantageous to give battle tomorrow or the day after with all the forces of the Fifth Army in concert with the British and the mobile forces from Paris against the German I and II Armies. Please advise whether your Army is in condition to do this with a chance of success. Reply immediately.

Joffre

From the beginning Joffre had preferred the plan of an attack against Von Kluck's outer flank to Berthelot's alternative of an attack from east to west, but unaware that Von Moltke had already decided to halt the German I Army's advance, he was inclined to agree with his subordinate that it would be better to wait until Von Kluck had committed himself further before opening the offensive. Assuming that the battle would not open until the 7th and that Von Kluck would continue to march towards the Seine, Maunoury's intervention to be effective would have to take place along the south bank of the Marne in the vicinity of Lagny. Accordingly when General Clergerie telephoned a second time from Paris, shortly after noon, to inquire about the position of the Fifth Army, Lieutenant-Colonel Pont, Chief of the Operations Section, told him that it seemed preferable to move the Sixth Army along the south bank of the Marne, and a telegram from Joffre to Galliéni, sent a few minutes later, confirmed this :

Of the two proposals which you made to me with regard to the use of General Maunoury's forces, I consider that the more advantageous one consists in moving the Sixth Army on the left (south) bank of the Marne south of Lagny.

Please come to an understanding with the Field Marshal Commanding in Chief the British Army for the execution of this movement.

Joffre

The telegram indicated that at the time it was sent, about noon on September 4th, Joffre had no doubt of the desirability of an advance by Maunoury's Army. The selection of the south rather than the north bank of the Marne as the zone of its operations represented a concession to Berthelot's view that it would be preferable to hold off the general offensive until the 7th, in the belief that by that time Von Kluck would have reached an even more hazardous position, and that in any case the Fifth Army would not be ready for a general advance any sooner.   Later in the day, as a result of Franchet d'Esperey's action, Joffre found it necessary to revise this decision.

Though Galliéni did not receive Joffre's telegram until late in the afternoon, Clergerie's conversation with Pont told the Military Governor all he needed to know for the moment of the Commander in Chief's intentions, and taking Clergerie and Maunoury with him, he set out for Sir John French's Headquarters at Melun to secure the co-operation of the British.   Unfortunately both Sir John French and Sir Henry Wilson were away when he arrived, and of all high-ranking British officers, Sir Archibald Murray, with whom he talked, was the least sympathetic to the French point of view and the least receptive to suggestion.   Despite the urgence of Galliéni's representations, Murray took refuge in the time-honoured formula of his own impotence in his chief's absence, and refused any positive assurance of participation by the British Army in the proposed advance against Von Kluck.   The best Galliéni could obtain was a memorandum setting forth a plan of co-operation in somewhat tentative terms, subject to Sir John French's approval.

Plan of Co-operation between the British Army and the French Sixth Army, subject to the approval of Field Marshal French.

In conformity with the instructions of the French Commander in Chief, the French Sixth Army and the British Army decide to combine their efforts against the German Army that has crossed the Marne.

For this purpose, during the day of September 5th, the Sixth Army will be put on the march towards the east, in such fashion that in the evening the heads of its columns will be on the Marne between Lagny and Meaux.

The same day the British Army will change front so as to occupy the general line Mauperthuis-Faremoutiers-Tigeaux-Chanteloup, in such a way as to leave the Sixth Army the room it needs.

September 6th, the Sixth Army will cross the Marne, directing its course towards the east.   The same day, the British Army will continue its movement and will pivot on its right wing, either the 6th or the 7th, its left joining the right of the Sixth Army.   The two armies will then be ready to act in conjunction.

This memorandum, a copy of which was forthwith sent to Joffre, was far from satisfactory, even supposing it received Sir John French's approval.   It provided, indeed, for the action of the French Sixth Army south of the Marne, in conformity with the instructions that Galliéni had received through Clergerie before leaving Paris, but it contained no definite assurance that the British would join in the concerted offensive, and it deferred all possibility of offensive action until September 7th at the earliest. It did not fulfil Joffre's hope of firm support from his ally, nor did it conform to Galliéni's own views, but the latter could not wait longer for Sir John French and was obliged to regain his Headquarters in Paris.

Apparently wholly oblivious of the strategic significance either of Von Kluck's advance south of the Marne or of the plans of the French High Command to take advantage of it, Murray seems to have attached little importance to the memorandum prepared with Galliéni, or else to have felt confident that French would not approve it, for two hours later, at 6:35 P.M., without waiting for the British Field Marshal's return to Melun, he issued orders to the British Army to continue its retreat towards the southwest, fixing the positions to be reached on September 5th as the line Ormeaux-Les Chapelles Bourbon-Ozoir la Ferrière, some ten to fifteen kilometres behind the line specified in the memorandum.

Happily for the Allies, another conference with more positive results was in progress at almost the same time. The day before Franchet d'Esperey, newly appointed to the command of the Fifth Army, had arranged a meeting with Sir John French at Bray-sur-Seine, but the British Commander in Chief, delayed at a meeting with his Corps Commanders sent in his stead his Deputy Chief of Staff, Sir Henry Wilson. Conspicuously wearing a British decoration, as an outward and visible sign of good feeling, Franchet d'Esperey impatiently paced the road-side at Bray at the appointed hour. While he was waiting,[2] Joffre's telegram reached him and he had it in his hand when Wilson at length arrived.

"I am going to answer that my Army is ready to attack," said Franchet d'Esperey, coming at once to the point. "I hope you will not oblige us to do it alone."

In contrast to Sir Archibald Murray, Wilson had always been the readiest of British leaders to fall in with French views, and it required only a brief discussion to persuade him to accede to d'Esperey's request. It was soon agreed that the French Fifth Army and the British should attack shoulder to shoulder in the general direction of Montmirail, the British approaching it from the west and the French Fifth Army from the south, while north of the Marne the French Sixth Army simultaneously advanced eastward towards Château Thierry. Unaware of Berthelot's views or Joffre's tem-

[2] Wilson was late. With true Irish gallantry, he had stopped along the way to help a lady in distress, whose automobile had run out of gasolene while she was fleeing from the Germans. He did not feel it necessary, however, to explain the cause of the delay to the irascible French commander.

porary acquiescence in them, D'Esperey and Wilson fixed September 6th as the date of the attack and agreed that Maunoury's Army should proceed along the north bank of the Marne, debouching generally from the line of the Ourcq. For the moment, the adherence of the British seemed to be won, though Wilson warned D'Esperey of the difficulty he expected in securing the ratification of Sir John French and particularly the approval of Sir Archibald Murray.

While Galliéni was conferring with Murray at Melun and Franchet d'Esperey was meeting Wilson at Bray, Joffre waited anxiously at his Headquarters at Bar-sur-Aube for the news that he knew might decisively affect the outcome of the campaign. From Maunoury's Army word came of strong enemy columns crossing the Marne, headed southeast, a further indication that Von Kluck had become irrevocably committed to the course that gave the Allies their great strategical opportunity.

To insure the effective co-operation of the Third and Fourth Armies, in case of a final decision to launch a general offensive immediately, Joffre issued during the afternoon a General Instruction No. 5, addressed to these armies and to Foch's Army Detachment, fixing their composition, determining their zone of action, and converting Foch's command into the Ninth Army as of September 5th.

The first of the reports for which Joffre was waiting came with the return of Lieutenant-Colonel Paquette from Foch's Headquarters, bringing word that Foch would be ready to take the offensive on the morning of the 6th or any time thereafter.

Shortly after six, as Joffre was at dinner, the message he was eagerly awaiting came at last from Franchet d'Esperey. There were two memoranda, the first of which embodied the understanding reached with Wilson :

1. The battle cannot take place until the day after tomorrow, the 6th.
2. Tomorrow, the 5th, the Fifth Army will continue its retirement to the line Provins-Sézanne. The British Army will execute a change of direction towards the east on the line Changis-Coulommiers and further south, on condition that its left flank is supported by the Sixth Army, which should come along the line of the Ourcq, north of Lizy-sur-Ourcq tomorrow, the 5th.
3. The 6th, the general direction of the British offensive should be Montmirail ; that of the Sixth Army should be Château Thierry ; that of the Fifth Army should be Montmirail.

D'Esperey

The second memorandum dealt with conditions precedent to the proposed offensive :

The following are necessary for the success of the operation:

1. Close and absolute co-operation from the Sixth Army, debouching from the left (east) bank of the Ourcq, northeast of Meaux on the morning of the 6th.

   It must reach the Ourcq tomorrow, September 5th. If not, the British will not march.

2. My Army can fight on the 6th, but is not in brilliant condition. The three Reserve divisions must not be relied upon.

3. It would furthermore be well for Foch's detachment to participate vigorously in the action in the direction of Montmort.

Franchet d'Esperey's communications, with their almost brusque phrasing, had a definite tone that brought Joffre keen satisfaction.

With that intelligent audacity that is found only in the souls of great leaders — Joffre wrote in his memoirs — Franchet d'Esperey splendidly seized the situation and did not hesitate to answer "Yes" to a question that would have caused most men to flinch. I could not help thinking that if his predecessor had still been at the head of the Fifth Army, the answer I had just received would probably have been quite different.

With British co-operation seemingly secure, and with Franchet d'Esperey, Foch and Galliéni in substantial agreement, there seemed no reason to postpone final action, and Joffre directed Gamelin, who had already provisionally drafted orders, to reduce them to final form along the lines Franchet d'Esperey had indicated.

While Gamelin was engaged in this task, Galliéni, who had just arrived in Paris after his unsatisfactory meeting with Murray at Melun, called on the telephone and insisted in speaking with Joffre personally. In the conversation that ensued — the third that day between G.H.Q. and the Military Government of Paris relative to the proposed advance of the Army of Paris, but the only one in which either Joffre or Galliéni took part — admirers of Galliéni have pictured the Military Governor of Paris as imperatively urging the Commander in Chief to order his armies to assume the offensive.

No official record of the conversation was kept, but the accounts of Joffre and Galliéni in their respective memoirs, both written long after the event and characterized — no doubt in consequence — by numerous minor inaccuracies, are in substantial agreement as to what was said. Neither indicates that Galliéni exercised a determining influence on Joffre's decision, which had already been taken, but on the contrary tend to show that it was Joffre who reassured Galliéni as to British participation in the operation, and consented that the Sixth Army should move along the north bank of the Marne, as Galliéni thought best, instead of along the south bank as Joffre had originally planned, inasmuch as this too had already been arranged by Franchet d'Esperey and Wilson.

There is little justification for the wide-spread popular opinion that the Military Governor of Paris in effect compelled Joffre to order a general offensive against his judgement, and it seems a poor compliment to Galliéni's military ability to suppose that, with the meagre information in his possession at the time, he would have done so.   No positive orders of any kind had as yet been issued to the French Sixth Army.   On the contrary, it had been instructed to take no detailed dispositions until Maunoury's return from Melun where he had accompanied Galliéni.   The visit to British Headquarters had been distinctly unsatisfactory and inconclusive, and Galliéni was obviously aware after his talk with Murray that he could not count upon British support with any degree of assurance — so much is apparent from the text of the memorandum which he had sent to Joffre.   Galliéni had no information as to the ability or readiness either of Franchet d'Esperey or of Foch to take part in a general action, and with no very high regard for the quality of the forces at Maunoury's disposal, it can hardly be supposed that he would have advocated throwing them unsupported against Von Kluck's five seasoned army corps, with the risk of defeat under the very walls of the capital.   In the light of the situation as it must have appeared to Galliéni at the time he called Joffre on the telephone in the early evening of September 4th, it is incredible that a leader of such acumen and experience should have unreservedly urged the Commander in Chief to order an offensive.

Joffre's information on the other hand was considerably more complete, and he already knew that he had the instruments at hand to carry out the offensive, for he had assurance from Foch that the Ninth Army would play its part, and most important of all, he had already received the memorandum from Franchet d'Esperey that he could count, not only upon the Fifth Army, but upon the British as well.   Furthermore, in the same memorandum Franchet d'Esperey, in agreement with Wilson, had fixed the north bank of the Marne as the zone of action for the Army of Paris.

Despite the assertions of those eager to bring homage to the memory of the Military Governor of Paris, the evidence leads inescapably to the conclusion that it was Franchet d'Esperey's memorandum, rather than any impulsion by Galliéni, that led Joffre to take the final decision to open the great counter-offensive which constituted the culmination of the strategy he had followed since August 25th, and to sign the battle order for the Marne :

G.H.Q. September 4, 1914.
10 P.M.

General Instructions No. 6

I. It is desirable to take advantage of the exposed position of the German I Army to concentrate against it the strength of the Allied left wing armies.

All dispositions will be taken during the day of September 5th with a view to launching an attack on the 6th.

II. The dispositions completed on the evening of September 5th will be:

(a) All available forces of the Sixth Army northeast of Meaux ready to cross the Ourcq, between Lizy-sur-Ourcq and May-en-Multien in the general direction of Château Thierry.

All available elements of the Cavalry Corps which are in the vicinity will be restored to the command of General Maunoury for this operation.

(b) The British Army, established on the front Changis-Coulommiers facing east, ready to attack in the general direction of Montmirail.

(c) The Fifth Army, contracting its front slightly on its left, will establish itself on the general front Courtaçon-Esternay-Sézanne, ready to attack in the general direction from south to north.

Conneau's Cavalry Corps will maintain liaison between the British Army and the Fifth Army.

(d) The Ninth Army (General Foch) will cover the right of the Fifth Army, holding the boundaries of the Marshes of St. Gond and moving a part of its forces forward on to the plateau north of Sézanne.

III. The offensive will be taken by the respective armies on the morning of September 6th.

J. Joffre

The Major General   *General Commanding in Chief*
Belin

In general design the orders for the Marne conform to the plan that Joffre had formulated the day after the Battle of the Frontiers and to which, in spite of temporary set-backs, he had held unswervingly ever since. In detail they follow with close fidelity the memorandum prepared by Franchet d'Esperey as a result of his meeting with Wilson at Bray, and bear eloquent testimony to the share, second only to that of Joffre himself, that justly accrues to the commander of the French Fifth Army in the foundation of the Allied victory.

The orders issued on the night of September 4th made no provision for the parts to be played in the general scheme by the French

Third and Fourth Armies, already foreshadowed in some degree by the General Instruction No. 5 which Joffre had sent out earlier in the day. To De Langle and Sarrail separate orders went from Berthelot the following morning,[3] directing the Fourth Army to halt its retreat and stand its ground, preparatory to resuming the offensive, and the Third Army, combining its action with that of the Fourth, to attack towards the west against the left flank of the enemy forces supposed to be marching south through the Argonne Forest.

With the issuance of his General Instructions No. 6 in the evening of September 4th, Joffre stood committed to a decisive course from which there could be no turning back. Upon the outcome depended the military destiny of the campaign and perhaps the political destiny of his country as well, and of this the French Commander in Chief was fully aware.

[3] See Appendix XII.

CHAPTER XXVI

THE MEETING AT MELUN

THOUGH the decision to embark upon the great counter-offensive had been taken irrevocably, the day of September 4th ended at Joffre's Headquarters upon a disquieting note. At 11 P.M. Lieutenant-Colonel Brécard arrived from Melun, bringing with him a copy of the memorandum drawn up that afternoon by Galliéni and Murray,[1] and at almost the same time a message from Huguet informed Joffre that in view of constant changes, Sir John French preferred to reconsider the whole situation before committing himself as to the British attitude. In the meanwhile, the British were continuing their retirement.

On receipt of Huguet's message, Joffre dispatched Captain de Galbert, his personal aide, to British Headquarters with a copy of General Instructions No. 6, and directed him to explain matters, if necessary, to the Field Marshal, never doubting that by relating the sequence of events De Galbert could clear up the confusion, more apparent than real, that seemed to exist.

A telephone message from the Military Government of Paris at about noon on the 4th had given Sir John French his first word of the proposed advance of Maunoury's Army, and at that time the British Commander in Chief had given the French Mission at his Headquarters to understand that his Army would hold its positions as long as possible, ready to co-operate with either the Fifth or Sixth French Armies, or both, in an offensive towards the east. He had then left his Headquarters, and on his return in the early evening had found three documents awaiting him : Joffre's letter, written the night before, the memorandum of Galliéni's conference with Murray that afternoon and the memorandum of Wilson's conference with Franchet d'Esperey at Bray. He also found that his Chief of Staff had already issued orders prescribing a further retreat during the night for the British Army of from ten to fifteen kilometres. These orders French left unaltered.

Late Friday night (September 4th) — French wrote Kitchener on September 7th, explaining this retreat — Joffre asked me to retire 12

[1] See pg. 214.

miles in order to make room for his Fifth Army [sic] south of the Marne. I had half completed the movement when he determined to keep the Fifth Army north of the river and asked me to retrace my steps and get in touch with that Army.[2]

It is comprehensible that French may have been puzzled by the apparent inconsistencies in the various communications received on September 4th from the French High Command ; but it is hard to understand how, in good faith, the British Commander in Chief could have arrived at so muddled an impression of his ally's desires and purposes as that indicated in his letter to Kitchener.[3]   Though differing in detail, the communications from Joffre, Galliéni and Franchet d'Esperey were at one on the essential point, that the French armies were about to take the offensive and wished the British to co-operate by advancing eastward between the Marne and the Seine against Von Kluck's flank.   One may search in vain for any suggestion that the British should retire 12 miles (19 kilometres), and it is difficult to understand what possible purpose such a retirement could serve in an offensive movement.   It was certainly not necessary to make room for the French Sixth Army south of the Marne, for Galliéni with this in mind had suggested the front Mauperthuis-Faremoutiers-Tigeaux-Chanteloup as the British line for September 5th.   Franchet d'Esperey, on the hypothesis that the Sixth Army would operate north of the Marne, had suggested the line Changis-Coulommiers, still farther to the east.   With full knowledge of both memoranda and of the assurance given earlier in the day by Sir John French himself to the French Mission, Sir Archibald Murray had prepared and sent out orders pulling the British Army back to the line Ormeaux-Les Chapelles Bourbon-Ozoir la Ferrière from which it was physically impossible for the British to reach in time the starting point envisaged by Joffre in his General Instructions No. 6.

The truth seems to be that with Murray always figuratively tugging at his coat-tails, French was again yielding to his deep-seated reluctance to take part in any offensive operations, taking refuge behind inconsistencies that a few minutes' telephone conversation would have sufficed to clear up, in order to justify his attitude.

On his arrival at Melun, on the morning of the 5th, De Galbert found to his dismay that he could not see the British Commander in Chief personally and heard that Sir John French's personal baggage was on its way to Fontainebleau.   Sensing that he lacked the

2 See Appendix XIII.
3 An article by Major-General Sir W. D. Bird, *A Crisis of the Campaign in France* 1914 ; British Army Quarterly, April 1934, deals from the British view-point with the conduct of the British High Command on September 4, 1914.

rank and authority his mission required, he returned forthwith to Joffre, bearing a message from Huguet that in the latter's opinion only Joffre's personal intercession could dissuade French from continuing his retreat and could secure British co-operation in the offensive.

At the first signs of French's reluctance to co-operate, Joffre had already sent Millerand an urgent telegram, asking him to act upon the British Commander in Chief through diplomatic channels,[4] and he now set out for Melun, accompanied by Gamelin, Captain Muller and Lieutenant-Colonel Serret, the last French Military Attaché at Berlin before the war, whom he proposed to leave with French as special liaison officer during the forthcoming operations.

It was a little after two when the French Commander in Chief arrived at British Headquarters. Sir John French, with Sir Archibald Murray and Sir Henry Wilson, received him in a little Louis XV salon of the Château Vaux-le-Pénil, which had been stripped of its furnishings and equipped instead with a long board table and a few camp-chairs.

Though the ostensible purpose of Joffre's visit was to thank French for his co-operation, it soon became apparent that he had come upon a mission of far greater importance. Standing before the window, his officers grouped around him, the French Commander in Chief stated his case, speaking slowly, in simple, measured phrases, while the British Field Marshal, leaning slightly forward, with his hands resting on the table, listened intently to Wilson's translation of Joffre's words.

"So far as the French Army is concerned," Joffre concluded, "my orders have been given, and whatever the result, I intend to throw my last company into the balance to win a victory and to save France. It is in her name that I come to you to ask for British aid, and I urge it with all the power that is in me. I cannot believe that the British Army, in this supreme crisis, will refuse to do its part — history would judge its absence severely. Monsieur le Maréchal, the honour of England is at stake !"

An awkward silence fell as the French Commander in Chief finished speaking, his great earnestness and evident sincerity carrying more weight than any flight of eloquence. The moment of tension was broken by Sir John French, who had straightened up and flushed slightly at Joffre's last words.

"I will do all I possibly can," he said in a voice that was low and charged with emotion, and then, in true Anglo-Saxon fashion, he ordered tea.

4 See Appendix XIV (2). This was done in such a way as to ruffle the British Commander in Chief's dignity and compel an apology from Joffre.

"I distinctly felt," Joffre relates, "the emotion that seemed to grip the British Commander in Chief; above all I had noticed the tone of his voice and I felt, as did all the witnesses to the scene, that these simple words were the equivalent of an agreement signed and sealed."

Relieved by the assurance of British support, yet sober in the consciousness of the overwhelming responsibility that now rested upon him, Joffre returned to his Headquarters, which had been moved during the day to Châtillon-sur-Seine.

In a letter to Millerand, Joffre had already revealed his appreciation of the momentous nature of the decision he had taken.

The strategic situation is excellent and we cannot hope for better conditions for our offensive. . . The struggle in which we are about to engage may have decisive results, but it may also have very serious consequences for our country in case of a reverse. I am determined to engage all our forces without stint and without reservation to achieve victory.

With all preparations made and with all precautions taken, the outcome rested in the hands of the combatants and depended in large measure on the presence of those moral qualities which Joffre had never doubted could be called upon at need. For the first time, the Commander in Chief addressed a direct appeal [5] to the officers and men under his command:

September 6, 1914.

As we engage in the battle upon which the safety of our country depends, all must remember that the time for looking backward has passed; every effort must be devoted to attacking and driving back the enemy. Troops that can no longer advance must hold ground won at any cost, and die in their tracks rather than retreat. In the present circumstances no weakness can be tolerated.

Joffre

Through every rank of the French army, Joffre's words met with vibrant response. For the moment, sufferings, fatigue and grievances were alike effaced in a common determination to avenge defeat and to wipe out humiliation by a victory that all realized could come only from the sum of the efforts of each individual. As a measure of the French soldier, with an unconquerable faith in the destiny of his country attested in the face of death, the days that followed stood as an example through the years of war to come, and will endure in the annals of the nation.

[5] The necessity for secrecy prevented Joffre's Order of the Day from being issued until the morning of September 6th, so that it did not reach many units before the battle had started. Nevertheless, its text, taken from a copy picked up on the battlefield, was in the hands of the German High Command by evening.

CHAPTER XXVII

JOINDER OF BATTLE

AT THE very time that Joffre was making his supreme effort at Melun to secure Sir John French's adherence to his plan, the battle had already opened to the north unexpectedly to all concerned.

The French Commander in Chief's General Instructions No. 6 specified the line of the Ourcq River between Lizy-sur-Ourcq and May-en-Multien as the starting point for the offensive movement to be launched by Maunoury's Army in the direction of Château Thierry on the morning of September 6th. To reach positions within striking distance of the line so designated the French Sixth Army [1] began its march towards the east in the early morning of September 5th in the apparent expectation that it would find the area along the west bank of the Ourcq clear of combatant troops. Though rumours had circulated widely through Maunoury's Army that the long retreat was over and that the turning point had come at last, the troops had received no official notification of the purpose of their march and no hint that they might expect opposition from the enemy.

Von Kluck, in his headlong pursuit of the retreating French, had given scanty thought to the possibility of a flank attack from the Entrenched Camp of Paris, but he had nevertheless left north of the Marne, to cover his communications, the 4th Reserve Corps and one division of Von der Marwitz' cavalry. Von Gronau's Corps was the only reserve unit in the German I Army, and its share in Von Kluck's victories had thus far been largely vicarious. Except for a few hours' engagement in the late afternoon at Le Cateau, it had seen little action, and beginning with the detachment of a brigade to garrison Brussels, it had successively furnished details for guard duty along Von Kluck's line of march, until on Septem-

---

[1] Order of Battle of French Sixth Army from left to right (north to south): 7th Army Corps (Vautier), comprising the 14th Division and 63rd Reserve Division, Group of Reserve Divisions (De Lamaze), comprising the 56th and 55th Reserve Divisions, Native Moroccan Brigade, Cavalry Brigade. In Army Reserve, 45th (Algerian) Division.

On September 7th, Maunoury's Army was reinforced by Sordet's Cavalry Corps and the 61st Reserve Division from the Paris garrison, and again on the 8th by the 7th Division of the 4th Corps (Boelle).

ber 5th, the strength of its infantry had been reduced from the original 25 battalions to the equivalent of only 16. The Army Commander had placed no aviation at Von Gronau's disposal, and he was compelled to rely for information upon reconnaissances of the 4th Cavalry Division. This division, which had been very roughly handled by the British at Néry on the 1st, had lost seven of its twelve guns and had also sustained very heavy casualties during the course of the long march through Belgium and France, so that its combatant effectives, normally 5200 officers and men, did not exceed 1200. Such was the force that stood between Maunoury's Army and the Ourcq.

Von Kluck's orders for September 5th, issued before he had received Von Moltke's General Directive, required the 4th Reserve Corps, comprising the 7th and 22nd Reserve Divisions, to march south from Nanteuil and Bois-Fresnoy to Marcilly, Barcy and Chambry. Alike unaware of the change in plans of the German High Command and of the activity in the French camp, the 4th Reserve Corps had already reached its objectives before noon and was looking forward to an afternoon of rest, when a decision of the Corps Commander profoundly altered its plans.

A series of disquieting reports had come to Von Gronau since early morning, notably from Von Garnier, commander of the 4th Cavalry Division. French cavalry in force had appeared to the west, and German patrols found themselves blocked at every turn by enemy outposts. Areas recently reported as clear or only feebly held now teemed with troops of all arms, and as a climax to the disturbing accumulation of information, a strong column was observed marching eastward along the road to Montgé. A succession of wooded crests, running north and south from St. Soupplet through Monthyon to Penchard, blocked the western horizon of the area occupied by the German 4th Reserve Corps and divided it from the plateau across which the French Sixth Army was marching. At his Headquarters at Barcy, Von Gronau realized that something of unusual significance was going on beyond this ridge, but with his cavalry admittedly powerless to give him precise information, he had no way of learning more by the usual channels. Whatever was afoot on the flank of the army corps, the indications were too serious to be ignored. There was only one way out and Von Gronau took it.

"Colonel, there's no use delaying further," he said to his Chief of Staff, Lieutenant-Colonel von der Heydt. "We must attack."

It was a bold decision and a wise one,[2] which as events proved went

---

[2] Von Gronau's decision to attack has often been compared to that of General von Alvensleben at the Battle of Vionville in the campaign of 1870.

far towards saving the German I Army from its commander's rashness and towards negativing Joffre's strategy by eliminating the important element of surprise. Shortly after 11 o'clock, Von Gronau ordered the 7th Reserve Division to occupy the line of heights to the west, and supported by Von Garnier's troopers, to attack any enemy forces approaching it, while the 22nd Reserve Division remained temporarily in reserve. Scarcely more than an hour later the German guns opened fire from the western slope of the heights of Monthyon on the French in the plain below.

Instead of falling upon Von Kluck's right flank and taking the enemy unawares as Joffre had planned, it was the French Sixth Army that was taken by surprise, when the Battle of the Marne opened eighteen hours before its appointed time. After a dusty march in the morning heat, the reservists of De Lamaze's group and the Moroccans of Ditte's native brigade had reached the villages of Cuisy, Iverny and Neufmontiers, and had settled down to prepare their noonday meal. Their objectives for the day, the very heights from St. Soupplet through Monthyon to Penchard that had obstructed Von Gronau's view, were a scant two kilometres away, and with no suspicion of an enemy in the vicinity the French felt confident of reaching them early in the afternoon. But the Germans reached them first.

A burst of 77 mm. shells gave the French their first warning of the enemy's presence, and his sudden apparition threw them momentarily into confusion ; but they soon recovered, and the Reserve divisions which Maunoury had brought with him from the Army of Lorraine proved that they were not the undisciplined, demoralized troops Galliéni had pictured them to be. Though they had not expected to fight to reach their objectives, they were wholly willing to do so, and it was not long before the German 4th Reserve Corps was fully engaged from St. Soupplet to Penchard.

The struggle that ensued continued with undiminished violence throughout the afternoon, and when ended by darkness had brought no decisive results to either side. Two German Reserve divisions and a Cavalry division were pitted against two French Reserve divisions and a native Moroccan brigade. The Germans found compensation for a slight inferiority in numbers in the presence on the field of an able and energetic Corps Commander, co-ordinating and directing the efforts of his troops, while the French fought a disconnected battle, never fully overcoming the handicap of their early surprise, and lacking the benefit of any controlling superior authority. At his Headquarters at Thieuze, eight kilometres from the battlefield, De Lamaze knew little of what was going on until after nightfall, when the fighting had already ended, and neither Maunoury nor Galliéni provided any guiding direction or seem to have appreciated the significance of the encounter.

Soon convinced that it was no mere reconnaissance with which he had to deal, but rather a force determined to advance, which might readily overwhelm the German 4th Reserve Corps, Von Gronau ordered his men not to press forward beyond Iverny and Plessis-L'Evêque. Whether they could have done so in any case seems at best conjectural ; but the Germans stood their ground and more, repulsing the Moroccans' attack on Penchard, temporarily dislodging the French 55th Reserve Division from Iverny and finally, in the dusk, retaking St. Soupplet, where the French 56th Reserve Division had gained a temporary foothold. When night brought the combat to an end, the Germans still held the line of heights from which they had started, and the French still had their objectives to attain.

With a rare appreciation of the strategic realities, Von Gronau realized that despite his momentary success ultimate defeat was imminent if he attempted to stand his ground, and with a caution no less admirable than his earlier boldness, he ordered the 4th Reserve Corps to fall back across the little valley of the Thérouanne to take up new positions almost ten kilometres to the east between Puisieux, Etrépilly and Vareddes. Disorganized and exhausted, the French made no attempt to follow, nor did they even perceive the enemy's withdrawal. Had they done so, an exceptional opportunity lay open to them, for the German units had suffered severely and during their night march became intermingled in great disorder, but there was no pursuit, and Von Gronau reached his goal unmolested. A message to Von Kluck, which arrived at the Headquarters of the I Army late in the evening, brought the 2nd Corps (Von Linsingen) hastening back north of the Marne, and its arrival early the following morning put an end, temporarily at least, to the threat of disaster.

At ten o'clock in the evening, the French 56th Reserve Division moved forward in the bright moonlight to attack St. Soupplet, which it had abandoned just before sun-down. It was a blow in the air, for they found the village and the crest abandoned, and the enemy nowhere to be seen. Learning of the neighbouring division's experience, Leguay of the French 55th Reserve Division ordered a similar effort against Monthyon, and at two in the morning an infantry company started from Iverny on a reconnaissance. As it crept cautiously across the plain that had been so hotly contested during the afternoon, it was guided by the light of blazing farms around Monthyon, but not a shot greeted its advance. Nevertheless, it was not until two and a half hours later that the company entered the village that had been the division's objective for the previous day, only to find it evacuated, except for a dressing-station in the church filled with Germans too badly wounded to be transported. A runner, sent back to report that the enemy had abandoned Monthyon, lost his way, and it was after six in the morning before the main body of the 55th Reserve Division realized that it no longer had an enemy before it.

The afternoon of September 5th had not been an auspicious opening for Joffre's great counter-offensive, and Von Gronau's bold decision precipitating the battle had been an extremely fortunate one from the German point of view.

"For us," Von Kuhl has written, "the engagement was of great importance ; it uncovered the enemy's hand."

In fact, though Von Kluck was slow to realize its import, it gave the German I Army timely warning of the nature of the French manoeuvre, and enabled it by successive withdrawals of army corps north of the Marne to build up a wall of opposition that narrowly but effectively prevented Maunoury's advance from achieving the strategic advantage that Joffre had hoped and expected to attain.

Conversely from the French point of view, the action of September 5th proved both a misfortune and a lost opportunity. While two Reserve divisions and the Moroccan brigade fought for more than five hours in a series of inconclusive attacks and counter-attacks, the French 7th Corps (Vautier) rested on its arms barely ten kilometres away at Ver, Eve and Rouvres, while on the opposite flank a cavalry brigade remained idly in reserve along the Marne. The energetic intervention of these forces on the flanks of the German 4th Reserve Corps could hardly have failed to encompass its complete defeat and possibly even its destruction ; but the opportunity passed not to recur again.

It seems evident that neither the Military Governor of Paris nor the Commander of the French Sixth Army had any expectation that the German 4th Reserve Corps would be encountered in the afternoon of September 5th. Both Galliéni's and Maunoury's orders envisaged the movement towards the Ourcq as preparatory to the offensive set for the following day, and neither contained any intimation of the proximity of the enemy, nor did they suggest the likelihood of immediate contact. Even after the engagement had started its significance seems wholly to have escaped the French High Command.

Maunoury's Army has advanced. There has been a small successful engagement near St. Soupplet (10 kilometres north of Meaux).

Thus Galliéni reported to the Minister of War at 6:50 P.M., and even more strikingly reported to the Commander in Chief at 11:55 P.M. :

Apart from covering elements in the region of Meaux, Lizy-sur-Ourcq and May-en-Multien, the I (German) Army has apparently only parks and convoys on the right (north) bank of the Marne. The movement of this army towards the south is accentuating.

Certain admirers of Galliéni, somewhat rashly it would seem, have affected to discern in the engagement of September 5th an added proof of his military talent.   It is true that in his memoirs the Military Governor of Paris has claimed to have foreseen the engagement against the German 4th Reserve Corps at the time it actually took place,[3] but it seems likely that the writer's memory played him false, for there is certainly nothing in Galliéni's orders or reports for the day of September 5th, or in the conduct of the battle itself, to indicate that it was anticipated on the French side.   It is incredible that had either Maunoury or Galliéni expected the encounter, more effective measures would not have been taken to secure the complete victory that for the only time during the Battle of the Marne lay within their grasp.[4]

[3] Galliéni, *op. cit.*, pg. 129.
[4] On the engagement of the French 55th and 56th Reserve Divisions, see Commandant Michel's *Monthyon* (Berger-Levrault, Paris, 1931) and Gen. de Dartein, *op. cit.* See also Von Kuhl, *op. cit.*, Lieut.-Col. Koeltz, *L'Armée Von Kluck à la Bataille de la Marne* (Lavanzelle, Paris, 1931) and Commandant Duché's *La Bataille de la Marne a-t-elle été engagée vingt-quatre heures trop tôt ?* ; Revue Militaire Française, June 1, 1925.   A more intimate and personal account is Capt. Wirth's *Von Saale bis zur Aisne* (Hesse & Becker, Leipzig, 1920).

CHAPTER XXVIII

THE BATTLE OF THE OURCQ

THOUGH Von Gronau's retreat during the night of September 5th averted for the time the danger of envelopment that threatened both flanks of his Army Corps, the defensive positions he had originally chosen for the right of his line did not favourably impress the German Corps Commander, for the chance that the French might outflank him from the north still gave him some concern. For greater security he ordered a further retirement, abandoning the village of Puisieux in favour of the line of heights to the east of it. This movement, carried out without incident, brought the German 4th Reserve Corps to its new positions shortly after six in the morning, where it settled down along a line running north and south from Vincy through Etrépilly to Vareddes on the Marne. It was a front of more than 15 kilometres, far too extended for effective defence by a single army corps with incomplete effectives, but Von Gronau determined to hold it as best he could while waiting for the reinforcements he knew were on the way. With all dispositions taken and with orders issued to every unit to resist resolutely, if attacked, Von Gronau established his Headquarters by a road-side behind the centre of his front and stretched himself out in the ditch along the highway for a nap.

In the meanwhile the German 2nd Corps (Von Linsingen), which had been aroused by Von Kluck's order shortly after midnight, had marched most of the rest of the night and was approaching the Marne from the south. It was five o'clock when the Corps Commander at the head of his leading division reached the river near Trilport. From the heights of Binche, southeast of the town, a natural observatory, Von Linsingen surveyed the region to the north through his field-glasses in an effort to discern where his forces might most usefully be employed. In the distance he saw five strong columns of French infantry marching east towards Vareddes. It was the Moroccan Brigade and the right brigade of the 55th Reserve Division, advancing against the left wing of Von Gronau's Corps. Von Linsingen acted without hesitation. Ordering his artillery forward to bring the French under its fire, he directed General von Trossel, commander of the 3rd Division, to march rapidly on Germigny and Vareddes to attack the enemy, while the other division of the corps, the 4th, continued northwards along the west bank of the Ourcq. At the same time he dispatched a messenger in all haste to call up three battalions which he had left as a rear-guard along the Grand Morin River.

The battle which opened early at the southern extremity of the German line soon spread along the whole front as French units, all marching eastward, successively came into contact with Von Gronau's positions. Between Vareddes and Etrépilly, the German 22nd Reserve Division with the aid of the newly arrived 3rd Division managed to stand its ground against the Moroccans and the French reservists, but north of Etrépilly the situation soon became fraught with danger as Von Gronau had feared. One after another elements of Vautier's 7th Corps, the left wing of Maunoury's Army, arrived on the line of battle, and the danger that the German flank might be turned from the north became momentarily more pronounced. Widely separated, in an effort to hold the maximum possible front, the battalions of German reservists slowly gave way, unable to withstand the weight of the French assaults. Von Gronau, who had been aroused from his improvised bed by a visit from Colonel von Bergmann, Von Kluck's Quartermaster-General, had already engaged his last reserves and was waiting in helpless anxiety when Von Linsingen joined him soon after eleven o'clock. As senior Corps Commander, the latter assumed command of all the German forces between Maunoury and the Ourcq, and forthwith determined to engage the 4th Division of his own Army Corps on the northern extremity of the line.

Until mid-afternoon, the French held the upper hand, but though obliged to remain on the defensive, the Germans defended themselves vigorously, and Maunoury's Army advanced only step by step at a heavy price. The arrival of the German 4th Division altered the situation. With the 4th Reserve Corps bracketed between the two divisions of the 2nd Army Corps, Von Linsingen resolved to regain the initiative and ordered a general counter-attack. To the north, around Acy-en-Multien, the German 4th Division, despite its weariness, first halted, then rolled back the French 14th Division, which had been striving all day to push around the German flank. In the centre the 7th Reserve Division and the 22nd Reserve Division, the latter reduced to the strength of only five battalions, drove De Dartein's 56th Reserve Division out of Etrépilly, and on the left, Von Trossel's 3rd Division threw back the Moroccans and the French 55th Reserve Division, which had been the most severely tried of all the French Sixth Army.

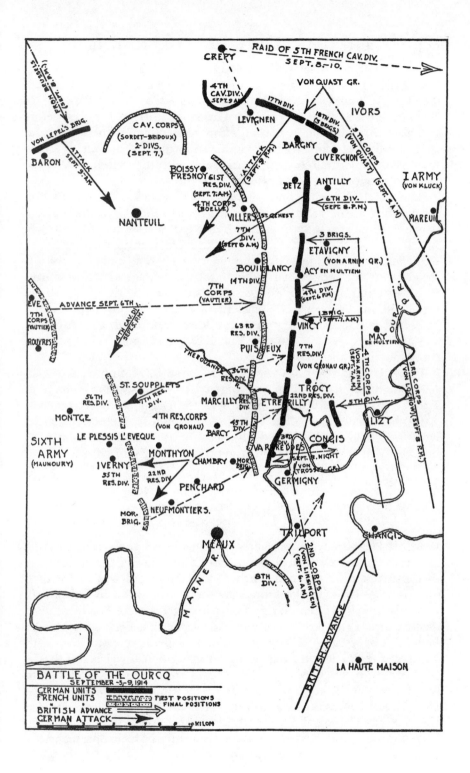

RAID OF 5TH FRENCH CAV. DIV.
SEPT. 8-10.

CREPY

VON QUAST GR.

4TH CAV. DIV.
SEPT. 9 A.M.

17TH DIV.

18TH DIV.
(3 BRIGS.)

IVORS

LEVIGNEN

(VON BRUSSELS)
(SEPT 9 P.M.)

VON LEPEL'S BRIG.

BARGNY

CUVERGNON

9TH CORPS
(VON QUAST) (SEPT. 9 A.M.)

I ARMY
(VON KLUCK)

CAV. CORPS
(SORDET-BRIDOUX)
2-DIVS.
(SEPT. 7.)

ATTACK
SEPT. 9 A.M.

ATTACK
(SEPT. 9 P.M.)

ANTILLY

BETZ

BARON

BOISSY
FRESNOY

61ST
RES. DIV.
(SEPT. 7 A.M.)

6TH DIV.
(SEPT. 8 P.M.)

MAREUIL

NANTEUIL

4TH CORPS
(BOELLE)

VILLERS

ST. GENEST

3 BRIGS.

ETAVIGNY
(VON ARNIM GR.)

7TH
DIV.
(SEPT 8 A.M.)

BOUILLANCY

ACY EN MULTIEN

EVE

7TH
CORPS
(VAUTIER)

ADVANCE SEPT. 6TH.

14TH DIV.

7TH
CORPS
(VAUTIER)

4TH DIV.
(SEPT. 6 P.M.)

OURCQ R.

ROUVRES

4TH CAV. DIV.
(SEPT. 5 P.M.)

63 RD
RES. DIV.

VINCY

I BRIG.
(SEPT. 7 A.M.)

MAY
EN MULTIEN

PUISIEUX

7TH
RES. DIV.
(VON GRONAU GR.)

4TH CORPS
(VON ARNIM)
(SEPT. 7 A.M.)

3RD CORPS
(VON LOCHOW)(SEPT 8 P.M.)

THEROUANNE R.

36TH
RES. DIV.

ST. SOUPPLETS

56TH
RES. DIV.

7TH RES.
DIV.

MARCILLY

53RD
RES.
DIV.

TROCY
22ND RES. DIV.

5TH DIV.

LIZY

ETREPILLY

MONTGE

LE PLESSIS L'EVEQUE

4TH RES. CORPS
(VON GRONAU)

BARCY

45TH
DIV.

VARREDDES

3RD DIV.
SEPT. 8. NIGHT

CONGIS

SIXTH
ARMY
(MAUNOURY)

IVERNY

55TH
RES. DIV.

MONTHYON

22ND
RES. DIV.

CHAMBRY

MOR.
BRIG.

GERMIGNY

VON
KROSSEL GR.

PENCHARD

MOR.
BRIG.

NEUFMONTIERS.

TRILPORT

SHANGIS

MEAUX

MARNE R.

8TH
DIV.

2ND CORPS
(VON LINSINGEN)
(SEPT. 6 A.M.)

LA HAUTE MAISON

BRITISH ADVANCE

BATTLE OF THE OURCQ
SEPTEMBER 5-9, 1914

GERMAN UNITS
FRENCH UNITS   FIRST POSITIONS
                      FINAL POSITIONS
BRITISH ADVANCE
GERMAN ATTACK
                      10 KILOM.

In spite of the success of his counter-offensive all along the line, Von Linsingen entertained no illusions as to the nature of his advantage.   Convinced that he was confronted by forces superior to his own, he was fearful — as Von Gronau had been the day before — that with night coming on an effort to exploit his success too far might lead to disaster.   Checking his subordinates' ardour, the German commander halted their attacks, and with the twilight the battle died down along the whole front.

The day had been a hard one for both armies.   Thanks to Von Gronau's strategic retreat, Maunoury could report a substantial advance by the French Sixth Army, but it had not succeeded in reaching the line of the Ourcq, which was to have been its starting point, and the day had ended with the enemy in the ascendancy.   For a second time Maunoury had failed to take advantage of all the means at his disposal, for the 45th Division, the best in his Army, whose weight might have proved sufficient to break Von Gronau's fragile line, had remained all day in Army Reserve unused, and before it was at last engaged on the 7th, Von Kluck had again reinforced his forces north of the Marne.

If the day had not been wholly satisfactory to Maunoury and Galliéni, nightfall found Von Linsingen likewise far from confident. For the first time since the opening of the campaign the German I Army had been compelled to fight an anxiously defensive battle, with its eyes always turned to the rear for the coming of reinforcements.   Von Linsingen called urgently on Von Kluck for aid :

The combat engaged on the line Etavigny-north of Vareddes is still maintained by powerful enemy artillery.   The 4th Reserve Corps having suffered heavily and the 2nd Corps having before it superior forces, it is essential that the 4th Corps should intervene at 5 o'clock in the morning.

At his Headquarters at Charly on the Marne, the German Army Commander remained still not wholly convinced of the seriousness of the struggle in progress north of the river, and was inclined to view it as an effort to check or delay the I Army's southward march. Nevertheless, he responded to Von Linsingen's appeal, and the 4th Army Corps (Von Arnim) which had reached La Ferté-sous-Jouarre late in the evening, in execution of the plan agreed upon with Hentsch the day before, was again set in motion towards the battlefield at 11:30 P.M.   At three o'clock in the morning, Von Arnim arrived in person at Von Linsingen's Headquarters to arrange for the entry of his divisions into line.   The tactical situation required that the 4th Corps, like the 2nd, should be divided, and Von Linsingen inserted one brigade on the right centre of his front, using the other three to prolong his line to the north, in order to parry the ever-present danger of envelopment from that quarter. With all semblance of corps organization destroyed, Von Linsingen divided his forces into three groups, the northern group commanded by Von Arnim, the centre group by Von Gronau and the southern group by Von Trossel.

The arrival of the German 4th Army Corps did not change the relative balance of the opposing forces, however, for during the night Maunoury received equivalent reinforcements. The arrival of the 61st Reserve Division from the Paris garrison extended the front of the 7th Corps to the north, and in the centre, the 45th Division, hitherto in reserve, partially relieved the exhausted units of the 55th Reserve Division between Etrépilly and Vareddes. Thus strengthened Maunoury retained the advantage in numbers he had enjoyed from the outset, but the margin proved still insufficient for the execution of his offensive mission.

The moon was setting and the first light of dawn was streaking the sky when the leading units of Von Arnim's Corps moved into position on the right of Von Gronau's centre group.[1] Two hours later the battle reopened, raging before the heights of Trocy, with the little village of Etrépilly as the prize.

The addition of the 15th Brigade of the 4th Corps infused Von Gronau's battle-worn reservists with new life, and they fought with a vigour that almost proved disastrous to the French 63rd Reserve Division. A violent bombardment preceding a counter-attack threw the French infantry into disorder, and they hurried back from their lines on the verge of panic under the impression that enemy shells, arriving from an angle, were fired from their own artillery. Colonel Nivelle — who two years later succeeded Joffre as Commander in Chief of the French armies, but on September 7, 1914, was commander of the 5th Artillery Regiment — perceived the danger and the likelihood that in their precipitate flight the infantry might not only open a gap in the front, but might leave the battery positions unprotected. Taking two groups of batteries, fortunately hitched up and in the act of changing their emplacements, under his orders, he boldly directed them towards the enemy, instead of ordering a retreat, as a less courageous chief might have done. Riding with the guns as they wheeled into position in front of the wavering infantry, he directed the fire which they opened at almost point-blank range against the advancing Germans. Firing at a maximum speed of twenty rounds to the minute, the French 75's cut wide swaths in the on-coming ranks, until at last the enemy halted and fell back,

[1] Two personal accounts of the operations of the German 4th Army Corps during the Battle of the Ourcq by junior officers are: Risse's *Meine Erlebnisse also Mitkämpfer* (Schiller, Berlin) and Schubert's *Meine Erlebnisse auf d. Vormarsch d. I Armee* (Reinecke, Magdeburg).

while the French infantry, taking courage from Nivelle's intrepid example, followed in their wake to re-occupy the positions they had abandoned.

Attacks and counter-attacks succeeded each other on the front of the German centre group, in one of which a German battle-flag remained in French hands,[2] but nightfall found the opposing positions virtually unchanged, with Etrépilly still in the Germans' possession.

In the sector close to the Marne, before Von Trossel's 3rd Division, the battle which had opened vigorously at daybreak died down in the middle of the day only to resume as evening approached. Fighting strictly on the defensive, Von Trossel managed to hold his ground before repeated assaults, but at nine o'clock in the evening, after the fighting had ceased at other points, a sudden attack by the Moroccans gained a temporary foothold in the German lines. The German artillery, hastily alerted, intervened with decisive effect, however, and averted an imminent panic, sweeping the French back with crushing loss under the fire of heavy batteries.

To the north, in the vicinity of Acy-en-Multien, Von Arnim gained a more conspicuous success. Attacking furiously, the German 16th Brigade met the French 61st Reserve Division in headlong collision, and drove the reservists from the Paris garrison back in confusion. Only the firmness of the French 7th Corps before the remainder of Von Arnim's group prevented the realization of the envelopment for which both sides had been striving continuously ; but the German 16th Brigade was in no position to exploit its advantage alone and had to be content with a partial victory.

When nightfall again brought the fighting to a close, the third day of battle still left the issue in doubt. The German commanders, gravely concerned, dispatched Von Arnim's Chief of Staff to Von Kluck's Headquarters to urge the immediate intervention of the remaining two corps of the I Army.

Early the same morning, September 7th, a message from Von Moltke had dispelled all doubt at German I Army Headquarters as to the character of the opposition north of the Marne, for a copy of Joffre's Order of the Day had been found on the battlefield on the front of the III Army, and Von Hausen's Chief of Operations, Lieutenant-Colonel von Werder, realizing its capital importance, had promptly telephoned its text to Luxembourg. Von Moltke, in turn, lost no time in passing on the word to his armies :

[2] At Nogéon Farm, near Vincy, Private Guillemard of the 298th French Infantry (63rd Reserve Division) captured the flag of the 2nd Battalion of the 36th German Infantry (8th Division) after a desperate hand-to-hand struggle in which the German colour-guard was wiped out.

According to an order of Joffre's found today (September 6th), decisive battle has been ordered for today for all the French armies.

With Maunoury's advance at last revealed in its true character as a major offensive operation, Von Kluck appreciated the necessity of turning his whole attention to the protection of the right flank of the German armies ; but he still had three possible methods by which this primary mission might be fulfilled. The first was to fall back east of the Ourcq on Château Thierry, breaking off the battle already engaged. Though this course would close the wide gap that already existed between Von Linsingen's forces north of the Marne and the right of Von Bülow's II Army, and would establish close contact between the two German right wing armies, a retreat after two days of fighting could hardly fail to be interpreted as a confession of defeat and to have a depressing effect upon the weary German troops and a correspondingly encouraging effect on Maunoury's Army ; aside from the technical difficulties of drawing off while in close contact with the enemy.[3]

A second possibility was to execute a short withdrawal to the east bank of the Ourcq and to stand defensively in the angle formed by the two rivers, the Ourcq and the Marne. This was a half-measure. It would have narrowed the breach between Von Kluck and Von Bülow without fully closing it, and would have been easier of execution than the longer retirement to Château Thierry, but it would also have left the German I Army in a cramped situation that raised many objections from a tactical stand-point.

The third possibility was to continue the battle on the ground where it had started, taking the offensive as soon as circumstances permitted, and ending the menace to the German right flank by the complete defeat of Maunoury's Army. This solution, the boldest of the three, was also the one most in keeping with the character of the German Army Commander, and, it seemed to him, also most in keeping with the instructions received from Von Moltke to "resist offensively" all enemy attacks debouching from Paris. It nevertheless involved inconvenient features, for it had already become abundantly evident that the three army corps under Von Linsingen's command could not by their unaided efforts accomplish the desired result. Victory over the French Sixth Army could be achieved only through the timely intervention of the two remaining corps of the I Army which at nightfall on September 6th were still far south of the Marne in the region west of Sézanne.

[3] This solution was the one that Von Bülow would have preferred and that he apparently expected Von Kluck to adopt.

Though Von Kluck had expected that September 6th would be a day of relative repose for his 3rd and 9th Corps, both had instead been violently engaged against the French Fifth Army, which had advanced from the south.   To assure the security of the right flank of the II Army, Von Kluck had originally intended to leave these two corps where they were, placing them temporarily under Von Bülow's orders, and to defer the execution of Von Moltke's orders until the unlooked-for enemy advance had been checked ; but the receipt of Von Moltke's message in the early morning of the 7th threw a new light on the whole situation, and at 9 A.M. he sent Von Bülow a radio :

The 2nd, 4th and 4th Reserve Corps are engaged in a hard combat west of the lower Ourcq.   Where are the 3rd and 9th Corps ?   What is your situation ?

At almost the same time Von Bülow was sending a message that crossed Von Kluck's :

The II Army is continuing the battle.   So far no decision.   What is your situation ?   Reply urgent.

In spite of the knowledge thus gained that the II Army too was in action, Von Kluck determined to recall the 3rd and 9th Corps north of the Marne to unite his forces for a crushing blow against Maunoury.   Though he realized that this action necessarily entailed increasing the gap between the I and II Armies and adding to the difficulties of Von Bülow's right flank, he relied heavily upon the supposed inability of the British Army to exploit the advantage that lay open to it, trusting to the two cavalry corps to hold any British advance in check.   Two hours after his first message Von Kluck sent another :

Intervention of the 3rd and 9th Corps on the Ourcq immediately necessary.   The enemy is reinforcing seriously.   Please start both corps marching for La Ferté Milon and Crouy.

This communication left Von Bülow no choice but to accede reluctantly to his colleague's demand.   Convinced that the I Army must be in a situation of deadly peril, the commander of the II Army responded at once, and the 3rd and 9th Corps left the area where they had been fighting in liaison with the right wing of the II Army and started to march northward to take part in the Battle of the Ourcq.

Lack of adequate communications with G.H.Q. at Luxembourg

or with the Headquarters of the II Army at Montmort, obliged Von
Kluck on September 7th to take the decision that in its strategic consequences proved the most important of the campaign, without consulting either Von Moltke or Von Bülow.   It is entirely likely, however, that had he done so, the result would have been the same, for
in his determination to rob Peter to pay Paul, Von Kluck based his
decision upon a misconception which Von Moltke and Von Bülow
shared with him : that the British Army could not and would not
fight.   The development of the breach between Von Kluck's and
Von Bülow's Armies, the exploitation of which is the key to the
German defeat, may be traced primarily to the withdrawal of the
3rd and 9th Corps.

If Von Kluck could have been transported to Maunoury's Headquarters on the night of September 7th, he would have found much
to comfort him.   The 61st Reserve Division, which had given
ground at the close of the day on the northern extremity of the
French front, had continued its retreat in disorder as far as Nanteuil,
and to make matters worse, Sordet's Cavalry Corps, which had arrived on the extreme left of the Sixth Army, as usual in an exhausted
condition, had also seen fit to fall back through a mistaken notion
of its commander that he might thus gain rest for his men and horses.
With consternation the French Army Commander learned of these
movements, which had temporarily completely uncovered his Army's
northern flank, and he forthwith issued peremptory orders to remedy
the situation, sending both the Cavalry Corps and the 61st Reserve
Division back to their respective posts.[4]   In support of the Reserve
division and to stiffen its resistance, he also sent the 7th Division of
the 4th Army Corps (Boelle) to the left of his line.[5]

The transportation of a part of this division to the front during
the night of September 7th forms the basis of one of the most colourful stories of the war, the use of the Paris taxicabs.   The incident
has been exaggerated to legendary dimensions, and has been related
so many times with such a variety of elaborations and embellish-
ments, that in the mind of the general public, and apparently in the
view of some historians as well, it has come to be regarded as one
of the principal events not only of the Battle of the Marne, but of
the whole war.   The facts are simple and from a military point of
view relatively unimportant.   The staff, the services, the artillery and
the greater part of the infantry of the French 7th Division travelled

[4] The following morning Maunoury summarily relieved Sordet of his command, replacing him at the head of the Cavalry Corps with General Bridoux, commander of
the 5th Cavalry Division.
[5] The other division of the 4th Army Corps, the 8th Division, Galliéni had placed
on the south bank of the Marne, near Meaux, in liaison with the British Army to
cover and support its left flank.

from Paris to the battlefield of the Ourcq by rail in the conventional way, but to make sure that in case of a break-down in the railway line a part at least of the much-needed reinforcements would arrive, the Military Governor of Paris decided to send two infantry regiments by automobile. For this purpose 1200 of the 10,000 taxicabs of Paris were utilized, the majority of them requisitioned on the streets of the city by the police during the day of the 7th.

A fleet of 500 of these cabs made its way in mid-afternoon, empty, from the Invalides down the Champs Elysées and thence across the city, following the principal avenues and filling the population of the capital with astonishment and curiosity. At Gagny and other designated centres, the waiting infantry battalions embarked, and the cabs proceeded with their passengers in military formation — or as near to it as the temperament of Paris taxi-drivers would permit — through Dammartin to the vicinity of Nanteuil, where they arrived at daybreak after a journey of more than 50 kilometres. Whatever may be said of the efficiency of this method of conveyance, the arrival of troops on the line of battle in taxicabs constituted a unique contribution to the history of military transportation, and it seems not unfair to assume that the dramatic quality of the event, and above all its publicity value, did not escape the Military Governor of Paris or his astute collaborators.[6]

For the day of September 8th, Maunoury centred his attention upon an effort to outflank his adversary from the north, abandoning all thought of driving eastward to the Ourcq, which had been his principal objective for the preceding two days ; [7] but the arrival of the 7th Division did not suffice to turn the scales. Combined with the 61st Reserve Division under the orders of the commander of the 4th Army Corps, General Boelle, it succeeded in recovering substantially all the ground that the French reservists had relinquished the night before, but failed to make headway before Von Arnim's defensive positions which were reinforced during the afternoon by the arrival of the 6th Division of the German 3rd Corps (Von Lochow).

In the centre of the front, another French assault against the heights that offered access to the plateau of Trocy became so menacing that Von Linsingen felt compelled to call upon the 9th Cavalry Division of Von der Marwitz' Corps, assembled along the Marne, to rush to Von Gronau's aid, and Von Kluck likewise diverted the 5th Division from the 3rd Corps to bring support to his hard-pressed centre. The precautions proved unnecessary, however, for the French attack, like those that had preceded it, broke down before

[6] In *La véritable histoire des taxis de la Marne* (Chapelot, Paris, 1927), Commandant Carré has given a complete and authoritative account of this episode and of the use of taxicabs by the Military Government of Paris.
[7] See Joffre's General Instructions No. 7, Appendix XV (1).

the German artillery massed around Trocy, and though forced to abandon Etrépilly, which remained unoccupied between the lines, Von Gronau retained the heights to the east of it.

At the southern extremity of the front, Von Trossel found himself under constant pressure and threatened momentarily by an attack against his flank from the south bank of the Marne.   Availing himself of permission already granted by the Army Commander the evening before, he withdrew his 3rd Division from the positions it had defended for three days to the heights of Congis, evacuating Vareddes and destroying the Marne bridges that lay upon his left flank.

Despite minor advantages thus gained at several points by the French Sixth Army, September 8th ended indecisively.   In both armies, the losses suffered, the efforts expended and the confusion that had resulted, had brought the troops to the verge of ultimate exhaustion.   Neither fully realized the plight of the other, but each knew that its own position was critical in the extreme.

Though the German I Army had stood on the brink of disaster since the afternoon of September 5th, Von Kluck did not yet despair of snatching a last-minute victory, pinning his faith upon the newly arrived 3rd and 9th Corps for the final decisive attacks intended to end the resistance of Maunoury's Army, and upon the hardly less welcome reinforcement provided by the timely arrival, northwest of Nanteuil, of a brigade of the 4th Reserve Corps, which had been left nearly three weeks before as a garrison in Brussels.

The decision will be obtained tomorrow — Von Kluck's orders to his Army read — by an enveloping attack on the north wing under the orders of General von Quast (9th Corps, 6th Division, 4th Cavalry Division) starting from the region of Cuvergnon.

Late in the evening, he reported to Von Moltke on the situation of the I Army and his intentions for the next day :

The I Army again held its positions against superior forces west of the Ourcq on the front Antilly-Congis.   The 3rd and 9th Corps arrived in the afternoon on our right wing and will attack by envelopment early tomorrow.   The line of the Marne, Lizy-Nogent, is held by the 2nd Cavalry Corps (Von der Marwitz) and a mixed brigade against an attack debouching from Coulommiers.[8]   The right wing of the II Army has fallen back from Montmirail on Fontenelle.

Whatever opinion one may entertain of Von Kluck's conduct of his Army from a strategical stand-point, it is impossible not to ad-

_____

[8] A recognition of the increasing danger created by the British advance towards the Marne.   The mixed brigade referred to (two infantry regiments and an artillery detachment) was Kräwel's force which had been left along the Marne by the German 9th Corps.

mire the resolute confidence with which, after four days of desperate battle, he held to an unflinching determination to attain victory.

When Galliéni conferred with Maunoury at the latter's Post of Command at St. Soupplet on the afternoon of September 8th, both French commanders took a frankly gloomy view. For four days the French Sixth Army had dashed itself vainly against the German defensive positions centred on Trocy, only to be hurled back again and again by counter-attacks, and since the morning of the 6th, it had made negligible progress. Reports of columns marching north to join Von Kluck — in fact the German 3rd and 9th Corps — gave reason to believe that the enemy would soon be substantially reinforced. It seemed evident that Maunoury's role must necessarily be a defensive one, until the British advance towards the Marne, which was slowly but surely progressing, could produce its effect.

"It is essential," Galliéni wrote Maunoury on the evening of the 8th, "that tomorrow you maintain your positions and hold your ground with all your energy."

Realizing that the safety of Paris ultimately depended on the success of the Sixth Army, Galliéni unhesitatingly drew upon his only mobile forces to provide Maunoury with a second line of defence, for use in case retreat became unavoidable, and he established the 62nd Reserve Division, the Marine Brigade, two depot regiments of Zouaves and a brigade of Spahi cavalry along a line between Dammartin and Montgé. At the same time, with Joffre's permission, the 8th Division of the 4th Army Corps, hitherto protecting the British left flank along the Marne, was turned northward to strengthen Maunoury's Army.

At the close of the day Maunoury informed Joffre of his intention to remain on the defensive :

I have all my forces engaged on the front Champu-les Andelys-Betz. My enveloping manoeuvre to the north is no longer possible of execution by reason of the extension of the enemy's front as far as Thury and the wood 3 kilometres east of Cuvergnon. Important concentrations at Lizy-sur-Ourcq, May-en-Multien, Rouvres, Saint-Gongoulph, Neuilly-Saint-Front, (latter remains to be confirmed). I am resisting on my positions. If too sharply attacked, I shall refuse my left little by little, in such a way as to march later towards the north when the pressure against me has been relieved by the offensive of the British and the Fifth Army.

Have taken two flags and numerous prisoners ; heavy losses.

In a secret order, Maunoury prepared his subordinates for the possibility of a retreat towards Paris, and specified the positions to be occupied by the respective units of the French Sixth Army in case such a movement became necessary.

In summary, as the last and decisive day dawned on the field of the Ourcq, the tide seemed to have turned in the Germans' favour. Von Kluck adhered to his determination to renew the offensive which he expected would bring decisive success, while Maunoury had become committed to a definitely defensive attitude. Yet victory eluded the German I Army, despite the iron will of its commander and the heroic efforts of its troops, for it had paid too dearly for the advantage that it held. Developments elsewhere on the front, before Franchet d'Esperey and Sir John French, had already doomed the German armies to certain defeat.

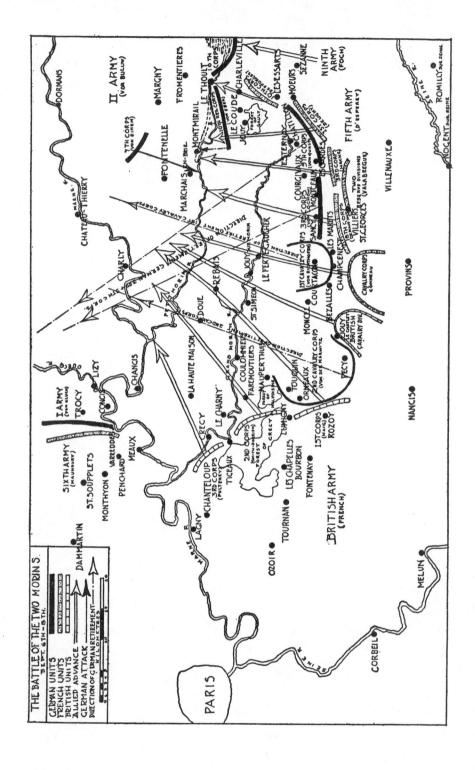

THE BATTLE OF THE TWO MORINS
SEPT. 6TH–9TH.

GERMAN UNITS
FRENCH UNITS
BRITISH UNITS
ALLIED ADVANCE
GERMAN ATTACK
DIRECTION OF GERMAN RETIREMENT

PARIS

MELUN

CORBEL

DAMMARTIN

SIXTH ARMY
(MAUNOURY)

ST. SOUPPLETS
MONTHYON
PENCHARD
VARREDDES
MEAUX
LIZY
CONGIS
TROCY

I ARMY
(VON CLUCK)

CHATEAU-THIERRY

DORMANS

MARGNY
FROMENTIERES

II ARMY
(VON BULOW)

7TH CORPS
(VON EINEM)

LE THOULT
CHARLEVILLE
MONTMIRAIL

LE COUDE
JOUY
FOREST

LES ESSARTS
MOEURS
SEZANNE

NINTH ARMY
(FOCH)

FONTENELLE
FONTENELLE

MARCHAIS-EN-BRIE

ESTERNAY
CHATILLON

COURGIVAUX
9TH CORPS
MONT FRU

3RD CORPS
DANS

LES MARETS
6TH CORPS
(VILLIERS)
ST. GEORGES

TWO DIVISIONS
(RESERVE DIVISIONS)
(VALABREGUE)

VILLENAUXE

FIFTH ARMY
(D'ESPEREY)

PROVINS

NANGIS

CRECY
LA HAUTE MAISON
DOUE
REBAIS

ST SIMEON
LE FERE-EN-TARDENOIS

CHAMPENE

BEZALLES

MONCEL
COULOMMIERS
FAREMOUTIERS
MAUPERTHUIS

TOUQUIN
ORMEAUX

CHOISY

VILLIERS

CAVALRY CORPS
CONNEAU

JOUY
BRITISH
CAVALRY DIV.

PECY

COULY

CHANCIS

LE CHARNY
CHANTELOUP
TICEAUX

2ND CORPS
(SMITH-DORRIEN)
FOREST
OF
CRECY

LES CHAPELLES
BOURBON
FONTENAY

LUMIGNY

1ST CORPS
(HAIG)
ROZOY

BRITISH ARMY
(FRENCH)

TOURNAN

OZOIR

CORBEL

ROMILLY SUR SEINE

NOGENT SUR SEINE

CHAPTER XXIX

THE BATTLE OF THE TWO MORINS

THE troops of the French Fifth Army received with high satisfaction Franchet d'Esperey's order announcing that at last the agonizing retreat had ended and the decisive moment, so long awaited, was at hand :

Tomorrow September 6th, the Fifth Army will attack the front of the German I Army, while the British and the Sixth Army will attack its flank and will threaten its retreat. . . It is important for each soldier to realize that the honour of France and the safety of our country depend upon the energy he brings to tomorrow's combat.

With its depleted ranks filled by reinforcements newly arrived from the depots, the Fifth Army gladly prepared for the struggle ahead. The rapidity of its retreat had brought the main body of the army almost to the Seine, and had resulted in a complete loss of contact with the German II Army, its opponent on the Sambre and at Guise-St. Quentin ; but two army corps, the 3rd and 9th, of Von Kluck's Army had kept doggedly on its traces, and at nightfall on September 5th still remained in contact with the outposts of Franchet d'Esperey's left wing. It was therefore against Von Kluck's left wing, rather than against Von Bülow, that the French expected to direct their efforts as Joffre's counter-offensive opened.

Wholly unsuspicious of any offensive intentions on the part of their adversary, the commanders of the German 3rd and 9th Corps planned to dedicate the day of September 6th to the execution of Von Kluck's orders, in accordance with Von Moltke's most recent General Directive. For the 3rd Corps (Von Lochow) this involved a short march northward as far as La Ferté Gaucher, and for Von Quast's 9th Corps a welcome day of rest in its positions near Esternay, pending the arrival of the 10th Reserve Corps (Von Eben) of Von Bülow's Army.

Some of the units of the German 3rd Corps were already beginning their march, while Von Quast's men were settling down in their cantonments to enjoy the promised repose, the first they had had since the opening of the campaign, when the artillery bombardment that presaged the advance of the French Fifth Army rudely broke their tranquillity.   Both corps stood to arms, and though it seemed to the Corps Commanders that this unexpected activity could hardly be more than a demonstration, possibly intended to cover the passage of the enemy's main body across the Seine, Von Lochow halted his retirement so as to cover the 9th Corps' right flank in case of need, while Von Quast sent out an aerial reconnaissance to ascertain, if possible, the enemy's intentions.

The explanation was not long deferred.   The French were no longer retreating, Von Quast's aviators reported, but columns estimated at an army corps or more were marching northward towards Esternay, heading for the front of the 9th Corps.   True to the offensive tradition that dominated the German army hardly less than the French, Von Quast ordered his corps forward to attack the advancing enemy.[1]

Along the whole front, from Sancy to Chatillon, the two German army corps were soon in contact with the three left wing corps of Franchet d'Esperey's Army.   Though completely taken by surprise, the Germans moved forward boldly to meet the French attack.   From noon until after dark, a fierce combat raged around Montceaux, where Von Lochow's infantry came to grips with De Maud'huy's 18th Corps and Pétain's 6th Division on its right, and it was not until late in the evening that the French at last occupied the village, flaming brightly from the bombardment of both artilleries.   Farther to the east, Mangin's 5th Division did not meet with equal success, for after occupying Courgivaux early in the afternoon, it was driven out by a series of counter-attacks that forced the French lines back two kilometres to the south as far as Escardes.   Around Chatillon, the French 1st Corps (Deligny) collided with the attack of Von Quast's 17th Division and battled inconclusively until dark, when the Germans, suddenly relaxing their grip, fell back to Esternay on the line of the Grand Morin River.

On the right of the French line, the 10th Corps (Defforges) supported by the 51st Reserve Division, advanced throughout the morning without opposition, for its line of march lay east of the sector held by the German 9th Corps. It arrived northeast of the Forest of Gault, on the line Jouy-La Recoude and as far east as Charle-

[1] On the morning of September 6th, the German 3rd Corps (Von Lochow) to the west occupied Sancy (5th Division) and Montceaux (6th Division), farther to the east, the 9th Corps (Von Quast) held Neuvy (18th Division) and Retourneloup (17th Division) near Esternay.   *Order of Battle of French Fifth Army*, from left to right (west to east) : Conneau's Cavalry Corps, in liaison with the British, 18th Corps (De Maud'huy), 3rd Corps (Hache), 1st Corps (Deligny), 10th Corps (Defforges) with 51st Reserve Division.   In reserve, group of 2 Reserve divisions (Valabrègue).

ville before coming in contact with the enemy. In obedience to orders from the Army Commander, the French 10th Corps had halted on the positions thus attained when a powerful attack launched by the German 10th Reserve Corps (Von Eben) [2] struck its line.

With no expectation of encountering the enemy during the day, Von Eben had been on his way to the positions assigned him by the Army Commander between Montmirail and Le Gault,[3] when word reached him that the 10th Corps (Von Emmich) on his left had met with serious resistance in the region Le Thoult-Soizy aux Bois.[4] To bring support to his neighbour, the German Corps Commander determined to disregard temporarily the objectives set for him by Von Bülow, and instead to deliver a blow against the left flank of the forces which were checking Von Emmich's advance. Crossing the Petit Morin River during the morning, Von Eben's two divisions, the 2nd Reserve Division of the Guard to the east and the 19th Reserve Division to the west, advanced towards the southeast, in a direction that brought them by early afternoon obliquely against the line held by the French 10th Corps between Jouy and Charleville. An engagement, carried on with the greatest vigour on both sides, drove back the French front during the afternoon an average of some five kilometres, to the southeastern edge of the Forest of Gault, though one brigade of the French 20th Division succeeded in retaining possession of Charleville.[5]

In the first day of battle, the French had advanced some five kilometres along the whole front of Franchet d'Esperey's Army, taking up the slack between the main bodies of the retreating and pursuing forces ; but the Germans had held stubbornly on their main line of resistance before the French 18th, 3rd and 1st Corps, and to the east had gained a distinct, though hardly decisive, advantage over Defforges' 10th Corps. Shortly after noon, when Franchet d'Esperey learned that his Army was in contact along its entire front with positions which the Germans were evidently resolved to defend, he ordered the advance to halt and his troops to entrench themselves

[2] Von Eben had replaced Count von Kirchbach in command of the 10th Reserve Corps on August 30th. In contrast to the manifold changes on the French side this was the only important shift in the German High Command during the campaign.

[3] Von Bülow's orders for the 6th assigned the following objectives to the German II Army : For the 7th Corps (right) Château Thierry-Fontenelle, for the 10th Reserve Corps, Montmirail-Le Gault, for the 10th Corps, Les Essarts-Moeurs, for the Guard, Gaye-Marigny le Grand.

[4] From the French 42nd Division on the extreme left of Foch's Ninth Army.

[5] The operations of the French 10th Army Corps from Sept. 6th–9th are followed in detail in Col. Valarché's monograph, *Le Combat du Petit Morin* (Berger-Levrault, Paris, 1929). The action of De Cadoudal's Brigade of the 20th Division in holding its ground at Charleville was of the greatest importance in sustaining the left wing of Foch's Ninth Army. See pg. 260.

solidly, substantially on the positions then held.   It was a fresh illustration of the instinctive understanding of the psychology of his
men that made the commander of the Fifth Army an outstanding
leader of troops.   Well aware of the terrible ordeal from which
they had only just emerged, he appreciated the importance of opening the new phase of operations with a success that would lend encouragement to further efforts, and conversely he understood the
unfortunate moral consequences of an initial reverse.   In the course
of the morning the army had advanced far enough without serious
loss to register clearly the fact that the long retreat had ended and
the advance begun.   Despite the importance of moving forward as
quickly as possible, it would not do to set the men a task beyond
their strength.   It was enough, if they could hold the ground already
won and could end the day feeling they had successfully carried out
the mission assigned them.   At nightfall, though the 3rd Corps had
been forced back from Courgivaux and the 1st Corps had not yet
reached Esternay, and despite the 10th Corps' loss of ground, a general feeling of satisfaction and confidence pervaded the French Fifth
Army that justified the wisdom of Franchet d'Esperey's course.   He
had taken a long step towards converting the depressed and dejected
force Lanrezac had turned over to him into an army confident of
its own power and convinced of its ability to conquer.   For the next
day, September 7th, the Army Commander ordered a renewal of
the offensive in the general direction of Montmirail, again refraining
from setting any specific objectives to be attained by the respective
units.

   To the High Command of the German I and II Armies the situation presented itself unfavourably, though the outcome of the combats south of the Grand Morin had, on the whole, been satisfactory.
All three army corps engaged had sustained heavy losses, and the
execution of Von Moltke's General Directive had been wholly dis-
rupted.   Moreover the state of affairs to the west contained serious
possibilities of danger.   There, Von Richthofen's and Von der Marwitz' cavalry divisions, instead of pushing forward in pursuit of a
retreating enemy, had been brought to bay by Conneau's French
Cavalry Corps and by the British, and a serious engagement had
been fought against the latter near Rozoy.   Von Kluck and Von
Bülow both felt deep anxiety for the security of the right flank of
their forces, left unprotected by the withdrawal of the 2nd and 4th
Army Corps north of the Marne.   Reports from the front were not
encouraging for a renewal of the offensive.   Von Eben's Corps in
particular had been sorely tried, and General von Susskind, commander of the 2nd Reserve Division of the Guard, had rendered a
pessimistic report to his Corps Commander :

The division is very exhausted.   Though still able to resist an attack, it is no longer in condition to continue its offensive.

In the light of this report and others like it, and on the insistence of Von Kluck, Von Bülow determined to withdraw the 3rd and 9th Corps, temporarily placed under his orders, as well as the 10th Reserve Corps of his own Army northward, behind the shelter of the Petit Morin River.   At 2 A.M. he notified Von Moltke by radio of his intentions.

In view of the contact with the enemy at Rozoy, the 3rd and 9th Corps are retiring behind the Petit Morin.   Left wing of the II Army [6] remains offensive.   Support by the III Army with all available forces immediately necessary.

Von Bülow's decision to withdraw the 3rd, 9th and 10th Reserve Corps behind the Petit Morin, a retreat of fifteen to twenty kilometres, *before* Von Kluck's order of the next morning recalling his two corps north of the Marne, is rarely emphasized and often not mentioned in either French or German accounts of the battle.   The reason is not far to seek, for it tends to negative the favourite German thesis that the action of Franchet d'Esperey's Army was a factor of negligible importance, and also to controvert the tendency of many French writers to minimize the importance of British intervention.   In fact, it seems to show that as a result of the joint action of the French Fifth Army and the British on September 6th, the commanders of the German right wing armies decided to withdraw a very substantial fraction of their forces between fifteen and twenty kilometres to the rear — a result by no means inconsiderable for the operations of one day.

In the last hours of darkness, the German 3rd and 9th Corps began their northward movement in accordance with Von Bülow's orders, leaving behind them only rear-guard detachments at Sancy and Esternay ; but though the retreat of the two corps of Von Kluck's Army was accomplished without serious loss, Von Eben was not so fortunate.

A battalion of the 19th Reserve Division, which had moved into position after nightfall along the southern boundary of the Forest of Gault, near Guebarré Farm, did not receive the order to withdraw, and at daybreak remained isolated, without artillery support and with no hope of reinforcement, while its comrades on the other side of the forest marched unconcernedly northward.   The battalion commander had chosen his position in the dark, without adequate

[6] The Guard (Von Plettenberg) and the 10th Corps (Von Emmich) fighting with Von Hausen against Foch's Army.

knowledge of the exact position of the enemy, and he had failed to
observe the farm buildings some five hundred yards to the west which
completely dominated the shallow trench the battalion dug for its
protection. In one of these buildings the French installed a machine-
gun group of six guns, which opened fire when daylight revealed
the long line of grey figures, lying unsuspecting and all but helpless
in their trench, sweeping the German position from end to end.
With a concentrated bombardment, the French artillery seconded the
efforts of the machine-gunners. Gallantly but futilely attempting to
reply, the luckless battalion lay pinned to the ground under a storm
of fire that beat upon it mercilessly from front and flank. A few
endeavoured to escape to the woods, only to be shot down like rab-
bits as they crossed the open space between the trench and the edge
of the forest. Soon white handkerchiefs tied to the muzzles of rifles
began to appear above the parapet of the trench, but the French fire
continued unheeding and unrelenting. When at length it ceased,
six officers and 87 men, uninjured or only slightly wounded, crawled
out to surrender, while more than 450 lay dead or helpless in the
trench.[7]

The combat or, more accurately, the massacre of Guebarré Farm
constituted the only noteworthy action along the front of Franchet
d'Esperey's Army during the day of September 7th. Meeting opposition only from isolated detachments left to harass them, the French
moved forward, but they advanced cautiously and only the 1st
Corps made any substantial progress beyond the Grand Morin River.
It was not until the following afternoon, September 8th, that the
main body of the French Fifth Army again gained contact with the
enemy. By that time the German 3rd and 9th Corps, marching
towards the Marne in response to Von Kluck's urgent appeal, were
far away, and only one division [8] of the German 7th Corps (Von
Einem) and the 10th Reserve Corps (Von Eben) remained along
the Petit Morin, before Montmirail and to the west of it, to oppose
the advance of Franchet d'Esperey's three army corps [9] and two Reserve divisions.

Frontal attacks during the afternoon made little impression against
the German positions of Montmirail, but farther to the west De
Maud'huy forced the passage of the Petit Morin and by a night at-

[7] The German unit was the 3rd Battalion of the 74th Reserve Infantry Regiment,
with its Machine-gun Company, the 5th Company of the 73rd Reserve Infantry Regiment and a section of the 10th Pioneer Battalion.

[8] The 13th Division. The other division, the 14th, Von Bülow's Army Reserve,
had been sent to support the left wing of the II Army in its battle against Foch. The
13th Division itself comprised only one brigade, the other brigade having been left
behind to besiege Maubeuge.

[9] The 10th Corps on Franchet d'Esperey's right had turned to the support of Foch's
Army, and its operations on September 8th and 9th were linked to the Ninth Army
rather than the Fifth.

tack broke the lines of the German 7th Corps and captured Marchais-en-Brie.

If it were necessary to select a single spot on the whole battlefield of the Marne and say, "There the battle was won," it might well be the little village of Marchais-en-Brie, two kilometres northwest of Montmirail.   In itself the action was a minor one, though brilliant in tactical execution.   A night bombardment, suddenly unleashed — an unconventional procedure at this stage of the war — threw terror into a few infantry companies of the German 7th Corps and opened the way to a brigade of the French 36th Division [10] that rushed boldly forward and established itself north of the town before the enemy could recover.

The immediate consequence of the capture of Marchais-en-Brie was to render Montmirail indefensible, for the positions of the German 10th Reserve Corps were thenceforth completely flanked and dominated from the west.   But the strategic consequences were much more far-reaching for both the German I and II Armies.   With his right flank, already inadequately protected, now further jeopardized, Von Bülow ordered his 7th and 10th Reserve Corps to fall back to the line Margny-Le Thoult, a position running from north to south.   It was a retreat of ten kilometres towards the east, which left the right wing of the German II Army facing west instead of south, and it ended all further possibility of closing the breach between Von Bülow and Von Kluck.   Even a retreat by the I Army on Château Thierry would no longer suffice, and the path to the Marne lay open to the left wing corps of Franchet d'Esperey's Army.[11]

The right flank of Von Bülow's Army was no longer threatened, it was turned.   Nothing but an immediate victory by the left wing against the French Ninth Army could save it from defeat, and though Von Bülow viewed the operations of the German 10th Corps and the Guard with more satisfaction than events on his right wing, it was still a far cry to decisive victory.

---

[10] The 18th and 49th Infantry Regiments.
[11] On the operations of the French Fifth Army, see Col. Grasset's *La Bataille des Deux Morins* (Payot, Paris, 1934).

CHAPTER XXX

THE BRITISH MARCH INTO THE BREACH

WHILE Maunoury's attacks compelled Von Kluck to recall his army corps, one after another, north of the Marne, and Franchet d'Esperey's advance forced Von Bülow to fall back, first to the Petit Morin and finally farther to the east, the British Army marched steadily into the ever-widening breach that was developing between the German I and II Armies.

True to his word, Sir John French halted the retreat of the British Army and ordered it forward on the morning of September 6th ; but it began its march from the general front Tournan-Fontenoy-Rozoy, fifteen to twenty kilometres behind the line from which Joffre had hoped it would start. The withdrawal of the German 2nd Corps during the night of September 5th and of the 4th Corps the following morning, left only two cavalry divisions [1] of Von der Marwitz' Corps, supported by four battalions of Jäger infantry and a cyclist battalion, to oppose the British advance, a force of hardly more than 10,000 men. Farther to the east, the German 1st Cavalry Corps (Von Richthofen) covered Von Bülow's right flank opposite the front held by Conneau's French Cavalry Corps.

Assuming that the Allied armies would continue their retreat, both German cavalry commanders had offensive intentions for September 6th. To cover the retirement of Von Kluck's 2nd and 4th Army Corps, Von der Marwitz proposed to push forward south of the Aubetin, a small tributary of the Grand Morin, to attack Lumigny and Rozoy, leaving the passages of the Aubetin and the Grand Morin guarded by his Jäger battalions. Von Richthofen, under Von Bülow's orders, had a more ambitious mission, to press forward in pursuit of the enemy, south of the Seine, to cut the main line of the Paris-Lyons-Méditerranée Railway between Melun and Nogent-sur-Seine and to send out reconnaissances in the direction of Caen, Alençon, Le Mans, Tours and Bourges, as Von Moltke had prescribed in his General Directive of the 5th.

[1] The 2nd and 9th Cavalry Divisions. The 4th Cavalry Division, the third of Von der Marwitz' Corps, was engaged against the French Sixth Army north of the Marne.

The British 3rd and 2nd Army Corps, respectively on the left and centre of Sir John French's line, encountered no opposition as they methodically began their march on the morning of the 6th; but on the British right Haig's 1st Corps ran almost immediately into Von der Marwitz' cavalry, attacking between Vaudoy and Pécy, just east of Rozoy.   Before a vigorous onslaught, the British successively abandoned Pécy, Touquin and Pezarches, and Haig, fearing enemy concentrations in the ominous Forests of Creçy and Malvoisine on his left, halted his advance, waiting for Smith-Dorrien's 2nd Corps to close in on his left near Lumigny.   When at last, upon Sir John French's insistence, Haig resumed his advance in mid-afternoon, he found the German positions evacuated, for in the meantime Von der Marwitz had learned of the enemy's strength and had fallen back behind the Aubetin.

In the engagement around Rozoy, Von der Marwitz fully attained his tactical objective, for he enabled Von Arnim's 4th Corps to draw off towards the north unperceived and unmolested.   Moreover, although only a fraction of the German 2nd Cavalry Corps had been engaged, it had sufficed to check the march of the British 1st Army Corps, and nightfall found Haig still twelve kilometres from the positions which the British Commander in Chief had expected him to reach.   Nevertheless, the British had displayed an aggressive attitude quite inconsistent with Von Kluck's preconceived notion of their capabilities.

"The I Army is fighting on two fronts," Von Kluck's Chief of Staff, General von Kuhl, told Von der Marwitz' liaison officer, when the latter presented himself at Charly to receive instructions for the day of the 7th.   "The 2nd Army Corps and the 4th Reserve Corps are attacked by an enemy debouching from Paris; the 3rd and 9th Army Corps are fighting south of Montmirail; the 4th Army Corps is on its way to the Paris front.   The mission of the 2nd Cavalry Corps is to prevent the enemy from advancing between Meaux and La Ferté Gaucher."

Thenceforward Von der Marwitz had a purely defensive mission: to hold the British in check until the I Army could win a decisive victory over Maunoury.   Von Kluck hoped to combine the efforts of Von der Marwitz' two divisions with those of the two divisions of Von Richthofen's Corps, and to this end he communicated with Von Bülow, suggesting that a common mission be assigned the two cavalry corps, but though the commander of the German II Army at first agreed in principle, no effective co-operation resulted, for when the 3rd and 9th Army Corps withdrew from Von Bülow's right on the morning of the 7th, he used the 1st Cavalry Corps almost wholly for the protection of his own Army's flank, with the result that in the succeeding days little contact existed between the two German cavalry corps.

On September 6th, while Von der Marwitz was fighting the British around Rozoy, Von Richthofen, in conformity with Von Bülow's orders, endeavoured to push southward towards Provins ; but one division [2] soon ran against strong French forces moving northward from Villiers St. Georges [3] and became involved in an engagement that checked its further progress and held its attention throughout the day. Farther to the west, the Guards Cavalry Division at first met better success, driving the French 10th Cavalry Division back from Courtaçon, but soon after, enemy resistance proved too strong and it halted for the night. The line attained by the Guards Cavalry Division at nightfall on September 6th, Maretz-Champcenest-Bezalles, marked the extreme southern limit of the German invasion of France during the war.

With the retirement of Von Bülow's line back of the Petit Morin, during the night of the 6th, Von Richthofen's mission, like Von der Marwitz', became a purely defensive one, the protection of the flank of the II Army, left exposed by the withdrawal of Von Kluck's two army corps, and all further thought of a reconnaissance south of the Seine was perforce abandoned.

When Sir John French's Army again moved forward on the morning of September 7th, it encountered little opposition and apart from cavalry skirmishes at Moncel, Faujus and Le Charnois the day passed uneventfully on the British front. Heartened by the arrival of replacements from England, the men tramped along the road in high good humour, singing "It's a long way to Tipperary," in a mood very different from that of the woe-begone army of a week before. But though Von der Marwitz made no serious effort to defend the crossings of the Grand Morin, which the British 2nd and 3rd Corps had passed by nightfall, the army as a whole moved slowly and with needless caution. Sir John French, weighted with age and conscious of his great responsibility, was no longer the dashing cavalry leader who had pressed to the relief of Kimberley fourteen years before, and despite reports brought by his aviators of German columns moving northward and of open country ahead, he remained assailed by doubts and disturbed by Murray's skepticism.

Actually, our own troops, though the men were very keen, moved absurdly slowly — General Charteris, then Chief of Haig's Intelligence Service, has written — and D. H. (Douglas Haig) spent the day going from one Divisional H.Q. to another to try to urge them forward. The

[2] The 5th Cavalry Division.
[3] The left wing of the French 18th Corps (De Maud'huy).

cavalry were the worst of all, for they were right behind the infantry. This was gall and wormwood to him, for he had always been first and foremost a cavalry officer.[4]

By nightfall on the 7th, Gough's cavalry brigades had entered Rebais, Pulteney's 3rd Corps had crossed the Grand Morin and had arrived in the vicinity of La Haute Maison, Smith-Dorrien held Coulommiers and a bridge-head northeast of it with the 2nd Corps, but Haig, on the Army right, had not yet crossed the Grand Morin, remaining south of the river between Jouy and St. Simeon, and Allenby's Cavalry Division was likewise south of the river near Choisy.

With the French Commander in Chief urging haste for the benefit of Maunoury's hard-pressed Army, the British made somewhat better speed the following day, and by noon on the 8th had arrived at the Petit Morin. There, however, Von der Marwitz made a stand in a determined effort to halt their progress.

"The ground was ideally suited to a rear-guard action," the British Official History states, "and the enemy's positions were well-chosen and most skilfully and gallantly defended."

In the face of staunch opposition, the British succeeded in forcing a passage of the river and in gaining some ground beyond it, but in the late afternoon a torrential rain ended operations for the day before even advance-guards could reach the banks of the Marne.[5] The British were not yet in position to lend Maunoury effective aid, though from the outskirts of La Ferté-sous-Jouarre Pulteney's heavy artillery brought the southern extremity of Von Kluck's positions north of the Marne under its fire. The British bombardment, however, constituted a threat and a warning to the Germans, rather than an actual danger.

Though Sir John French's advance during the three days from September 6th to 8th did not fully correspond to the possibilities that lay open to him, his Army had nevertheless reached a position just south of the Marne, where on the decisive day it held the strategic key to the battle. In not unnatural anxiety for the fate of Maunoury's Army, bitter criticism of the slowness of the British march emanated from Galliéni's Headquarters in Paris,[6] and these criticisms have been reflected, somewhat unfairly, by many writers since. It is undeniable that though out-numbering the opposing enemy forces in a ratio of almost 10 to 1, the British consumed three days in covering a distance of barely twenty-five miles ; but it must be remembered that Franchet d'Esperey's Fifth French Army, on

---

[4] Brigadier-General J. Charteris, *At G.H.Q.* (Cassell, London, 1932).
[5] See Joffre's message to French, Appendix XV (4).
[6] See Appendix XV (2), message from Galliéni to Joffre.

the British right, moved on September 7th and 8th with almost equal caution towards the Petit Morin, and in particular, that Conneau's cavalry, though virtually unopposed, constantly lagged behind Allenby.

On the evening of September 8th, Von der Marwitz made ready to defend the line of the Marne, with the aid of Kräwel's mixed brigade left behind by Von Quast's 9th Corps. The British advance into the gap between the German I and II Armies had produced a situation that made a decision a matter, not of days, but of hours. Both German armies were in analogous situations : for Von Kluck, it had become imperative to defeat Maunoury before the British could break down Von der Marwitz' resistance and strike the German I Army's left flank ; Von Bülow's problem was to defeat Foch, with Von Hausen's aid, before Franchet d'Esperey could exploit the dangerous situation created by the retirement of the II Army's right wing. The fate of both German armies, the result of the campaign, and indeed the outcome of the war itself, depended upon whether Maunoury and Foch could hold their ground, and upon what use the Allies could make of the breach in the German front that had opened before them.[7]

[7] In a remarkable series of articles : *La défense de la brèche Kluck-Bülow par les corps de cavalerie Marwitz et Richthoven ;* French Revue de Cavalerie, May–June 1932, to November–December 1933, Lieut.-Col. Pugens has dealt with the operations of the British and the left wing of the French Fifth Army and of the German forces opposed to them.

CHAPTER XXXI

THE MARSHES OF ST. GOND

THE French Ninth Army formed the pivot of the Allied left wing manoeuvre, and the results Joffre hoped to obtain from the offensives of the Sixth and Fifth Armies and the advance of the British depended in large measure upon Foch's ability to stand fast.

On the morning of September 6th, Foch's line of battle [1] faced east of north from La Villeneuve to Sommesous. On his extreme left, the zone of action of the 42nd Division was linked to that of the 10th Army Corps on the plateau of Brie, a broken country of woods, small hills and cultivated fields, sprinkled with villages and farms. In the centre, the Marshes of St. Gond, a broad belt of swamp land in which the Petit Morin River rises, extended from east to west for 19 kilometres, with an average width of 3 kilometres. Two main highways flank the marshes at either extremity and five lesser roads and three foot-paths cross them from north to south, but they are otherwise impassable, forming a military obstacle of the first importance. The heights of Mondemont and Allemant dominate the marshes from their southeastern corner and also overlook the great Catalaunic plain which stretches eastward for almost sixty kilometres, unbroken save for the eminence of the Mont Août. The positions of Foch's right wing extended across these barren, chalky flats, east of the Marshes of St. Gond, a region ideal for infantry manoeuvres and practice marches, but difficult to defend in war, for it has little cover and few observatories. The beds of numerous small streams, dry in September from the summer heat, cut across it, but have only mediocre value either as obstacles or as protection, and the few villages, with houses of fragile construction, offer poor possibilities as centres of resistance. Only the town of Fère Champenoise, somewhat larger and more solidly built than its neighbours, constitutes a useful rallying point.

It is a region rich in military history, for here, fifteen hundred

---

[1] Order of Battle of French Ninth Army, from left to right (west to east): 42nd Division, 9th Corps (Dubois), 11th Corps (Eydoux), 9th Cavalry Division. In reserve, behind the 9th Corps, 52nd Reserve Division and behind the 11th Corps, 60th Reserve Division, and on September 7th, the 18th Division. Army H.Q.: Plancy.

years ago, the common ancestors of the French and the Germans together turned back the hordes of Attila, and in the last century, the
Emperor Napoleon, at last brought to bay by the combined armies
of Europe, fought his brilliant Campaign of 1814. Now, a century
later, a new chapter was destined to be added, as Foch turned his
Army to face the advancing enemy.

To fulfil the primary role which Joffre had assigned to the Ninth
Army, the protection of Franchet d'Esperey's right flank, Foch as-
signed an offensive mission to his 42nd Division, while the 9th Corps
(Dubois) in the centre stood its ground north of the Marshes of
St. Gond and the 11th Corps (Eydoux), on the Army right, likewise
remained on the defensive between Morains-le-Petit and Lenharée.

The extreme right of the French Ninth Army seemed a particularly vulnerable point, for a distance of nearly twenty kilometres
separated the right of the 11th Corps from the nearest unit of De
Langle's Fourth Army to the east.   Only the 9th Cavalry Division
was available to fill this gap until the reinforcement of De Langle's
Army by the arrival of the 21st Corps (Legrand-Girarde), then on
its way from Lorraine.   As events proved, this situation which at
the time seemed fraught with danger, need not have caused Foch
undue concern, for a breach almost exactly corresponding to the one
in the French front existed in the line of the German III Army, by
reason of the necessity in which Von Hausen found himself to di-
vide his forces in order to lend aid to the Duke of Wurtemburg on
his right.

The memoirs of Baron von Hausen [2] reveal him as a guileless
soldier, with an elemental faith in the righteousness of his cause, a
trustful belief in the efficiency and sincerity of the German military
hierarchy, and an inordinate respect for royal personages.   This
combination of qualities, admirable enough in their place, had made
Von Hausen an easy mark throughout the campaign for the more
subtle and ambitious Von Bülow and for the royal Duke who commanded the German IV Army.   Again and again, Von Hausen had
displayed a spirit of co-operation unique among the German Army
Commanders, turning aside obligingly to left and right in response
to appeals for support from his neighbours, and expressing no more
than hurt surprise when his own similar requests met blunt refusals.
Invariably Von Hausen's eager willingness to comply with the wishes
of his imperious colleagues had operated to the disadvantage of his
own Army, and occasionally, as on the Sambre, had seriously preju-
diced the German strategy.   It seems difficult to say whether the III
Army Commander's weakness resulted from temperamental over-
affability, or from fear of the consequences that might flow from an

[2] *Erinnerungen an den Marnefeldzug* (Kohler, Leipzig, 1920).

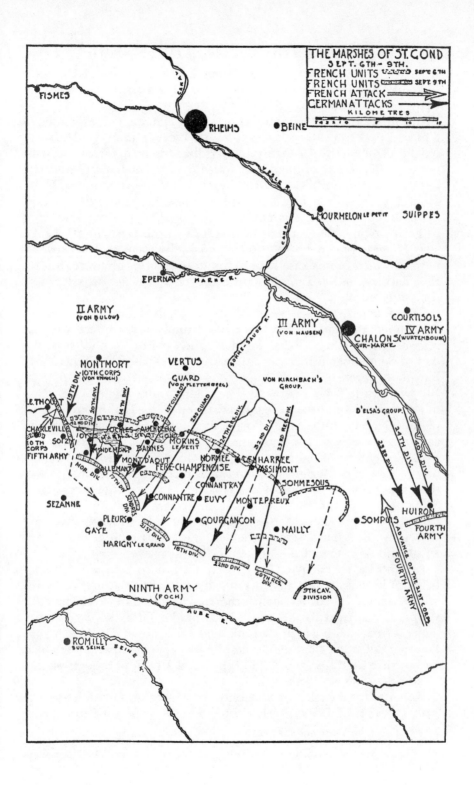

THE MARSHES OF ST. GOND
SEPT. 6TH - 9TH.
FRENCH UNITS ········ SEPT 6TH
FRENCH UNITS ▬▬▬▬ SEP 9TH
FRENCH ATTACK ➡
GERMAN ATTACKS ➡
KILOMETRES

FISHES

RHEIMS

BEINE

MOURMELON LE PETIT   SUIPPES

EPERNAY   MARNE R.

II ARMY
(VON BULOW)

III ARMY
(VON HAUSEN)

COURTISOLS

IV ARMY
(WURTEMBOURG)

CHALONS
SUR-MARNE

MONTMORT
16TH DIV. 10TH CORPS
(VON EMMICH)   20TH DIV.

VERTUS

GUARD
(VON PLETTENBERG)

VON KIRCHBACH'S
GROUP.

1ST GUARD   2ND GUARD

D'ELSA'S GROUP.

LE THOULT

CHARLEVILLE
10TH CORPS   SOIZY
FIFTH ARMY

OYES   JOCHES   AULNIZEUX
MAROLS   ST GOND   MORINS
BANNES   LE PETIT
MONDEMENT   MONT D'AOUT
ALLEMANT   FERE-CHAMPENOISE
MOR. DIV.   17TH DIV.
NORMEE
CONNANTRAY
ST PRIX   LE CONNANTRE
DIV.   EUVY

24TH DIV.   23RD RES. DIV.

LENHARREE   VASSIMONT

SOMMESOUS

MONTEPREUX

34TH DIV.   40TH DIV.

HUIRON

FOURTH
ARMY

SOMPUIS

SEZANNE

PLEURS

GAYE

MARIGNY LE GRAND

21ST DIV.

18TH DIV.

GOURGANCON

MAILLY

ADVANCE OF THE 21ST CORPS
FOURTH ARMY

22ND DIV.   32ND DIV.

NINTH ARMY
(FOCH)

AUBE R.

22ND DIV.

60TH RES.
DIV.

9TH CAV.
DIVISION

ROMILLY
SUR SEINE   SEINE R.

impolitic resistance by a Saxon general to the wishes of the most influential of Prussian commanders and of a scion of the reigning house of Wurtemburg.

In a final display of neighbourliness, Von Hausen had responded to a new appeal from the 8th Corps (Von Tschepe und Weidenbach) on the right of the IV Army by dividing his own forces into two groups, joining one of them, the 19th Corps (Von Laffert) and one division of the 12th Corps, to the Duke of Wurtemburg's battle around Vitry-le-François, and sending the other, the 12th Reserve Corps and the other division of the 12th Corps, against the right wing of Foch's Army.   As a result of this split in the German III Army, Von Hausen was in no position to take advantage of Foch's weakness, of which in any case he appears to have been unaware, but on the contrary, he lived in constant dread of a French attack through the same breach.

The Saxon Army had rested south of Châlons during the day of September 5th and as a result had virtually lost contact with its retreating adversary, so that for the right wing of Foch's Army, the day of September 6th passed in relative calm ; but the centre and left of the French Ninth Army stood directly in the path of Von Bülow's two left wing corps.[8]   The night before General von Emmich, the conqueror of Liége, had mapped the southward march of the German 10th Army Corps, fixing Les Essarts and Sézanne as the objectives of his 19th and 20th Divisions respectively, and Von Plettenberg, Commander of the Guard, had similarly designated Gaye and Marigny-le-Grand as the respective destinations of the 1st and 2nd Divisions of the Guard.[4]   Early in the morning of September 6th, the two German army corps, attacking resolutely under the impression that they had to deal only with an unusually tenacious rear-guard, struck the left and centre of Foch's Ninth Army and soon forced the French to the defensive.

Around La Villeneuve, Grossetti's 42nd French Division, far from being able to open the way to Franchet d'Esperey's Army, found itself in serious difficulties against the 19th Division of Von Emmich's Corps, and turned to the 10th Corps of the Fifth Army for help. The obstinacy with which De Cadoudal's Brigade of the French 20th Division defended Charleville, despite its exposed situation, enabled Grossetti to hold his ground, and the 42nd Division, though unable to advance, was not forced back.

North of the Marshes of St. Gond, the Moroccan Division and the 17th Division of Dubois' 9th Corps came to grips with the enemy

_____
[8] The 10th Army Corps and the Guard.
[4] In view of German claims of complete victory, it seems worthy of note that on the afternoon of September 9th, when the battle ended, none of these objectives had yet been reached.

even before they had succeeded in reaching the positions Foch had assigned them. By noon both had fallen back to the southern border of the marshes, between Oyes and Bannes, and Foch had no choice but to resign himself to a defensive attitude in the centre of his Army, ordering the 9th Corps to hold its positions and to "maintain close, absolute, indisputable liaison" with the 42nd Division on its left and with the 11th Corps on its right.

Contrary to legendary accounts, which depict the German Guard as caught floundering in the morasses of St. Gond under the French artillery fire and hurled back with staggering loss, neither the Guard nor the 10th Corps made any serious effort to follow the Moroccans and the 17th Division across the marshes. Weary and disorganized after the morning's combat, the Germans were satisfied to consolidate their positions on the northern bank, and only isolated patrols attempted further progress.

In the substance of its results, September 7th became a repetition of the preceding day. Again around La Villeneuve, Soizy and north of Mondemont, the French 42nd and Moroccan Divisions exchanged blow for blow with the German 10th Corps, meeting every attack with a counter-attack no less violent, and losing ground for the moment only to retake it soon afterwards. Though at nightfall the Germans held Soizy and Oyes, at the western extremity of the marshes, Grossetti still occupied La Villeneuve, with the French 10th Corps at Charleville on his left.

On Foch's right, two Saxon divisions of Von Hausen's Army, with the Guard supporting them, pressed against Eydoux's 11th Corps, but their attacks made little progress and the French succeeded in maintaining their principal positions. Nevertheless, disturbing signs of weakness began to appear in Eydoux's Corps which led Foch to place the 18th Division, newly arrived from De Castelnau's Army in Lorraine, behind its front in reserve. Through a combination of errors, the reinforcements so provided took their place immediately behind the line of combat without adequate provision for liaison and apparently, in some instances, without notice to the front-line units of the arrival of new forces back of them. The unfortunate results became apparent the next morning.

In the centre, where the marshes separated the opposing lines, both sides limited themselves to long-range artillery duels, and it seemed evident to Commandant Jette, the Chief of Staff of the 17th French Division, that both Von Emmich and Von Plettenberg were concentrating their efforts at the extremities of the marshes, holding the positions immediately to the north only by weak detachments supported by artillery. This conviction led him to urge upon his Division Commander the desirability of a reconnaissance in force along the northern edge of the marshes, and General Moussy, some-what reluctantly, consented to allow an infantry company to attempt the crossing.   Almost immediately a vigorous fire halted its progress and drove it back ; but Jette persisted.   Taking three companies of the 90th Infantry under his personal command, he led them across the marshes and into the village of Aulnizeux on the northern bank, driving its defenders out in hand-to-hand combat ; but German reinforcements, hastily summoned, counter-attacked, forcing the French back to Bannes, whence they had started, leaving the Divisional Chief of Staff dead on the field.

This brief and apparently unsuccessful excursion provided a diversion that relieved to some extent the pressure against the French 11th Corps, but it had another and far more important effect upon the general situation.   Jette had been right in his estimate, and his impromptu move against Aulnizeux called the attention of the two German Corps Commanders to a serious weakness in the centre of their front.   Fearing that a more serious effort by the French might jeopardize their positions to the east and west, Von Emmich and Von Plettenberg persuaded Von Bülow to employ the 14th Division to fill the gap.   The Army Commander had previously decided to restore this division, theretofore in Army Reserve, to the 7th Corps (Von Einem) to which it belonged, in order to strengthen his right wing, and it was already on the march towards the west, but as a result of Jette's initiative, the 14th Division retraced its steps during the night of September 7th, arriving the following morning to take its place between the 10th Corps and the Guard along the northern boundary of the Marshes of St. Gond.   Though this decision compelled the French Ninth Army to face an additional enemy division, it left Von Einem, commander of the German 7th Corps, with only one brigade of the 13th Division to cover Von Bülow's right flank and the weakness contributed not a little to De Maud'huy's success at Marchais-en-Brie the following night.

As darkness brought the second day of battle to a close, Foch viewed the situation optimistically in his report to the Commander in Chief :

On the front of the Ninth Army, the troops have maintained their positions without difficulty.   The enemy offensive carried two positions (Vassimont and an isolated farm) which were re-taken during the evening.

The commanders of the German II and III Armies differed in their estimates of the situation.   Filled with anxiety by the withdrawal of Von Kluck's two corps, Von Bülow resolved to abandon the offensive that Von Emmich had hitherto carried on west of the marshes, and to recall the 10th Corps behind the Petit Morin where it could lend support to the defence of the positions of Montmirail. Despite the Corps Commander's protest, the German 10th Corps was compelled to abandon during the night the ground it had won at heavy cost during the day, evacuating Soizy and Oyes, and falling back between Le Thoult and Joches.

Von Hausen on the other hand made aggressive plans. Though without precise information as to developments at other points along the front, the commander of the III Army knew of Von Bülow's successive retirements and concluded, though no explanation had been vouchsafed him, that they must have resulted from the action of French forces debouching from Paris, as Von Moltke's General Directive had warned. With a surprisingly just appreciation of the general situation in view of the meagre information at his disposal, Von Hausen perceived that a rapid decision on his own front would provide the best possible response to the enemy's manoeuvre, and decided upon vigorous action for the day of the 8th.

In two days of inconclusive fighting the French artillery had already taken heavy toll among the Saxon infantry, and to avoid its devastating effects, Von Hausen ordered a surprise attack in the last hour before dawn, conducted without artillery preparation, and pressed at the point of the bayonet as far as the French artillery emplacements. When General von Hoeppner, Chief of Staff of the III Army, broached the plan to Von Plettenberg, and asked for the co-operation of the Guard, it seemed to Von Plettenberg fantastic. An orthodox Prussian soldier, the commander of the Guard instinctively mistrusted any scheme of Saxon origin. The operation Von Hoeppner suggested was well enough for a raid by a few companies, he thought, but wholly unsuitable on the front of four divisions against objectives four kilometres away. Nevertheless, Von Hausen stuck to his unconventional project, and at 3 o'clock in the morning, the German infantry, with fixed bayonets and unloaded rifles, advanced by moonlight against the French 11th Corps.[5]

Completely surprised, the French 21st and 22nd Divisions were swept back by the unexpected assault, falling in confusion into the midst of the 18th Division immediately behind them and carrying it with them in disorderly flight. For a time it seemed that the whole right wing of the French Ninth Army had collapsed beyond redemption. Capturing 28 guns [6] and carrying the villages of

[5] The Saxon 32nd Division and 23rd Reserve Division, and the 2nd Division of the Guard, all grouped under the orders of General von Kirchbach attacked according to Von Hausen's plan. Out of deference to Von Plettenberg's objections, the 1st Division of the Guard did not attack until half an hour later, at 3:30 A.M.

[6] These guns, mostly taken from the French 22nd Division, were not removed from the field and were recaptured when the French advanced three days later.

Sommesous and Connantray, and finally Fère Champenoise itself, the Saxons and the Guard advanced a full five kilometres before the momentum of their drive slackened.   But though three French divisions had been temporarily placed beyond the possibility of organized resistance, the Germans did not lack opposition.   At many points, officers and men of all arms and of different units banded together behind hastily improvised defences, resisting desperately and inflicting heavy losses on their assailants.   Yet it was not the courageous self-sacrifice of these isolated groups that at last halted the German advance, nor the timely intervention of the artillery of the 52nd Reserve Division to the west, nor the fierce energy with which the French officers strove to restore order ; rather it was the result of long days of marching followed by two days of uninterrupted combat that had brought the German infantry to the limit of human endurance, and their advance halted of its own accord, before the ridge south of the main highway, running through Fère Champenoise and Connantray, and on the southern outskirts of Montepreux.

Von Hausen had gained an incontestable victory over the right wing of the French Ninth Army, and the arrival of the Saxon 24th Reserve Division, which had been delayed by the siege of Givet and had only just rejoined the III Army, gave rise to legitimate hopes for the next day ; but he had not yet attained the decisive result he sought.   Though three French Active divisions and one Reserve division had been reduced to little more than remnants, the front of Foch's Army remained unbroken.   On the contrary, late in the afternoon, elements of the 52nd Reserve Division acting on Foch's peremptory orders counter-attacked Fère Champenoise, and though the attempt failed, some fractions penetrated the German lines and even entered the town.[7]

In the meanwhile, the left wing of the French Ninth Army had also been in action since early morning.   Learning of the success obtained by the Saxons and the Guard, Von Emmich had not been able to reconcile himself to the passive attitude Von Bülow had prescribed, and the German 10th Corps again advanced in an effort to recover the ground it had voluntarily abandoned during the night. Against stout opposition from Grossetti's Division, aided on its flanks by the Moroccans and by the French 10th Corps of Franchet d'Esperey's Army, Von Emmich made little progress, and night found him still short of Soizy and Mondemont, the objectives he had set.

In the centre, however, the Germans had obtained a measure of

---

[7] For a description of this counter-attack, see Commandant Bienfait's *Comme ceux de Quatre-vingt-treize* (Meininger, Mulhouse, 1920).

success that created a new source of anxiety for the French Army Commander. In the middle of the day, while Dubois' 9th Corps was exerting all its efforts to support Grossetti on its left and to stem the retreat of the all but shattered 11th Corps on its right, the German 14th Division debouched from Joches and Coizard, sweeping across the Marshes of St. Gond with a resistless impetus that hurled back the defenders along the southern shore. Much seems to have been expected from this attack on the German side, for when General von Einem, commander of the 7th Army Corps, had sent a liaison officer to Von Bülow's Chief of Staff to protest against this use of a division that had originally been intended to reinforce the 7th Corps, Von Lauenstein curtly dismissed the objection with the remark :

"Tell Von Einem that His Excellency General von Bülow will be at Sézanne tonight."

But though the 14th Division successfully crossed the great swamp and installed itself along the southern boundary, it could not progress farther and the road to Sézanne remained barred, for French artillery fire from the heights of Allemant and the Mont Août concentrated upon it and held it fast.

The day of September 8th had been a particularly hard one for the French. The Ninth Army heavily engaged on its left, with its centre yielding and its right almost broken, had engaged every available battalion and no further reserves remained. In vain Foch appealed to De Langle, his neighbour to the east. The Fourth Army too was fighting a desperate battle around Vitry-le-François and had no means of lending support. The 21st Army Corps (Legrand-Girarde) which Joffre had brought from Lorraine to fill the gap between the Fourth and Ninth Armies was still ten kilometres away at nightfall. Much might happen before it could make its presence felt.

It was at this crisis that Foch is reported to have sent his celebrated dispatch to Joffre :

Hard pressed on my right. My centre is yielding. Impossible to manoeuvre. Situation excellent. I am attacking.[8]

Indeed, during such a day there was little that an Army Commander could do towards the tactical direction of the battle, for the situation at the front was changing too rapidly and the confusion was too great to permit of accurate judgements or of timely decisions

[8] In an address on the occasion of Foch's induction as a member of the French Academy on February 5, 1920, Poincaré referred to this dispatch as follows : "Serious authors have given this text as authentic. I have not the heart to disillusion them. If you never wrote these optimistic words, you thought them, and better still, you translated them into action."

from Army Headquarters ; but one thing Foch could and did do —
keep constantly before the combatants the decisive nature of the
struggle in which they were engaged.   Though many of his series of
orders directing immediate attacks or counter-attacks proved impossible of execution, they nevertheless served his main purpose, for his
subordinates loyally strove to carry them out and in so doing gave
no thought to retreat, but kept their faces constantly towards the
enemy.   This was the primary object Foch had in mind.

Though official records contain no trace of Foch's famous message
to the Commander in Chief, it truly reflected his attitude during the
battle, an attitude that requires no comment and that was worth
an army corps to the French Ninth Army.[9]

[9] The Battle of the Marshes of St. Gond has called forth an abundant literature.
In addition to official accounts and to the memoirs of Von Hausen, Von Bülow and
Foch already cited, among the most important are : on the German side, Gen. Baumgarten Crusius' *Die Marneschlacht* 1914 (Lippold, Leipzig, 1919) and Gen. von
François' *Marneschlacht und Tannenberg* (Scherl, Berlin) : on the French side, Capt. Villate's *Foch à la Marne* (Lavauzelle, Paris, 1933), Gen. Dubois' *Deux ans de commande-
ment sur le front de France* (Lavauzelle, Paris, 1921), Gen. Bujac's *Le Général Eydoux
et le 11ie Corps* (Nantes, 1924), Col. de Ligny's *La Division du Maroc aux Marais de
St. Gond* (Lavauzelle, Paris, 1933).   See also *Die Krisis an der Marneschlacht* by Col.
Bircher, Swiss Army, and articles by Lieut.-Col. Lucas, *Le 10ie Corps et la 42ie D.I. à
la bataille de la Marne*, Revue Militaire Générale, October 1924, and by Lieut.-Col.
Lestien, *L'Action du Général Foch à la bataille de la Marne*, Revue d'histoire de la
Guerre Mondiale, April 1930.

CHAPTER XXXII

THE MISSION OF LIEUTENANT-COLONEL HENTSCH

DURING the first three days of the decisive battle upon which the outcome of the campaign depended, not a single order or even suggestion came to the German armies from the High Command at Luxembourg.

From the time he signed his General Directive on the morning of September 5th, Von Moltke rigidly observed the policy his uncle had adopted during the campaign of 1870, and contented himself with a passive role, leaving developments wholly to the initiative of his Army Commanders and waiting anxiously at his distant Headquarters for such news as might come to him. The major decisions of the battle — Von Bülow's retirement behind the Petit Morin, Von Kluck's withdrawal of two army corps from the Petit Morin, north of the Marne, Von Hausen's division of his Army into two groups, and the night attack of September 8th — all were taken by the Army Commanders concerned without prior consultation with the High Command, and Von Moltke might count himself fortunate if he obtained a belated report that enabled him to mark the situation on the great map that hung in his office in Luxembourg.

One move of high strategic importance Von Moltke did make, the transfer of the VII Army from Lorraine to the north. Disturbed by reports of activity on the part of the Belgian forces bottled in Antwerp, of the British landing on the Belgian coast and of French concentrations around Lille, the Chief of Staff belatedly came around to Schlieffen's original plan of reinforcing his right wing by forces drawn from the left.[1]

The news that Joffre had ordered a general offensive, which reached Luxembourg in the evening of September 6th, did not provoke any change of attitude on the part of the German High Command. Indeed, it seemed to Von Moltke and his staff that the enemy was playing into their hands. At last the elusive French had

[1] The VII Army as newly constituted included two army corps from Lorraine, the forces besieging Maubeuge, and the forces covering Antwerp, all under the command of General von Heeringen. It was originally intended to include also a corps from the VI Army, but this was blocked by Von Dellmensingen's vigorous objection.

dropped their unsporting tactics and would stand and fight it out ; at last the German armies would have a chance to demonstrate their superior fighting qualities. The General Directive of September 5th had fixed the principal objectives to be attained, and there seemed nothing for the High Command to do but wait until the Army Commanders carried them out. Tappen was jubilant and looked forward to the result with the utmost confidence ; but Von Moltke was not so sure. Doubts began to assail him, and the thought of his responsibility oppressed him.

Today destiny will deliver a great decision — he wrote his wife on September 7th — Since yesterday the whole German army from Paris to Upper Alsace is at grips with the enemy. If I could give my life to achieve victory, I should do it with infinite joy, following the example of thousands of our brothers who are fighting today and of thousands of others who have already fallen. What torrents of blood have flowed ! Into what incalculable despair innumerable innocent people have been plunged whose houses and farms have been burned and devastated ! I shudder sometimes at the thought ; I have the impression that I am responsible for all these horrors, and yet I could not do otherwise.

It was hardly the conventional attitude of a Warrior-Chief en-flamed by the joy of battle, nor even of a manly soldier to whom millions were looking for leadership and guidance in a moment of crisis. Nevertheless there was some justification for Von Moltke's pessimism. In the afternoon of September 7th, in response to a re-quest from Luxembourg, Von Bülow reported on his situation :

The II Army is engaged in battle with the issue still in doubt on the line of the Petit Morin between Montmirail and Normée (northeast of Fère Champenoise).

The 7th at noon the 3rd Corps was sent north of the Marne on the insistent demand of the I Army. The 9th Corps is pushing its advance-guards towards Chezy. The III Army is only supporting us feebly. To produce a decisive change, it is necessary that it should intervene with important forces.

The British are reported at noon on the 7th from Coulommiers to Choisy, the French from the southwest at Esternay, Sézanne and Fère Champenoise. The cavalry division which was to have been trans-ferred to the III Army has not yet been sent as it is engaged on the other wing.

Von Moltke took no action on this report. He knew it was use-less to urge Von Hausen to intervene more vigorously, for half of the III Army was already fighting with the Duke of Wurtemburg around Vitry-le-François and the Saxon commander had no other forces available.

In the small hours of the morning of the 8th, a message from Von Kluck, dispatched the afternoon before, threw new light on the position of the right wing armies :

Following the arrival of the 4th Army Corps on the right wing, the action of the 2nd and 4th Reserve Corps progressed on the line east of Nanteuil-Meaux. The 3rd and 9th Corps are on the march towards the battlefield. The attack will be continued tomorrow with prospects of success. The Cavalry Corps is covering the front from Meaux to Coulommiers, where no important enemy force has advanced. The enemy has been using a great quantity of heavy artillery probably brought from Paris. Enemy : British forces [2] and it seems the 5th and 7th French Army Corps.

This word from the I Army seemed reassuring, but another report from Von Bülow, that arrived soon after, was less optimistic :

Have so far maintained positions against superior forces. The 8th, a new attack on the left wing with the support of two Saxon divisions. As a result of heavy losses the II Army has no more than the combatant strength of three army corps.

Two short messages intercepted by the radio station at G.H.Q. in the early morning of the 8th led the Chief of Staff to doubt whether in fact Von Kluck's impression was correct that no important enemy forces were advancing between the I and II Armies. The first came from Von Bülow addressed to Von Richthofen :

Right wing north of Montmirail. Absolutely necessary to cover right flank against the British.

Two hours later came Von Richthofen's reply :

Position on the Grand Morin from Villeneuve to Orly has been broken. The Cavalry Corps is retiring slowly behind the Dolloir.

A glance at the map sufficed to show Von Moltke that the enemy was beginning seriously to exploit the gap between Von Bülow and Von Kluck. To consider the situation, he called into his office his principal advisers, Lieutenant-Colonel Tappen, Lieutenant-Colonel von Dommes and finally Lieutenant-Colonel Hentsch, who became a central figure in the events of the next few days.

After Tappen had explained the positions of the various armies

---

[2] It seems that the Germans mistook the khaki uniforms of the native Moroccan Brigade for British. Actually there were no British north of the Marne.

so far as they were known to the Operations Section, a general discussion ensued in which it appears to have been the consensus of opinion that the situation did not justify a retreat by the right wing armies, but on the contrary, that they should maintain their positions. Nevertheless, the breach that had developed between Von Kluck and Von Bülow, into which the British were slowly advancing, required the High Command to take the possibility of retirement into its calculations. Apparently realizing at last that a lack of first-hand information was preventing the High Command from assuming its proper role, Von Moltke determined to send Hentsch to the front, at the same time authorizing him, in the event that a movement in retreat had already been initiated, to endeavour to direct it in such a way as to close the breach between the I and II Armies, and to direct the retirement of the I Army on the line Soissons-Fismes, while the II Army simultaneously fell back behind the Vesle. For some unaccountable reason, Von Moltke failed to reduce Hentsch's instructions to writing.

Few episodes of military history have given rise to so much discussion as the mission of Lieutenant-Colonel Hentsch, and notably in Germany it has called forth a literature almost as voluminous and controversial as that of the Dreyfus case in France. The popular view outside Germany is perhaps best expressed by General Peyton C. March, a former Chief of Staff of the United States Army, who describes Hentsch as "a perfectly unknown Lieutenant-Colonel of his (Von Moltke's) General Staff — Hentsch by name — who intervened in the battle, giving orders far exceeding his authority, which seem to have been obeyed without question by generals commanding armies," and somewhat facetiously suggests that the Allies should erect a monument to Hentsch's memory.[3]

To the German army, Hentsch was far from "perfectly unknown"; on the contrary, he enjoyed a wide reputation as one of the most brilliant and promising of the younger officers of the General Staff. Before the war he had been the Chief of the Operations Section, from which he had been transferred on the outbreak of hostilities to Chief of the Intelligence Section. General von Kuhl, who as Quartermaster-General had Hentsch under his direct orders for a number of years, has described him as a "very intelligent, very prudent and very reserved officer in whom one could place absolute confidence." This statement becomes the more significant from the fact that it was written after the war by the officer who, as Chief of Staff of the I Army, appeared in the light of Hentsch's principal antagonist in the controversy that followed.

[3] *The Nation at War* (Doubleday Doran, New York, 1932), pgs. 16–17.

Von Moltke selected Hentsch in preference to Von Dommes, who volunteered to go, because the former was well known personally both to Von Bülow and Von Kuhl, and also because, three days before, he had already visited the Headquarters of the I and II Armies when he took Von Moltke's General Directive of September 5th to Von Kluck, so that he was already familiar with the attitude and point of view of the officers of both Army Staffs. Though it may well be debated whether the situation did not require Von Moltke to go in person, assuming that he was not to do so, he could hardly have selected a more suitable emissary than Hentsch.

Despite the welter of controversy, it now seems settled that in his subsequent conduct Hentsch did not exceed the verbal authority conferred upon him by the Chief of Staff at the memorable conference in Luxembourg on September 8th. Though the accounts of those present differ materially, this was the conclusion reached by a military Court of Inquiry appointed at Hentsch's request in 1917, after he had been promoted to the rank of Colonel and designated Chief of Staff of Von Mackensen's Military Government of Rumania. The findings of the Court, which considered the evidence of Von Moltke, Von Dommes and Tappen as well as of Hentsch himself, were approved by Ludendorff, and were confirmed in substance by an exhaustive independent investigation after the war conducted by Lieutenant-Colonel Müller-Loebnitz, formerly of the General Staff and at the time Chief of the Service of Military Archives of the German Reich.[4]

Leaving Luxembourg by automobile at about eleven o'clock in the morning, Hentsch stopped briefly on his way successively at the Headquarters of the V, IV and III Armies. From the Duke of Wurtemburg's Headquarters at Courtisols, he telephoned Tappen to give a favourable account of the situation on the front of the IV and V Armies, proceeding thence to Châlons, where he met Von Hausen and his Chief of Staff, Von Hoeppner. Learning with satisfaction of the successful attack executed before dawn against Foch's right wing, he radioed Von Moltke :

Situation and point of view entirely favourable at the III Army.

It was 7:45 in the evening when Hentsch finally arrived at Montmort, the Headquarters of the II Army. Von Bülow was still at Fromentières, his advance Post of Command, but returned soon after Hentsch's arrival. With the Army Commander and his Chief

---

[4] *Die Sendung des Oberstleutnants Hentsch* (Mittler, Berlin, 1922). See also Brig.-Gen. J. S. Edmonds' article, *The Scapegoat of the Battle of the Marne*, British Army Quarterly, January 1921.

of Staff, Von Lauenstein, and Lieutenant-Colonel Matthes, Chief of the Operations Section, Hentsch and the two junior officers accompanying him sat down to a conference that was destined to exercise a profound influence upon the fate of the German armies.

CHAPTER XXXIII

VON BULOW'S DECISION

WHEN General von Bülow arrived at Montmort on the evening of September 8th, he was not in a happy frame of mind. He had spent most of the day at Fromentières, barely five kilometres behind the front lines, and what he had seen there had given him small ground for encouragement. Late in the afternoon, a momentary panic had given the Army Commander a few moments of serious alarm, and he had even suggested to General von Einem that it might be advisable for the II Army to retire behind the Marne. When it turned out that the disorder at the front was less important than at first reported and that the French had not taken advantage of it, he had not insisted, but it was evident to him that Von Eben's two Reserve divisions had no more than a precarious hold on their positions around Montmirail in the face of greatly superior forces. The situation of the II Army's right flank especially worried Von Bülow. As reports came in from Von Richthofen's cavalry units that they were falling back before an advancing enemy, and aviators reported hostile columns marching into the breach that separated the II Army from Von Kluck, Von Bülow had addressed a pressing appeal to Von Hausen for an attack from the east that might divert the enemy :

1st Division of the Guard already at Fère Champenoise. Vigorous action by Von Kirchbach's three divisions right wing Connantre immediately indicated. Enemy is attempting to envelop the right wing of the II Army. No reserves available.[1]

To this communication Von Hausen had responded only by relinquishing control of the 2nd Division of the Guard, which had temporarily been placed under Von Kirchbach's orders, restoring it to Von Plettenberg and thus placing another division at the disposal of the II Army, but he could do nothing further, for the Saxons were already exerting their strength to the limit.

Von Bülow was aware of the success achieved by the Guard and the Saxon divisions against the French Ninth Army's right wing, but he knew also that despite an advance of five kilometres and the cap-

[1] This message was intercepted at Luxembourg and received by Von Moltke after Hentsch's departure.

ture of Fère Champenoise, the enemy's resistance remained unbroken and the final outcome was still in doubt.   Farther to the west, the situation of his army corps became progressively worse.   At the western extremity of the Marshes of St. Gond, Von Emmich's 10th Corps had made negligible progress.   On the line of the Petit Morin, the 10th Reserve Corps was barely holding its own, and finally, on the right flank, Von Einem's 7th Corps, reduced to a single brigade of infantry, was in grave danger from the French forces that had crossed the river.   Such in substance was the point of view Von Bülow expressed to Hentsch and to the officers of the II Army staff, as they assembled at his Headquarters in the Château of Montmort.

"As a result of all that we have been through and of the hard combats of the last few days," Von Bülow said, "the II Army has naturally lost a considerable part of its combat value.   It is no longer capable of forcing a decisive victory.   As a result of the transfer of two army corps from the left to the right wing of the I Army, a gap has been created which forms an immediate danger to the inner wings of both the I and II Armies.   I am informed that enemy columns, brigades or divisions, are on the march into this breach, and I have no reserves left to attack the enemy or to hold him off."

"The enemy has two alternative courses open to him," the Army Commander continued, "either to turn against the left wing of the I Army or to march against the right wing of the II Army.   Because of our lack of reserves, either movement might lead to a catastrophe. If the enemy compels a retreat by force of arms, the withdrawal would have to be made through a hostile country and the consequences to this Army might be incalculable.   It should therefore be considered whether it would not be better, viewing the situation as a whole, to avert the danger by a voluntary concentric retreat of the I and II Armies." [2]

As the discussion became general and continued on the basis indicated by the Army Commander, an orderly called the Chief of Staff, General von Lauenstein, to the telephone.   It was Von Einem of the 7th Corps, reporting the loss of Marchais-en-Brie as a result of De Maud'huy's night attack and the consequent menace to Montmirail.   Forthwith, Von Bülow decided to draw back the II Army's right wing towards the east to the line Margny-Le Thoult, thereby placing it temporarily at least, beyond the danger of envelopment.

The conference went on until nearly midnight, and it was decided to make no further alteration in the orders issued for the following day ; the Guard to continue its offensive in conjunction with Von

[2] See article by Captain Koeppen, one of the officers who accompanied Hentsch, *The Battle of the Marne, 8th and 9th of September 1914,* British Army Quarterly, July 1934. See also Müller-Loebnitz, *op. cit.*

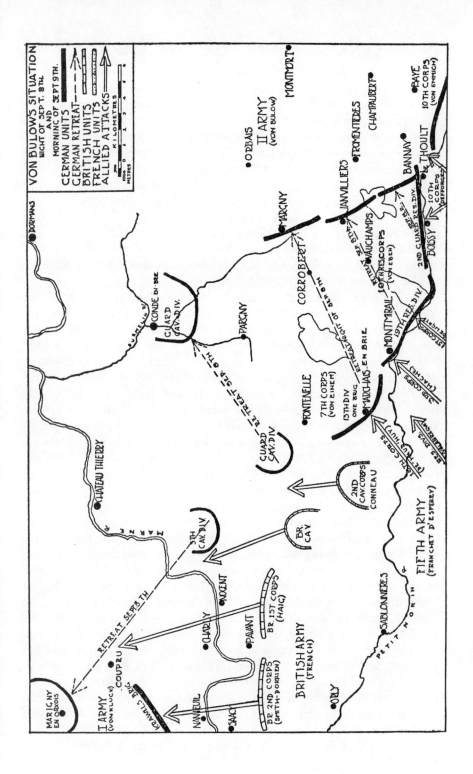

Hausen, while the rest of the army awaited developments. Nevertheless the trend of opinion seems to have been generally pessimistic and the view accepted that unless some way could be found to close the breach between the I and II Armies, either by the withdrawal of the I Army to the east or otherwise, a retirement behind the Marne had become inevitable. Hentsch made no effort to combat this conception or to urge the point of view expressed the same morning by Von Moltke, Tappen and Von Dommes that no retreat was necessary. On the contrary, it seems that he fully acquiesced in what he found to be the prevailing opinion at the Headquarters of the II Army, and took no steps to inform himself more precisely as to Von Kluck's situation.

Late at night, as the meeting broke up, Hentsch sent a message to Von Moltke by radio :

"Situation serious, but not desperate, at the II Army," was all he thought it necessary to say. It seems incomprehensible that Hentsch should have limited himself to this brief communication, which must have seemed maddeningly cryptic to the officers at Luxembourg, so eagerly waiting for news. Between midnight and dawn an officer might readily have covered the 200 kilometres between Montmort and Luxembourg by automobile and have brought to the Chief of Staff a full report on the position of the II Army, with the views of its commander and of Hentsch himself ; but no such action was deemed necessary, and except for the single sentence of Hentsch's report, the High Command received no word from the II Army on its operations during the day of September 8th.

At 5:30 the following morning, September 9th, Hentsch again conferred with Von Lauenstein and Matthes, to canvass the situation in the light of the night's reports from the front. The Chief of Staff expressed his belief that the II Army could hold its ground only provided the I Army was able to disengage itself from its battle against Maunoury and could retreat eastward, along the north bank of the Marne, far enough to effect a junction with the left wing of Von Bülow's Army. All concurred that such procedure would be difficult if not impossible, and it was determined then and there, for the safety of the II Army, that it should retire behind the Marne and ultimately behind the Vesle. It was agreed that Hentsch should proceed immediately to the Headquarters of the I Army at Mareuil-sur-Ourcq and bring about its retreat in such a direction as to close the breach existing between the two armies. Von Bülow was not present at this early morning meeting, but there seems to have been no doubt in the minds of those present that he would ratify the conclusion reached, for Hentsch did not see him again before leaving Montmort.

While Hentsch was on his way to the Headquarters of the I Army, 80 kilometres from Montmort, Von Bülow confirmed Von Lauenstein's decision and issued orders for the general retreat of the German II Army behind the Marne. In a laconic message he informed Von Kluck and Von Hausen :

Aviator reports four long columns marching towards the Marne. Heads at nine o'clock at Nanteuil-sur-Marne, Citry, Pavant, Nogent l'Artaud. II Army is beginning retreat, right wing Daméry.[3]

It is of little moment to determine the exact time when the German Army Commander decided to order the retreat, though this is a matter that has been sharply debated. Whether the order came as a result of a determination that had been ripening in Von Bülow's mind since the night before — and there seem many indications that such was the case — whether it was the result of Von Lauenstein's persuasion after the latter's talk with Hentsch in the early morning, or whether it was brought about by the report of British columns approaching the Marne as indicated in Von Bülow's dispatch to his colleagues, will probably never be known. The principal thing is to note that the decision was taken, and taken by the Army Commander himself. It seems quite clear, and Ludendorff's Court of Inquiry so found, that Hentsch did not order or purport to order the retreat of the German II Army.

This fact, however, hardly suffices to exonerate Hentsch from all responsibility. Knowing, as he did, the opinion of his superior, Von Moltke, and of his colleagues, Tappen and Von Dommes, the conclusion is inescapable that Hentsch agreed too readily in the view taken by the commander and the Chief of Staff of the II Army, without making any serious effort to impress upon them the point of view of the High Command. It seems certain that Hentsch was personally convinced that the part of wisdom required the retreat of the II Army. Nevertheless, with knowledge that other views prevailed at Luxembourg, he should at least have made every effort to present these views fully to the II Army Commander, and conversely the views of the II Army to the Chief of Staff, before acquiescing in so momentous a decision. By failing to do so, and by yielding too readily to his personal convictions, Hentsch performed less than his full duty.

Whatever the faults of Von Moltke during the Campaign of the Marne, he cannot fairly be charged with having initiated the retreat of the German armies, for Hentsch did not communicate again with Luxembourg until he sent a radio from Fismes in the middle of the

[3] It was actually Dormans, farther west, that was meant. The error was corrected in a later message.

afternoon of September 9th, after both the I and II Armies had begun their retirement, and Von Bülow himself did not inform the High Command of his decision until the movement of the II Army had started beyond possibility of recall.

The wisdom of the retreat of the II Army, which entailed within a few hours that of its neighbours to the right and left, must be judged objectively, apart from the manner in which it was done and from the reasons alleged in justification after the event. Von Bülow's decision has been generally denounced by German military critics and soldiers, who have almost unanimously taken the position that he regarded the situation on the morning of September 9th with undue pessimism and that nothing warranted his determination. The German thesis is based on the assumption that the right wing of the German II Army, after its withdrawal to the line Margny-Le Thoult, had nothing to fear from the enemy, and that its left wing, with Von Hausen's three divisions, was on the verge of inflicting a decisive defeat on Foch, while Von Kluck was similarly about to bring his battle against Maunoury to a decisively victorious conclusion.

In fact Von Bülow was confronted with a race against time. If Von Hausen and the left wing of the II Army could defeat Foch before Franchet d'Esperey could strike the German II Army's right wing, and if Von Kluck could defeat Maunoury before the British could strike the I Army's left wing, all might have yet been well, but the risk involved was enormous. The French Fifth Army outnumbered Von Bülow's right wing in the ratio of 11 divisions to $2\frac{1}{2}$ — even allowing for the two divisions which Franchet d'Esperey had turned over to Foch — and it was hardly likely, with all due recognition of the fighting qualities of the German soldier, that the two divisions and one brigade which had failed to hold the line of the Petit Morin would be able to stand for any length of time against odds of more than four to one, on the much less formidable tactical positions to which they had fallen back during the night of September 8th.

By staying where he was for another twenty-four hours, Von Bülow incurred grave danger of seeing the right wing of his Army crushed beneath the weight of numbers, and it was far from a foregone conclusion that either Von Kluck or Von Hausen could push their respective battles to a victorious result during the day of September 9th. While the Guard and the Saxons had undeniably gained the upper hand over Foch's right wing during the day of the 8th, the French were still far from completely defeated. Though severely tried, the French Ninth Army was not broken, and with the aid received from Franchet d'Esperey, Foch was by no means ready

to concede defeat.   The second corps of Von Bülow's left wing, Von
Emmich's 10th Corps, had made only insignificant progress, and the
Army Commander had ordered it to stand defensively on September
9th substantially on the same ground where the battle had been engaged three days before.

The outcome of the Battle of the Ourcq was no less doubtful.   As
the German II Army was beginning its retreat, three British army
corps were already forcing the passages of the Marne, with French
cavalry on their right, and were already coming into position to
strike Von Kluck's line of communications.

Reading between the lines in the story of the Campaign of the
Marne, much appears that is unattractive in the personality of General von Bülow, and it is easy to understand his unpopularity with
his colleagues and their subordinates.   It is but simple justice to
state, however, that in the light of all the facts of which he had knowledge on the morning of September 9th — and the situation was actually no better than he supposed — Von Bülow's decision to order
the retreat of the German II Army was a sound one.

Though his Army might, and probably could, have maintained its
positions for another twenty-four hours, the situation at the end of
that time would have become so precarious that it is doubtful
whether complete disaster could have been averted.   The errors of
the German High Command and of the German Army Commanders
had combined with the dispositions of the French Commander in
Chief to place the German armies in a strategically impossible situation from which, though tactically undefeated, their only escape lay
in timely retreat.   Von Bülow was first to realize the danger on the
fourth day of battle, and, characteristically without consulting either
his colleagues or his superiors, he issued the orders that marked the
beginning of the end of the Battle of the Marne.[4]

4 Virtually all of the German writers who have dealt with the strategy of the Campaign of the Marne have discussed Von Bülow's decision in detail, and the great preponderance of German military opinion has condemned it as unjustified.   For biographical sketches of Von Bülow, see Dr. Otto Kracke's *Generalfeldmarschall von Bülow*
(Scherl, Berlin), and Gen. von Gebsattel's *Generalfeldmarschall Karl von Bülow*
(Lehmanns Verlag, Munich).

CHAPTER XXXIV

THE CLIMAX ON THE OURCQ

WHILE Lieutenant-Colonel Hentsch was making his way from the German II Army Headquarters at Montmort to Von Kluck's Headquarters at Mareuil-sur-Ourcq, the Battle of the Ourcq had begun anew. On the northern extremity of the German line, between Vaumoise and Cuvergnon, the 9th Army Corps and the 6th Division of the 3rd Corps had assembled, forming a new group under the orders of General von Quast. These troops, some of whom had arrived in the afternoon of the 8th and the remainder early the following morning, gave Von Kluck the means to carry out the attack on which he relied to attain a rapid and final decision over Maunoury. In spite of the fatigue of the troops, brought from the battlefields of Montceaux and Esternay by two days of continuous marching, officers and men looked forward courageously to the attack in which they were to participate, with the support of the 4th Cavalry Division on their right and of Von Arnim's group on their left.

In the French camp, Maunoury was aware of the danger that threatened him from the north and of the reinforcements that Von Kluck had received. The safety of his Army, the security of Paris, and above all, the success of Joffre's great offensive depended on his ability to hold out until the British could cross the Marne from the south and intervene against Von Kluck's flank. The French 8th Division was already on the march to join him, and on the morning of the 9th Joffre sent word that a new division, the 37th of the 3rd Army Corps, was likewise coming to his aid,[1] but these reinforcements could hardly arrive in time to help against the imminent attack, which the arrival of Von Lepel's Brigade northwest of Nanteuil made all the more formidable.

Informed of the Sixth Army's difficult position, Joffre had approved Maunoury's decision to remain on the defensive, and had telephoned from his Headquarters :

While awaiting the arrival of reinforcements which will enable you to resume the offensive, avoid any decisive action by withdrawing your left, if necessary, in the general direction of the Entrenched Camp of Paris.

[1] See Appendix XV (8).

The early morning of September 9th passed without infantry activity but both sides maintained a continuous cannonade. At Mareuil, Von Kluck waited impatiently for Von Quast to complete his preparations to attack, but in the meanwhile disquieting news began to come from the southern flank along the Marne. Two divisions of Von der Marwitz' Corps with Kräwel's Brigade from the 9th Corps and elements of the 5th Division held the line of the river covering the left flank of the German I Army against the British advance. The 5th Cavalry Division of Von Richthofen's Corps had withdrawn to Marigny-en-Orxois, nearly ten kilometres northwest of Château Thierry, and the retirement during the night of the right wing of Von Bülow's Army from Montmirail to Margny-Le Thoult had left the forces along the Marne beyond the possibility of assistance from the II Army. The path to the Marne lay open, not only to the British, but to Conneau's cavalry and to De Maud'huy's 18th Corps on the left of the French Fifth Army as well.

It was 9:30 A.M. when Von Kluck received two messages in quick succession from his cavalry :

Strong infantry and artillery at Charly, across the bridge of the Marne.

The second message was no less disturbing :

Strong infantry on the march by Charly and Nanteuil-sur-Marne ; 5th Cavalry Division and 2nd Cavalry Division have orders to attack.

A third message began with a repetition of the second, but broke off abruptly with the words : "I must leave at once."

To Von Kluck it seemed evident that the British had already crossed the Marne in force, and that the southern extremity of his line, facing west from Congis parallel to the Ourcq, was seriously menaced. A crisis would be reached in this quarter before Von Quast's attack, even if completely successful, could accomplish its result. Without abandoning the plan for an attack by his right wing, Von Kluck decided to pull back his left to the general line May-en-Multien-Coulombs, so as to face the danger from the south, and at 11 o'clock he issued the necessary orders to initiate this movement.

The effect of this retirement by the German I Army's left wing was to abandon the positions from Congis northward along the plateau of Trocy that had hitherto been so stalwartly defended, and to establish Von Gronau's and Von Trossel's groups, respectively in the centre and on the left of the I Army, on a new line roughly parallel to the Marne instead of at right angles to it. By thus altering the front of his left wing from west to south, Von Kluck safe-guarded the flank and rear of his Army against the British, but he also surrendered the principal advantage of Von Quast's attack, for thenceforth Maunoury was free to manoeuvre with the right wing of the French Sixth Army, either by following the retreating Germans and effecting a junction with the British, or by wheeling northward to reinforce the resistance of the 4th and 7th Army Corps against Von Quast.   The encirclement of Maunoury's Army had become impossible, and the danger to the French from the concentric attack by Von Lepel from the northwest, by Von Quast from the north and by Von Arnim from the northeast was materially lessened.   A simple retreat southward against the second line organized by Galliéni sufficed to secure Maunoury from decisive defeat.

It was just before noon — as Von Quast and Von Arnim were setting their forces in motion on Von Kluck's right wing to begin their long-expected attack, and Von Linsingen was simultaneously directing the retirement of the left wing of the German I Army — when Hentsch arrived at Mareuil.   Instead of the two hours ordinarily required for the trip by automobile from Montmort, he had spent five hours on the road.   All along the way, he had met convoys, trains, ambulances, stragglers and wounded from various units, all hastening northward seeking safety beyond the Marne from the advancing British.   At one point a report of enemy cavalry in the vicinity had compelled him to make a wide detour, and the impression he had gained was one of confusion, defeat and imminent disaster, strengthening his resolution to avoid it by compelling the timely retreat of the I Army.   Reporting to the Chief of Staff, Hentsch quickly explained the situation at other points along the front : the blocking of the Crown Prince's Army before Verdun, the failure of Rupprecht of Bavaria to break through around Nancy, and lastly the critical situation of the II Army and Von Bülow's determination to retreat. While they were talking, the radio from the II Army arrived announcing that its retreat had started [2] and the message confirmed what Hentsch had said.   To his suggestion that the I Army should immediately retreat to the line Soissons-Fismes, where it could reestablish contact with Von Bülow's right wing, Von Kuhl objected strenuously, urging — somewhat inconsistently it would seem — the favourable tactical situation of the I Army and its prospects of success, and at the same time the difficulty of the movement Hentsch proposed.

I pointed out — Von Kuhl wrote in a memorandum prepared next day, jointly with Colonel von Bergmann, Quartermaster-General of the I

[2] See pg. 277.

Army — that we were in the midst of an attack, that a retreat would be a very delicate operation, that the elements of the Army were intermingled and also very much worn out.

Nevertheless, Hentsch insisted, finally invoking his authority as a representative of the High Command and in its name ordering the retreat of the I Army.

All the possibilities of continuing the battle to a decisive victory were considered — Von Kuhl has written — nevertheless, when it was settled that the decision of the II Army had been taken in the morning, that its troops were already in full retreat in the afternoon and that there was no chance of revoking this decision, the High Command of the Army could only yield. Even a victory over Maunoury could not have prevented us from being outflanked on our left wing by superior forces and from being cut off from the main body of the army. The I Army was thenceforth isolated.

General von Kuhl's line of reasoning seems difficult to follow, for the I Army was already separated from the II by more than 50 kilometres, with the whole of the British Army and the French Fifth Army in between, and it seems, therefore, that the retreat of the II Army could hardly have affected the situation of the I to the extent suggested. The I Army would have been in no better posture, even if Von Bülow had stood his ground.

Hentsch's own view of the position of the I Army is summarized in the report he made to Von Falkenhayn on September 14th :

I was convinced that by reason of the situation of the II Army on the 9th of September, the I Army was obliged to retreat to avoid being cut off completely by the British and driven back towards the west. The commander of the 2nd Cavalry Corps [3] and the Quartermaster-General of the Army also shared this conviction. I cannot judge of the importance of the progress realized against the French on the line Nanteuil and to the south ; the confidence and calm that prevailed in the staff of the I Army justified a hope of success, but even if I had not given the order, a retreat would have become inevitable by reason of the general situation.

In the light of all that is known today, it seems hard to dispute Hentsch's conclusion that on the afternoon of September 9th, the retreat of the German I Army had become a military necessity which even the success of Von Quast's attack could not have altered.

Nor can it be questioned that in issuing the order to retreat in the

[3] Hentsch did not in fact see General von der Marwitz and this statement in his report is erroneous.

name of the High Command, Hentsch acted within the scope of his authority, whatever criticisms may be levelled against him on other grounds.   The retreat of the II Army fulfilled the condition precedent which brought his plenary powers into existence, for a movement in retreat had already been initiated.   If anything more than the findings of Ludendorff's Court of Inquiry and the investigations of Lieutenant-Colonel Müller-Loebnitz is needed to vindicate the memory of a conscientious officer from such charges as General March and others have heedlessly brought against him, it may be found in Von Kuhl's own statement :

In the light of what has gone before, one is bound to concede that Lieutenant-Colonel Hentsch did not exceed his authority.

Once the retreat of the I Army had been finally decided, Hentsch left the Army Headquarters and started on his return journey, strange as it may seem, in the light of the momentous character of the decision, without having seen the I Army Commander personally.

While Hentsch and Von Kuhl debated at Mareuil, Von Quast launched his attack.   Convinced that not only the fate of the army but the success of the campaign depended upon them, the German infantry pressed gallantly forward, heedless of the fatigues and privations they had already endured and happily ignorant of the futility of their efforts.   Though at first delayed by the artillery of two French cavalry divisions,[4] Von Quast's group soon swept forward, driving the French 61st Reserve Division before it.   First Bargny, then Boissy-Fresnoy and Villers-St. Genest fell into German hands, while at the same time from Baron and Rozières, Von Lepel's Brigade pushed forward to the western outskirts of Nanteuil.   Then, suddenly, the German drive halted.   Astonished but grateful for this unlooked-for respite, the disorganized French re-formed their lines, hastily entrenching to meet the next blow which they could only believe had unaccountably been postponed.

But the end had come.   At two o'clock a telephone call from Army Headquarters informed Von Quast of the decision to retreat. The Army liaison officer, Captain Buhrman, himself incredulous, brought the news to the commander of the 9th Corps : the attack

---

[4] The 1st and 3rd Cavalry Division's of Bridoux's Corps.   The third cavalry division, the 5th, was at the time engaged in a gallant and dramatic, but strategically unimportant, raid behind the lines of Von Kluck's Army.   For accounts of this raid, the only cavalry operation of its kind on the western front during the course of the war, see J. Héthay (Gen. de Cornulier-Lucinière), *Le rôle de la cavalerie française à l'aile gauche de la première bataille de la Marne* (Perrin, Paris, 1919) and Gen. Pelecier's *Un raid de Cavalerie* (Lavauzelle, Paris, 1923).   See also S. T. Tyng's article, *A French Cavalry Raid at the Marne ;* U. S. Cavalry Journal, September–October, 1934.

must be broken off, a general retreat had been ordered.   Thunder-struck, Von Quast insisted on calling back Army Headquarters for confirmation and not till he had spoken with Von Kuhl himself could he credit the news.   Even then, having failed to move the Chief of Staff, he refused to accept the decision as final, and at his instance, his aide, the Grand Duke of Mecklenburg-Schwerin — one of the royal personages who abounded at the higher German Head-quarters — appealed personally to the Army Commander ; but Von Kluck was adamant.[5]   The last resort had failed and Von Quast could only accept the inevitable.   With a heavy heart, he halted his troops on their positions.

On the afternoon of September 9th, Paris was saved and the fight-ing along the Ourcq came to an end.   It was the turning point of the Battle of the Marne, for though the struggle in the east continued for two days more with unabated fury, the ultimate issue was no longer in doubt.

[5] Many German military writers have expressed the view, despite the opinions of Von Kluck and Von Kuhl, that the commander of the German I Army should have de-liberately ignored Hentsch's order and permitted Von Quast to continue his attack. See notably Gen. von Francois' *Marneschlacht und Tannenberg* (Scherl, Berlin) and Lieut.-Col. Müller-Loebnitz' *Der Wendepunkt des Weltkrieges* (Mittler, Berlin).

CHAPTER XXXV

FOCH STANDS FIRM

THE DAY of September 9th, so momentous for Von Bülow and Von Kluck, proved no less crucial in the struggle that Von Hausen's Saxons and the German Guard were waging against Foch. The powerful surprise attack on the morning of the 8th had so weakened the right wing of the French Ninth Army as to render its capacity for sustained resistance at least doubtful ; against its centre the German 14th Division had overcome the obstacle of the Marshes of St. Gond and had ensconced itself on the southern shore; even on the left, where Grossetti and Humbert's Moroccans had fought a valiant drawn battle against Von Emmich's 10th Corps, the situation left much to be desired, for both French divisions had suffered greatly.

The position of his right wing, however, mainly disturbed the French Army Commander. To withstand the inevitable renewal of the Saxon onslaught, he knew it must be strengthened and he had no means with which to do so. In his extremity Foch turned to Franchet d'Esperey, requesting that the 10th Corps on the right of the Fifth Army relieve the 42nd Division on the left of the Ninth, so that the latter could be transported to the aid of the faltering right wing. Sensing at once the seriousness of a situation that led Foch to make such a request, Franchet d'Esperey replied immediately and generously, placing two divisions [1] of the 10th Corps, with the corps artillery, at Foch's disposal for the day of the 9th.

Forthwith, the commander of the Ninth Army directed the 10th Corps to take over the 42nd Division's positions at dawn and to continue with its task of attacking in the direction of Bannay and Baye, while Grossetti led his command back of the front into place behind the 11th Corps at the opposite end of the line. The manoeuvre that Foch proposed was by no means an easy one, for it presupposed a relief in close contact with the enemy, a long march for the 42nd Division behind a none too stable front, and finally the ability of the French Ninth Army's right wing to stand its ground, or at least

[1] The 20th Division and the 51st Reserve Division. On the operations of these Divisions, see Gen. Requin's article *La journée du 9 Septembre 1914 à la gauche de la 9ie Armée*, Revue Militaire Française, November 1930.

to avoid disintegration, until the 42nd Division arrived. It was a make-shift arrangement at best, but no better solution offered.

The orders to the German II Army for the day of September 9th, issued while Hentsch was at Von Bülow's Headquarters at Montmort, directed Von Emmich's 10th Corps and the 14th Division south of the marshes to hold their ground, while the Guard pressed its attack in liaison with Von Kirchbach's group of the III Army. The Saxons had been reinforced by the belated arrival of the 24th Reserve Division, and Von Hausen was confident that he could complete the work so auspiciously begun the previous day.

At dawn the German bombardment opened upon the five shattered divisions [2] that formed Foch's right wing and soon after six o'clock the assault began. Although this time there was no element of surprise involved, the French were no longer in condition to offer well organized resistance, and the Germans, pushing forward with renewed vigour, successively carried line after line. On the right of the attacking group, the 1st Division of the Guard, with all its four regiments in line, stormed the French positions on the Mont Août, and before noon the whole hill that overlooked the eastern portion of the battlefield was in German hands. From its crest, the artillery of the Guard poured its fire mercilessly into groups of red-trousered infantry that dotted the plain below, while in the meanwhile the grey attacking waves moved relentlessly on into the villages of Mailly, Oeuvy, Gourgançon and Connantre, as the French resistance became increasingly disconnected and ineffective. Though still retaining some semblance of cohesion, by mid-afternoon the French Ninth Army had come perilously close to the breaking point. Only by the intervention of fresh troops did it seem possible to save the situation, but Foch still waited in an agony of apprehension for Grossetti's coming.

In the meanwhile, on the French left, the 10th Corps had relieved the 42nd Division without serious mishap, but it had proved a difficult business which took longer in the field than on the paper calculations of sanguine staff-officers, and it was after ten o'clock before Grossetti was fully on his way. Difficulties of the Moroccan Division around Mondemont had complicated and delayed the operation.

The position of Mondemont was one of the greatest value, for it offered access to the ridge of Allemant which dominated the whole broad plain to the east and south.[3] Once securely established there, the German guns would hold the French Ninth Army at the mercy of an enfilading fire, and its capture had been one of the principal objectives of the German 10th Corps the previous day.

[2] The 18th, 21st and 22nd Divisions and the 52nd and 60th Reserve Divisions.
[3] The position of Mondemont may be compared to that of Little Round Top at Gettysburg.

"His Excellency General von Emmich attaches the highest importance to the capture of Mondemont," Colonel von Lambsdorff, the Corps Chief of Staff, had told Captain Purgold, who commanded the 2nd Battalion of the German 164th Infantry. "He orders the 164th to gain possession of the Château and the village at any price, whatever the losses."

But the objective had not been attained. A confusing series of misunderstandings at Corps, Division, Brigade and Regimental Headquarters, orders lost or misunderstood, ambiguous orders or orders not issued at all, had contributed to the failure and had caused the abandonment of a projected night attack. It had not been Purgold's fault, for he was a gallant and competent officer who had borne a major share in such success as the German 10th Corps had obtained, but he was nevertheless chagrined at his inability to execute the mission so definitely indicated to him, and without waiting for further instructions from higher authority or for assurances of coöperation from neighbouring units, he resolved to carry out his task alone. At six in the morning, through a cold mist following a rainy night, Purgold led two battalions out of Oyes up the slope of Mondemont towards the Château on its crest. Except for the roar of the Saxon bombardment farther to the east, no sound broke the early morning stillness as nine infantry companies with two machine-gun sections advanced on the French outposts, men of the Moroccan Division who were standing on the parapet of their shallow trench stamping their feet for warmth. Before a sudden outburst of German fire, they fled, and a few minutes later the French guns opened vigorously. Hastily dispatching a runner to request reinforcements and artillery support, Purgold stood his ground and when at last the German artillery began, somewhat lazily, to bombard the Château and the woods around it, he led his men in a desperate rush up the heights and through a breach in the walls into the Château itself. Inexplicably the French had left it unoccupied and undefended, but its heavy masonry walls constituted a veritable fortress, almost invulnerable except to heavy artillery. The Germans lost no time in organizing the defence, distributing their companies in the Château and in the out-buildings adjacent to it.

For the rest of the day the left wing of the French Ninth Army concentrated its efforts upon the recovery of Mondemont. Realizing — somewhat belatedly it would seem — the significance of the loss, Humbert, commanding the Moroccan Division, appealed to his Corps Commander, Dubois, for aid in recovering the precious foothold to the key-position of the French battle-line. Dubois hastened to send his only reserve, the 77th Infantry Regiment.

"Retake Mondemont at any cost. The result of the battle depends upon it," such was the substance of the orders Colonel Lestoquoi received as he hurried with his regiment to meet the emergency. Two regiments of the 51st Reserve Division, two battalions of Chasseurs, four artillery groups of the 42nd Division and finally the 77th Infantry, all converged against the position that Purgold grimly held with two battalions, sweeping the French lines on either side with a murderous fire.

Determined at all costs to prevent the Germans from extending their success or from exploiting it by installing artillery on the heights, the French guns kept up a constant bombardment on the Château and its surroundings. Shells crashed through the roof ; the upper story became enveloped in flames ; but the French 75's could make little headway against the thick stone-work of the lower walls, and the defenders clung tenaciously to their position.

It was early afternoon before the whole of the 77th had assembled in the woods around the Château ready to deliver the main assault. Under the trees, along the road to Broyes, Commandant de Beaufort drew up the 2nd Battalion assigned to lead the attack. Erect, white-gloved, immaculate he stood before his men and called from the ranks a corporal, Father Gallard,[4] inviting all who desired to receive absolution. Almost without exception, the battalion — devout Catholics from the Vendée — knelt in prayer while overhead French shells roared, bursting around the Château a few hundred yards away. The pause was only for a moment, for as the guns with one accord ceased their bombardment, the battalion fixed bayonets and to the strident call of the bugle rushed towards the Château, De Beaufort in the lead. The French light artillery, so deadly in the open, had produced little effect upon the thick walls that sheltered Purgold's men. The defenders were alert, and from every window, from every angle of the walls, German rifles and machine-guns spat forth angrily. In the front rank of the charging column, pointing his way with his cane, De Beaufort fell among the first, and though a few French reached the Château and some even penetrated the gate, it was a task beyond human power, and the leaderless battalion flowed back in disorder to the protecting woods.

Convinced of the futility of further attempts at direct assault, Colonel Lestoquoi sought other means. Two guns, laboriously dragged by hand, were set up less than 500 yards from the Château. It was nearly six o'clock in the evening before they were ready to open fire, but when they did, the shells at point-blank range soon

4 In France, since the enactment of the secularization laws, holy orders do not confer exemption from military service, and only a relatively small proportion of priests or ministers are assigned to duty as chaplains.

crashed yawning breaches in the walls. In less than half an hour, Lestoquoi again ordered his men forward through the gathering dusk.

Despite heavy losses and the fierce bombardment that beat upon the Château without cessation, Purgold had kept his little force at its post throughout the afternoon with dogged fortitude. Under a devastating fire, a volunteer runner had carried back to Oyes an imperative demand for reinforcements and munitions, and the German Brigade Commander had ordered two companies to Purgold's aid, but they had been prevented from leaving Oyes by the intensity of the French bombardment. Although a caisson of much-needed ammunition and later a group of eighty men had eventually reached Mondemont, the gallant detachment which had all but thrown the left wing of the French Ninth Army into disarray had received little succour or support. In the late afternoon, a non-commissioned officer sent back with another appeal for assistance returned with the discouraging intelligence that the German 20th Division had been ordered to retreat and was already abandoning Oyes. With no alternative but to give up the position he had so courageously defended, Purgold began to evacuate his wounded, and though wounded himself, remained to the end. Under the last furious French bombardment, the defenders of Mondemont moved out towards the north, and as Lestoquoi's infantry finally burst into the court-yard of the Château, they saw of the enemy only a few shadowy figures retreating through the twilight down the northward slope. Whether the retreat was wholly voluntary or whether it was impelled by the final desperate bombardment and assault, the fact remains that in the capture and defence of Mondemont against overwhelming odds, Captain Purgold and his men have written a glorious page in the annals of the German infantry.[5]

In the meanwhile, farther to the east, events had moved swiftly to a climax. Throughout the day Foch had issued a series of ringing appeals to his wavering troops, calling attention to the favourable developments to the west, on the front of the Fifth Army, and exhorting his men to give the last ounce of their strength and courage in order to reap the benefit of victory so near at hand. As Grossetti's Division approached the scene of action, Foch determined to launch it at once into an attack, supported by the elements of his right wing in the measure of their ability. A general counter-attack, mounted by every available unit of the French Ninth Army, seems to have been the Army Commander's conception from a reading of

[5] In his book *D'Esternay aux Marais de Saint-Gond* (Lavauzelle, Paris, 1930), Lieut.-Col. Koeltz has given an account of the episode of Mondemont from the German side that is at once clear, concise and eminently fair.

his orders, and the legend has persisted of a great counter-attack, executed by seven divisions, sweeping the enemy before it and turning the tide of battle.

The reality was much more modest. Weary, disorganized and scattered, the elements of the 9th and 11th French Corps were no longer capable of an offensive movement on a grand scale, and Weygand, the Army Chief of Staff, whom Foch sent personally to supervise the organization of the supreme effort, has expressly disclaimed any expectation on his chief's part that such an offensive could be executed.[6] Nevertheless, the issue of the battle depended upon not giving way ; at all costs the offensive spirit had to be maintained, and the best means seemed to be by ordering a counter-attack. An attempt had to be made, but the 42nd Division which was to furnish the nucleus did not arrive. The attack planned for four o'clock was deferred, first until five, then until six, in the hope that Grossetti might come, but the light was beginning to wane and further postponement became impossible. For nearly two hours the vigour of the enemy's pressure had unaccountably relaxed and prospects seemed favourable, when at last, shortly after six, one brigade of the 17th Division moved forward. Even imperative orders from Army Headquarters and from intermediate commanders produced little effect in other units and the counter-attack so often celebrated was actually executed by only five battalions instead of by eighty-four. In fact it was a blow in the air, for as the French infantry somewhat hesitantly advanced, it encountered no opposition. The German III Army was already in full retreat, and the enemy had gone. As for the 42nd Division, it did not arrive on the line from which it had been supposed to debouch until after nightfall and took no part in the operation.

At Von Hausen's Headquarters the atmosphere of confident optimism with which the day had started upon news of Von Kirchbach's early successes had changed to one of deepest gloom. The news of Von Bülow's retreat, which arrived at noon, left the Saxon Army Commander bewildered and amazed, for he was wholly in the dark as to the reasons for his colleague's decision, and hesitated to credit it, until a message from Von Kirchbach that he had received an order to retreat direct from Von Bülow brought confirmation.

Once convinced that the II Army had embarked irrevocably on its retirement, Von Hausen had no choice but to conform, for without the Guard, Von Kirchbach's three divisions could not continue their operations independently, and furthermore it would not do to leave the II Army's flank exposed. On the other hand, although the Duke

6 See Gen. Weygand's preface to Capt. Villate's book, *Foch à la Marne* (Lavauzelle, Paris, 1933).

of Wurtemburg had made no notable progress around Vitry-le-François, there seemed no indication that the IV Army contemplated retreat, and the withdrawal of D'Elsa's three divisions from its right wing would place it in grave jeopardy. Accordingly, late in the afternoon, Von Hausen directed Von Kirchbach to halt and fall back, but issued no corresponding order to the easterly group of the III Army, pending further information of the wishes of the High Command.

Alone of the three German right wing Army Commanders Von Hausen seems to have been troubled with doubts as to whether his action conformed to Von Moltke's intentions and desires. A difficult choice lay before him : if he did not retreat, he would lose contact with Von Bülow and expose his own right flank ; if he did retreat, he would imperil the Duke of Wurtemburg's Army. At 5:30 P.M. he reported to Von Moltke that he was retiring north of the Marne and in the evening received telephone instructions through the IV Army to remain south of the Marne ready for a new offensive. Fearful lest the High Command did not fully understand the situation, Von Hausen sought advice from Hentsch, telephoning him at Courtisols, the Headquarters of the IV Army, as he arrived there on his return journey to Luxembourg.

"The order of the High Command to remain south of the Marne can no longer be carried out literally," Hentsch replied to Von Hausen's request for an interpretation of Von Moltke's order. "The situation of the II Army is different from what it must have appeared to the High Command when it sent its message."

Upon his own responsibility Hentsch therefore authorized Von Hausen to take such measures as he might deem necessary with due regard for the II Army, with an obvious implication that Von Hausen should meet Von Bülow's wishes and withdraw in such fashion as to maintain close liaison with him. While Von Hausen considered whether to follow Hentsch's suggestion or Von Moltke's order, another message arrived by radio direct from Luxembourg :

The III Army will remain south of Châlons-sur-Marne. The offensive will be resumed September 10th as soon as possible.

With all doubts thus dispelled, Von Hausen determined to adhere to his original plan of a partial withdrawal by his right wing before Foch's Army, while his left remained in position in liaison with the Duke of Wurtemburg, and he accordingly radioed Von Moltke :

The combats of the 8th and 9th have been difficult and costly. We have captured 50 cannon, machine-guns and some hundreds of prisoners. The 10th the Army will remain south of Châlons. Advance elements, Pierre-Morains, Sommesous, Sompuis, Huiron.

Von Bülow's decision to withdraw his Army northwards towards the Marne thus halted the advance which Von Hausen had confidently expected would produce decisive victory over Foch. Whether or not it would have done so, and whether the Von Kirchbach's group of the German III Army would have been able to crush the right wing of the French Ninth Army must forever remain conjectural. Many military writers, especially in Germany, have categorically affirmed that Foch was defeated, but the same has been said with elaborate proof of Wellington at Waterloo. Like the mythical hero of antiquity who was killed in battle, but failing to perceive he was dead continued to fight, Foch failed to recognize defeat, and like many another great captain in similar case, events proved him justified.[7]

[7] The numerous biographies of Foch all deal, in more or less detail, with the Battle of the Marshes of St. Gond. In addition to the authorities already mentioned, Le Goffic's *Les Marais de Saint-Gond* (Plon, Paris, 1917) gives a vivid, non-technical, but not wholly accurate, account from the French view-point.

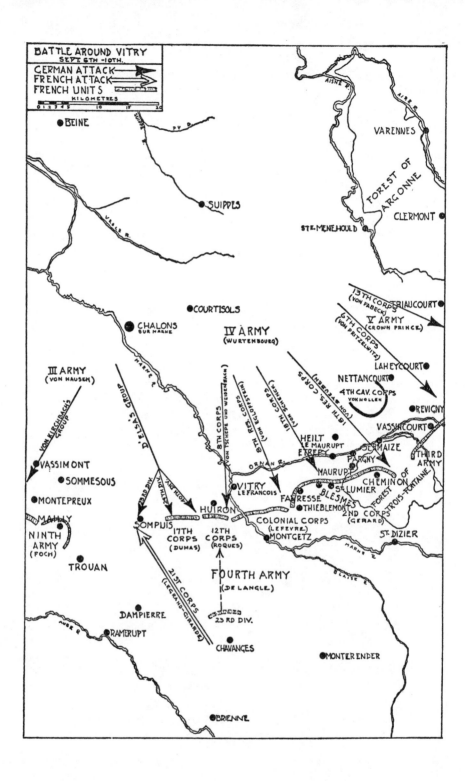

BATTLE AROUND VITRY
SEPT. 6TH -10TH.
GERMAN ATTACK
FRENCH ATTACK
FRENCH UNITS
KILOMETRES
0 1 2 3 4 5   10   15   20

BEINE

VARENNES

AISNE R.

AIRE R.

FOREST OF
ARGONNE

SUIPPES

VESLE R.

STE.MENEHOULD

CLERMONT

13TH CORPS STRIAUCOURT
(VON FABECK)

COURTISOLS

IV ARMY
(WURTEMBOURG)

V ARMY
(CROWN PRINCE)

6TH CORPS
(VON PRITZELWITZ)

CHALONS
SUR MARNE

LAHEYCOURT

NETTANCOURT
4TH CAV. CORPS
(VON HOLLEN)

REVIGNY

III ARMY
(VON HAUSEN)

MARNE R.

8TH CORPS
(VON TSCHEPE UND WEIDENBACH)

8TH RES. CORPS
(VON KIRCHBACH)

18TH CORPS
(VON SCHENCK)

18TH RES. CORPS
(VON STEUBEN)

D. ELSA'S GROUP

VON KIRCHBACH'S GROUP

VASSINCOURT

VASSIMONT

SOMMESOUS

HEILT
LE MAURUPT
ETREPY

SERMAIZE

THIRD
ARMY

MONTEPREUX

ORNAN R.

PARGNY

CHEMINON

FOREST OF

MAURUPT

MAILLY

NINTH
ARMY
(FOCH)

23RD DIV.

60TH DIV.

VITRY
LE FRANCOIS

HUIRON

SOMPUIS

17TH
CORPS
(DUMAS)

12TH
CORPS
(ROQUES)

FARESSE

ST.LUMIER

BLESMES

THIEBLEMON

TROIS-FONTAINE

2ND CORPS
(GERARD)

ST. DIZIER

COLONIAL CORPS
(LEFEVRE)
MONTGETZ

MARNE R.

TROUAN

21ST CORPS
(LEGRAND-GIRARDE)

FOURTH ARMY
(DE LANGLE)

BLAISE R.

DAMPIERRE

RAMERUPT

AUBE R.

23 RD DIV.

CHAVANGES

MONTER ENDER

BRIENNE

CHAPTER XXXVI

THE BATTLE AROUND VITRY

WHILE the events described in the preceding chapters were taking place, another struggle was in progress farther to the east, equally violent, if somewhat less dramatic. When Joffre's order of September 5th,[1] directing De Langle to halt his retreat and stand his ground, reached the French Fourth Army it had arrived on a line that described an arc running from Hambauville, southwest of Vitry-le-François to a point between Sermaize and Revigny northeast of it. On neither flank was De Langle's Army in close contact with its neighbour. On its left a gap of some twenty kilometres, the Gap of Mailly, stretching across the flats of Champagne, separated it from Foch's right wing, and on its right another gap, the Gap of Revigny, less extensive but no less vulnerable, lay between it and the left of Sarrail's Third Army.

Both breaches thus existing in the French front offered the enemy tempting avenues to success. Through the Gap of Mailly, Von Hausen and the Duke of Wurtemburg might turn the left flank of the French Fourth Army and open a free path to the rear of the forces defending the line of the Moselle against the Bavarian Crown Prince, and similarly the Gap of Revigny opened a corridor through the hills surrounding Verdun which would lead the German Crown Prince direct to Bar-le-Duc, his main initial objective. To prevent the exploitation of either gap without forces sufficient to close them became the principal mission of the two eastern French Armies as the decisive battle opened.

The danger arising from the exposed flanks of the French Fourth Army had not escaped Joffre's attention, however, and to meet it he had withdrawn on September 3rd two army corps from Lorraine, the 15th and the 21st from the Second and First Armies respectively, both of which were on their way when the Battle of the Marne began.

Since crossing the Meuse on August 29th, the German IV Army had steadily advanced, meeting only the opposition of rear-guard detachments, but the Duke of Wurtemburg's almost daily bulletins of victory had led Von Moltke to pin his faith upon his ability, in conjunction with the German Crown Prince, to achieve a decisive

[1] See pg. 220 and Appendix XII.

victory when the German right wing armies seemed no longer able to do so.   In the General Directive of September 5th, Von Moltke assigned a definitely offensive role to the IV and V Armies, ordering them to drive forward in a southeasterly direction to open the passages of the Moselle to the VI and VII Armies which were still floundering indecisively before the fortified positions around Nancy. With no thought of any change of attitude on the part of his adversary, the Duke of Wurtemburg prepared to carry out his instructions on the day of September 6th and directed his Army to march towards the southeast, debouching from Vitry-le-François and the line of the Marne-Rhine Canal with Montceltz, Thiéblemont, Maurupt and Sermaize as its objectives.[2]

On a front of fifty kilometres the battle opened with a violence that led the German commander to believe that the French, at the end of their strength, had resolved on a last despairing stand, but aviation reports of enemy columns coming up from the south [3] altered his view and brought the realization that the decisive battle, which he thought had already been fought and won, was at last engaged.   The exposed situation of the 8th Corps (Von Tschepe und Weidenbach) on the right flank of the IV Army determined the Duke of Wurtemburg to appeal to Von Hausen for aid, with the result already noted that the 19th Corps (Von Laffert) and the 23rd Division of the 12th Corps (D'Elsa) of the Saxon Army were turned to aid the IV Army's imperilled right wing.   Although this division of the German III Army into two separate groups involved a substantial change in its mission as prescribed by the General Directive of September 5th, it was characteristic of the attitude of the German Army Commanders throughout the campaign that neither Von Hausen nor the Duke of Wurtemburg deemed it necessary to consult Von Moltke or to obtain his approval.

It was De Langle's plan, in accordance with Joffre's instructions, to remain on the defensive until the arrival of the 21st Corps (Legrand-Girarde) on his Army's left put an end to any possibility that the enemy might exploit the Gap of Mailly.   For three days, without interruption, the French Fourth Army beat off the attacks of the German IV Army and of the three Saxon divisions fighting with it, yielding little ground despite a momentary weakness by the Colonial Corps.[4]

[2] Order of Battle from southwest to northeast: *German IV Army* (Wurtemburg): 8th Corps (Von Tschepe und Weidenbach), 8th Reserve Corps (Von Egloffstein), 18th Corps (Von Schenck), 18th Reserve Corps (Von Steuben). *French Fourth Army* (De Langle): 17th Corps (Dumas), 12th Corps (Roques), Colonial Corps (Lefévre), 2nd Corps (Gérard).

[3] The 23rd Division of the French 12th Corps.

[4] For an account of the operations of the Colonial Corps, see Gen. Puyperoux's *La 3e Division Coloniale dans la grande guerre* (Fournier, Paris).

In spite of General d'Elsa's urging, the Duke of Wurtemburg rejected as too unorthodox Von Hausen's plan for a bayonet attack on a large scale, executed in the dark without artillery preparation, and the assault so successfully carried out against Foch's right wing on the morning of September 8th, was deferred on the front of the German IV Army until after daybreak and then delivered only following the conventional bombardment.   With the French alert and waiting, the attack made no material progress, and at nightfall De Langle summarized his situation to Joffre in encouraging terms :

Very sharp fighting along the whole front with varying degrees of success.   Particularly violent on the front of the 17th Corps which lost a little ground but is in good condition at the end of the day.   The general situation at the close of the day is good.

The battle has been very hot today.   It seems that the enemy has thrown in all his forces.   Aviators report no more troops approaching the battlefield from the rear.   The entry of the 13th Division (21st Corps) into line, southwest of Sompuis, occurred too late in the afternoon to produce any effect.   Tomorrow the attack of the 21st Corps, disposing of its full strength, against the enemy right has a good chance of bringing about a decision.

Physical condition of troops good.   Morale, much improved, is now excellent.   Post of Command maintained at Chavanges.

De Langle

The report thus rendered to the Commander in Chief after three days of violent battle fairly reflected the state of mind prevailing in the French Fourth Army.   Neither the Duke of Wurtemburg nor D'Elsa's group of divisions had made appreciable progress, and at the end of the fighting on September 8th, the lines of the opposing forces remained substantially the same as when battle had been joined on the morning of the 6th.

The arrival of the 21st Corps (Legrand-Girarde) turned the tide. Uncertainty in the French High Command as to the exact use to be made of this corps resulted in some confusion in the orders issued to it and in the imposition, needlessly it would seem, of some twenty kilometres additional marching, so that it did not arrive on the field either as soon as De Langle had hoped or in as fresh condition.[5] Nevertheless, with the entry of both its divisions into line, the left wing of the French Fourth Army took the offensive against D'Elsa's Saxons, and with no further reason to fear that their flank might be turned through the Gap of Mailly, the French seized and retained the initiative.   Though the progress made did not fully satisfy De Langle, by nightfall on the 10th the 21st Corps held Sompuis and

[5] The 21st Corps after its withdrawal from the First Army was first assigned to the Third Army, then reserved at the disposal of the Commander in Chief and finally sent to the Fourth Army.   On its part in the battle, see Gen. Legrand-Girarde, *op. cit.*

had established firm contact with Foch's Ninth Army which by that time was advancing on the left.

While events around Vitry-le-François, on the left and centre of the French line, had taken a favourable turn for De Langle's Army, the situation of its right wing remained obscure and unsatisfactory. No real contact existed between Gérard's 2nd Corps and the left wing of Sarrail's Third Army, and the Gap of Revigny still presented a real source of danger. The arrival of the French 15th Corps (Espinasse) in the evening of September 7th did not suffice wholly to close the breach between the two French armies, and the enemy's efforts in this quarter gained in intensity as his inability to progress farther to the southwest became increasingly apparent.

From the outset of the battle the German Crown Prince had striven to induce the Duke of Wurtemburg to concentrate against De Langle's right wing and to co-operate with the German V Army in an effort to force the Gap of Revigny instead of pressing his attacks around Vitry-le-François. A sharp disagreement arose between the two royal Army Commanders, for Wurtemburg on the contrary was convinced that his wisest course lay in an effort to envelop De Langle's left flank, and for this purpose he even contemplated withdrawing one division of Von Schenck's 18th Corps in order to reinforce his right. The Crown Prince appealed to the High Command to adjudicate the difference, but the response gave him scant comfort, for Von Moltke's innate respect for royal dignity, and perhaps also his fear of the consequences of taking sides in a quarrel between his princely subordinates, led him to dodge the issue in a brief and cautious message :

It is desirable that the IV and V Armies should lend one another mutual support. Acknowledge receipt.

Von Moltke

Though the Duke of Wurtemburg abandoned his design of withdrawing the division that was covering the Crown Prince's right flank, it was not until two days later — September 9th — that he consented unreservedly to co-operate by joining the action of his 18th Reserve Corps (Von Steuben) to that of the V Army. It was a fortunate circumstance for De Langle, because Gérard's 2nd Corps, holding a front of twenty kilometres with no reserves available, had all it could do as it was to stand its ground.

In the first day's fighting the French 4th Division had lost Sermaize and had fallen back to the woods around Cheminon. The following day, under pressure from Von Schenck's 18th Corps, it had abandoned Pargny. From end to end of Gérard's front, German attacks followed one another in swift succession, and the days of

September 9th and 10th, when the German armies to the west were already in full retreat, brought no relief. Before Blesmes and St. Lumier, the French 3rd Division won a notable local success, driving back the German 8th Reserve Corps (Von Egloffstein) in disorder, but on the Corps right, despite desperate fighting, the 4th Division could not hold the key positions of Maurupt and Le Montoy, and its situation became critical in the extreme.[6]

All but resigned to the abandonment of the ground so heroically defended against heavy odds, Gérard warned De Langle, in the afternoon of the 10th, that his Corps was reaching the limit of its endurance, and at the same time issued secret instructions to his subordinates preparatory to a retirement south of the Marne. But the necessity which seemed imminent did not arise. The expected German attacks did not materialize, and at sundown an unwonted calm, lasting throughout the night, fell along the front of the French 2nd Corps. As the weary French units toiled feverishly to reorganize their lines and to construct defences against the assault they felt sure would break upon them at dawn, a strange rumble came through the stillness to the ears of the watchful outposts. It was not the accustomed roar of cannon, but the distant sound of iron-shod wheels rolling over cobbled roads.

At daylight observers in a church steeple at Blesmes noted clouds of dust mounting along the roads behind the enemy lines and forthwith pointed them out as targets for the French artillery. The enemy responded with a vigorous fire, and the battle seemed about to reopen along the whole front ; but General Cordonnier, commanding the French 3rd Division, observed that the German bombardment was not concentrated upon any particular sector, as if in prelude to an assault, but fell impartially along the whole line and to the rear. More significant still, the firing seemed at long range and entirely from the north. From a front-line observation post, Cordonnier studied the situation through his glasses, and at length called over to him an earnest-eyed youngster, an Aspirant [7] commanding an infantry section.

"You seem to be an Aspirant, young man," the General said. "Would you like to get your commission ?"

"Yes, sir."

"Over there, behind those trees, is a farm."

"I know it, sir. It's the Sorton Farm."

"Take as many men as you need, your whole Section, if you like,

---

[6] In *L'Obéissance aux Armées* (Lavauzelle, Paris, 1924), Gen. Cordonnier has given a dramatic, detailed account of the operations of the right wing of De Langle's Army.
[7] This rank, analogous to *Fähnrich* in the German service, has no exact equivalent in the United States Army. It may be placed between Cadet and commissioned officer — a student-officer.

and go to that farm. Find out whether it is strongly held. Don't let yourself be held up by a patrol. Tell me whether the enemy is there or whether he's retreating. I want to know what you find out the very minute you get the information. You'll get your commission if you do your work well. Go ahead."

Eagerly the Aspirant set out, and similar parties were dispatched towards other points, while the Division Commander impatiently paced the ground behind the lines of his infantry. A half hour passed ; then shots rang out around the Sorton Farm, and in a few minutes a breathless runner appeared with a hastily scribbled note. Sorton Farm had been held only by a weak patrol which was falling back towards Etrepy ; the Aspirant was following with his section. It was the fulfillment of Cordonnier's hopes. The enemy was retreating.

All along the front of the French Fourth Army the experience was the same on that morning of September 11th. The German main bodies had broken contact under cover of the darkness and were retreating towards the north. The bitter struggle was over for De Langle, as two days before it had ended for Maunoury, Franchet d'Esperey and Foch.

CHAPTER XXXVII

THE GAP OF REVIGNY

THE French Third Army, commanded by Sarrail, held the eastern extremity of the great semi-circular battle-line on which Joffre launched the Allied counter-offensive. During its two weeks' retreat, it had slowly pivoted around the fortress of Verdun, so that on September 5th, instead of occupying the region northeast of the great stronghold in which it had fought its opening battle against the German Crown Prince, it had reached the region southwest of the fortress.

Anticipating that in the coming manoeuvres Sarrail might be forced to abandon contact with Verdun in order to maintain liaison with the Fourth Army on his left, Joffre had strengthened the garrison and at the insistent request of the Governor, General Coutanceau, had compelled Sarrail to relinquish control of the mobile forces from the fortress which he had temporarily taken under his command. In addition to the Reserve division and Territorial battalions normally attached to the large fortresses, Coutanceau had at his disposal three Active infantry regiments and a reserve brigade, constituting in the aggregate a force of considerable proportions, which was destined to play a part by no means negligible in the impending operations.[1]

The Crown Prince at the head of the German V Army had followed Sarrail across the Meuse and turned southward through the Argonne Forest, keeping always at a respectful distance from the fortifications of Verdun and detaching substantial forces to cover his lines of communication against a possible sortie by the garrison. With no knowledge of Von Moltke's Directive of September 5th, Joffre assumed that the German V Army would continue its southerly course, and on this assumption planned to have Sarrail execute a flank attack from the east, the counterpart of Maunoury's manoeuvre against Von Kluck.

"Debouching from the east," Sarrail's orders read, "The Third

[1] On the role of Verdun in the Battle of the Marne, see *Dix ans de souvenirs* (Chastanier, Nîmes) by Gen. Nayral de Bourgon, Coutanceau's Chief of Staff ; also *Devant Verdun*, Revue Hébdomadaire, October 1917, by Louis Madelin of the French Academy who served as a lieutenant in the garrison.

Army will attack the flank of the enemy forces that are marching south, west of the Argonne Forest." [2]

With two army corps, a group of three Reserve divisions and a cavalry division, exclusive of the 15th Army Corps (Espinasse) which was on its way but had not yet arrived, Sarrail made ready to carry out the Commander in Chief's orders, with the aid of the garrison of Verdun which planned a simultaneous demonstration against the German Crown Prince's lines of communication.

When the battle opened on the morning of September 6th, however, it did not assume the form that Joffre expected, for in accordance with Von Moltke's orders the German V Army had deflected its course in the general direction of Bar-le-Duc, and instead of a flank attack against an enemy moving south, the French offensive developed into a frontal clash with the main body of the enemy advancing towards the southeast.[3]

The French Army Commander expected that while the main attack was being delivered by the 6th Corps (Verraux) in conjunction with the Reserve divisions and the garrison of Verdun on its right, the 5th Corps (Micheler) on the Army left would cover the advance and maintain contact with De Langle's Army in the vicinity of Sermaize. Matters did not work out according to Sarrail's plan, however, for the French 5th Corps, widely extended in an effort to cover the Gap of Revigny, was compelled to face the spear-head of the German V Army's drive towards Bar-le-Duc, when soon after daybreak Von Pritzelwitz' 6th Corps — the same that had scored so signal a victory over the unfortunate Colonials at Rossignol — struck Micheler's line of battle from Revigny to Laheycourt. Thenceforth the left wing of the French Third Army, and particularly the gap that separated it from De Langle's right, became the focal point of the battle.

Inadequately supported by artillery, one division — the 10th — of the French 5th Corps gave way precipitately before Von Pritzelwitz' onslaught, and the enemy, following closely, pressed the retreating infantry as far as divisional Headquarters, where in the ensuing struggle a majority of the division staff fell or became prisoners, and the Division Commander himself [4] was shot down at point-blank range by a German trooper. For a time confusion reigned throughout the division, thus suddenly deprived of leadership, and though a

---

[2] See Appendix XII.

[3] Order of Battle from south to north: *German V Army* (Crown Prince): 4th Cavalry Corps (Von Hollen), 6th Corps (Von Pritzelwitz), 13th Corps (Von Fabeck), 16th Corps (Von Mudra), 6th Reserve Corps (Von Gossler). North of Verdun, 5th Reserve Corps (Von Gündell), east of Verdun, 5th Corps (Von Strantz). *French Third Army* (Sarrail): 7th Cavalry Division, 5th Corps (Micheler), 6th Corps (Verraux), Group of 3 Reserve Divisions (Paul Durand). Reinforced September 7th by 15th Corps (Espinasse).

[4] General Roques.

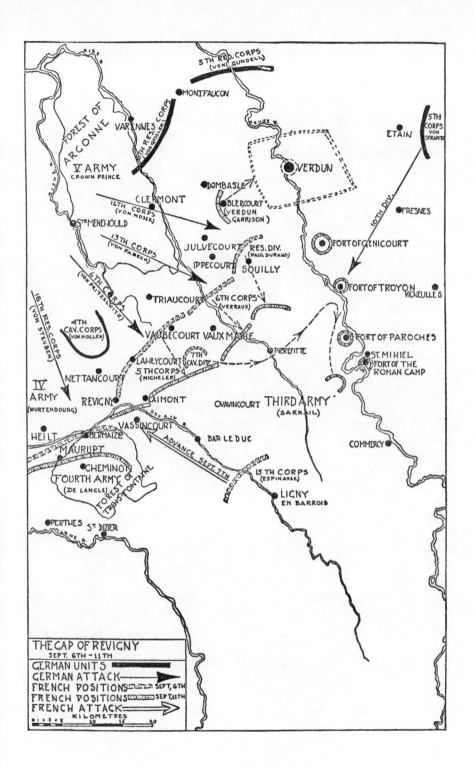

5TH RES.CORPS
(VON RUNDELL)

MONTFAUCON

FOREST OF ARGONNE

VARENNES

5TH RES. CORPS
(VON GROSSLER)

ETAIN

5TH
CORPS
VON
STRANTZ

V ARMY
CROWN PRINCE

VERDUN

CLERMONT

16TH CORPS
(VON MOSER)

DOMBASLE

BLERCOURT
(VERDUN
GARRISON)

FRESNES

St-MENEHOULD

13TH CORPS
(VON FABECK)

JULVECOURT

RES. DIV.
(PAUL DURAND)

FORT OF GENICOURT

10TH DIV.

IPPECOURT   SOUILLY

5TH CORPS
(VON PRITZELWITZ)

TRIAUCOURT   6TH CORPS
(VERRAUX)

FORT OF TROYON
VIGNEULLES

18TH RES.CORPS
(VON STEUBEN)

4TH
CAV. CORPS
(VON HOLLEN)

VAUBECOURT VAUX MARIE

PIEREFITTE

FORT OF PAROCHES

LAHEYCOURT
5TH CORPS
(MICHELER)

7TH
CAV. DIV

ST. MIHIEL
FORT OF THE
ROMAN CAMP

IV
ARMY
(WURTEMBOURG)

NETTANCOURT

REVIGNY

LAIMONT

OVAVINCOURT

THIRD ARMY
(SARRAIL)

VASSINCOURT

ORNAIN R.

BAR LE DUC

COMMERCY

HEILT   SERMAIZE

ADVANCE SEPT 7TH

MAURUPT

CHEMINON

FOURTH ARMY
(DE LANGLE)

FOREST OF
TROIS-FONTAINE

15TH CORPS
(ESPINASSE)

PERTHES   ST DIZIER

MARNE R.

LIGNY
EN BARROIS

THE GAP OF REVIGNY
SEPT. 6TH - 11TH
GERMAN UNITS
GERMAN ATTACK
FRENCH POSITIONS   SEPT. 6TH
FRENCH POSITIONS   SEPT. 11TH
FRENCH ATTACK
KILOMETRES
0 1 2 3 4 5   10   15   20

Brigade Commander at last succeeded in restoring order, the whole line fell back, leaving Revigny, Laheycourt and finally Laimont in the enemy's hands and severing the tenuous liaison that existed between the French Third and Fourth Armies.[5]

Though events at first developed more favourably in the centre and on the right of Sarrail's Army, gains made during the morning were wiped out in the afternoon, when the French were forced to give ground before powerful attacks of the German 13th and 16th Corps. Taken as a whole the battle opened indecisively with such advantage as there was at the end of the first day on the German side.

The two days that followed — days of unremitting effort and danger for the combatants of both armies and of constant anxiety for the opposing High Commands — brought no material alteration in the situation. The arrival of Espinasse's 15th Corps on the left of the French Third Army strengthened and relieved the 5th Corps, but did not suffice to conjure the danger of the breach between Sarrail and De Langle towards which the Crown Prince increasingly bent his efforts. Nevertheless, though forced to fight on the defensive along its whole front and repeatedly obliged to give ground, the front of the French Third Army remained unbroken, and at nightfall on September 8th, the German V Army was still far from the objectives it had to attain in order to accomplish the decisive results that Von Moltke expected of it.

Though the danger from the Gap of Revigny did not escape Sarrail's attention and he repeatedly urged De Langle to close it, he made no effective effort in that direction himself, preferring to remain in contact, however slight, with the fortress of Verdun on his right. The Third Army Commander's apparent willingness to sacrifice the solidarity of the Allied front for the uncertain advantage of keeping liaison with Verdun constituted a grave source of anxiety to Joffre, for the success of the whole plan on which he relied to roll back the German invasion depended upon the close cooperation of each army with its neighbour, and a serious breach between Sarrail and De Langle might well have nullified this plan by jeopardizing the rear of De Castelnau's Army during its defence of Nancy and opening the way to a complete victory for the Bavarian Crown Prince — the very end that Von Moltke was seeking.

If the German Crown Prince succeeded in penetrating the gap between the French Third and Fourth Armies with substantial forces, the most serious strategical consequences would almost in-

[5] The loss of Sermaize by the 4th Division of the French 2nd Corps on De Langle's right (see pg. 298) materially increased the danger of a German penetration between the two French armies through the Gap of Revigny.

evitably follow, but it was by no means equally important that the right wing of the French Third Army should remain in contact with Verdun. With its great ring of forts, its powerful artillery and its strong garrison, resolutely commanded, the fortress had little to fear from the Crown Prince's Army, even though completely isolated, so long as the French field armies remained undefeated and united in the vicinity. Provided Sarrail retained intimate contact with De Langle and avoided decisive defeat, it was incredible that the German Crown Prince would attempt a collateral operation of the magnitude of a siege of Verdun, any more than Von Kluck would have attempted a direct assault against the Entrenched Camp of Paris without having first disposed of the Allied armies operating around it.

In short, Verdun was in no real danger and could be placed in danger only by the very eventuality that Joffre feared — a breach between the Third and Fourth Armies, compelling De Langle to retreat, exposing De Castelnau's rear, and isolating Sarrail by throwing him back upon Verdun.

These considerations Joffre pointed out to Sarrail, both through liaison officers at the Third Army Headquarters and by two dispatches, the first of which he sent on the afternoon of the 7th :

I call your attention to the unfortunate consequences that would follow from allowing yourself to be cut off from the Fourth Army by the enemy column you report is marching from Nettancourt on Sermaize. Just as the Fourth Army must support the right of the Ninth Army, it is your duty in the same way to make your action felt on the right of the Fourth Army, at the same time covering yourself against attempts of the enemy against your right flank.

The following evening, in somewhat more emphatic form, Joffre again pointed out the danger of the Third Army's position, authorizing Sarrail, if it came to a choice, to break contact with Verdun in order to maintain his liaison with De Langle :

I authorize you, if you judge it expedient, to withdraw your right, so as to cover your communications and to lend power to the action of your left wing. It is important not to allow yourself to be cut off from the Fourth Army.

Upon the slim foundation of these two dispatches rests the story of the so-called "order to abandon Verdun," and Sarrail's claim, largely fostered in political circles long after the event, to the title of "Saviour of Verdun." In fact there was no such order — Joffre was careful in making his recommendation not to restrict his subordinate's liberty of action — and far from saving Verdun, Sarrail actually increased its peril by ignoring Joffre's advice and clinging to the fortress.

It seems impossible to escape the conclusion that Joffre was right and Sarrail was wrong. In the light of the strategic situation, the part of wisdom required, above all, united action by the mobile armies, and in his failure to heed the Commander in Chief's counsel, Sarrail assumed a needless risk, with no corresponding benefit to his own Army or to the general cause. Only the fortunes of war, and the failure of the Duke of Wurtemburg to respond to the German Crown Prince's importunities for united action against the Gap of Revigny prevented the French Third Army Commander's decision from leading to disastrous consequences.[6]

Another danger, almost as grave, threatened Sarrail, for the German Crown Prince, perceiving an opportunity to take his antagonist from the rear, ordered the 5th Corps (Von Strantz) which was covering the eastern front of Verdun to deliver an attack from the east against the line of the Meuse.

Along the Heights of the Meuse, between Verdun and St. Mihiel, four forts, Génicourt, Troyon, Les Paroches and the Roman Camp, afforded protection against an attack debouching from Metz and the plain of the Woevre, forming the connecting link between the fortifications of Toul and Verdun, though not within the perimetre of either fortress. They were no more than *forts d'arrêt,* centres of resistance, neither equipped nor intended to withstand a serious siege without the aid of mobile forces, but Von Strantz's attack while the Third Army was fully engaged to the west imposed an unexpected responsibility upon the four little forts and compelled them to play a part of a strategic importance out of all proportion to their strength.

With the intention of crossing the Meuse and striking the rear of Sarrail's Army, the Germans concentrated their efforts on the Fort of Troyon, which covered the passages of the river some fifteen

[6] Sarrail, who had powerful political affiliations among the radical groups of "the Left," was relieved of his command by Joffre in July 1915, and immediately became openly hostile to the Commander in Chief and bitterly critical of him. He became the rallying point of the political elements who sought to discredit the Government's conduct of the war, and sought — in the end successfully — to obtain Joffre's removal from chief command. After his departure from the western front, Sarrail had sufficient influence to obtain an appointment as Commander in Chief of the Allied forces at Salonika, from which command Clemenceau finally removed him in the fall of 1917. In a series of articles, *Souvenirs de 1914–1915,* Revue Politique et Parlementaire, May–July 1921, Sarrail defended his record and virulently attacked the High Command. In a subsequent book, *Ai-je Trahi Sarrail?* (Les Etincelles, Paris, 1930), Gen. Cordonnier offers illuminating comments on Sarrail's conduct at the Battle of the Marne, which he had already discussed in *L'Obéissance aux Armées,* already cited. An interesting character sketch of Sarrail, among other leading French commanders, that is on the whole sympathetic appears in Lieut.-Col. Mayer's *Nos Chefs de 1914* (Stock, Paris, 1930).

kilometres south of the principal line of fortifications of Verdun. If successful, the blow might easily have proved fatal, and to parry it, Sarrail dispatched his 7th Cavalry Division to the left bank of the Meuse, facing east, while Joffre called on De Castelnau, hard pressed as he was, for the aid of the 2nd Cavalry Division and a brigade from the garrison of Toul to make a demonstration against the attacking forces' lines of communication with Metz. Unexpectedly to all concerned, however, the best obstacle proved to be the little Fort of Troyon itself.

At eight o'clock in the morning of September 8th, a civilian refugee warned the Governor of the fort, Commandant Toussaint, that German columns were approaching from the east, and barely twenty minutes later a bombardment opened which continued, almost without interruption, for the next five days. Through the heavy smoke of German shells that enveloped the defences and obscured the gunners' view, Troyon replied staunchly, and when, twenty-four hours later, Von Strantz presented a formal demand for the surrender of the fort, Toussaint promptly refused. In the late afternoon of the 9th, the German infantry advanced to the assault, its skirmishers creeping forward behind sheaves of wheat in the historic manner that Birnam Wood came to Dunsinane. Undismayed by the losses it had suffered, the little garrison manfully stood to its combat positions, bringing the fort's complement of two machine-guns into action, and within a few minutes turned the attacking waves back to their trenches, along the edge of a wood to the east, to await the effects of a further bombardment before renewing the attempt.

For five days and nights the German guns hammered away, with only occasional intervals which the weary garrison turned to account to repair their crumbling defences. A heavy calibre shell crashed through the masonry roof of the fort's magazine and touched off sixty 90 mm. shells stored there, depleting the scanty store of munitions and all but wrecking the defences. Five times the defenders beat off the onslaughts of advancing infantry. Nevertheless, the fort held out, taking advantage of every lull to return the enemy's fire with its fast diminishing artillery. To the right and left the guns of Les Paroches and Génicourt lent such aid as they were able, and the artillery of the 7th Cavalry Division, on the west bank of the Meuse, gave moral support.

"Hold out to the last extremity. The general situation is very good ; the fall of Troyon would jeopardize it," General Coutanceau, Governor of Verdun, telegraphed Toussaint, on the 9th, and Toussaint, though reporting his situation as desperate, kept his colours flying.

At last, at two o'clock in the morning of September 13th, the German fire ceased as abruptly as it had begun, and for the first time the garrison learned that the battle was over and the victory had been won. The exploit of Commandant Toussaint and the garrison of Troyon, a single infantry company, exclusive of an artillery detachment, with no more than a dozen cannon and two machine-guns, in holding a whole German division [7] at bay for nearly a week constitutes one of the most notable achievements of the French army during the Campaign of the Marne.

In the meantime, while Von Strantz's guns pounded at the Heights of the Meuse at Sarrail's back, the battle raged with undiminished vigour along the front of the French Third Army. During the day of September 8th, the artillery of the French 6th Army Corps regulated from the air under the direction of General Herr, once again demonstrated the efficacy of the French 75's by the virtually complete destruction of eleven batteries (66 guns) of the German 16th Army Corps.[8] Like Von Hausen, the German Crown Prince resolved to spare his men the devastating effects of the French fire by means of a night attack, mounted by three army corps, the 6th, 13th and 16th, which had already borne the brunt of the fighting and supported by elements of the 5th and 6th Reserve Corps as well as by the 18th Reserve Corps of the Duke of Wurtemburg's Army. The attack, set for the hours just before daybreak on September 10th, was intended for a decisive blow, and the High Command of the German V Army counted heavily upon its crushing effect.

Unlike most of the German armies, a direct telephone wire connected the Crown Prince's Headquarters at Varennes with Luxembourg, which permitted the plan to be submitted to Von Moltke, who gave it his sanction ; but in this case the facility of communication proved a doubtful blessing, for on learning of the difficulties of the I and II Armies during the day of the 9th, and believing a general retreat to be imminent, Von Moltke changed his mind and ordered the night attack to be abandoned in view of the general situation. In face of the protests which the Crown Prince and Von Knobelsdorff showered upon Tappen, Von Moltke finally relented and permitted the attack to proceed, but meanwhile the German preparatory bombardment had slackened, and the French, who had had ample warning that something unusual was in the wind, had regulated the fire of their guns so as to enable them after dark to concentrate not only upon the German artillery emplacements, but also upon likely points of infantry concentration.

[7] The German 10th Division.
[8] One of the earliest and most notable instances of combined action by aviation and artillery. It served as a model and example in developing the co-operation that became a commonplace later in the war.

When the German infantry assembled in the darkness of a cold, rainy night, the French artillery beat upon it with deadly effect at Vaux-Marie and other points, and on the front of the French 5th and 6th Corps, the German assault which began at three in the morning and continued until after daylight made only limited progress, out of all proportion to the magnitude of the effort and the casualties sustained.   On the French right, however, against the three Reserve divisions through which Sarrail had managed to maintain a tenuous contact with Verdun, the efforts of Von Mudra's 16th Corps were better rewarded.   Though the French reservists, after a period of confusion, managed to retain the solidity of their front, they were forced back so that the right wing of the French Third Army no longer faced west but north, and the liaison with Verdun, for which Sarrail had risked so much, was definitely severed.[9]

A success on the left wing, however, where the 30th Division of the 15th Corps carried out a spirited counter-attack, compensated in some measure for the turning of Sarrail's right flank, and although it did not fully suffice to relieve the right wing of the Fourth Army from danger, it neutralized the threat of an attack debouching from Sermaize, which De Langle and Gérard so greatly feared during the day of the 10th.

September 10th, which had been a day of victory and pursuit for the Allied left wing armies, had been a hard one for the French Third Army, as it had been for the Fourth, but by evening the fighting had gradually come to an end, and in substance the German Crown Prince had only minor local gains to show for all the effort and losses of his great attack.   The French Third Army, despite its perilous situation in the morning, had on the whole improved its position by nightfall, and Sarrail was able to report to Joffre : "The situation is satisfactory."

Despite the relative lack of success that had attended what was expected to be the supreme effort of the German V Army, the Crown Prince was not yet ready to give up hope, and looked forward to a continuation of the battle when Hentsch, on his return journey to Luxembourg, stopped at Varennes on the morning of September 10th.   According to the Crown Prince's story,[10] the representative of the High Command after painting a gloomy picture of the situation of the German western armies, ordered or at least strongly urged

9 In his articles cited above (pg. 306), Sarrail accused the Reserve divisions of undue precipitation in their retreat.   See in reply, and with respect to the operations of the Reserve divisions generally, Gen. Bizot's article *A propos des souvenirs 1914–1915 du Général Sarrail,* Revue Politique et Parlementaire, May 10, 1922.

10 *Meine Erinnerungen aus Deutschlands Heldenkampf* (Mittler, Berlin, 1923), and also see *Récit du Kronprinz Guillaume, Les Deux Batailles de la Marne* (Payot, Paris, 1928).

the immediate retreat of the V Army.   The Crown Prince has stated that in the absence of written instructions he met this suggestion with a categorical refusal and that Hentsch thereupon left.   This incident affords an example of the strange divergences of fact that sometimes appear in the accounts of principal German participants in the Campaign of the Marne, for Hentsch himself, in his report, not only fails to mention having sought to bring about the V Army's retreat, but states that he recommended to Von Moltke that its position remain unaltered, and on this point General Tappen has confirmed Hentsch's statement.

In the afternoon of September 10th, Von Moltke after conferring with Hentsch directed the V Army to remain on its positions, and ordered a continuation of the attack against the Heights of the Meuse to the east.   Throughout the day of September 11th, the German V Army, battered and exhausted, held its lines, watching its no less weary adversary, but making no effort to do more, while Von Strantz still hammered against Troyon.   But events to the west had already determined the fate of the Crown Prince's Army.   During the evening, it slowly drew off to the north, unmolested and unpursued, but forced at last to acknowledge its inability to master its enemy, and the following night Von Strantz too abandoned his efforts.[11]

[11] In addition to authorities already cited, see Gen. von Gossler's *Erinnerungen* (Breslau, 1919) and an article by Sarrail's Chief of Staff, Gen. Tanant, *Souvenirs d'Etat-Major*, Revue de Paris, April 1, 1922.

CHAPTER XXXVIII

THE HEIGHTS OF NANCY

POPULAR interest in the Campaign of the Marne has naturally focussed upon events around Paris, and military writers, intent upon following the development of the Schlieffen Plan, have largely concentrated their attention upon operations on the western portion of the front, so that the importance of the great battles in Lorraine in which the French First and Second Armies were pitted against Rupprecht of Bavaria have been often overlooked, and their place in the strategic scheme of the Battle of the Marne has been neglected. Though the mastery of the French capital was not at stake and the outcome of these battles might not have served to save the German right wing armies from the necessity of retreat, a victory by the German VI and VII Armies over Dubail and De Castelnau would have robbed the Allies of the main fruits of victory and dealt a blow to the military power of France in the end no less mortal than the loss of Paris.

The Bavarian Crown Prince's titanic effort to crash through the French defensive line of the Moselle between Toul and Epinal and to engulf Nancy, the ancient capital of Lorraine, began on August 24th, the day after the Battle of the Frontiers ended, and continued, with a brief interruption from August 28th to September 3rd, until after the issue of the Battle of the Marne had been decided. In general, it comprised three principal phases, the so-called Battle of the Trouée de Charmes, in which the French met the initial Bavarian drive with a powerful counter-offensive, a period of recuperation, during which Joffre withdrew a substantial part of the strength of his easternmost armies, and the final assault, lasting eight days and nights, primarily directed against the Grand Couronné de Nancy, with the possession of the city as the prize.

The vigour with which the German VI and VII Armies pressed their pursuit after their victories at Sarrebourg and Morhange hardly corresponded to Von Dellmensingen's impetuous eagerness to exploit their success, and it was not until four days later, that they again gained contact with the main bodies of the French First and Second Armies. In the meanwhile, Dubail and De Castelnau had reached a front that formed a pocket, facing generally northeast, extending from the Vosges on the right to the heights of Nancy on the left, with the centre of the line dipping to the south between the Meurthe and the Moselle. It is a hilly country, in the main heavily wooded, intersected by three main watercourses, the Meurthe, the Mortagne and the Moselle, all flowing from east to west and each in turn fed by a series of smaller streams. From a military point of view, the natural advantages all lie with the defenders, and in addition the French derived the same benefit of familiarity in peace-time manoeuvres that the Germans had enjoyed at Morhange and Sarrebourg.

On August 24th, the Bavarians marched into the pocket, three army corps strong. It was their intention to pierce the French front through the Trouée de Charmes, between Toul and Epinal, forcing their way across the Moselle and dividing the French armies into two fractions one of which they planned to drive east towards the Swiss frontier and the other towards the west, investing Nancy and eventually the other eastern French fortresses. It was an ambitious program, but the favourable outcome of the battles fought on the 20th encouraged Prince Rupprecht and his Chief of Staff to have faith in its feasibility.

In the brief respite allowed them, Dubail and De Castelnau had reorganized their shattered forces with admirable energy and efficiency, and foreseeing the German manoeuvre, had prepared to parry it by a counter-offensive, launched towards the east by the right wing of the Second Army, while the left wing of the First Army simultaneously advanced north from the bottom of the pocket.

With no suspicion that the French armies, which seemed to have been so decisively beaten, would be capable of another offensive effort, the main body of the German VI Army advanced towards Charmes on the Moselle, leaving only covering detachments to protect it towards Nancy to the west; but on the morning of August 24th, the French 20th Corps (Foch) with Fayolle's 70th Reserve Division on its left, began a northeasterly march towards the region north of Lunéville. Crossing the Meurthe during the morning, Foch[1] established contact with advance detachments of the enemy shortly after mid-day, and receiving strong artillery support, found little difficulty in reaching Fainville, where he halted for the night.

Convinced from reports received during the day that their forecast of the German plan of action had been correct, the French Army Commanders opened the battle in earnest the following morning. Resolutely fixing the line of the Meurthe, fifteen kilometres

---

[1] It will be recalled that it was not until four days later, August 28th, that Foch left the 20th Corps to take command of the Army Detachment that ultimately became the Ninth Army.

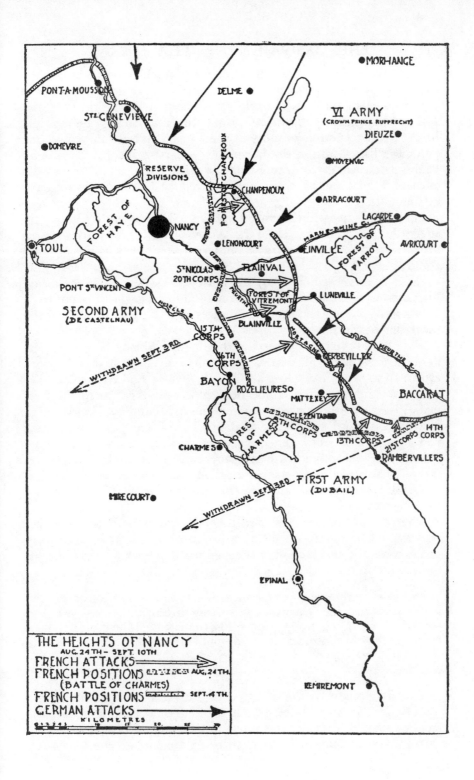

MORHANGE

PONT-A-MOUSSON

DELME

Ste GENEVIEVE

VI ARMY
(CROWN PRINCE RUPPRECHT)

DOMÈVRE

DIEUZE

RESERVE
DIVISIONS

MOYENVIC

CHAMPENOUX

ARRACOURT

FOREST OF
HAYE

NANCY

LENONCOURT

LACARDE

MARNE-RHINE CANAL

TOUL

St NICOLAS
20TH CORPS

PLAINVAL

EINVILLE

FOREST OF
PARROY

AVRICOURT

PONT St VINCENT

FOREST OF
VITREMONT

LUNEVILLE

SECOND ARMY
(DE CASTELNAU)

Moselle R.

15TH
CORPS

BLAINVILLE

MEURTHE R.

16TH
CORPS

GERBEVILLER

WITHDRAWN SEPT. 3RD.

BAYON

ROZELIEURESO

MATTEXEY

BACCARAT

CLEZENTAINE
15TH CORPS

14TH
21ST CORPS CORPS
13TH CORPS

FOREST
OF
CHARMES

CHARMES

RAMBERVILLERS

MIRECOURT

WITHDRAWN SEPT. 3RD.

FIRST ARMY
(DUBAIL)

EPINAL

REMIREMONT

THE HEIGHTS OF NANCY
AUG. 24TH – SEPT. 10TH

FRENCH ATTACKS ⟶

FRENCH POSITIONS ▭▭▭▭▭ AUG. 24TH.
(BATTLE OF CHARMES)

FRENCH POSITIONS ▭▭▭▭▭ SEPT. 4TH.

GERMAN ATTACKS ⟶

KILOMETRES

away, as his objective, Dubail drove his two left wing corps against the 2nd Bavarian Corps and the German 21st Army Corps as they advanced from the north, while De Castelnau threw his 15th and 16th Corps against the Bavarians' right wing and flank.   Though the battle did not open favourably to the French and at more than one point the issue hung in the balance by a narrow margin, the action of the Second Army on the Bavarians' flank soon began to have its effect and the threat of envelopment forced the Germans to successive retirements.

Under the unsparing impulsion of Dubail, who would tolerate no suggestion of weakness, the First Army pressed unremittingly forward, while the Second Army hammered relentlessly at the enemy's flank.

"Forward everywhere — to the limit !"   De Castelnau exhorted his Corps Commanders, and his words found an eager response from Espinasse, Taverna and their men, eager to efface the memory of the black day of Morhange.

The battle that continued without intermission from August 25th until the night of August 28th, quickly assumed a very different aspect from what the Bavarian Crown Prince had expected.   Far from breaking the French line between Toul and Epinal, the German VI Army, facing a rejuvenated enemy, found itself obliged to give ground until the pocket on Dubail's and De Castelnau's front had been wiped out.   The left wing of the French First Army, though not able to reach the Meurthe, established itself firmly along the left bank of the Mortagne, and De Castelnau reached the outskirts of Lunéville and an area northwest of it, adding materially to the security of the positions around Nancy.

The conduct of the First and Second Armies brought Joffre his only ray of comfort in the midst of the desperate trials that beset him to the west, and he recognized their efforts in a dispatch issued to all the armies on the 27th :

The First and Second Armies are now setting an example of tenacity and courage that the General Commanding in Chief is pleased to call to the attention of the troops under his command. These armies have been fighting for fourteen days without an instant's respite with an unshakable confidence in the victory that always rewards the most tenacious.

The first phase of the struggle in Lorraine, the Battle of the Trouée de Charmes, ended on August 28th, and from that date the front remained virtually stabilized until the attacks against Nancy began on September 3rd.   It resulted in a complete check to Rupprecht of Bavaria's plans and for the second time demonstrated the justice of Schlieffen's foresight.

More than ever determined to justify their early enthusiasm, Rupprecht and Von Dellmensingen worked feverishly to complete preparations for a renewal of the battle, urgently demanding more heavy artillery and successfully preventing Von Moltke from withdrawing any forces from their armies for the benefit of the Russian front.

The Bavarian representative at Luxembourg, General von Wenniger, strove with some embarrassment to explain the reasons for the delay in the VI Army's victorious advance, and to account for the unexpected difficulties that had arisen. He found his listeners sympathetic and disposed to overlook the failure of early prophecies to materialize, for the German High Command had committed itself to an offensive policy on its left wing — Schlieffen to the contrary notwithstanding — and its military reputation was engaged.

In Von Moltke's conception, the success of the campaign now depended no less upon the left wing armies than upon the right, and he belaboured Von Dellmensingen with messages urging him to resume his attacks, for the uncomfortable fact could not be avoided, that somehow or other Prince Rupprecht's plans had gone awry and the situation in Lorraine had reached a stalemate.

While Joffre withdrew division after division to lend strength to the Allied left wing, Rupprecht of Bavaria was maturing his preparations, and at last, on the night of September 3rd, launched a new attack, directed this time squarely against the powerful fortified positions of the Grand Couronné around Nancy. With the strength of his Army seriously depleted, De Castelnau had grave doubts of his ability to withstand a serious assault, and in anticipation that a retreat might become unavoidable, submitted to Joffre a memorandum specifying the direction of his retirement and the positions to be taken by the Second Army, in case of necessity.

The successive reports received at the French Second Army Headquarters during the night of September 4th and on the morning of the 5th both from Leon Durand's Reserve divisions and from Balfourier's 20th Corps confirmed De Castelnau's fears, and at 2:30 P.M. on the 5th, he telegraphed Joffre suggesting the evacuation of Nancy :

The enemy has been attacking me violently since last night on the Couronné de Nancy, towards Cerceuil and Haraucourt. The enemy artillery, which has brought up siege equipment, is superior in number, power and range. I cannot depend upon a very prolonged resistance.

In case the enemy presses me vigorously, I can resist on my present positions as long as I am able, but in that case the units of the army remaining will have very little future value ; or, on the other hand, I can execute a timely withdrawal on the first position : Forest of Haye-Saffais-Belchamp-Borville, then on to another position. I will try to hold out and to cover the right flank of the group of armies. I prefer this second solution ; I am preparing to carry it out while awaiting your orders.

De Castelnau

De Castlenau's discouraging message arrived at French G.H.Q. at the very time when Joffre was at Melun, interviewing Sir John French in an effort to secure complete co-operation from the British in the counter-offensive about to open.

The suggested retirement of the Second Army did not fit into the strategical pattern of the Commander in Chief's plans, for the manoeuvre envisaged for the Allied left wing armies was necessarily based upon the right wing as a pivot, and its success depended upon the pivot's remaining in place. Nor would the abandonment of Nancy have constituted an auspicious start for the decisive battle on which so much depended. Though Joffre was wholly willing to sacrifice territory and to risk the demoralization involved in retreat whenever such a course seemed to offer proportionate advantages, he was convinced that he had at last attained the strategic superiority over his adversary for which he had striven so hard, and he was in no mood for further concessions. Confident that he held the upper hand at last, the French Commander in Chief was resolved to hazard all, perhaps even the outcome of the war, on the fighting power of his men. Such was the sense of his reply to De Castlenau the next day :

The principal mass of our forces is engaged in a general battle in which the Second Army, too remote from the scene of operations, cannot take part. I consider it preferable that you maintain your present positions pending the outcome of this battle. I shall then be able to give you general instructions. However, if you are compelled to abandon the Grand Couronné of Nancy, I approve the intentions you express in your note SC1910 of September 4th.

Joffre

Though the civil authorities of Nancy had already begun to prepare for the evacuation of the city upon De Castelnau's order, the troops defending the Grand Couronné had remained in place pending receipt of word from the Commander in Chief, and successfully held their lines of resistance against violent attacks pressed throughout the day of September 5th. Though the group of Reserve divisions to the north and east of Nancy yielded some ground, on the French right the offensive was completely checked.

The German Emperor, who had spent the day at Crown Prince

Rupprecht's Headquarters at Dieuze hoping to be present at a great victory, returned at nightfall to Luxembourg disappointed.[2] His presence there had not been wholly without effect, however, for when a message arrived from Von Moltke, announcing the purpose of the High Command to withdraw a part of the VI Army to the north in order to form the new VII Army, he joined his protests to that of the Bavarian Crown Prince and Von Dellmensingen. Against the personal opposition of the Supreme War Lord, Von Moltke felt bound to yield, and to consent to a continuation of the Bavarian attack with undiminished forces.

On the 6th, as the Battle of the Marne opened farther to the west, the assaults against Nancy continued unabated, and though the French 20th Corps (Balfourier) executed a counter-attack that temporarily improved De Castelnau's tactical situation, the front of Durand's Reserve divisions remained a point of danger. The next day, September 7th, the battle reached the climax of its intensity. Before the threat of an attack debouching from the north, a battalion of the 59th Reserve Division abandoned the position of Ste. Geneviève, a dominating height that overlooked the Grand Couronné northwest of Nancy. With this eminence in the hands of the enemy, German guns would hold the city, as well as the flank and rear of the French Second Army, at their mercy.

Word of the loss of Ste. Geneviève reached De Castelnau just after news had come that one of his sons had fallen on the battlefield. Overcome with grief and momentarily discouraged, the Army Commander directed his Chief of Staff to prepare orders for the retreat of the Second Army and the evacuation of Nancy. Realizing the grave purport of the decision his chief had taken in a moment of great emotional stress, General Anthoine, on his own responsibility immediately telephoned Berthelot who lost no time in informing Joffre. In response to a personal telephone call from the Commander in Chief, the Commander of the Second Army painted a dark picture of the situation that confronted him.

"If I try to hold out where I am," De Castelnau said, "I feel that my Army will be lost. We have got to face the idea of retreating immediately behind the Moselle."

"Do nothing of the kind," Joffre replied. "Wait twenty-four hours. You do not know how things are going with the enemy. He is probably no better off than you are. You must not abandon the Grand Couronné, and I formally order you to hold your present positions."

[2] The story, originating in France, that the Emperor waited attired in the white dress-uniform of the Cuirassiers of the Guard, expecting to make a triumphal entry into Nancy, is apocryphal.

For the third time, by Joffre's personal intervention, the abandonment of Nancy was thus prevented.

In fact, De Castelnau's pessimism turned out to be unfounded. The enemy did not observe the evacuation of Ste. Geneviève and made no effort to occupy it. In the afternoon, a French reconnaissance discovered that the attacking forces had fallen back of their own accord and Ste. Geneviève was re-occupied without a combat.

The German drive against Nancy continued for three days more, but after the morning of September 8th, it became little more than a half-hearted effort. Convinced at last of the futility of further efforts to break through the French defensive line, Von Moltke resolved to abandon the attempt and to transfer a substantial part of Rupprecht of Bavaria's forces to aid his hard-pressed right wing armies. At almost the same time on September 8th that Lieutenant-Colonel Hentsch left Luxembourg on his celebrated mission to the right wing armies, another officer of Von Moltke's Operations Section, Major Roeder, set out for Dieuze, bearing instructions to the VI Army to break off its attacks and to prepare for a withdrawal towards the frontier.

By chance, Rupprecht of Bavaria crossed him on the road, for the Army Commander went in person the same day to Luxembourg to voice a protest against a previous order which had deprived him of six trains of munitions for the benefit of the German Crown Prince. Thus he had no knowledge of the decision of the High Command when he entered Von Moltke's office shortly after six o'clock in the evening. In his conversation with the Chief of the General Staff, the Bavarian Crown Prince obtained for the first time a true picture of the difficulties that beset the right wing armies, in whose uninterruptedly victorious progress he had theretofore implicitly believed, and he learned too of the increasingly critical attitude that the High Command was adopting towards the operations of the forces under his own command. Strangely enough, however, Von Moltke made no mention of the order which was even then on its way to Dieuze or of Major Roeder's mission.

Before leaving, Prince Rupprecht agreed to turn over a battery of heavy mortars to the V Army for use in bombarding Verdun, but he parted with Von Moltke and went to pay his respects to the Emperor under the impression that in substance he had gained his point, that his Army would not be weakened and that Von Moltke approved a continuation of the attacks against Nancy. There is no more striking illustration of Von Moltke's weakness of character which proved so detrimental to the fortunes of the German armies during the course of the campaign.

On returning to his Headquarters the next morning, Rupprecht learned with surprise and disappointment of the written order that had arrived in his absence. Its terms seemed wholly irreconcilable with the impression he had gained from his talk with Von Moltke, and he forthwith called Luxembourg on the telephone to find out what the views of the High Command really were.

It is easier to have someone else give unpalatable news to a royal prince over the telephone than it is to do so oneself, face to face, and Von Moltke had no hesitation in directing Tappen to tell the commander of the VI Army that he must govern himself by the written order delivered by Major Roeder. With bitterness and disillusion, mingled with contempt, the Crown Prince of Bavaria accepted the decision. The German attacks against Nancy slackened, then ceased altogether, and during the night of September 10th, the German VI Army sullenly began to retrace its steps towards the frontier.

The operations of the German left wing armies in Lorraine, though perhaps not strictly a part of the Campaign of the Marne, were an important factor in determining its outcome.[3] The ill-advised effort to break through the French defensive line between Toul and Epinal and to capture Nancy cost heavily in lives and munitions; but more than that, it held the exclusive attention of large German forces that might better have been employed — which were, indeed, sorely needed — elsewhere. Not only did Rupprecht of Bavaria fail to attain the objectives he had set, but he permitted Joffre to withdraw from the forces opposing him strength sufficient to turn the balance of numbers at the opposite extremity of the front, thereby forfeiting the primary advantage which the Germans had enjoyed at the outset of the campaign and in the Battle of the Frontiers. Schlieffen's justification was a brilliant one, but one for which his country paid a heavy price.

[3] On operations in Lorraine generally, see Rupprecht of Bavaria, Von Dellmensingen, Dubail, Foch, De Castelli and Legrand Girarde, *op. cit.*; also, dealing with Leon Durand's Reserve divisions, Rolin's *La bataille qui sauva Nancy-Champenoux* (Berger-Levrault, Paris, 1930).

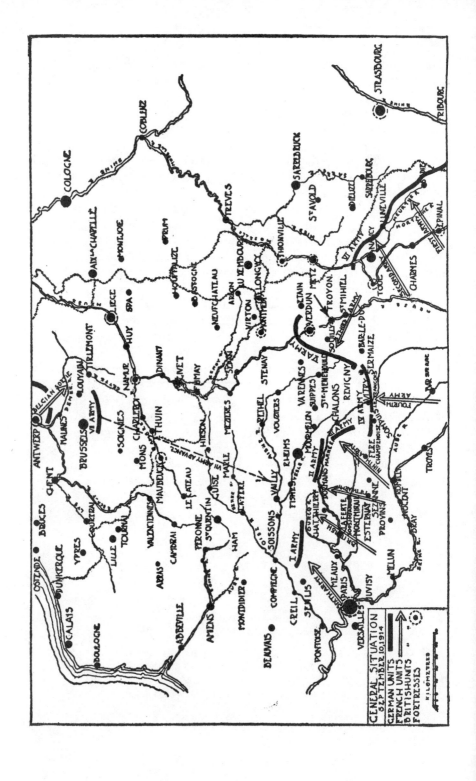

GENERAL SITUATION
SEPTEMBER 10,1914
GERMAN UNITS
FRENCH UNITS
BRITISH UNITS
FORTRESSES
KILOMETRES

CHAPTER XXXIX

EBB-TIDE

ON THE night of September 9th, the issue of the Battle of the Marne had been decided. The German I and II Armies and the right wing of the III had broken contact with the enemy and had started their northward march ; Von Kluck towards Soissons on the Aisne, Von Bülow towards Dormans on the Marne and Von Hausen towards the region south of Châlons. The next night, the rest of the III Army and the Duke of Wurtemburg followed suit, while Rupprecht of Bavaria, abandoning his ill-starred offensive, began his withdrawal to the frontier of Lorraine. At last in the night of September 11th, the German Crown Prince retreated as well.

At every point the carefully laid plans of the German High Command to bring the war to a speedy conclusion by crushing France had ended in a forced admission of failure ; yet in the main the combatant troops of the German armies felt no consciousness of defeat. They were weary to the point of exhaustion ; for days they had had little food and less rest ; their munitions had run low ; they had suffered terribly in killed and wounded ; they were disorganized, as the best troops must become disorganized after days of continuous battle ; but they were not beaten. They knew they had not accomplished what they had set out to do, and that they still had a powerful and undefeated enemy before them, but they had not given up hope and were quite willing to have another try. When the order to retreat came, they obeyed as disciplined soldiers should, without fully understanding the reason, with some relief, perhaps, but also with real regret. In short, the Battle of the Marne, like the Battle of the Frontiers, was a strategic rather than a tactical or moral victory, which left the victors masters of the field, but did not impose on the vanquished the sense of hopeless inferiority that is the mark of decisive defeat. If proof be needed, it may be found in the conduct of these same German soldiers in the weeks that followed on the Aisne, in Artois, in Flanders, before Ypres and on the Yser.

In the High Command, the Great General Staff which had been the proudest boast of Imperial Germany, it was another story. At Luxembourg on September 9th, Von Moltke passed a day of doubt,

confusion and finally dismay as news came to him that one by one
his armies were leaving the battlefields where they had struggled
for nearly four days.   Though he received no direct word from
Von Bülow, Von Kluck, or even from his own representative
Hentsch, until the middle of the afternoon, the Chief of Staff formed
an approximate estimate of the situation as it developed through
radio messages intercepted by G.H.Q.   Thus he learned first of the
retirement of the II Army, and at once foresaw that the withdrawal
of the whole line must almost inevitably follow as the strategic
consequence.

Convinced that orders should immediately be issued for the retreat of all five armies, Von Moltke presented this point of view to
the Emperor when he made his daily report, but to his surprise the
titular Commander in Chief strenuously demurred and forbade any
order for a general retirement until more complete reports had been
received from the right wing armies.   The Emperor, backed in his
opinion by General von Plessen[1] and by Von Stein the Quartermaster-General, stuck to his guns despite all Von Moltke's efforts to
dissuade him, and the Chief of Staff returned crestfallen to his office,
feeling he had lost his sovereign's confidence.

In mid-afternoon Von Moltke at length received a message from
Von Bülow :

The I Army is retreating, left wing Coulomb-Gandelu.[2] The II
Army, in agreement with Hentsch, is suspending its attack which was
progressing slowly, and is retiring to the north bank of the Marne, right
wing Dormans.   Reinforcements extremely urgent and necessary.

Filled with forebodings that as a result of Von Bülow's action a
general retreat would ultimately become unavoidable, Von Moltke
directed Tappen to draft the necessary orders ; nevertheless, he determined to follow the Emperor's wishes, which coincided with the
advice of Tappen and others, and to adhere for the present to the
policy of the General Directive of September 5th, namely to obtain
a decision by the action of the IV and V Armies, while the right wing
armies retired to more secure defensive positions, holding the enemy
in check and — so he hoped — closing the dangerous breach that
had opened between them.   General Tappen has summarized the
conception that prevailed in the German High Command in the
evening of September 9th :

In the evening of September 9th, the High Command believed, basing
its views upon reports received, that there was not yet any occasion to
contemplate a general retreat in order to obtain more favourable defensive

---

[1] The Emperor's personal aide.
[2] Von Bülow evidently referred to the retirement of the I Army's left wing in the
morning of September 9th. See pg. 281.

conditions in positions further to the rear, but on the contrary, that the IV and V Armies, and if possible the III as well, should take the offensive. It was the opinion that in this very tense situation, victory would belong to the one who held out longest.

In pursuance of the foregoing intentions, Von Moltke telephoned through Courtisols to the III, IV and V Armies at 9:30 P.M.:

The III Army will remain south of Châlons, ready for a new offensive; the V Army will attack during the night of the 9th to the 10th; the IV Army will also attack, if it has prospects of success. To this end, establish liaison with the III Army.[3]

An hour later, through the medium of Von Bülow's radio station, Von Moltke issued his orders to Von Kluck:

The II Army has retired behind the Marne, right wing Dormans. The I Army will echelon itself to the rear, ready to oppose offensively any attempt to envelop the right wing of the II Army.

Thus, despite the outcome of the Battles of the Ourcq, of the two Morins and of the Marshes of St. Gond, the German High Command saw no occasion to alter the plan for its right wing armies formulated on September 2nd, the I Army remaining as a flank guard in echelon behind the right wing of the II, with both of them maintaining an aggressively defensive attitude, while the burden of obtaining a decision rested upon the IV and V Armies.

Though outwardly endeavouring to maintain an attitude of calm resolution, Von Moltke gave way to the anguish of despair in a letter to his wife:

Things are going badly. The battles east of Paris are turning against us. One of our armies must retreat and the others will have to follow. The great hopes that the beginning of the war gave us have been dashed. I must submit to events and I will stand or fall with my country. We shall finally wear ourselves out in this struggle on two fronts! What a difference from the brilliant beginning of our campaign! Now it is a cruel disillusion. And we must pay for all this devastation!

The fear of incurring a further manifestation of Imperial displeasure caused Von Moltke to refrain from any definite action, pending Hentsch's return from the front: but the reports received from Von Kluck and Von Bülow early in the morning of the 10th

---

[3] See pg. 292. A confirmatory radio was later sent direct to the III Army.

offered little encouragement. For the I Army, Von Kluck reported on the events of the preceding day as follows :

The right wing of the I Army was driving back the enemy in the direction of Nanteuil ; the centre and left wing were maintaining their positions. The 2nd Cavalry Corps (Von der Marwitz) was holding the enemy in check on the Marne at La Ferté and above. The I Army retired in conformity to an order of the High Command, not pressed by the French, on the line Crépy-en-Valois, La Ferté Milon, Neuilly. The British are progressing beyond the Marne in the region La Ferté-sous-Jouarre, Château Thierry. Intention for the 10th, to continue the movement north of the Aisne. Army H.Q. today : La Ferté Milon.

While Von Kluck ascribed the retreat of his Army solely to an order of the High Command, Von Bülow presented matters in a somewhat different light :

In agreement with Hentsch, I judge the situation as follows : the retreat of the I Army behind the Aisne was required by the strategical and tactical situation. The II Army must support the I north of the Marne, if the right wing armies are not to be crowded together and taken on the flank. Will reach today (10th) Dormans-Avize, with a strong rear-guard south of the Marne in liaison with the III Army. Awaiting orders.

The divergence in the versions of the two right wing Army Commanders is apparent, as each endeavoured to divest himself of responsibility on the very day of the retreat. Neither report is wholly disingenuous in the light of facts actually within the knowledge of the respective commanders. While it is true that the right wing of Von Kluck's Army (Von Quast's group) had been progressing favourably at the time the retreat was ordered, the centre and left of the Army were by no means maintaining their positions, but on the contrary were in the act of executing a change of front from west to south in response to the threat of the advancing British. Along the Marne, Von der Marwitz had been only partially successful in his efforts, for in the early morning two British army corps had crossed the river without serious opposition. In a similar way, Von Bülow glossed over or wholly omitted facts unfavourable to his own Army, neglecting to mention the precarious situation of his right wing and its retirement to Margny-Le Thoult, in his effort to assign the necessity of supporting the I Army north of the Marne as the primary, if not the sole, reason for his retreat.

More serious from the point of view of the High Command, however, than the differences between the Army Commanders, was the indication that the danger from the breach between the I and II

Armies had not even yet been averted, for the distance from Dormans on the Marne to Soissons, towards which Von Kluck was evidently retiring, is forty kilometres, hardly less than the extent of the breach which had originally caused the retreat. The situation of the right wing armies therefore remained insecure and Von Kluck's unaccountable silence, despite repeated appeals for information, accentuated Von Moltke's fears. Determined that Von Bülow should be protected on his right flank, Von Moltke at last took a drastic step, and soon after noon on the 10th, sent Von Kluck a curt radio:

The I Army will be subordinated, until further orders, to the commander of the II Army.

To Von Kluck and his staff, already resentful at Von Bülow's action which they deemed had snatched away a victory within their grasp, Von Moltke's message came as a crowning humiliation. It must indeed have seemed cruelly undeserved, for whatever may be said of Von Kluck's conduct of his Army in the manoeuvres prior to September 6th, once the battle was engaged he had conducted it in a manner and with a resolution that has elicited grudging admiration even from his adversaries; but to Von Moltke this seemed the only practical way to assure the closing of the breach that constituted so grave a source of peril. Once again Von Bülow became the dominant figure in the operations of the German right wing armies as he had been at the outset of the campaign.

It was nearly two o'clock in the afternoon of September 10th before Hentsch at last arrived at Luxembourg to give Von Moltke a first-hand account of the situation of his armies. Coldly and impersonally, he rendered his report to the assembled officers who received it without criticism, and at the conclusion of the conference Von Moltke issued a new set of orders to all the armies :

His Majesty orders :
The II Army will retire behind the Vesle, left wing Thuizy. The I Army will receive its instructions from the II Army. The III Army, maintaining contact with the II, will hold the line Mourmelon-le-Petit — Francheville-sur-Moivre. The IV Army, in liaison with the III, will hold positions north of the Rhine-Marne Canal as far as Revigny. The V Army will remain on the positions it has attained. The 5th Army Corps and the General Reserve from Metz will attack the forts of Troyon, Les Paroches and the Roman Camp. The positions reached by the respective armies will be organized and held.
The first elements of the VII Army — 15th Corps and 7th Reserve Corps — will reach approximately the region of St. Quentin — Sizy by noon on September 12th. Liaison will be established at the latter point by the II Army.

In summary, while the right wing armies fell back and remained on the defensive, awaiting the arrival of the new VII Army, the IV Army was to execute a short retirement to prevent loss of contact with the III and the V Army was to discontinue its attacks and hold its positions, but was not to retreat.

But Von Moltke had not yet come to the end of his troubles. From Brussels, Von Heeringen reported that a Belgian sortie from Antwerp had obliged him to engage a part of the 15th Corps in the vicinity of Louvain and further that a railroad accident might delay the arrival of the rest of the VII Army approximately twenty-four hours. Messages from Von Kluck and Von Bülow confirmed his worst fears that the I Army, instead of closing the breach with the II, was retiring due north, leaving Von Bülow as much exposed as ever. The Duke of Wurtemburg reported a sharp check at Blesmes and negligible progress elsewhere, while the German Crown Prince urgently demanded reinforcements. Von Strantz had not succeeded in overcoming the resistance of the Fort of Troyon, and finally word came from Von Hindenburg, on the eastern front, that his victory over Rennenkampf did not seem as complete as at first reported, coupled with a request for reinforcements.

Faced with a situation that seemed momentarily becoming more discouraging, Von Moltke determined to adopt Hentsch's suggestion that he go to the front and see for himself whether the measures already taken sufficed or whether a further withdrawal of the IV and V Armies seemed desirable.

In the cold, misty dawn of September 11th, a group of automobiles left Luxembourg along the Longwy road, bearing the Chief of the General Staff, accompanied by Tappen and Von Dommes, on his first and last visit to the Headquarters of the German field armies. It was barely eight o'clock when he arrived at Varennes, the Headquarters of the V Army, where the Crown Prince received him. Downcast and despondent to the verge of tears, Von Moltke presented a pitiable figure, picturing the German armies as beaten and on the point of collapse. Nothing that the Crown Prince or his officers could say or do sufficed to restore his confidence or to convince him that an immediate retreat was unnecessary.

Without issuing any definite orders to the V Army, however, Von Moltke next proceeded to Suippes to visit Von Hausen. There he found a general attitude more consistent with his own impressions and expectations, for the commander of the III Army was suffering from dysentery and on the verge of collapse, and the Army staff was disillusioned and demoralized. The evening before, near Connantray, Foch's advance-guards had caught up with the 24th Reserve Division, taking it by surprise and administering a sharp check, and the Saxons had only extricated themselves with difficulty after hard fighting. The III Army was stretched out across a front of more than forty kilometres, with no reserves behind it, and consisted of hardly more than a cordon, highly vulnerable to any serious attack. Ordering Von Hausen to hold his front at any cost, Von Moltke hastened to the Headquarters of the IV Army at Courtisols, where he obtained the Duke of Wurtemburg's consent to take over a part of the Saxon Army's over-extended line.

The Chief of Staff was still conferring with the commander of the IV Army when a radio message, addressed to Luxembourg but intercepted at Courtisols, arrived from Von Bülow. In positive terms it gave warning of a new danger, a serious enemy advance directed against the right wing and centre of the III Army. Theretofore Von Moltke had been mainly concerned over the breach that still existed between the I and II Armies, but now another, even more serious, possibility presented itself, for if Von Bülow's fears proved well-founded, the rear and the communications of the IV and V Armies might be threatened, the right wing armies might both be isolated and disaster would be imminent. Despite the objections of General von Lüttwitz, the Duke of Wurtemburg's Chief of Staff, Von Moltke resolved to order a general retreat without delay. Before doing so, however, he decided to return to Suippes to find out whether reports at the III Army Headquarters bore out what Von Bülow had said.

With Von Hausen too ill to be disturbed and the Army Chief of Staff and the Quartermaster-General both away, Von Moltke could only talk with the Chief of the Operations Section, but a brief conversation convinced him that Von Bülow had sound grounds for his alarm ; a strong column of enemy infantry was reported marching from Villeseneux towards Châlons and other important forces were on their way towards Vitry-le-François and Maison-de-Champagne.

Certain that the situation made the further retreat of the III, IV and V Armies an imperative necessity, at 2:30 P.M. on September 11th, Von Moltke issued his last general orders to the German armies :

Reliable information leads to the conclusion that the enemy intends to execute an attack with important forces against the left wing of the II Army and the III Army.

His Majesty therefore orders :

The armies will reach the following lines: III Army, Thuizy (exclusive) — Suippes (exclusive) ; IV Army, Suippes (inclusive) — Ste. Menehould (exclusive) ; V Army, Ste. Menehould (inclusive) and to the east.

The lines so reached will be fortified and defended. In the course of the retirement, the armies will maintain contact with one another.

After dispatching Von Dommes to carry this order to the IV and V Armies, Von Moltke set out with Tappen for Rheims to meet Von Bülow. After a brief personal conversation between the Chief of Staff and the commander of the II Army, Von Lauenstein, the Army Chief of Staff and Matthes, Chief of its Operations Section, joined them and reviewed the situation in the light of the latest reports. All concurred in the wisdom of Von Moltke's action, and in the necessity for the order he had just issued. During the conference at Rheims Von Moltke placed the VII Army as well as the I under Von Bülow's orders, constituting him in effect the commander of a Group of Armies embracing the whole German right wing. In the evening, without stopping to see Von Kluck, Von Moltke returned to Luxembourg.

During the night of September 11th, all the German armies from the Oise to the Swiss border were in retreat. In the darkness, under an icy rain, the field-grey columns trudged northward, weary in body and depressed in spirit ; Von Kluck towards the Aisne, Von Bülow and Von Hausen towards the Vesle, the Duke of Wurtemburg towards the plateau between the Marne and the Aisne, the German Crown Prince into the Argonne and Rupprecht of Bavaria towards the frontier of Lorraine.

The retreat of the German armies after the Battle of the Marne was mainly a matter of reaching an understanding between the several High Commands as to the defensive line to be finally adopted — for it was virtually unmolested by the Allies — yet it was not accomplished without difficulty. Three times the Saxon III Army reached the positions assigned to it, only to receive orders obliging it to move on again, still farther to the rear. The Duke of Wurtemburg and the German Crown Prince found themselves once more at odds over the lines to be held by their respective armies. The differences extended to the lower echelons of command, and Von Laffert, commanding the 19th Corps of Von Hausen's Army, engaged Von Tschepe und Weidenbach, commander of the Duke of Wurtemburg's 8th Corps, in a sharp road-side altercation in which bitter recriminations were exchanged.

On September 12th, Von Kluck's whole Army crossed to the north bank of the Aisne, between Attichy and Soissons, while Von Bülow's right wing still remained on the northern outskirts of Rheims. The breach between the German I and II Armies thus subsisted, and although the following day Von Kluck extended his left wing eastward as far as Vailly, it was not until the arrival of the 7th Reserve Corps (Von Zwehl), released by the fall of Maubeuge,[4] and of elements of

---

[4] On the operations of the 7th Reserve Corps, including the siege of Maubeuge and the arrival of the VII Army north of the Aisne, see Gen. von Zwehl's *Maubeuge, Aisne, Verdun* (Curtius, Berlin, 1921).

the 15th Corps (Von Deimling), which had come from Lorraine by way of Belgium, that the danger was finally averted. With the French and British once more hammering at Von Kluck and Von Bülow on the day of the 13th, their coming saved the situation with no more than a matter of minutes to spare.

As a measure of further security, Von Moltke arranged to withdraw one army corps each from the III, IV and V Armies and for the transfer of the 1st Bavarian Corps from Crown Prince Rupprecht's forces ; but it was not the reinforcements thus tardily provided that saved the German armies from suffering the full consequences of the strategic disadvantage in which the ineptitude of their own High Command and the skill of Joffre's counter-manoeuvre had placed them. Rather it was the energy and ability displayed by the German local commanders in conducting their retreat, and the notable lack of power behind the Allied pursuit.

On September 14th, despite minor frictions, the German armies at last arrived upon the positions which they were destined to hold without substantial change until the spring of 1918 ; but Von Moltke had still to drain the dregs of his cup of humiliation, for this day was his last as Chief of the German General Staff.

At the suggestion, it is said, of the younger officers of Von Moltke's own Operations Section who had lost all confidence in their chief, and impelled by the officers of the Imperial military household, the Emperor summoned Von Moltke and informed him that the state of his health was too precarious for the heavy responsibilities devolving upon him. The same day Von Falkenhayn, the Prussian Minister of War, assumed the duties of the Chief of the General Staff, and Von Stein, superseded by Von Freytag-Loringhoven as Quartermaster-General, was sent to command an army corps. To avoid the unfavourable comment and criticism which a summary removal of the Chief of Staff immediately following a general retreat would inevitably have provoked, Von Moltke retained his title for several weeks before Von Falkenhayn formally succeeded him, remaining however a mere figure-head, in the role of a spectator, where he had formerly exerted supreme authority. At last, on November 1st, Von Moltke left the field Headquarters of the German armies forever.

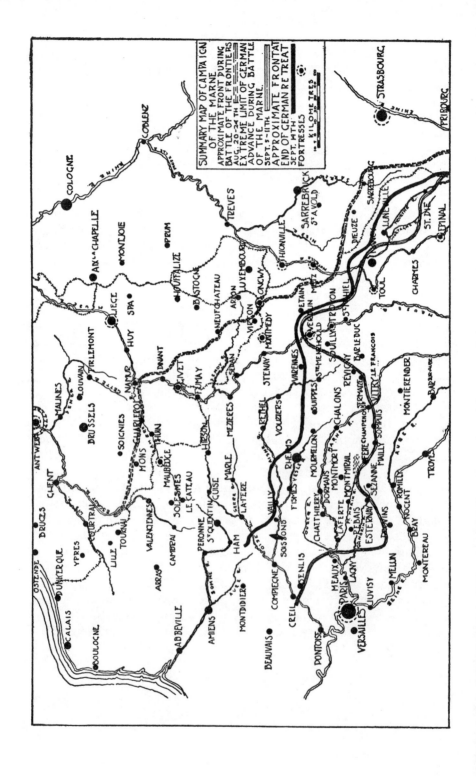

SUMMARY MAP OF CAMPAIGN
OF THE MARNE
APPROXIMATE FRONT DURING
BATTLE OF THE FRONTIERS
AUG. 20-24TH ≡≡
EXTREME LIMIT OF GERMAN
ADVANCE DURING BATTLE
OF THE MARNE.
SEPT. 5-11TH
APPROXIMATE FRONT AT
END OF GERMAN RETREAT
SEPT. 14TH
FORTRESSES

KILOMETRES

CHAPTER XL

THE PURSUIT

THE German armies retreated from the battlefield of the Marne practically unmolested, in many cases unperceived by their opponents, and were able to settle down upon their new positions before the main bodies of the Allied armies could resume contact. In efforts to explain the Allies' failure to exploit the victory so dearly bought to its fullest extent, many reasons have been assigned : the weather, which changed on September 9th from clear and hot to cold and rainy, the exhaustion of stocks of munitions, the destruction of bridges across the Marne and other streams, and the congested conditions of the roads ; but though all these no doubt contributed in some degree, the most important single cause lay in the condition of the victorious troops themselves. A natural reaction from the fatigue of a long retreat, followed by days of battle fought under highest tension, made them incapable of greater effort. It was not the will, but the physical strength that lacked, and orders from the High Command, however peremptory or inspiring, could not supply it.

On the front of Maunoury's Sixth French Army, Von Kluck's retirement was not observed for more than twelve hours. Though Von Quast's attack in the early afternoon of the 9th, hardly produced the effect that some German writers have claimed for it, it left the French severely shaken and during the hours of darkness, while Von Kluck was already pulling away towards the north, Galliéni and Maunoury were anxiously preparing for a renewal of the defensive battle at dawn.

Galliéni's observation of the enemy's retreat did not equal the vigilance with which he had noted Von Kluck's advance, for on the morning of September 10th, he telephoned pessimistically to the Minister of War in Bordeaux,[1] and it was not until afternoon that

---

[1] Galliéni's insistence on communicating directly with the Government at Bordeaux instead of through military channels at G.H.Q. was a source of irritation to Joffre who had little faith in the discretion of civilian officials and feared that useful information might reach the enemy. As a result of a message sent from Paris on the 7th giving the military situation with dangerous completeness, Joffre requested Galliéni not to communicate direct with Bordeaux on military matters. Galliéni recognized the justice of the request and agreed to comply with it, but he nevertheless continued to furnish the Government with direct telephonic reports.

the High Command of the French Sixth Army fully realized that it no longer had an enemy before it. When at last the all but exhausted French troops were ordered forward in pursuit, the German I Army had already gained a head-start of nearly twenty-four hours.

The withdrawal of the German II Army, which started three or four hours before that of Von Kluck's Army, was sooner observed by the French, but Von Bülow's withdrawal of his right wing during the night of the 8th had already given him an important initial advantage, and he had no more difficulty than Von Kluck in escaping his adversary's clutches. In part, this was due to the fact that Franchet d'Esperey, knowing of Foch's desperate plight, had oriented the 1st Corps (Deligny) towards the east to lend the Ninth Army aid, but it was also due to a failure on the part of local commanders to recognize their advantage and to remain close on the heels of the retreating enemy.

The responsibility for the failure of the Allies to obtain benefits corresponding to the magnitude of their strategical victory rests primarily, however, at the door of the British and of Conneau's French Cavalry Corps, for they, above all, failed to profit by their opportunities.

In the early morning of September 9th, Haig on the right and Smith-Dorrien in the centre of Sir John French's line crossed the Marne without serious difficulty, thanks in no small degree to an inexplicable failure on the Germans' part to destroy the bridges. As the British 1st Corps, continuing its march north of the river, reached Le Thiolet and Coupru some eight kilometres away, aviators informed Haig of seemingly important enemy forces congregated to the north and northeast. The mere announcement of the presence of these forces, which in fact were the German 5th Cavalry Division [2] and the trains and convoys of the German 9th Corps, sufficed to cause the British to halt and to remain in their positions until nightfall, though their right flank was covered both by Allenby's cavalry and by the approach of Conneau's French Cavalry Corps. In the meanwhile, Smith-Dorrien's 2nd Corps, which had crossed the Marne at Nanteuil-sur-Marne and Saacy, likewise came to standstill when its 5th Division encountered Kräwel's mixed Brigade near Montreuil. Though a determined advance by the whole corps might readily have turned the German position, which was defended by substantially inferior forces, the afternoon was spent in a series of inconclusive efforts to dislodge Kräwel, and it was almost dark

[2] This division crossed to the north bank of the Marne in the evening of September 8th. During the day of the 9th, it executed a series of complicated manoeuvres north of the river, but was not seriously engaged and had no apparent desire to give battle.

before the enemy fell back, clearing the way for a further advance. Against Kräwel's two infantry regiments, supported in the afternoon by advance elements of the German 5th Infantry Division, Smith-Dorrien engaged only two out of the three brigades of the British 5th Division and two infantry companies of the 3rd Division, while the rest of the 2nd Army Corps rested on its arms awaiting the outcome of the fight.

On the British left, around La Ferté-sous-Jouarre, Pulteney's 3rd Corps encountered more serious opposition, for there the bridges of the Marne had been destroyed and the German 2nd and 9th Cavalry Divisions of Von der Marwitz' Corps defended the opposite shore resolutely. Not until long after dark, after Von der Marwitz had at length fallen back in conformity with the general order to retreat, could the bridges be repaired sufficiently to permit Pulteney to cross with his main body to the northern bank.

In general, it may be said that the forces Von Kluck scratched together to defend the line of the Marne, though suffering from a lack of unity of command, effectively fulfilled their mission against vastly superior numbers even though they did not defend the line of the river itself as Von Kluck had intended they should. It hardly seems possible to accept General Kräwel's statement made after the war [8] that except for the order to retreat, he could have held the British at bay for another day, but it is a fact that at the point of greatest strategic significance and at the crucial moment of the battle, Sir John French's Army exercised no effective intervention. The British advance into the breach between Von Kluck and Von Bülow remained no more than a threat which was never translated into decisive action.

The record of Conneau's cavalry on the British right was no more brilliant. Following in the wake of the British Cavalry Division, the French Cavalry Corps arrived south of the Marne in the afternoon of September 9th, in the vicinity of Château Thierry without encountering opposition. There it halted, apparently paralyzed as Haig had been by the spectre of the German 5th Cavalry Division to the north. With all the roads beyond the Marne already congested with German convoys, retreating northward, the French cavalry waited south of the river while elaborate reconnaissances were sent out in all directions.

It was De Maud'huy, commander of the French 18th Corps, who finally spurred the French cavalry into belated action. Hurrying towards Château Thierry, whither he was pushing a brigade of his 38th Division as fast as he could, he came upon the 10th French Cavalry Division halted by the road-side. Astonished to find it still

8 Militär-Wochenblatt, No. 74, 1919.

south of the Marne, he inquired as to the enemy's position, only to be informed that as yet the cavalry had no information. In a fury De Maud'huy sought the commander of the cavalry division.

"It's a disgrace to the French cavalry," he cried, "My divisional cavalry has already told me there is no one at Château Thierry and you tell me you know nothing ! You're good for nothing ! I am going to take Château Thierry with a regiment of my Zouaves, and you can follow behind if you like, but at least don't get in my way !"

Stung into action by the Corps Commander's tirade, the advance-guard of the 10th Cavalry Division started for Château Thierry and succeeded in wresting possession of the bridge from a weak rear-guard detachment of the enemy before the leading battalion of De Maud'huy's Zouaves arrived ; but it was already late afternoon by the time the enemy had been cleared out of the town. A squadron pushing north of Château Thierry along the main road to Soissons progressed for seven kilometres without meeting resistance other than a few shots from an isolated Uhlan patrol.

"I have nothing before me," the squadron commander reported at 7 P.M. ; but the main body of the division had already bivouacked in Château Thierry for the night and did not follow. The reconnoitering detachment could only fall back.

Actually, at that very moment, the convoys of the German 3rd and 9th Army Corps were painfully making their way along the Soissons road, virtually unprotected, almost within rifle-shot of the French reconnaissance. A vigorous advance would inevitably have resulted in their capture, but the days of Murat and Lasalle had passed.

In the same way, after an afternoon of hesitation and delay, the French 4th Cavalry Division [4] also crossed the Marne after night-fall, and Conneau's whole Corps spent the night in and around Château Thierry with the advance-guard of De Maud'huy's 18th Corps. For a few brief hours in the afternoon and evening of September 9th, the French Cavalry Corps, like the British, had within their grasp a chance to write the word "decisive" before the victory already won, perhaps even to convert into a reality the disaster that Von Bülow and the German High Command so greatly feared, but the moment was allowed to slip away, and the German I and II Armies eluded their pursuers.

Foch, De Langle and Sarrail obtained hardly more impressive results, and the German III, IV and V Armies, like the right wing, carried out Von Moltke's orders to retreat without serious hindrance. So slow was the French Third Army, in particular, in following its

[4] For an account of the operations of this division, see Capt. Langevin's *Cavaliers de France* (Crés, Paris).

retiring adversary, that Joffre testily ordered an inquiry, telegraphing Sarrail on the 13th :

I have received your report of 1 P.M. I do not understand how the enemy was able to get away 48 hours ago without your being informed of it. Kindly institute an inquiry immediately on this matter and let me know the result at once.

Everywhere the Allied armies marched through villages strewn with wreckage, along roads lined with litter of every kind, with broken-down wagons, and with dumps of abandoned munitions and supplies. Frequently they came upon evidences of hasty flight, where the invaders had waited until the last minute before taking their departure, and often in houses or churches they found improvised hospitals filled with Germans too badly wounded to be transported. Stragglers abounded, men who had lost their way or were too weary or discouraged to follow their comrades, but of the armed forces that were destined to spend another four years on French soil they saw little sign. No serious actions between any considerable forces marked the period of retreat and pursuit, until at last the German armies halted, in their own time, upon positions of their own choosing.

With a conservatism in marked contrast to the over-optimism at the opening of the campaign, it was not until September 11th that the French High Command spoke in terms of victory. Then, in a general order, Joffre conveyed his congratulations to his officers and men :

G.H.Q., September 11, 1914.

General Order No. 15

The battle which has been in progress for five days is ending in an indisputable victory. The retreat of the German I, II and III Armies is accentuating before our left and our centre. The enemy IV Army in turn is beginning to fall back north of Vitry and Sermaize.

The enemy is everywhere leaving behind numerous wounded and quantities of munitions. Everywhere prisoners are being taken. As they gain ground, our troops are noting signs of the fierceness of the struggle and the magnitude of the effort the Germans put forth in their endeavour to resist our drive. The vigorous resumption of the offensive brought about our success.

All — officers, non-commissioned officers and men — responded to my appeal. You have all of you deserved well of our country.

Joffre

During the course of the Battle of the Marne and the German retreat that followed it, the Allied left wing armies advanced approximately ninety kilometres ; yet only 11,717 prisoners, three flags, 30 cannon and some 100 machine-guns fell into the hands of the seven French armies, to which may be added some 3500 prisoners and a few guns taken by the British.   The relative insignificance [5] of these tangible evidences of victory afford the best proof of the thesis upon which German writers have strenuously insisted, that the Battle of the Marne was not a great tactical defeat for the German armies. Yet it was certainly not a victory, nor can the German withdrawal be considered a voluntary one.   Rather it may be said that the retirement was forced by the strategic situation and was undertaken in the nick of time, forestalling at the last possible moment a disaster which Von Bülow alone of all the German Commanders realized was impending.

In the course of the whole great conflict, which ultimately engulfed all the great nations of the world, no clash of the opposing forces was attended by greater or more significant consequences, both strategic and political than the Battle of the Marne.   Just as the death-knell of the Confederacy had sounded when Lee's Army marched away from the field of Gettysburg, strategically defeated, so when the tide of invasion rolled back from the Marne, Germany's great plan for a prompt and decisive victory, leading to world domination, broke down once for all.   In the words of Winston Churchill, in his preface to General Spears' admirable book, *Liaison 1914* :

"No part of the Great War compares in interest with its opening. The measured silent drawing together of gigantic forces, the uncertainty of their movements and positions, the number of unknown and unknowable facts made the first collision a drama never surpassed.   Nor was there any other period in the war when the general battle was waged on so great a scale, when the slaughter was so swift or the stakes so high.   Moreover in the beginning our faculties of wonder, horror and excitement had not been cauterized or deadened by the furnace fires of years.   In fact the war was decided in the first twenty days of fighting, and all that happened afterwards consisted in battles which, however formidable and devastating, were but desperate and vain appeals against the decision of fate."

[5] For purposes of comparison, it may be recalled that in the unsuccessful offensive of April 1917, the French took 28,815 prisoners, 187 guns, 465 machine-guns and 149 trench mortars.   During the same period (Arras-Vimy) the British took 20,271 prisoners and 484 guns.

CHAPTER XLI

THE MARNE IN RETROSPECT

THE Campaign of the Marne did not bring about the complete defeat of the German armies, nor did it even accomplish all the immediate results hoped for by the French High Command. Nevertheless it ranks deservedly as the greatest strategical victory of the whole conflict, for it put an end to the possibility of achieving a rapid decision in the west by the defeat of France which had been the basic idea of the German plan of operations at the outset of the war.

It seems idle to debate what might have happened had Von Moltke applied the Schlieffen Plan entirely in accordance with the conception of its author. Much has been written to demonstrate that such a course would have given Germany complete victory ; but there are too many speculative factors, too many possible variations of circumstances, and too much depends upon how Joffre and other Allied leaders would have acted under different sets of assumed conditions, to permit of a positive conclusion. It has been said that Schlieffen, trained in the school of Prussian invincibility, underestimated the calibre of his adversaries' High Command and did not sufficiently allow for the fighting qualities of the French and British soldiers. However that may be, it seems certain that he did not reckon with the inertia of his own countrymen, and did not expect that after the opening of the campaign, the reins of leadership would be allowed to fall slack in limp hands. Whether any plan of operations, however well conceived and minutely prepared, could have survived such treatment, it is reasonable to doubt.

The development of the campaign served to demonstrate in striking fashion the soundness of the dying Schlieffen's injunction, "Make the right wing strong !" But this, above all, was the point the importance of which Von Moltke failed to appreciate. The whole tendency of his modifications introduced before the war in the plans of the German General Staff was to decrease the power of the right wing armies for the benefit of the left, and the two earliest and most important decisions taken by the German High Command after the campaign had started were to the same effect.[1] The first of these,

[1] In his reminiscences, *Aus Meinem Leben* (Hirzel, Leipzig, 1920), Von Hindenburg mentions first the weakening of Schlieffen's conception in enumerating causes for the German failure in 1914.

based on an over-sanguine view of the nature and extent of the victories at Sarrebourg and Morhange, was the unfortunate acquiescence in Rupprecht of Bavaria's offensive in Lorraine, and the second, for which excessive optimism was likewise in part responsible, was the dispatching of two army corps to the eastern front immediately after the Battle of the Frontiers.

Remembering the slight margin by which Maunoury held Von Kluck in check and by which Foch gained the advantage over Von Hausen, it requires little effort of the imagination to picture what might have happened, if the German right wing had been reinforced by a second echelon, as Von Schlieffen intended, and if the German II and III Armies each had been strengthened by the Army Corps of which Von Moltke had deprived them.

Not all the faults which contributed to the collapse of the German plan of command are directly imputable to Von Moltke and the High Command, however, for on at least four occasions the Army Commanders, on their own responsibility, took decisions of vital consequence which turned out unfortunately. The first of these was Von Bülow's insistence that Von Kluck and Von Hausen should limit the scope of action of their respective Armies by converging on the flanks of the II Army before and during the Battle of the Sambre. As a result, the Sambre and Mons, either or both of which might readily have been converted into decisive victories, became no more than inconclusive successes.   Again, after Le Cateau, Von Kluck continued his march towards the southwest, instead of pursuing the retreating and disorganized British, so that Sir John French was enabled to escape the destruction that might well have befallen him and could reorganize his forces to take a decisive part in the later stages of the campaign.   Similarly, on August 31st, partly at Von Bülow's instigation but also because he himself underestimated the French forces assembling to the west, Von Kluck changed his course sharply, this time towards the southeast, thereby leaving Maunoury free to complete the organization of the French Sixth Army outside his flank. Lastly, on September 3rd, the commander of the German I Army pressed forward across the Marne into the region east and southeast of Paris, disregarding through insufficient information the instructions he had received from Von Moltke to fall in behind the II Army in echelon.   In consequence, he exposed his right flank to the blow of Maunoury's Army and gave Joffre the opportunity for which he had been waiting.   It is easy with the full knowledge now available to criticize the wisdom of these decisions ; but in the fog of war each of them seemed reasonable at the time it was made.   All four profoundly affected the development of the campaign and contributed in no small degree to its outcome.

The errors of the German High Command and of the Army Commanders as well, whatever their apparent justification at the time, rested upon a common foundation — a failure of the Military Intelligence to provide accurate and complete information of the strength, dispositions and character of the enemy, and an inadequacy of communication between the higher echelons of command. Whatever may be said in criticism of the French General Staff for its failure, before the war, to forecast the dispositions and action of its adversary, there can be no doubt that after the campaign opened the French far surpassed the Germans in the efficiency both of their Intelligence and of their Communications. All the undeniable qualities of the German soldiers and the technical skill of their leaders did not suffice to compensate for these deficiencies, and the vital importance of these factors constitutes one of the primary military lessons of the Campaign of the Marne.

Material or physical disadvantages likewise played a major part in the collapse of the German strategical scheme. In the first place, the logic of numbers was against them. Along the main battle-front, from Paris to the Swiss border, the Allies engaged 13 cavalry divisions against 9 German cavalry divisions, 54½ Active infantry divisions against 42½ Active German infantry divisions, and 21½ Reserve divisions against 26 German Reserve and Ersatz divisions — a total of 76 infantry divisions against 68½.[2] Even allowing for the greater youth and superior military training of the German troops, this discrepancy, which was accentuated by the replacements the French units had received from their depots, constituted a heavy burden. Hardly less important was the lack of transportation facilities. Operating far within a hostile country, across which the retreating Allies had, so far as possible, destroyed or impeded roads, railways, bridges and means of communication, the German armies found themselves many miles from their principal rail-heads with no transversal lines behind their front, and with no means, except by road, to bring forward reinforcements, munitions or supplies. Even had Von Moltke desired to reinforce his right wing armies by withdrawals from his left, he could have done so only by the circuitous route of Aix-la-Chapelle, while Joffre had unimpeded use of a number of railway lines. In granting the Allies full credit for the skill displayed in the use of the facilities of transportation and communication at their command, it must not be forgotten that the advantage they derived was proportionately increased from the fact that the Germans could only improvise or do without such facilities.

In seeking the explanation for the outcome of the Campaign of

2 See Appendix IX for analysis of this computation.

the Marne, one cannot look solely to short-comings on the German side, or to disabilities under which the invading armies laboured, important as these undoubtedly were. Once the Battle of the Frontiers had ended, Joffre conducted the retreat and the regrouping of the Allied armies with an ability that rarely has been rivalled in military history. The end of the retreat and the beginning of the Allied offensive came, not as the result of any lightning stroke of genius by one of his subordinates, but after a deliberate survey of the whole situation had convinced him that no better opportunity would be likely to offer, and after a careful appraisal of the strength of his own forces and of the ability of his ally to co-operate gave him reasonable hope of victory.

It cannot be said that Joffre foresaw the form of the Battle of the Marne. To have done so before Von Kluck led his Army east of Paris on September 3rd and 4th, would have required a gift of divination beyond the range of mortal fallibility. Still less did he deliberately lead the German armies into a trap where he could strike at their flank. But neither were the positions of the opposing forces when the battle opened merely the result of a fortuitous combination of circumstances. They were rather the logical outcome of the German plan of operations and of the dispositions taken by the French Commander in Chief to counteract it : the manoeuvre in retreat, the formation of Maunoury's Army outside the German western flank and the judicious strengthening of the Allied left wing. By September 4th, unless the Germans halted their advance along the Marne, regrouped their forces and devised a new strategical combination,[3] it had become inevitable that a chance for a resumption of the offensive would present itself, before the Allied armies reached the line of the Seine, the extreme limit of retreat which Joffre had fixed.

The Miracle of the Marne belongs to the realm of fiction ; but if a miracle must be found, it lies in the willingness and ability of French and British soldiers, after a series of devastating defeats and incredible hardships during two weeks of continuous retreat, to turn about and resume the offensive with a power and ferocity that amazed and confounded their pursuers.

Taken as a whole, the Campaign of the Marne finds no parallel in military history, either in the size of the forces engaged, in the geographical extent of the area over which it developed or in the rapidity with which its three major phases succeeded one another.

---

[3] This is the course that a number of high-ranking German officers, writing after the war, among them General von Kuhl, have come to the conclusion should have been adopted.

Never again in the course of the Great War did the opposing sides
enjoy the same mobility and freedom of manoeuvre, nor did the
stakes of ultimate victory again rest so clearly in the balance.[4]

[4] Dealing with the campaign of the Marne as a whole from a German point of view,
the works of Gen. von Kuhl and of Gen. Baumgarten-Crusius, already cited, are of exceptional interest and merit. Two other works, both by distinguished officers, deserve
especial mention : *La Bataille de la Marne* (Fournier, Paris, 1918) by the French Gen.
Canonge, and *Forty Days in 1914* (Little, Brown, Boston, 1919), relating mainly to the
British forces, by Major-Gen. Sir Frederick Maurice. Though both these books were
written before a large part of the documentation now existing became available, the
accuracy of their estimates and judgements highly attest their authors' professional ability. More voluminous popular accounts are, Gabriel Hanotaux of the French Academy's *La Bataille de la Marne* (Plon, Paris, 1922) and Gen. Palat's (Pierre Lehautcourt)
Le Grande Guerre sur le front occidental, vols. I–VI (Chapelot, Paris).

CHAPTER XLII

LEGEND AND FACT

It is inevitable that a wealth of legends should have grown up around the Campaign of the Marne. Most of them are harmless enough, of the Washington-and-the-Cherry-Tree variety, stories invented by journalists seeking to lend "colour" to a prosy narrative of military operations, which are objectionable for one reason only, a minor one, that they do not happen to be true. Some are based on the supernatural, like the Angel of Mons and various apparitions of Joan of Arc at critical moments ; others, like the tale of the German flag twenty metres long, specially woven to fly from the Eiffel Tower, and the ten cars of medals loaded and ready behind Von Kluck's front to commemorate the capture of Paris, bear on their face the patent marks of absurdity. Of still another type is the anecdote of the famous council of war, held on the eve of the Battle of the Marne, where Joffre after listening to the discussion and arguments of his officers, is said to have brought his fist down on the table and remarked : "Gentlemen, we shall fight it out on the Marne."

But there are legends of another sort, more sinister and more cruel, in that they tend to detract from honour bravely won and to give credit where none is due. So rapidly have some of these grown and so widely have they gained credence, that they cannot be ignored, for it is the function and the duty of the honest chronicler, not only to state the truth, but to combat falsehood and misconception.

Two of these found their origin in the campaign of criticism, almost of defamation, started against Joffre in 1915, which continued with ever-increasing vigour and volume until, at the end of the following year, he was promoted Marshal of France and superseded as Commander in Chief. The first is the statement that he ordered the evacuation of Nancy and that only De Castelnau's refusal to obey saved the city from falling prey to the invaders. This is the exact reverse of the facts. On three separate occasions, on August 21st, after the defeat at Morhange, on September 4th and again on September 7th, De Castelnau prepared to evacuate Nancy and even recommended its abandonment. Each time the fulfilment of his purpose was blocked by Joffre's direct intervention, when the French Commander in Chief unhesitatingly took the grave responsibility of over-ruling his Army Commander. Nancy was saved from hostile domination, and the credit belongs personally to Joffre.

Similar in tenor, but more dangerous because it is based upon history's most formidable enemy, the half-truth, is the legend that Joffre ordered Sarrail to abandon Verdun and that only the disobedience of the commander of the Third Army saved the great fortress from falling into the enemy's hands. No order to abandon Verdun was ever given. It is true that Joffre authorized Sarrail, if it came to a choice, to break contact with Verdun in order to preserve the infinitely more important contact with De Langle's Fourth Army, and that Sarrail did not follow this advice. But even if the Third Army's right wing had been withdrawn as the Commander in Chief suggested, or if the suggestion had been put in the form of an order, it does not follow that the fortress would have fallen. On the contrary Verdun was quite capable of taking care of itself in the face of such forces as the Crown Prince would have had available to bring against it. On September 2nd, Joffre had peremptorily compelled Sarrail to strengthen the garrison of Verdun out of the forces under his command when the Third Army Commander had been reluctant to do so, and it seems apparent that Joffre, to a greater extent than Sarrail, appreciated the importance of providing for the adequate defence of the fortress and of endowing it with sufficient means for its security.

The legends of Nancy and Verdun, apparently based upon an effort to discredit the French Commander in Chief and to minimize his share in the victory of the Marne, have derived authority and gained circulation from Galliéni and his admirers; [1] but the third and most wide-spread of all the legends of the Marne concerns Galliéni himself and the part that he played at the critical juncture of the campaign.

It has often been stated that Joffre's decision on September 4th to take the offensive and to fight the Battle of the Marne came as the result of a series of telephone calls from the Military Governor of Paris, in which Galliéni is represented as insisting that the Commander in Chief launch the great counter-offensive and virtually compelling him to do so.

"The Battle of the Marne was won over the telephone," is the way the story has sometimes been phrased, and the inference has been drawn that Galliéni rather than Joffre is entitled to credit for the victory.

The story of the four telephone calls between the Military Govern-

[1] See *Les Carnets de Galliéni* (Michel, Paris, 1932) pg. 201.

ment of Paris and Joffre's Headquarters on the crucial day of September 4th has already been told in detail.[2]   In only one of them — after Galliéni's fruitless trip to Melun — did the Military Governor of Paris talk with the Commander in Chief ; the others were between subordinate officers of their respective staffs.   At the time of this one conversation, Galliéni, as we have already seen, was in no position to press the Commander in Chief to take general offensive action, for he had in his possession no information which might reasonably justify such a course.   No orders had as yet been issued to the Sixth Army, except in the most tentative, preparatory way ; the arrangements with the British were indefinite and Galliéni did not know anything of the situation of either Franchet d'Esperey or Foch.   Under the circumstances, while Galliéni undoubtedly appreciated the strategic advantage which Von Kluck's advance had given the Allies, it seems inconceivable that he should have ventured to force his point of view upon the Commander in Chief.   There seems no reason, on the other hand, to doubt Joffre's statement that the Battle Order for the Marne was already in course of preparation, based on Franchet d'Esperey's memorandum, when Galliéni telephoned and that the decision had already been taken.

Apart from Joffre himself, the French commander entitled to the principal credit for the decision to fight the Battle of the Marne was not Galliéni, but Franchet d'Esperey.   It was his agreement with Sir Henry Wilson that determined the date of the battle and the participation of the British Army, and it was he and not Galliéni who determined the zone of action of the French Sixth Army north of the Marne.   A study of the documents abundantly proves from internal evidence that Franchet d'Esperey's memorandum was the source and the basis for General Instructions No. 6, as indeed Joffre has said.   That Joffre's personal intervention later became necessary to secure Sir John French's ratification of the agreement made by Sir Henry Wilson in no way diminishes Franchet d'Esperey's credit for having obtained it, or for having, on his own part, guaranteed the readiness of the French Fifth Army to do its share.

Galliéni's role in the Campaign of the Marne was an important one.   He must receive full credit for the energy and capacity he displayed in organizing the defences of Paris and in sustaining the morale of its inhabitants, for the aid he brought Maunoury in turning the Sixth Army into an effective fighting force, for his ready appreciation of the strategic significance of Von Kluck's movement south of the Marne and for his desire to take advantage of it, and lastly for his willingness, during the battle, to depart from the con-

[2] See Ch. XXV.

ventional role of a governor of a fortress by engaging his forces without reservation outside the immediate zone he had been charged to defend. The value to the Commander in Chief of so energetic and able an collaborator must not be minimized, but there seems small basis for the claim that it was Galliéni who initiated the offensive of the Marne or determined its time or scope.

At the outbreak of the war, Galliéni was regarded as France's most distinguished soldier, largely by reason of his long and successful period of colonial pacification and administration in Madagascar, where he had had Joffre under his orders. Once the war opened, however, his participation in active military operations was virtually confined to a period of three days, between September 3rd and the beginning of the Battle of the Marne. Before that time, Galliéni's duty was limited to preparing the capital for defence, and after the battle had started, it was Maunoury rather than Galliéni who directly controlled the operations of the French Sixth Army. Frustrated through no fault of his own in the ambition of a life-time, which his career had amply justified, and denied an opportunity to command French troops in battle against their historic enemy,[3] Galliéni seems to have magnified in his own mind the importance of the part he actually played, by a process of self-deception almost pathetic in a man of such undeniable qualities and strength of character.

Just as for many soldiers in the humbler walks, the whole war became epitomized in the experiences of some engagement or raid, not even dignified by mention in the communiqué, for Galliéni the whole Battle of the Marne became centred around these three days, with himself as the central figure. Worn out by illness and fatigue, after a disillusioning venture into political circles as Minister of War, Galliéni died in the spring of 1916, disappointed and embittered, but honestly convinced that he had been his country's saviour.[4]

Under the cloak of respect due to the memory of a great public servant, the legend of Galliéni has grown unchecked in France and in foreign lands. Friends of Galliéni and enemies of Joffre have

[3] In March 1915, when Maunoury was wounded and permanently disabled, Joffre offered Galliéni the command of the Sixth Army. At the time, Foch and Dubail each commanded a Group of Armies, but no Group Commander had been designated for the centre armies. Hoping to receive this appointment — which was eventually given to De Castelnau — Galliéni declined Joffre's offer on the ground that it was not commensurate with his seniority and reputation. Galliéni's conduct on this occasion contrasts with the attitude adopted by Gen. Michel (see pg. 198) and with that of De Maud'huy and Mangin, later in the war, each of whom accepted command of an army corps after having previously commanded an army.

[4] For a point of view wholly at variance with that expressed in the foregoing text, see P.-B. Gheusi's Galliéni (Fasquelle, Paris, 1922) and La Gloire de Galliéni (Michel, Paris, 1928); Leblond's Galliéni Parle (Michel, Paris, 1920) and Grandidier's Galliéni (Plon, Paris, 1931). See also Liddell Hart's The Real War (Little, Brown, Boston, 1931).

zealously fostered it.   Paris, which idolized Galliéni, is the journalistic even more than the political capital of France and has given it unrivalled opportunities for publicity ; until today it challenges the fairness of history.

CHAPTER XLIII

JOFFRE THE VICTOR

"JOFFRE was not a general, he was a national nerve sedative." [1] Thus an English writer has summarized the French Commander in Chief, but the phrase, cleverly turned, leaves an impression that is at once incomplete and misleading. It derives its inspiration, perhaps, from a description that Poincaré has given of his first visit to General Headquarters, soon after the Battle of the Marne :

We found Joffre in good health physically and mentally. He is the same as I have always seen him, just as he must have been formerly in Formosa, Tonkin and Timbuctoo, impassive, smiling, gently obstinate. His powerful, massive frame remains unchanged, his calm forehead, his great white moustaches, his light blue eyes shining under heavy brows. Everything about him gives the impression of balance and coolness ; that is to say, of those military virtues that are perhaps the rarest and the most essential in the uncertain times in which we are living. What would have become of us after Charleroi, with a chief richer in imagination, but nervous and impulsive ? [2]

An inscrutable, inarticulate calm, maintained under all circumstances, with the rarest exceptions, constituted superficially Joffre's most impressive quality. He would listen patiently to argument or discussion by those on whose advice he relied, rarely taking part, never committing himself until a decision became necessary, and then, whatever the stress, taking it only after mature reflection. Strongly imbued with a sense of the magnitude of his task and of the personal responsibility resting upon him, Joffre acted only on his own inward convictions, and did not hesitate to reject the views even of his principal advisers. He did not feel the need of "talking out" his problems, but reached his conclusions by a process of inner deliberation that he never offered to analyze or explain. At times the result came slowly, so slowly as to try the patience of his subordinates — but never too late. There was no evidence of indecision or

[1] Liddell Hart, *Reputations Ten Years After* (Little, Brown, Boston, 1928).
[2] Poincaré, *op. cit.*

reluctance to embrace the full burden of responsibility.   From his determination, once taken, there could be no appeal.

The French journalist De Pierrefeu has described [8] an incident that illuminates Joffre's character.   An artillery officer, Lieutenant-Colonel Carence, visited the Commander in Chief to explain the situation of the heavy artillery and the urgency of remedying the shortages in guns and munitions.   Joffre listened silently to his exposition as he explained it with all the enthusiasm of a man wholly absorbed in his task, and at its conclusion dismissed him with only a friendly tap on the shoulder and the remark : "Good old Carence, always thinking about his guns.   That's fine."

Not a word of his own anxiety on the same subject, of his unheeded efforts before the war to wrest appropriations from a reluctant Parliament or of the long correspondence in which he had bombarded the Ministry of War with pleas and demands to accelerate the program of production and to supply the deficiency that gave Germany a continued advantage.   The information gained in the interview Joffre received gladly and stored in his reservoir of knowledge. Carence's interest and enthusiasm pleased him, and he valued it ; but the responsibility was his own.   It was something he could not share, and he saw no reason for discussing it.

Joffre belonged to no aristocratic, military caste.   Of modest, almost humble origin, he spent his life mainly in the colonies and in the garrisons of France and became a man of the simplest personal tastes.   Lacking almost completely in worldly graces, he had no interest in military pomp or smartness of dress.   He clung affectionately to a faded cap, the despair of his aides, rarely wore gloves and owned no spurs.   Nevertheless he accepted with great seriousness the high duties vested in him and regarded them as a solemn trust for which he, and he alone, could be held to account.   In this profound conviction of the personal nature of his responsibility, lies the explanation of Joffre's arbitrary exercise of the powers confided to him and of his refusal to share them with others in the slightest degree.

Though he resisted jealously efforts from any source to diminish his authority or to limit his prerogatives, he did so in the belief that only thus could he properly fulfil the responsibility laid upon him.   The modesty with which he permitted himself to be effaced after Nivelle succeeded him and his refusal to take any advantage of his own great popular prestige to force himself into a central role, sufficiently acquit him of any charge of personal ambition.   In retirement he steadfastly refused to be drawn into controversy, despite

[8] *G.Q.G. Secteur* 1 (Éd. Française Illustrée, Paris, 1920).

the strident clamours of his critics, maintaining the same imperturbable calm he had displayed in his days of power before the attacks, often envenomed, of Lanrezac, Sarrail and their satellites, and relying solely for his vindication on the light of history. In his memoirs, posthumously published, he has dealt with his detractors with exemplary moderation and forbearance.

It is perhaps small wonder that many writers, with agile minds and facile pens, seeking to translate history into terms of journalism, should see little of interest in the placid, unsophisticated character of the French Commander in Chief. Unable to fathom the source of his strength, they have turned upon him in caustic derision, finding an easy target in his unimaginative, humourless personality, and have depicted him as a bumbling old bourgeois, carried along by a tide of forces utterly incomprehensible to him and ending up as a hero, almost in spite of himself. In a more sentimental mood, they have created a fictitious character, "Papa Joffre," a venerable, lovable figure, shedding sweetness and light along the western front — a sort of Santa Claus in uniform — retaining however many of the traits of the bumbling bourgeois.

Nothing could be more unfair or wider of the mark than either of these conceptions. In the Campaign of the Marne, as indeed throughout the rest of his tenure of command, Joffre stands revealed as a leader, far-sighted, unsentimental, determined and at times peremptory. In the exercise of command his method differed sharply from Von Moltke's, for while the latter, following the tradition of his illustrious uncle, limited his intervention strictly to matters of general strategy, rigorously refraining from all attempts at executive control, Joffre, on the contrary remained in daily, almost hourly, touch with each of his armies. Misleading reports from German Army Commanders soon placed Von Moltke in an atmosphere of misconception and unreality, leading him first to an exaggerated belief that his adversaries' backbone had been broken, and later, as the error became apparent, to a reaction of profound pessimism. Under Joffre such a result was impossible. In spite of the unprecedented size of his armies and the extent of his front, he adhered in an amazing degree to the Napoleonic method of personal command, insisting on frequent reports from his subordinates, supplemented by the observation of liaison officers and by personal inspections.

While individual German Army Commanders were left to resolve their problems as best they could, within the broad and elastic lines of Von Moltke's general prescriptions, Joffre made his own the difficulties of each of his subordinates, issuing instructions or suggestions, and when occasion seemed to require, as for example before the Battle of Guise-St. Quentin, stretching out a directing hand in peremptory fashion.

There were many times during the course of the campaign and in the Battle of the Marne itself, when weakness on the part of one or another subordinate commander, or a failure to act, might have led to momentous consequences and even have altered the result of the campaign. It is hardly unnatural that many, remembering such occasions, should have seen in their own individual conduct the mainspring of victory. Some may honestly claim that but for them, the battle might have been lost ; but that is quite another thing from winning the battle.

Joffre himself showed no inclination to emphasize the degree of credit to which he was personally entitled for the outcome. After the war, friends of Messimy affected to see in the order issued on August 25th by the former Minister of War, calling for three army corps for the defence of Paris, the instrument of the strategical combination that brought about the victory. When Joffre was asked before the Briey Parliamentary Commission what effect this order had had upon his plans, he replied without hesitation :

"None whatever ; but I have no pride of authorship and if it gives him (M. Messimy) any pleasure, I will say that it was he who won the Battle of the Marne. It makes little difference so long as it was won."

"I don't know who won the Battle of the Marne," Joffre remarked on another occasion, "But if it had been lost, I know who would have lost it."

For the grave errors that led to defeat in the Battle of the Frontiers, Joffre must bear a major share of responsibility ; but he received what is vouchsafed to few in like circumstances, a second chance, and out of a desperate, almost hopeless case brought forth decisive victory. It is perhaps too much to say that Joffre had genius, if he had, it was the genius of Washington rather than of Bonaparte ; but the events of the Campaign of the Marne lead to the unavoidable conclusion that it is to Joffre, primarily if not solely, that France owes the first and most far-reaching of her great victories of the war.[4]

[4] No authoritative, fully documented life of Joffre has as yet (1935) appeared. A brilliantly written and wholly sympathetic character study is *Joffre et son destin* (Lavauzelle, Paris, 1931) by Lieut.-Col. Fabry, Deputy of Paris, who served as Joffre's *Chef de Cabinet* and accompanied him on his visit to the United States in 1917. An interesting popular biography is Raymond Récouly's *Joffre* (Editions des Portiques, Paris, 1931). Commandant Muller, who was one of the Commander in Chief's personal aides during the Campaign of the Marne, has given a vivid, intimate and discerning account of life at French G.H.Q. during that period in *Joffre et la Marne* (Crès, Paris, 1931). See also F. H. Simonds' illuminating estimate of Joffre in *They Won the War* (Harpers, New York, 1931).

Foch in his memoirs, has concluded his account of the Battle of the Marne in part as follows :

The Battle of the Marne was ended ; it was indeed a great victory.   It was the work of the man who planned for it from the 24th of August on, and pursued the realization of his plans to the end — of the General in Chief, Joffre.   The day after our reverses on the frontier, he perceived the errors that had been made and broke off the battle, to renew it vigorously as soon as our obvious weaknesses had been remedied.   With the intentions of the enemy at last revealed by the powerful manoeuvre across Belgium, and in spite of the deficiencies of certain commanders, he did not hesitate to regroup his forces, to form a mobile army in the west, to reorganize the High Command, to prolong his retreat until the favourable moment and when that moment came, to combine wisely an offensive and a defensive, after an about-face energetically directed. With one magnificent, halting stroke, he dealt a mortal blow to the invasion.

The judgement thus rendered seventeen years after the event by the greatest of Joffre's subordinates will be affirmed by history.

APPENDIX I

Plan of 1905

The German forces on the western front were to be divided into seven
field armies, and distributed as follows :

I. An Offensive Group of Armies (I to V Armies) aggregating 23
   Active army corps, 12½ Reserve corps, 7 cavalry divisions and 16
   brigades of Landwehr, concentrated into three groups and a flank
   guard, as follows :

   (a). *Northern Group* (I and II Armies) : 9 army corps, 7 Reserve
   corps, 5 cavalry divisions.
   Zone of Concentration : Region of Aix-la-Chapelle and along
   the Dutch frontier immediately to the north of it.
   Line of March : Across the southern tip of Dutch Limbourg
   and across Belgium to the left bank of the Meuse River, pivoting on the left to turn south between Namur and Brussels
   and thence into France, in a wide enveloping movement outside the left flank of the French line.

   (b). *Centre Group* (III Army) : 6 army corps, 1 Reserve division.
   Zone of Concentration : Along the German-Belgian frontier
   just north of Luxembourg.
   Line of March : Southwest across Belgium, striking the Meuse
   and entering France between Namur and Mezières.

   (c). *Southern Group* (IV and V Armies) : 8 army corps, 2 cavalry
   divisions.
   Zone of Concentration : In the region of Treves and in the
   fortified zone of Thionville-Metz.
   Line of March : Across Luxembourg and directly into France,
   striking the Meuse between Mezières and Verdun.

   (d). *Flank Guard :* 5 Reserve Corps.
   Zone of Concentration : The region of Metz, to cover the left
   flank of the German Offensive Group against any French
   counter-offensive debouching from the region Verdun-Toul.

II. A Defensive Left Wing Group (VI and VII Armies), aggregating
    3 Active army corps, 2 Reserve corps, 3 cavalry divisions and 10½

brigades of Landwehr, subject to reduction by 2 army corps to reinforce the Offensive Group.

Zone of Concentration : Along the frontier between Metz and the Swiss border.

Mission : To oppose defensively an anticipated French offensive into Alsace-Lorraine, limiting its action to retaining the maximum of enemy forces before its front without engaging in a decisive battle, and retreating if necessary to gain time for the completion of the right wing's enveloping manoeuvre ; after the successful completion of the envelopment by the right wing, to take the offensive against the French eastern fortresses.

III. Reinforcements provided for Offensive Group :
    (a). By the withdrawal of 2 army corps from the Defensive Left Wing as soon as possible.
    (b). By a second echelon composed of 6 Ersatz corps, to follow behind the right wing armies and relieve them of the necessity of diverting forces for secondary missions, such as besieging Antwerp, Maubeuge, etc., and to permit them to extend their action towards the west and south as might seem advisable without weakening their main bodies.

Plan of 1914

I. An Offensive Group of Armies (I to V Armies), aggregating 16 Active army corps, 10½ Reserve corps, 7 cavalry divisions and 12 brigades of Landwehr, distributed as follows :
    (a). *Northern Group* (I and II Armies): 7 army corps, 6 Reserve corps, 5 cavalry divisions.
    Zone of Concentration and *Line of March* substantially the same as under the original Schlieffen Plan, except that the neutrality of Holland was not to be violated, necessitating moving the area of concentration somewhat further south towards Aix-la-Chapelle and requiring the reduction by assault of the Belgian fortress of Liége.

    (b). *Centre Group* (III Army) : 3 army corps, 1 Reserve corps.
    Zone of Concentration and *Line of March* substantially unaltered.

    (c). *Southern Group* (IV and V Armies): 6 army corps, 4½ Reserve corps, 2 cavalry divisions.
    Zone of Concentration and *Line of March* substantially unaltered.

    (d). *Flank Guard* in region of Metz eliminated.

II. Defensive Left Wing Group (VI and VII Armies), aggregating 6 army corps, 2½ Reserve corps, 3 cavalry divisions, 6 Ersatz divisions and 2 brigades of Landwehr.

Zone of Concentration unchanged, but mission altered to provide for offensive resistance against anticipated French attack and a minimum surrender of territory.

III. Reinforcements provided for **Offensive Group** : **None.**

APPENDIX II

ORDERS OF BATTLE UPON COMPLETION OF CONCENTRATIONS

I

GERMAN ARMIES

From North to South :
I Army (Von Kluck) — H.Q. Grevenboich.
2nd Corps (Von Linsingen).
4th Corps (Von Arnim).
3rd Corps (Von Lochow).
9th Corps (Von Quast).
3rd Reserve Corps (Von Beseler) ; diverted to cover Antwerp, August 20th.
4th Reserve Corps (Von Gronau) ; one brigade diverted to garrison Brussels.
2nd Cavalry Corps (Von der Marwitz) ; 2nd, 4th and 9th Cavalry Divisions.

II Army (Von Bülow) — H.Q. Montjoie.
Guard (Von Plettenberg).
10th Corps (Von Emmich).
10th Reserve Corps (Count von Kirchbach).
7th Corps (Von Einem) ; one brigade diverted to besiege Maubeuge.
7th Reserve Corps (Von Zwehl) ; diverted to besiege Maubeuge.
Guard Reserve (Von Gallwitz) ; sent to Russian front, August 25th.
1st Cavalry Corps (Von Richthofen) ; Guard and 5th Cavalry Divisions.

III Army (Von Hausen) — H.Q. Prüm.
11th Corps (Von Plüstow) ; sent to Russian front, August 25th.
12th Reserve Corps (Von Kirchbach) ; one division diverted to besiege Givet.
12th Corps (D'Elsa).
19th Corps (Von Laffert).

IV Army (Duke Albrecht of Wurtemburg) — H.Q. Treves.
8th Corps (Von Tschepe und Weidenbach).
8th Reserve Corps (Von Egloffstein).

18th Corps (Von Schenck).
18th Reserve Corps (Von Steuben).
6th Corps (Von Pritzelwitz) ; transferred to V Army, August 28th.

V Army (German Crown Prince) — H.Q. Sarrebruck.
5th Corps (Von Strantz).
5th Reserve Corps (Von Gündell).
6th Reserve Corps (Von Gossler).
13th Corps (Von Fabeck).
16th Corps (Von Moser).
4th Cavalry Corps (Von Hollen) ; 3rd and 6th Cavalry Divisions.
33rd Reserve Division from Metz Garrison ; operated partly with VI Army.

VI Army (Crown Prince Rupprecht of Bavaria) — H.Q. St. Avold.
21st Corps (Von Below).
1st Bavarian Corps (Von Xylander).
2nd Bavarian Corps (Von Martini).
3rd Bavarian Corps (Von Gebsattel).
1st Bavarian Reserve Corps (Von Fasbender) ; transferred to VII Army,
   August 19th.
Guard, 4th, 8th and 10th Ersatz Divisions.
3rd Cavalry Corps (Von Frommel) ; 7th **Bavarian and 8th Cavalry** Divisions, latter to Russian front, August 25th.

VII Army (Von Heeringen) — H.Q. Strasbourg.
14th Corps (Von Hoiningen).
14th Reserve Corps (Von Schubert).
15th Corps (Von Deimling).
19th and Bavarian Ersatz Divisions.

II

FRENCH ARMIES

From West to East :
4th Group of Reserve Divisions (Valabrégue) — H.Q. Vervins.
51st, 53rd and 69th Reserve Divisions.

Fifth Army (Lanrezac) — H.Q. Rethel.
1st Corps (Franchet d'Esperey).
3rd Corps (Sauret) ; three divisions, including 37th Division from Africa.
10th Corps (Defforges) ; three divisions, including 38th Division from
   Africa.
18th Corps (De Mas Latrie) ; transferred from Second Army, August 15th.
Cavalry Corps (Sordet) ; 1st, 3rd and 5th Cavalry Divisions.

Fourth Army (De Langle) — H.Q. Ste. Menehould.
52nd and 60th Reserve Divisions ; transferred from Fifth Army, August
   15th.
9th Corps (Dubois) ; transferred from Second Army, August 19th.

11th Corps (Eydoux) ; transferred from Fifth Army, August 15th.
12th Corps (Roques).
17th Corps (Poline).
Colonial Corps (Lefévre).
2nd Corps (Gérard) ; transferred from Fifth Army, August 8th.
4th and 9th Cavalry Divisions.

Third Army (Ruffey) — H.Q. Verdun.
4th Corps (Boelle).
5th Corps (Brochin).
6th Corps (Sarrail) ; three divisions.
3rd Group of Reserve Divisions (Paul Durand) ; 54th, 55th and 56th Reserve Divisions.
7th Cavalry Division.

Second Army (De Castelnau) — H.Q. Neufchâteau.
20th Corps (Foch).
15th Corps (Espinasse).
16th Corps (Taverna).
18th Infantry Division ; originally part of 9th Corps.
2nd Group of Reserve Divisions (Leon Durand) ; 59th, 68th and 70th Reserve Divisions.
2nd and 10th Cavalry Divisions.

First Army (Dubail) — H.Q. Epinal.
8th Corps (De Castelli).
13th Corps (Alix).
21st Corps (Legrand-Girarde).
14th Corps (Pouradier-Duteil).
6th Cavalry Division.

Army of Alsace (Pau) — H.Q. Belfort.
(Not provided for in Plan XVII, but organized August 10th and dissolved August 26th.)
7th Corps (Bonnier, then Vautier).
44th Division, from the Army of the Alps, dissolved on Italy's neutrality.
1st Group of Reserve Divisions (Archinard) ; 58th, 63rd and 66th Reserve Divisions.
Group of Battalions (5) of Chasseurs.
8th Cavalry Division.
57th Reserve Division, from Belfort Garrison.

III

BRITISH ARMY (SIR JOHN FRENCH) — H.Q. LE CATEAU

1st Corps (Haig).
2nd Corps (Smith-Dorrien).

19th Infantry Brigade ; constituted August 23rd.
4th Division ; arrived from England, August 25th.
Cavalry Division (Allenby) ; 1st, 2nd, 3rd, 4th and 5th Cavalry Brigades.

IV

BELGIAN ARMY (KING ALBERT) — H.Q. LOUVAIN

Along Gette River :
1st Cavalry Division.
1st, 2nd, 5th and 6th Infantry Divisions.

At Liége :
3rd Infantry Division and 15th Brigade from 4th Infantry Division ;
 evacuated August 6th and rejoined main body of army on the Gette.

At Namur :
4th Infantry Division, less 15th Brigade (2 brigades) ; evacuated August
 23rd and rejoined main body of army in Antwerp.

Comparative Tables of Effectives

I

Total Effectives upon Completion of Concentration
German Armies

	Active Inf. Div.	Reserve or Ersatz Inf. Div.	Cav. Div.
I Army	8	4	3
II Army	7	5	2
III Army	6	2	—
IV Army	6	4	—
V Army	6	5	2
Total for Offensive Group	33	20	7
VI Army	8	6	3
VII Army	4	4	—
Grand Total	45	30	10

Note : In the II Army, the Reserve Corps of the Guard was composed of one Active division (3rd Division of the Guard) and one Reserve division (1st Reserve Division of the Guard).

No account is taken in the foregoing tabulation of 14 brigades of Landwehr allocated to the German field armies. These troops were in general assigned to guard the lines of communication, and except at the eastern extremity of the front took little part in active operations during this campaign.

Allied Armies

	Active Inf. Div.	Reserve Inf. Div.	Cav. Div.
French :			
Fifth Army	8	3	3
Fourth Army	10	2	2
Third Army	7	3	1
British	4½	–	2
Belgians	–	6	1
Total Forces opposing German Offensive Group	29½	14	9
French :			
Second Army	10	3	2
First Army	8	–	1
Army of Alsace	3	4	1
Grand Total	50½	21	13

Note : In the foregoing tabulation, no account is taken of the forces attached to the garrisons of the various French fortresses and forts, except the Reserve division of the Belfort garrison which operated with the Army of Alsace from the time of its organization, of French Territorial units, of units of the African Army which joined the French mobile armies after the Battle of the Frontiers or of the garrison troops of the Belgian fortresses of Liége, Namur and Antwerp. For tabulation showing inclusion of all these units which took part in the Battle of the Marne, see Appendix IX.

II

Comparative Effectives of German Right Wing Armies and of Allied Left Wing Armies at Battle of the Frontiers (i.e. Battles of the Sambre and of Mons)

	Active Inf. Div.	Reserve Inf. Div.	Cav. Div.
German (I, II, III Armies) :	18	6½	5
Allies (French Fifth Army and British) :	14½	3	5

Note : No account is taken of (a) the forces detached from the German I Army to cover Antwerp and to garrison Brussels or (b) the forces detached from the German II and III Armies to besiege Namur.

The British cavalry, although organized as one division, is rated as 2 cavalry divisions, which corresponds to its actual strength and into which it was subsequently divided.

III

Comparative Effectives of German Centre Armies and French Centre Armies at Battle of the Frontiers (i.e. French Offensive in the Ardennes)

	Active Inf. Div.	Reserve Inf. Div.	Cav. Dif.
German, (IV and V Armies) :	12	9	2
French, (Third and Fourth Armies) :	19	5	3

Note : On the French side, it must be recalled that the 9th Corps and 2 Reserve divisions of the Fourth Army were acting as a flank guard and did not actually take part in offensive operations. Similarly, on the German side, the 8th and 8th Reserve Corps of the IV Army did not reach the field until the action had virtually ended. The totals on both sides must therefore be reduced by 2 Active and 2 Reserve divisions in computing the forces actually engaged on August 22nd.

No account is taken of the French Army of Lorraine (6 Reserve divisions) which did not go into action until after the main battle had ended.

IV

Comparative Effectives of German Left Wing Armies and French Right Wing at Battle of the Frontiers (i.e. French Offensive in Lorraine)

	Active Inf. Div.	Reserve Inf. Div.	Cav. Dif.
German, (VI and VII Armies) :	12	11	3
French, (Second, First and Army of Alsace) :	17	5	4

Note : The 33rd Reserve Division, from the Metz Garrison, which fought on the left of the German Crown Prince's Army on August 24th, also took part in the Battle of Morhange on the right of Crown Prince Rupprecht's Army on August 20th. Four Landwehr brigades took an active part in the German operations in Lorraine.

Only a portion of the French Second Army (i.e. three army corps and a Reserve division) participated in the offensive movement.

APPENDIX III

INSTRUCTIONS FROM LORD KITCHENER TO SIR JOHN FRENCH — AUGUST 1914

OWING to the infringement of the neutrality of Belgium by Germany, and in furtherance of the Entente which exists between this country and

France, His Majesty's Government has decided, at the request of the French Government, to send an Expeditionary Force to France and to entrust the command of the troops to yourself.

The special motive of the Force under your control is to support and co-operate with the French Army against our common enemies. The peculiar task laid upon you is to assist the French Government in preventing or repelling the invasion by Germany of French and Belgian territory and eventually to restore the neutrality of Belgium, on behalf of which, as guaranteed by treaty, Belgium has appealed to the French and to ourselves.

These are the reasons which have induced His Majesty's Government to declare war, and these reasons constitute the primary objective you have before you.

The place of your assembly, according to present arrangements, is Amiens, and during the assembly of your troops you will have every opportunity of discussing with the Commander-in-Chief of the French Army, the military position in general and the special part which your Force is able and adapted to play. It must be recognized from the outset that the numerical strength of the British Force and its contingent reinforcement is strictly limited, and with this consideration kept steadily in view it will be obvious that the greatest care must be exercised towards a minimum of losses and wastage.

Therefore, while every effort must be made to coincide most sympathetically with the plans and wishes of our Ally, the gravest consideration will devolve upon you as to participation in forward movements where large bodies of French troops are not engaged and where your Force may be unduly exposed to attack. Should a contingency of this sort be contemplated I look to you to inform me fully and give me time to communicate to you any decision to which His Majesty's Government may come in the matter. In this connection I wish you distinctly to understand that your command is an entirely independent one, and that you will in no case come in any sense under the orders of any Allied General.

In minor operations you should be careful that your subordinates understand that risk of serious loss should only be taken where such risk is authoritatively considered to be commensurate with the object in view.

The high courage and discipline of your troops should, and certainly will, have fair and full opportunity of display during the campaign, but officers may well be reminded that in this their first experience of European warfare, a greater measure of caution must be employed than under former conditions of hostilities against an untrained adversary.

You will kindly keep up constant communication with the War Office, and you will be good enough to inform me as to all movements of the enemy reported to you as well as those of the French Army.

I am sure you fully realize that you can rely with the utmost confidence on the whole-hearted and unswerving support of the Government, of myself and of your compatriots, in carrying out the high duty which the King has entrusted to you and in maintaining the great tradition of His Majesty's Army.

Kitchener
Secretary of State

APPENDIX IV

JOFFRE'S INSTRUCTIONS TO THE FRENCH ARMIES AT THE OUTSET
OF THE CAMPAIGN

G.H.Q.
─────
3rd Bureau.

G.H.Q., Vitry-le-François, August 8th.

7 A.M.

General Instructions No. 1

Note : These instructions are strictly personal to the Generals commanding armies and to their Chiefs of Staff.

The instructions of the Commander in Chief must not be quoted in full in any order or instruction. Subordinate authorities must know only so much of them as is necessary for the execution of the part which devolves upon them, that is to say as much as concerns their own mission and the role of neighbouring units.

I. — Before the First and Second Armies, the enemy forces do not appear to exceed the equivalent of approximately six (6) army corps.

Around Metz, before Thionville and in Luxembourg seems to be the principal group of German armies, assembled to debouch towards the west, but also in position to converge to the south, resting on the fortress of Metz.

To the north, a German army in which elements of five (5) army corps have been identified has entered Belgium and is partly engaged against Belgian forces.

II. — The intention of the General Commanding in Chief is to seek battle, with all his forces united, resting the right of his general line of battle on the Rhine.

He will withdraw, if necessary the left of this line to the rear in order to avoid an engagement which might be decisive for one of the armies before the others are in a position to support it.

But it is also possible that we shall have time to advance our left wing, in the event that the German right is delayed before Liége or turns away from it towards the south.

Initially the assembly of the armies and the general offensive movement may be anticipated under the following conditions :

III. — The First Army will take as its objective the German army at Sarrebourg, Mt. Donon, the valley of the Bruche (River) and will seek to put it out of action by driving it back on Strasbourg and Lower Alsace.

The zone of action of the First Army will be limited on the north by the line (inclusive) Charmes, Saint-Germain, Borville, Moriviller, Gerbéviller, Fraimbois, Marainviller, Embermenil, Moussey, Dianne-Capelle, Fenestrange.

The 7th Corps will facilitate the attack of the main body of the army by advancing rapidly on Colmar and Schlestadt. It will assure its security on its right by destroying the bridges of the Rhine and by covering Neuf-Brisach. The 8th Cavalry Division will remain attached to it.

Later and successively, the 1st Group of Reserve Divisions, reinforced by the Reserve divisions from the Alps, will be charged with the surveillance of Neuf-Brisach, the investment of Strasbourg and the protection of Upper Alsace.

IV. — The Second Army, covering itself towards Metz, will act offensively in the general direction of Sarrebruck, on the front Dieuze, Château-Salins, Delme, maintaining contact with the First Army in the region of Les Etangs.

It will reserve at the disposition of the Commander in Chief its two left army corps in the region Bernécourt, Rosières-en-Haye, ready to engage them towards the north.

V. — The Third Army will establish itself on the front Flabas, Ornes, Vigneulles, Saint-Baussant, ready to act in a northerly direction, its left wing marching on Damvillers, or to counter-attack any forces debouching from Metz.

In the former case, the two left corps of the Second Army may be attached to the Third Army for the battle.

VI. — The Fourth Army assembled between Servon, Aubréville and Souilly will hold itself in readiness to attack, between the Meuse and the Argonne enemy forces which may have crossed the Meuse north of Vilosnes, or to cross the Meuse itself north of Verdun.

The 2nd Corps is hereby attached to the Fourth Army. The latter corps will avoid allowing itself to be held by superior forces and if threatened will fall back to the support of the fortress of Verdun keeping the greater part of its forces on the right bank of the Meuse between Sivry-sur-Meuse and Flabas.

VII. — The Fifth Army will concentrate its forces between Vouziers and Aubenton in such a way as to enable it to launch an attack in force against any force debouching between Mouzon and Mézières (inclusive) or, in case of necessity, to cross the Meuse itself between these two points.

VIII. — The zones of action between the Third, Fourth and Fifth Armies are limited by the road : Bar-le-Duc, Vavincourt, Chaumont-sur-Aire, Souilly, Verdun, Vacherauville, Flabas ;

And by the road : Souain, Tahure, Séchault, Senuc, Grand-Pré, Briquenay, Harricourt, Sommeuthe.

These two roads to the Fourth Army.

The 4th Corps will contract its front within the zone of its army to make room for the 2nd Corps.

IX. — At the outset the Cavalry Corps will cover the front of the Fifth Army. In the event that this corps is compelled to re-cross the Meuse, it will maintain itself on the left of the Fifth Army (region Mariembourg, Chimay) to protect the assembly of the British Army and the 4th Group of Reserve Divisions.

The 4th Cavalry Division will be restored to the command of the commander of the Fifth Army as soon as the Cavalry Corps begins to uncover the front of that Army.

X. — The 4th Group of Reserve Divisions will organize a fortified position around Vervins in such a way as to permit it to debouch either to the north or to the east. It will be transported into this region as and when it debarks and the work will be undertaken immediately.

XI. — The Army Commanders will begin at once with the preparation of their orders in view of the general offensive above contemplated, so that such orders can be issued upon receipt of telegraphic instructions. They will also immediately order preparatory movements calculated to facilitate the offensive and to render it overwhelming.

J. Joffre
General Commanding in Chief

APPENDIX V

FRENCH ESTIMATES OF THE GERMAN ORDER OF BATTLE

(1) August 16th

General Headquarters
Armies of the East   August 16, 1914.
_____
Staff
_____
2nd Bureau — 1076

German order of battle as estimated by the 2nd Bureau August 16th. From North to South.

Two Armies of the Meuse : 9th, 10th, 7th Corps — 2nd and 9th Cav.
  (Gen. von Bülow)   Div. 11th, 3rd, 4th, 6th Corps — 5th and Guard Cav. Div.

Army of Belgian Luxembourg : Guard, 19th, 12th Corps — 8th (?) Cav.
  (Gen. von Heeringen)   Div.

Army of Luxembourg-Thionville : 8th, 18th, 16th Corps — 6th and 3rd
  (Gen. von Eichorn)   (Saxon) Cav. Div.

Army of Lorraine No. 6 : 3rd Bav., 2nd Bav., 21st, 1st Bav. Corps —
(Prince Rupprecht of   7th and Bav. Cav. Div.
Bavaria)

Army of Alsace : 13th, 15th, 14th Corps (Disappeared for last three
(Prince Friedrich II   days.)
of Bavaria)

Russia : 1st, 20th, 2nd, 17th and 5th Corps — 1st, 4th Cav. Div.
Not identified : Reserve Corps of the Guard.

(2) August 23rd

German Order of Battle as estimated by the 2nd Bureau, August 23rd.
From North to South.
Two Armies of the Meuse : II Army : ½ 2nd, 4th, 9th, 7th, 10th and
Guard Corps, — 2nd, 9th and Guard
Cav. Div.
III Army : 11th, 3rd and 6th Corps, — 5th
Cav. Div. (Probably on right bank.)
Army of Belgian Luxembourg : IV Army : 12th, 19th, 18th Corps, —
3rd Cav. Div.
Army of Luxembourg : V Army : 8th, elements of 13th and 16th Corps,
— 6th and perhaps 7th Cav. Div.
(From the VI Army.)
Army of Lorraine : VI Army : 1st, 2nd and 3rd Bavarian, 21st Corps —
Saxon (No. 8) and Bavarian Cav. Div.
Army of Alsace : VII Army (a) Northern Group : Elements of the
13th, 14th, 15th Corps ; perhaps the
7th Cav. Div.
(b) Southern Group : Reserve and de-
pot units.
Not identified : Reserve Corps of the Guard.

(3) August 25th

General Headquarters
2nd Bureau   August 25th ; 6 P.M.

General situation of German forces on the date of August 25th.

In Belgium :
On the front Condé-sur-Escaut, Sart-la-Bruyère, Beaumont, Givet, are
the following army corps : 2nd, 4th, 9th, 7th, 10th, Guard, with two
Divisions of Cavalry on the right wing.
In the region of Givet, and still astride of the Meuse, are the group of
the 12th and 19th Corps.
The 3rd and 11th Corps are not yet located.

Note : It will be observed from the foregoing, that two days after the Battles of the
Sambre and of Mons, the French High Command had not yet identified the 4th, 7th,

10th and 12th Reserve Corps which formed part of the German right wing group of armies, nor the 3rd and 9th Reserve Corps which were covering Antwerp. In point of fact, at the date of this bulletin, the part of these forces comprising Von Kluck's Army was no longer in Belgium around Condé-sur-Escaut and Sart-la-Bruyère, but had entered France and marched south of Maubeuge to the vicinity of Le Cateau and Landrecies.

Between the Forest of the Ardennes and the region of Longuyon-Spincourt, from west to east :

8th, 8th Reserve, 6th and 6th Reserve Corps, and elements of the 5th and 13th Corps.

Columns of all arms are reported this morning marching respectively on Hargnies, Vress, Carignan, Margut, and Virton.

Between the region of Longuyon-Spincourt and Briey :

16th Corps, 2 brigades of Landwehr, the 33rd Reserve Division and the 6th Cavalry Division.

In Lorraine (between the Entrenched Camp of Metz and the Vosges) :

3rd Bavarian Corps, region of Delme.

Our Second and First Armies are actually in contact between Luneville and the Vosges with the 21st Corps, the 1st and 2nd Bavarian Corps, the 15th Corps and part of the 14th and 13th Corps.

In Upper Alsace :

Between Colmar and Huningue, on the left (west) bank of the Rhine : elements of Reserve and Landwehr forces.

In the region of Leopoldshöhe : elements of the 14th Corps.

Note : The extent of the misconception of the French High Command of the enemy's strength and dispositions at this period of the campaign (i.e. after the Battle of the Frontiers) may be appreciated when it is noted that in addition to the deficiencies already remarked on the German right wing, the following units had not been identified : 5th Reserve Corps (V Army), 1st Bavarian Reserve Corps and 14th Reserve Corps (VII Army). Thus on August 25th, the date of Joffre's General Instructions No. 2, the French High Command under-estimated the strength of the enemy armies actually engaged against them by a total of at least seven army corps.

APPENDIX VI

JOFFRE'S PRINCIPAL ORDERS TO THE ALLIED LEFT WING ARMIES PREPARATORY TO THE BATTLES OF THE SAMBRE AND OF MONS

(1)

Armies of the East
| General Staff |
| 3rd Bureau |
| 1011 |

G.H.Q., August 15, 1914 ; 3:30 P.M.

Special Instructions No. 10 to the Commanders of the Fourth and Fifth Armies and of the Cavalry Corps.

I. — The enemy appears to be directing his principal effort on his right wing north of Givet. Another group of forces seems to be marching on the front Sedan, Montmédy, Damvillers.

II. — The Fifth Army, leaving its right corps (11th Corps) in the region southwest of Sedan and its Reserve divisions (52nd and 60th Res. Div.) for the defense of the line of the Meuse, and leaving the 4th Cavalry Division at the disposition of the Fourth Army, will move the rest of its forces into the region of Mariembourg or Philippeville, to act in concert with the British Army and the Belgian forces against the opposing forces in the north.

The Cavalry Corps hereby passes under the orders of the commander of the Fifth Army.

The Group of Reserve Divisions at Vervins is likewise under the orders of the commander of the Fifth Army.

III. — The Fourth Army, to which the 11th Corps and the 52nd and 60th Reserve Divisions are attached until further orders, will establish itself facing northeast in such a way as to be able to debouch from the front Sedan, Montmédy in the general direction of Neufachâteau.

The 4th Cavalry Division hereby passes under the orders of the commander of the Fourth Army.

J. Joffre
General Commanding in Chief.

Note : This order was issued on the day of the German attack against Dinant, which was accepted at French G.H.Q. as a definite indication of the enemy's intention to cross in force to the left bank of the Meuse.

(2)

Armies of the East

General Staff   G.H.Q., August 18th ; 8 A.M.

3rd Bureau

No. 1269

Special Instructions No. 13 to the Commander of the Third, Fourth and Fifth Armies.
Communicated to : the Commander in Chief of the British forces ;
the Commander in Chief of the Belgian forces.

I. — The Third, Fourth and Fifth French Armies, acting in concert with the British and Belgian Armies, have as their objective the German forces assembled around Thionville, in Luxembourg and in Belgium.

These forces seem to comprise a total of 13 to 15 army corps. It seems that they are formed into two principal groups :

To the north, the enemy right wing group appears to include from 7 to 8 army corps and 4 cavalry divisions ; further to the south, the central group, between Bastogne and Thionville, may include from 6 to 7 army corps and 2 or 3 cavalry divisions.

Note : In fact, as of this date, the German right wing group included 16 army corps and 5 cavalry divisions, and the central group included 10 army corps and 2 cavalry Divisions.

II. — The Third and Fourth French Armies have already received their missions and their initial instructions for an offensive.

III. — So far as the French Fifth Army, the British Army and the Belgian Army are concerned, two possible eventualities may be envisaged :

(1) The enemy northern group, marching on both banks of the Meuse, may seek to pass between Givet and Brussels and even to accentuate its movement farther to the north.

In this eventuality, the French Fifth Army and the Cavalry Corps which is attached to it, operating in complete liaison with the British and Belgian Armies, will directly oppose this movement, by seeking to outflank the enemy from the north. The Belgian Army and the Cavalry Corps seem to be already in place for this outflanking action.

In the meanwhile, our center armies (the Third and Fourth) will first attack the enemy central group to put it out of action. When this result has been attained, the major part of the Fourth Army will immediately march against the left flank of the enemy northern group.

(2) The enemy may engage only a fraction of his right wing group north of the Meuse (i.e. on the left bank of the Meuse).

While his central group is engaged in a frontal action against our Third and Fourth Armies, the other part of his northern group, remaining south of the Meuse, may seek to attack the left flank of our Fourth Army.

In this second hypothesis, the Fifth Army, leaving to the British and the Belgian Armies the task of combatting the German forces north of the Sambre and the Meuse, will turn, by way of Namur and Givet, in the general direction of Marche or St. Hubert (i.e. east).

In view of this possibility, it will be appropriate to organize a strong bridge-head east of Givet, on a line marked by Falmagne, Finnevaux, Beauraing, Sevry Wood.

The Fifth Army's Group of Reserve Divisions may, in whole or in part, operate with the British Army north of the Meuse.

J. Joffre
General Commanding in Chief

(3)

August 21st ; 5 P.M.

Special Orders No. 15.

To the Commander of the Fifth Army and the Commander in Chief of the British Forces.

No. 1574.

I. — The first eventuality envisaged by my Special Instructions No. 13 seems to be realized.

II. — The Third and Fourth Armies are beginning today, August 21st, their march in the general direction of Neufchâteau (Fourth Army) and Arlon (Third Army) taking as their objective the enemy forces which have entered Belgian Luxembourg and whose movement seems to be directed towards the west.

III. — The Fifth Army, supported by the Meuse and by the fortress of Namur, will take as its objective the northern enemy group.

The Commander in Chief of the British forces is requested to co-operate in this action by remaining on the left of the Fifth Army and by initially advancing the main body of his forces in the general direction of Soignies.

The line of demarcation between the zones of march of the Fifth Army and the British Army will be determined by agreement between the Commander in Chief of the British forces and the commander of the Fifth Army.

Information obtained by the Cavalry Corps and, in a general way, by the Fifth Army will be communicated to British Headquarters and vice versa.

J. Joffre

Note : At the time the foregoing order was issued, the French Fifth Army was already engaged against Von Bülow along the Sambre, and the British Army was marching north from Le Cateau. The Belgian Army had already retreated into Antwerp.

APPENDIX VII

JOFFRE'S PLAN OF OPERATIONS FOR THE ALLIED ARMIES AFTER THE
BATTLE OF THE FRONTIERS

G.H.Q.
the Armies of the East   G.H.Q., August 25, 1914.
—————————————
Staff
————
3rd Bureau
————
2349

General Instructions No. 2

The Commander in Chief to the Army Commanders.

I. — Having been unable to carry out the offensive manoeuvre originally planned, future operations will be conducted in such a way as to reconstruct on our left a force capable of resuming the offensive by a combination of the Fourth and Fifth Armies, the British Army and new forces drawn from the east, while the other armies hold the enemy in check for such time as may be necessary.

II. — Each of the Third, Fourth and Fifth Armies, during its retreat, will take account of the movements of the neighbouring armies, with which they must remain in liaison. The movement will be covered by rear-guards left at favourable points in such fashion as to utilize all obstacles to halt the enemy's march, or at any rate to delay it, by short and violent counter-attacks in which artillery will be the principal element employed.

III. — Limits of zones of action among the different armies :
Army W. (British) : Northwest of the line Le Cateau, Vermand and Nesle inclusive.
Fifth Army : Between the latter line (exclusive) to the west and the line : Rocroi, Liart, Rozoy-sur-Serre, Craonne (inclusive) to the east.
Fourth Army : Between the latter line (exclusive) to the west and the line : Stenay, Grand-Pré, Suippes, Condé-sur-Marne (inclusive) to the east.
Third Army (including the Army of Lorraine) ; Between the line Sassey, Fléville, Ville-sur-Tourbe, Vitry-le-François (inclusive) to the west and the line : Vigneulles, Void, Gondrecourt (inclusive) to the east.

IV. — On the extreme left, between Picquigny and the sea, a defensive line will be held along the Somme by the Territorial divisions of the north (i.e. d'Amade's Group), having as reserve the 61st or the 62nd Reserve Divisions.

V. — The Cavalry Corps is on the Authie, ready to follow the forward movement on the extreme left.

VI. — Before Amiens, between Domart-en-Ponthieu and Corbie, or behind the Somme between Picquigny and Villers-Bretonneux a new group of forces will be constituted by elements transported by rail (7th Corps, four Reserve divisions, and perhaps another Active army corps) between August 27th and September 2nd.
This group will be ready to take the offensive in the general direction of St. Pol-Arras or of Arras-Bapaume.

VII. — The Army W. (British), behind the Somme from Bray-sur-Somme to Ham, will be ready to move either towards the north on Bertincourt or towards the east on Le Catelet.

VIII. — The Fifth Army will have its main body in the region Vermand, St. Quentin, Moy (offensive front) to debouch in the direction of the railway station of Bohain. Its right holding the line La Fère, Laon, Craonne, St. Erme (defensive front).

IX. — Fourth Army : behind the Aisne on the front Guignecourt, Vouziers, or in case this is impossible on the front Berry-au-Bac, Rheims, mountain of Rheims, always reserving means to take the offensive towards the north.

X. — Third Army : supporting its right on the fortress of Verdun and its left on the defile of Grand-Pré, or at Varennes, Ste. Menehould.

XI. — All the positions indicated should be organized with the greatest care, so as to offer the maximum resistance to the enemy.
We shall start from these positions on the offensive movement.

XII. — The First and Second Armies will continue to contain the enemy forces which are opposed to them.   In case of retirement they will have as zones of action :
Second Army : Between the road : Frouard, Toul, Vaucouleurs (inclusive) and the road : Bayon, Charmes, Mirécourt, Vittel, Clefmont (inclusive).
First Army : South of the road : Châtel, Dompain, Lampain, Montigny-le-Roi (inclusive).

J. Joffre

APPENDIX VIII

VON MOLTKE'S GENERAL DIRECTIVE TO THE GERMAN ARMIES AFTER THE BATTLE OF THE FRONTIERS

August 27, 1914.

The enemy, comprising three groups, has sought to check the German offensive.

On his northern wing, supported by the British Army and by elements of the Belgian Army, before our I, II and III Armies, he has adopted an attitude in the main defensive in the region Maubeuge-Namur-Dinant. His plan, which consisted in taking the German right wing on the flank, broke down before the outflanking movement of our I Army.

The central enemy group was assembled between Mezières and Verdun. His left wing took the offensive and moved beyond the cut of the Semoy against our IV Army.   This attack did not succeed.   He then sought to cut off the left wing of our V Army from Metz by an attack debouching from Verdun.   This attempt also failed.

A third powerful enemy group attempted to penetrate Lorraine and the valley of the Upper Rhine, in order to march towards the Rhine and the middle Main, passing on either side of Strasbourg.   Our VI and VII Armies succeeded in victoriously repulsing this effort after hard combats.

All the French Active army corps, including two newly formed divisions (the 44th and 45th) have already been engaged and have sustained heavy losses ; the majority of the French Reserve divisions have likewise been engaged and are severely shaken.   One cannot yet say what value must be given to the capacity for resistance that the Franco-British army still retains.

The Belgian army is in a state of complete disintegration ; there is no longer any question of its ability to take the offensive in the open field.

At Antwerp there may be about 100,000 Belgian troops, mobile forces as well as garrison. They are severely shaken and have little capacity for offensive enterprises.

The French, at least their northern and centre groups, are in full retreat in a westerly and southwesterly direction, that is on Paris. It is likely that in the course of this retreat they will oppose new and bitter resistance. All information from France indicates that the French army is fighting to gain time and that it is a question of holding the greatest possible part of the German forces on the French front to facilitate the Russian offensive.

The Anglo-French group of the north and centre may, after the loss of the line of the Meuse, offer a new resistance behind the Aisne, with their extreme left pushed perhaps as far as St. Quentin, La Fère and Laon and their right wing established west of the Argonne, about in the region of Ste. Menehould. The next line of resistance will probably be the Marne, with the left wing supported by Paris. It is also possible that forces will be concentrated along the lower Seine.

On the southern wing of the French army the situation is not yet clear. It is not impossible that in order to relieve his northern wing and centre, the enemy may resume the offensive in Lorraine. If this southern wing retreats, it will endeavour, resting on the fortified triangle Langres-Dijon-Besançon, constantly to attack the flank of the German armies by debouching from the south, or to hold its forces in readiness for a new offensive.

We must count upon the French army replacing its effectives and receiving new units. Although for the moment, it has only the class of 1914 available, outside of the weak resources of its depots, it must be envisaged that it will call up the next class of recruits and will transport to the front all available units from North Africa as well as naval units. The French Government will doubtless soon order the organization of bands of *francs-tireurs*.

England is also actively attempting to constitute a new army with volunteers and Territorials. However one need hardly expect that this army can be utilized before from four to six months.

It is therefore important, by moving the German army rapidly on Paris, not to allow the French time to recover, to prevent the creation of new units and to eliminate so far as possible the country's means of defense.

Belgium will be organized by a general government under German administration. It will serve as the Zone of the Rear for the I, II and III Armies for supplies of food, and will thus materially shorten our right wing's lines of communication.

His Majesty orders that the German armies advance in the direction of Paris.

The I Army, with the 2nd Cavalry Corps under its orders, will move towards the Lower Seine, marching west of the Oise. It will be ready to intervene in the actions of the II Army. It will be further charged with the protection of the right flank of the armies. It will prevent the formation of new enemy units within its zone of action. The elements left behind to besiege Antwerp will receive their orders from the High Command (3rd Reserve and 9th Reserve Corps). The 4th Reserve Corps is restored to the orders of the I Army.

The II Army, with the 1st Cavalry Corps under its orders, will cross the line La Fère-Laon and will move on Paris. It will besiege and capture Maubeuge and later La Fère and Laon, the latter place in concert with the III Army. The 1st Cavalry Corps will reconnoitre before the front of the II and III Armies. It will also give information to the III Army.

The III Army, crossing the line Laon-Guignecourt (west of Neuchatel) will march on Château Thierry. It will seize Hirson as well as Laon and the Fort of Condé, the two latter points in concert with the II Army. The 1st Cavalry Corps, operating before the fronts of the II and III Armies, will give information to the III Army.

The IV Army will march by way of Rheims on Epernay. The 4th Cavalry Corps under the orders of the V Army, will also give information to the IV Army. Siege material necessary for the capture of Rheims will be placed later at the disposal of this Army. The 6th Army Corps will pass under the orders of the V Army.

The V Army, to which the 6th Corps is henceforth attached, will march towards the front of Châlons-sur-Marne, Vitry-le-François. It will assure the protection of the left flank of the armies by echelons to the rear and to the left, until the VI Army is in a position to undertake this protection west of the Meuse. The 4th Cavalry Corps will remain under the orders of the V Army ; it will reconnoitre before the fronts of the IV and V Armies and will also report to the IV Army. Verdun will be invested. In addition to the 5 brigades of Landwehr on the Nied position, the 8th and 10th Ersatz Divisions will pass under the orders of the V Army when they are no longer indispensable to the VI Army.

The VI Army, with the VII Army and the 3rd Cavalry Corps under its orders, will have as its mission first, supporting itself on Metz, to oppose an enemy advance into Lorraine and Upper Alsace. The fortress of Metz is placed under the orders of the VI Army. If the enemy retires, the VI Army, with the 3rd Cavalry Corps under its orders, will cross the Moselle between Toul and Epinal and will advance in the general direction of Neufchâteau. The protection of the left flank of the armies will then devolve upon the VI Army. In this event the VI Army will be reinforced by elements of the VII Army (14th and 15th Army Corps, an Ersatz division). On the other hand it will yield the 8th and 10th Ersatz Divisions to the V Army. The VII Army will thereupon be independent.

The VII Army will remain initially under the orders of the VI Army. If the VI Army crosses the Moselle, the VII Army will become entirely independent. The fortress of Strasbourg and the fortifications of the Upper Rhine will remain under its orders. The mission of the VII

Army will be to prevent any enemy break-through between Epinal and the Swiss frontier.   It is recommended that it construct substantial defensive works before Epinal and thence to the Vosges, as well as in the valley of the Rhine, connecting them with Neuf-Brisach, and that it place the main body of its forces behind its right wing.   The 14th and 15th Corps, as well as one Ersatz division, will then pass under the orders of the VI Army.

Limits of zones of action. . .

All the armies must act in mutual co-operation and lend each other mutual support in overcoming the various obstacles of the terrain.   If the enemy presents powerful resistance along the Aisne and later along the Marne, it may become necessary to have the armies converge towards the south instead of southwest.

It is urgently desirable that the armies move forward rapidly, so as not to allow the French time to re-form and organize new resistance. Accordingly, the armies will report when they can begin their respective movements.

Von Moltke

APPENDIX IX

JOFFRE'S GENERAL INSTRUCTIONS AND ACCOMPANYING SECRET MEMO-RANDUM ISSUED AFTER IT BECAME EVIDENT THAT THE PLAN OF GENERAL INSTRUCTIONS NO. 2 COULD NOT BE FULLY CARRIED OUT

(1)

September 1st, 2 P.M.

No. 3205

General Instructions No. 4

I. — In spite of the tactical successes obtained by the Third, Fourth and Fifth Armies in the region of the Meuse and of Guise, the outflanking movement executed by the enemy on the left wing of the Fifth Army, insufficiently checked by British troops and by the Sixth Army, compels the whole of our line to pivot on the right.

As soon as the Fifth Army escapes the threat of envelopment against its left, the whole of our Third, Fourth and Fifth Armies will resume the offensive.

II. — The retirement may lead the armies to retreat for a certain time in the general direction from north to south.

The Fifth Army, on the marching wing, must in no event allow the enemy to reach its left ; the other armies, less hurried in the execution of their movement, may halt to face the enemy and to take advantage of every favourable opportunity to inflict a check upon him.

The movement of each army must, nevertheless, be so regulated as not to uncover the neighbouring armies, and the Army Commanders should constantly communicate to one another their intentions, their movements and their information.

III. — The lines separating the zones of march of the various armies are as follows :

Between the Fifth and Fourth Armies (Foch's Detachment) : the road Rheims, Epernay (to the Fourth Army), the road Montmort, Sézanne, Romilly (to the Fifth Army).

Between the Fourth Army and the Third Army : the road Grand-Pré, Ste. Menehould, Revigny (to the Fourth Army).

In the zone allocated to the Fourth Army, General Foch's Army Detachment will maintain constant liaison with the Fifth Army and with the main body of the Fourth Army under the protection of the 7th and 9th Cavalry Divisions of the Fourth Army and supported by infantry detachments furnished by that Army.

The Third Army will execute its movements covered by the Heights of the Meuse.

IV. — The limit of the retreat may be envisaged, without implying that this limit need necessarily be reached, when the armies reach the following positions :

A new Cavalry Corps behind the Seine, south of Bray.

Fifth Army behind the Seine, south of Nogent-sur-Seine.

Fourth Army (Foch's Detachment) behind the Aube, south of Arcis-sur-Aube.

Fourth Army (main body) behind the Ornain, east of Vitry.

Third Army north of Bar-le-Duc.

The Third Army will be reinforced at this point by the Reserve divisions, which will abandon the Heights of the Meuse in order to take part in the offensive.

If circumstances permit, fractions of the First and Second Armies will be recalled in opportune time to participate in the offensive ; finally the mobile troops of the Entrenched Camp of Paris may also take part in the general action.

J. Joffre

Note : The text of the foregoing order as issued to the French Army Commanders differs slightly from the text sent to Sir John French, but the differences do not seem material.

(2)

General Headquarters
of Armies of the East.

| Staff | G.H.Q., September 2, 1914. |

3rd Bureau

3463

Personal and Secret.
Memorandum for Army Commanders.

The general plan of operations which motivated the sending of Instruction No. 4 is aimed at the following points :

a. Withdrawing the armies from the pressure of the enemy and leading them to organize and fortify the zones where they will be established at the end of the retreat.

b. Establishing the whole of our forces on a general line marked by Pont-sur-Yonne, Nogent-sur-Seine, Arcis-sur-Aube, Brienne-le-Chateau, Joinville on which they will be reconstituted by replacements from the depots.

c. Reinforcing the right wing army by two Corps withdrawn from the Armies of Nancy and Epinal.

d. At this point taking the offensive along the whole front.

e. Covering our left wing by all available cavalry between Montereau and Melun.

f. Asking the British Army to participate in the manoeuvre :
(1) by holding the Seine from Melun to Juvisy ; (2) by debouching from that front when the Fifth Army attacks.

g. Having the garrison of Paris act simultaneously towards Meaux.

J. Joffre
General Commanding in Chief.

APPENDIX X

ORDERS OF BATTLE DURING THE BATTLE OF THE MARNE

(Italics indicate units newly constituted or transferred between August 24th and September 5th)

ALLIED ARMIES

From Left to Right (west to east):

French Sixth Army (Maunoury), organized August 26th :
Cavalry Corps (Sordet, then Bridoux), transferred from Fifth Army ; 1st, 3rd and 5th Cavalry Divisions.
7th Corps (Vautier), transferred from Army of Alsace ; with the 63rd Reserve Division replacing 41st Active Division.
Group of Reserve Divisions (De Lamaze), transferred from Army of Lorraine ; 56th and 55th Reserve Divisions.
45th Division (Algerian), transferred from North African Army.
Native Moroccan Brigade, transferred from North African Army.
Cavalry Brigade, transferred from Paris Garrison.
61st Reserve Division, transferred from Paris Garrison, arriving September 7th.
4th Corps (Boelle), transferred from Third Army, arriving September 8th. (Only 7th Division and Corps troops actively participated in Battle of the Ourcq ; 8th Division remaining south of the Marne in liaison with British left wing until September 9th.)

APPENDICES

British Army (Sir John French):
3rd Corps (Pulteney), organized August 30th; 19th Brigade and 4th
Division, which arrived from England August 25th.
Cavalry Detachment (Gough); 3rd and 5th Cavalry Brigades; designated
2nd Cavalry Division, September 16th.
2nd Corps (Smith-Dorrien).
1st Corps (Haig).
Cavalry Division (Allenby); 1st, 2nd and 4th Cavalry Brigades.

French Fifth Army (Franchet d'Esperey):
Cavalry Corps (Conneau), organized September 1st; 4th Cavalry Division,
8th Cavalry Division from Army of Alsace, 10th Cavalry Division from
Second Army.
18th Corps (De Maud'huy).
Group of Reserve Divisions (Valabrégue); 53rd and 69th Reserve Divisions.
3rd Corps (Hache).
1st Corps (Deligny).
10th Corps (Defforges).

Note: The 18th, 3rd and 10th Corps had three divisions each.

Ninth Army (Foch), organized September 5th:
(Originally constituted on August 28th, as an autonomous Army Detachment, comprising the left wing of the Fourth Army.)
42nd Division, transferred from the Third Army.
9th Corps (Dubois), transferred from the Fourth Army.
52nd Reserve Division, transferred from the Fourth Army.
11th Corps (Eydoux),   "   "   "   "   "
60th Reserve Division,   "   "   "   "   "
9th Cavalry Division,   "   "   "   "   "
18th Division, transferred from the Second Army, arriving September 7th.

Fourth Army (De Langle):
21st Corps (Legrand-Girarde), transferred from the First Army, arriving
September 8th.
17th Corps (Dumas).
12th Corps (Roques).
Colonial Corps (Lefévre).
2nd Corps (Gérard).

Third Army (Sarrail):
15th Corps (Espinasse), transferred from Second Army, arriving September 7th.
7th Cavalry Division.
5th Corps (Micheler).
6th Corps (Verraux), less the 42nd Division.
Group of Reserve Divisions (Paul Durand); 67th, 75th and 65th Reserve
Divisions.

Garrison of Verdun (Coutanceau) ; 72nd Reserve Division and brigade of
54th Reserve Division, comprising mobile forces.

Second Army (De Castelnau):
2nd Cavalry Division.
Garrison of Toul (Rémy) ; 73rd Reserve Division, comprising mobile forces.
Group of Reserve Divisions (Leon Durand) ; 59th, 68th and 70th Reserve
Divisions.
25th Corps (Balfourier).
74th Reserve Division.
16th Corps (Taverna).

First Army (Dubail):
6th Cavalry Division.
8th Corps (De Castelli).
13th Corps (Alix).
Temporary Army Corps (Delétoille), organized September 4th ; 44th
Division, a Colonial brigade and battalions of Chasseurs.
14th Corps (Baret).
Group of the Vosges (Toutée, then Bataille) ; 41st Division and 58th Reserve Division.
Garrison of Belfort (Thevenet) ; 57th Reserve Division and Active brigade
comprising mobile forces.
66th Reserve Division.
14th Dragoon Brigade.

GERMAN ARMIES

From Right to Left (west to east):

I Army (Von Kluck):
4th Cavalry Division.
4th Reserve Corps (Von Gronau).
2nd Corps (Von Linsingen).
4th Corps (Van Arnim).
3rd Corps (Von Lochow).
9th Corps (Von Quast).
2nd Cavalry Corps (Von der Marwitz) ; 2nd and 9th Cavalry Divisions.

II Army (Von Bülow):
1st Cavalry Corps (Von Richthofen) ; Guard and 5th Cavalry Divisions.
7th Corps (Von Einem), less one brigade left at Maubeuge.
10th Reserve Corps (Von Eben).
10th Corps (Von Emmich).
Guard (Von Plettenberg).

III Army (Von Hausen):
32nd Division
24th Reserve Division   }   Von Kirchbach's right wing group
23rd Reserve Division   (with II Army)

23rd Division   }   D'Elsa's left wing group
19th Corps (Von Laffert)   (with IV Army)

IV Army (Duke of Wurtemburg):
8th Corps (Von Tschepe und Weidenbach).
8th Reserve Corps (Von Egloffstein).
18th Corps (Von Schenck).
18th Reserve Corps (Von Steuben).

V Army (German Crown Prince):
4th Cavalry Corps (Von Hollen) ; 3rd and 6th Cavalry Divisions.
6th Corps (Von Pritzelwitz) ; transferred from IV Army.
13th Corps (Von Fabeck).
16th Corps (Von Mudra).
6th Reserve Corps (Von Gossler), covering west and northwest front of Verdun.
5th Reserve Corps (Von Gündell), astride of the Meuse, covering north front of Verdun.
5th Corps (Von Strantz), in plain of the Woevre, covering northeast and east front of Verdun.

VI Army (Crown Prince Rupprecht of Bavaria):
Garrison of Metz ; 33rd Reserve Division.
Guard, 4th, 8th and 10th Ersatz Divisions.
3rd Bavarian Corps (Von Gebsattel).
1st Bavarian Reserve Corps (Von Fasbender).
2nd Bavarian Corps (Von Martini).
21st Corps (Von Below).
1st Bavarian Corps (Von Xylander).
3rd Cavalry Corps (Von Frommel) ; 7th and Bavarian Cavalry Divisions.

VII Army (Von Heeringen):
14th Corps (Von Hoiningen).
15th Corps (Von Schubert).
14th Reserve Corps (Von Deimling).
19th and Bavarian Ersatz Divisions.
30th Reserve Division, from Strasbourg Garrison.

I

Total Effectives on Main Battle-front during Battle of the Marne

German Armies

	Active Inf. Div.	Reserve or Ersatz Inf. Div.	Cav. Div.
I Army	8	2	3
II Army	5½	2	2
III Army	4	2	–
IV Army	4	4	–
V Army	8	4	2
Total for Offensive Group	29½	14	7
VI Army	8	5	2
VIII Army	4	7	–
Grand Total	42½	26	9

Allied Armies

	Active Inf. Div.	Reserve Inf. Div.	Cav. Div.
French Sixth Army	4½	4	3½
British	5½	–	2
French Fifth Army	10	3	3
French Ninth Army	6	2	1
French Fourth Army	10	–	–
French Third Army	6	4½	1
French Second Army	4	5	1
French First Army	8½	3	1½
Grand Total	54½	21½	13

II

Comparative Effectives of German Right Wing and of Allied Left Wing at the Battle of the Marne

	Active Inf. Div.	Reserve Inf. Div.	Cav. Div.
German, (I, II and one-half of III Armies):	14½	6	5
Allies, (French Sixth, Fifth and Ninth Armies and British):	26	9	8½

III

Comparative Effectives of German Centre and of Allied Centre at the Battle of the Marne

	Active Inf. Div.	Reserve Inf. Div.	Cav. Div.
German, (One-half of III, IV and V Armies) :	15	8	2
Allies, (French Fourth and Third Armies) :	16	4½	1

IV

Comparative Effectives of German Left Wing and Allied Right Wing during the Battle of the Marne

	Active Inf. Div.	Reserve or Ersatz Inf. Div.	Cav. Div.
German, (VI and VII Armies) :	12	12	2
Allies, (French First and Second Armies) :	12½	8	1½

APPENDIX XI

VON MOLTKE'S GENERAL DIRECTIVE OF SEPTEMBER 5TH ISSUED TO THE
GERMAN ARMIES ON THE EVE OF THE BATTLE OF THE MARNE

G.H.Q., September 5, 1914.

The enemy has eluded the enveloping attack of the I and II Armies and has succeeded, with a part of his forces, in gaining contact with Paris. Reports from the front and information from reliable agents lead furthermore to the conclusion that he is transporting towards the west forces drawn from the line Toul-Belfort and that he is also proceeding to withdraw forces from before our Armies III to V. It is therefore no longer possible to roll up the whole French army towards the Swiss frontier in a southeasterly direction. We must rather expect to see the enemy transfer numerous forces into the region of Paris and to bring up new forces in order to protect his capital and to threaten the right flank of the German armies.

The I and II Armies must therefore remain before the eastern front of Paris. It will be their mission to oppose offensively any enemy effort coming from the region of Paris and to lend each other mutual support in these operations.

The IV and V Armies are in contact with important enemy forces. They must endeavour to drive these forces back without respite in a southeasterly direction, which will have the effect of opening the passage of the Moselle to the VI Army between Epinal and Toul. One cannot as yet predict whether this operation, conducted in concert with the VI and VII Armies, will have the result of throwing important enemy forces against the Swiss frontier.

The VI and VII Armies will initially conserve their present mission of holding the enemy forces which are before their front. They will advance as soon as possible to the attack of the line of the Moselle between Toul and Epinal, covering themselves towards these fortresses.

The III Army will march on Troyes-Vendoeuvre ; as circumstances dictate, it will be employed either to support the I and II Armies beyond the Seine in a westerly direction or to participate in a southerly and southeasterly direction in the operations of our left wing.

Accordingly, His Majesty orders :

I. — The I and II Armies will remain facing the eastern front of Paris to oppose offensively all enemy attempts starting from Paris : the I Army between the Oise and the Marne ; the crossings of the Marne below Château Thierry will be held to permit of passage from one bank to the other. The II Army between the Marne and the Seine ; the possession of the crossings of the Seine between Nogent and Méry is very important. It is recommended to the two armies to keep the main bodies of their forces far enough away from Paris to be able to retain sufficient liberty of action for their operations. The 2nd Cavalry Corps will remain under the orders of the I Army and will transfer one division to the 1st Cavalry Corps. The 1st Cavalry Corps will remain under the orders of the II Army and will transfer one division to the III Army.

The mission of the 2nd Cavalry Corps will be to observe the northern front of Paris between the Marne and the Lower Seine and to reconnoitre between the Somme and the Lower Seine as far as the coast. Distant reconnaissance beyond the Lille-Amiens railroad line will be undertaken by the aviation of the I Army.

The 1st Cavalry Corps will observe the southern front of Paris between the Marne and the Seine below Paris ; it will reconnoitre in the directions of Caen, Alençon, Le Mans, Tours and Bourges and should receive the aviation necessary for this purpose.

The two cavalry corps will destroy the railroad lines leading to Paris as near to the capital as possible.

II. — The III Army will march on Troyes-Vendoeuvre. A division of cavalry will be transferred to it by the 2nd Cavalry Corps. Reconnaissance towards the line Nevers-Le Creusot, aviation necessary for this mission should be attached to it.

III. — The IV and V Armies advancing resolutely towards the southeast will open the passage of the Moselle to the VI and VII Armies. Right wing of the IV Army by Vitry-le-François and Montierender, right wing of the V Army by Revigny-Stainville-Morlaix. With its left wing the V Army will cover the fortifications of the Meuse and will capture the Forts of Troyon, Les Paroches and the Roman Camp. The 4th Cavalry Corps will remain under the orders of the V Army. It will reconnoitre before the front of the IV and V Armies in the direction of the line Dijon-Besançon-Belfort. It will transmit information also to the IV Army.

IV. — The mission of the VI and VII Armies remains unchanged.

Von Moltke

APPENDIX XII

ORDERS TO THE FRENCH RIGHT WING ARMIES DEFINING THEIR ROLE IN THE BATTLE OF THE MARNE

I

General Headquarters
of Armies of the East.
———————————
Staff
———
3rd Bureau
————
3861

G.H.Q., September 5, 1914.
10:20 A.M.

Commander in Chief to General commanding the Fourth Army.

Tomorrow September 6th our left armies will attack the front and flank of the German I and II Armies.

Under these conditions, the Fourth Army, halting its movement towards the south, will stand its ground against the enemy and will endeavour by every means in its power to hold itself in readiness to resume the offensive joining its movement to that undertaken by the Third Army on its right.

The latter will debouch north of Revigny, marching west, to attack the enemy.

Attached is a copy of the order given to the left armies.

By order
Berthelot

3rd Bureau   II
_____
No. 3866
_____
Code telegram.   September 5th.
Received 2:40 P.M.

Commander in Chief to General commanding the Third Army.

Tomorrow September 6th our left armies will attack the front and flank of the German I and II Armies.

The Third Army, covering itself towards the north and northeast, will debouch towards the west to attack the left flank of the enemy forces which are marching west of the Argonne. It will combine its action with that of the Fourth Army which has been ordered to stand its ground. Acknowledge receipt.

Berthelot

APPENDIX XIII

LETTER FROM SIR JOHN FRENCH TO EARL KITCHENER

Headquarters, 7th September 1914.

My dear Lord K.

Thank you for your letters of September 5th received late last night.

I am very sorry to seem to have allowed you to lack information in the previous two days, but, as I explained to you in my telegram, the situation and the arrangements for our advance were so uncertain on Saturday [September 5th] that I was afraid of misleading you. For instance, on Friday night Joffre asked me to retire 12 miles in order to make room for his 5th Army south of the Marne. I had half completed the movement when he determined to keep the 5th Army north of the river and asked me to retrace my steps and get touch with that Army.

I think this was unavoidable, and on the whole his conception and his dispositions are really quite good. He tells me of the success in the advance of the 5th Army yesterday on my right and adds, "This result is certainly due to the advance of the English Forces towards the East. The continuation of your offensive will be of the greatest assistance to the attack of the 5th Army during the movement tomorrow."

He asked me to direct the march to-day a little more to the north, so as to be in closer touch with the 6th Army on the left.

As regards this latter Army, they have in front of them the 4th German Reserve Corps which has retreated north of the Marne and which they appear to be hammering pretty freely.

The 2nd German Corps was moving north all yesterday and at night-fall was watched by the aeroplanes into a large forest just south of the Marne from which we supposed them to be debouching, through Lizy, north of the wood to the north of the river.[1]

_____

(1) The reference is perhaps to the German 4th Corps. The 2nd Corps arrived north of the Marne early in the morning of September 6th, after a night march.

Joffre tells me that the 5th French Army have parts of the 9th and 3rd German Corps opposite them, and in rear of them are the 4th Regular Corps and parts of the 10th Corps.

As I told you, we pushed back considerable detachments of the enemy yesterday and hope to reach a much more forward line to-day.

I have been a great deal amongst the men and I find them in excellent spirits and good heart. Most of our casualties have now been replaced. I enclose you the returns for the 4th, 5th and 6th September; they have, of course, gone officially through the Lines of Communication.

We are refitting as quickly as we can, having regard to the forward movement and to the awful congestion of trains in the rear. This is now getting better, but it will be some days before we get our full requirement and our maxims and guns.

I am delighted to hear about the Indian Divisions. Who is to be the Indian Corps Commander?

Thank you for all your trouble about the 6th Division. I have not worried you about it because I know very well you are doing all you possibly can, and I much hope to get a wire from you to-night or to-morrow morning to say it is coming.

* * *

You ask my opinion as to German fighting characteristics. I will write to you on this subject in a day or two, as I must get this letter off by messenger; but I may say at once it will never do to oppose them with anything but very highly trained troops led by the best officers. All their movements are marked by extraordinary unity of purpose and mutual support; and to undergo the fatigues they have suffered they must be under an absolutely iron discipline. However, more of this to-morrow. At the same time I will tell you what I think of Gwynne's very useful letter.

I return the Prime Minister's note.

I have tried to write a bit of my despatch on every day when I could spare a few minutes. I have got the story fairly complete and accurate in despatch form up to our retirement from St. Quentin on Friday the 28th. That is practically when we threw off the bulk of the enemy after our first fight on the Mons position.[1]

This shall be finished off at once and will be with you in about three days; and it might be published on Thursday or Friday.

You say in your note enclosing P.M.'s letter, "I only sent one man to write." *No one* for writing purposes has arrived at the front. I should be delighted to have Percy.

Yours very truly
J. D. P. French.

(1) Although this statement is in accordance with the facts, it seems hardly consistent with French's communications to Kitchener of August 29th–31st. See Chapter XXI.

APPENDIX XIV

I

G.H.Q.
Staff
3rd Bureau   September 3rd.
No. 3523

Personal Memorandum for the Minister of War

During the day of September 2nd, the main bodies of the German armies were occupying the following positions :

I Army (4 Active and 1 Reserve corps) had crossed south of the region of Compiègne.

II Army (3 Active corps, 2 Reserve corps) had reached the region of Laon.

III Army (2 Active corps, 1 Reserve corps) had crossed the Aisne between Château Porcien and Attigny.

IV Army and V Army (amounting together to 6 Active corps and 4 Reserve corps) are in contact with our armies between Vouziers and Verdun.

From Belfort to Nancy, their VI and VII Armies (6 Active corps and numerous Reserve and Ersatz units) are entrenched before our right wing.

The German right wing is accordingly executing a sweeping enveloping movement against our left.

We had hoped to combat this manoeuvre by a powerful concentration of forces in the region of Amiens, thanks to the aid of the British Army and of the army formed under the orders of General Maunoury.

The rapid retreat of the British Army, carried out too soon to permit Maunoury's Army to intervene under favourable conditions, has had deplorable consequences for the left of Lanrezac's Army, which was northeast of Château Thierry on the afternoon of September 2nd.

The German cavalry, crossing the Oise by a bridge which the British could not destroy in time, were able to penetrate our lines of communication, capturing a convoy and even arriving in the night of September 2nd before Château Thierry where they have attacked the bridges.

To accept battle at this time with any one of the armies would inevitably involve the engagement of all our forces, and Lanrezac's Army would find itself held in a position which the advance of the German I Army makes extremely dangerous. The least reverse would create the greatest risk of an irretrievable rout in the course of which the rest of our armies would be thrown far back from the Entrenched Camp of Paris and completely separated from the British forces.

Our chances of success would be further diminished by the great fatigue of our troops who have been fighting constantly and who need to fill the gaps created in their ranks. The Army Commanders, who have been consulted, are not favourable to the idea of an immediate general engagement.

Moreover our situation in the coalition imposes on us the duty of holding out, to gain time by retaining the maximum possible German forces before us. We can do it only by avoiding being held to a decisive engagement, in which we should not have a great chance of success, and by wearing out the enemy by offensives undertaken at every favourable opportunity, as our armies have continually been doing.

The necessity of temporarily abandoning a still greater part of our territory to the enemy, however painful, is not sufficient reason to induce us to accept a general battle too soon, under unfavourable conditions.

These considerations have animated the decision I have taken :

To wait a few days before delivering battle, retiring as far as necessary to prevent our armies from being held to a general engagement.

To withdraw from our right wing armies at least two army corps, by assigning these armies strictly defensive missions.

To reconstitute and rest our troops to the greatest possible extent.

To prepare for an offensive in the near future, in liaison with the British Army and with the mobile garrison of Paris. The region for this offensive is so chosen that, by utilizing defensive organizations already prepared on certain parts of the front, we can be sure of a numerical superiority in the zone selected for our main effort.

Facing an enemy who will become weaker as he advances farther and farther into a country where the communications have in part been destroyed, we shall increase in large proportion our chances of victory.

J. Joffre

II

General Headquarters
of Armies of the East.

Staff
September 5, 1914.
3rd Bureau
No. 3845

Personal Memorandum for the Minister of War

The situation which led me at first to refuse a general battle and to withdraw our armies towards the south has been modified as follows :

The German I Army has abandoned the direction of Paris and has turned its march towards the southeast to seek out our left flank.

Thanks to the dispositions taken, it has not been able to find this flank and the Fifth Army is now north of the Seine, ready to gain contact with the front of the German columns.

At its left, the British forces are assembled between the Marne and the Seine, ready to attack. They will themselves be supported and flanked on the left by the mobile forces of the garrison of Paris, acting towards Meaux, in such a way as to relieve them of the fear of envelopment.

The strategic situation is therefore excellent and we cannot hope for better conditions for our offensive.

That is why I have decided to attack.

Field Marshal French has assured me that I can count upon his energetic co-operation. A question has arisen, however, with regard to the action of the British Army. His Chief of Staff had an interview at Melun with the Military Governor of Paris, while the Deputy Chief of Staff was seeing the commander of the Fifth Army at Bray.

The conclusions reached at these two interviews seem to me somewhat divergent, but I have adopted dispositions which can be adjusted to either one of the two solutions.

In any case, the struggle in which we are about to engage may have decisive results, but it may also have very serious consequences for the country in case of a reverse.

I am determined to engage all our forces without stint and without reservation to achieve victory. It is essential that the British Army do the same, and I count on you to be good enough to draw the Field Marshal's attention, through diplomatic channels, to the importance of unreserved offensive action.

If I could give orders to the British Army as I would give them to a French Army occupying the same position, I should attack immediately.

J. Joffre

APPENDIX XV

SOME ORDERS ISSUED BY THE FRENCH HIGH COMMAND DURING THE BATTLE OF THE MARNE

(1)

General Headquarters
of Armies of the East.

Staff

3rd Bureau

No. 4151

September 7, 1914; 3:45 P.M.

General Instructions No. 7

The German I Army seems to be retreating towards the northeast before the combined efforts of the Allied left armies.

The latter should follow the enemy with all their forces in such a way as to maintain the possibility of enveloping the German right wing.

The march will therefore be carried out in a general way in a north-easterly direction, with dispositions which will permit battle to be engaged, if the enemy halts and without allowing him time to organize solidly.

To this end the Sixth Army will successively gain ground towards the north on the right bank of the Ourcq.

The British forces will seek to cross successively [sic] the Petit Morin, the Grand Morin and the Marne.

The Fifth Army will accelerate the movement of its left wing and will employ its right to support the Ninth Army.

The latter will endeavour to hold the front it is occupying until the arrival of the reserve forces of the Fourth Army on its right (i.e. the 21st Corps) permit it to take part in the forward movement.

Limit of zones of action between the Fifth Army and the Army W. (British) : Dagny, St. Rémy, Sablonnières, Hondevilliers, Nogent-l'Artaud, Château Thierry (this road to Army W.).

J. Joffre
General Commanding in Chief.

Note : The German retirement above referred to is, of course, the withdrawal of the German 3rd and 9th Corps behind the Petit Morin River during the night of the 6th.

(2)

Telephone Message from General Clergerie, Chief of Staff to the Military Governor of Paris to Capt. de Galbert, personal aide to the Commander in Chief

September 8th, 8 A.M.

The British are not showing any offensive power [*mordant*] and are satisfied to follow ; all the German effort is directed against General Maunoury.

The latter received by rail and auto during the night all of the second division (7th Division) of the 4th Corps. General Galliéni is leaving the autos at General Maunoury's disposal and has sent him machine-gun automobiles.

General Sordet has been directed by General Maunoury to act vigorously against the enemy's rear.

(3)

Commander in Chief to the Chief of the French Mission at British Headquarters

Telephone message September 8th, 9 A.M.

With the support of British forces, the Fifth and Sixth Armies have continued to progress. In the centre and on the right our troops though sharply attacked have maintained their positions. Today the Third and Fourth Armies have resumed the offensive with the support of the reinforcements sent them.

In general the situation is very satisfactory on the whole front.

In accordance with telegram No. 4151, it is most important that British forces should cross as soon as possible north of the Petit Morin and the Marne, in order to make the enemy's retreat difficult and to prevent him from halting behind the obstacle which these two rivers provide.

J. Joffre

(4)

Commander in Chief of the French Armies to the Field Marshal commanding the British Armies.

Telephone message transmitted through French Mission.

September 8th, 3:30 P.M.

The German forces which were in front of the British Army are moving north against our Sixth Army. In order that the latter shall not be obliged to retreat, I consider it indispensable that the British forces attack on La Ferté-sous-Jouarre and debouch north of the Marne tonight.

J. Joffre

(5)

No. 4365

To : Sixth Army

    Fifth Army   September 8, 1914.

    Ninth Army

    Colonel Huguet (British)

    Military Governor of Paris.

Special Orders No. 19.

I. — Before the combined efforts of the Allied left wing armies, the German forces have retreated, forming two distinct groups.

One which appears to comprise the 4th Reserve Corps and the 2nd and 4th Active Corps is fighting on the Ourcq, facing west against our Sixth Army, which it is even seeking to envelop from the north.

The other, comprising the rest of the German I Army (3rd and 9th Active Corps) and the II and III German Armies remains facing south opposed to the Fifth and Ninth French Armies.

Contact between these two groups seems to be maintained only by several cavalry divisions, supported by detachments of all arms, facing the British troops.

II. — It seems essential to put the German extreme right out of action before it can be reinforced by other units which the fall of Maubeuge may have rendered available.

The Sixth Army and the British will take this as their mission.

For this purpose, the Sixth Army will hold before it the troops opposing it on the right bank of the Ourcq ; the British forces, crossing the Marne between Nogent-l'Artaud and La Ferté-sous-Jouarre will move against the left and rear of the enemy who is along the Ourcq.

III. — The Fifth Army will cover the right flank of the British Army by sending a strong detachment against Azy, Château Thierry.

The Cavalry Corps, crossing the Marne, if necessary behind this detachment and behind the British Army, will assure effective liaison between the British Army and the Fifth Army.

On its right the Fifth Army will continue to support the action of the Ninth Army, so as to permit the latter to take the offensive.

The main body of the Fifth Army, marching due north, will drive the forces opposed to it beyond the Marne.

IV. — Beyond the Marne the road Romény, Azy, Château Thierry, assigned to the British Army by General Order No. 7 of September 7th, is reserved to the Fifth Army.

J. Joffre
General Commanding in Chief

(6)

Commander in Chief to the Commander of the First Army.

No. 4407   September 9th ; 7:34 A.M.

The decisive point is on the left wing ; necessary to transport still another corps, 8th or 13th, towards Paris. Designate the one, report, take measures for its embarkation September 11th in the region Epinal, Châtel, Charmes.

Joffre

(7)

Commander in Chief to the Commander of the Third Army.

No. 4412   September 9th ; 8:45 A.M.

Code Telegram

It is important to take advantage of your success over the enemy's artillery to progress more and more towards the west, particularly on your left, so as to check the progress of the enemy and to relieve the right of the Fourth Army.

J. Joffre

(8)

Commander in Chief to the Commander of the Sixth Army.

No. 4448   September 9th ; 10:30 A.M.

Telephone message.

I am going to reinforce you by a division taken further from the right which will begin to entrain this afternoon from four o'clock on.

While awaiting the arrival of the reinforcements which will permit you to resume the offensive, you should endeavour to avoid all decisive action, withdrawing your left if necessary in the direction of the Entrenched Camp of Paris.

J. Joffre

(9)

Commander in Chief to the Commander of the Fifth Army.
No. 4469

Telephone message.   September 9th ; 2:10 P.M.

It is essential that the 18th Corps cross the Marne this very night in the vicinity of Château Thierry, so as to support effectively the British columns which have crossed the river. Your order of yesterday did not seem to correspond sufficiently to this necessity. The Cavalry Corps must act accordingly.

J. Joffre

(10)

Commander in Chief to the Chief of the French Mission at British Head-quarters.

No. 197A.

Telephone message.   September 9th ; 8:45 P.M.

Please express particularly to the Field Marshal my thanks for the services which the British aviation has daily been rendering us.

The precision, the accuracy, the regularity of the information it has furnished testify to its excellent organization as well as to the perfect efficiency of its pilots and observers.

J. Joffre

(11)

General Headquarters
of Armies of the East.

Staff   G.H.Q., September 9, 1914 ; 10 P.M.

3rd Bureau

No. 4550.

Special Orders No 20.

I. — As a result of the engagements during the days of September 8th and 9th, the enemy seems to have retreated, partly in the forests north of Champaubert, and on the Marne above Château Thierry, partly on the line Etrépilly, Courchamps, where he seems to be entrenching. These forces are prolonged to the left by those facing the Sixth Army.

II. — Tomorrow the Fifth and Sixth Armies, as well as the British forces, will place themselves in position to attack the enemy.

III. — For this purpose :

a. The British forces will endeavour to reach the heights of the south bank of the Clignon between Bouresches and Hervilliers and will organize their positions. They will be supported on their left by the 8th Infantry Division which will move north along the east bank of the Ourcq and on their right by the 18th Corps which will organize a bridge-head north of Château Thierry.

b. The Fifth Army will support the movement of the 18th Corps by driving the enemy back towards the north, while retaining its liaison with the Ninth Army by the 10th Corps. It will endeavour to reach the Marne between Château Thierry and Dormans and to prepare to cross it.

Conneau's Cavalry Corps, operating with the 18th Corps, will establish contact with the enemy and will seek to break through in the direction of Oulchy-le-Chateau.

c. The Sixth Army, resting its right on the Ourcq, will continue to gain ground towards the north to seek to envelop the enemy ; its action will be prolonged towards the north by Bridoux's Cavalry Corps which will seek the flank and the rear of the enemy.

IV. — The Ninth Army, retaining the 10th Corps at its disposal, will pursue the offensive begun on the 9th.

J. Joffre
General Commanding in Chief

(12)

General Headquarters
of Armies of the East.

Staff   G.H.Q., September 10, 1914.
3rd Bureau   4:50 P.M.
Operations-Priority.
No. 4653

General Commanding in Chief to the Minister of War, Bordeaux.

The offensive ordered for the 6th of September was assumed by our Armies with a fierceness which has only increased in four days of uninterrupted combat. It was reasonable to fear that the movement in retreat, which the strategic situation led me to order, from the Meuse almost to the Seine might have impaired the vigour of the Allied troops and broken their spirit. Everywhere, on the contrary, the morale of our soldiers has risen beyond praise, everywhere they have responded with all their energy to the first order of their leaders.

I have deliberately been very sparing of news before having definitely obtained indisputable results. Today I can announce to you the results of the Battle of the Marne. Before our left the enemy armies, in full retreat, have been driven beyond the Marne by the British Army and by Franchet d'Esperey's Army which have advanced more than 60 kilometres in four days of fighting.

Maunoury's Army has withstood, with admirable energy, the powerful effort that the Germans made against it to relieve their right. These troops, long subjected to the intensive fire of German large calibre shells, have succeeded in repelling all attacks and have resumed their movement towards the north, pursuing a retreating enemy.

This morning the German centre has commenced to give way. Foch's Army is progressing towards the Marne, finding along its way signs of the precipitate retreat of the enemy, whose army corps, notably the Guard, have sustained very heavy losses.

On our right we are vigorously resisting very violent attacks and everything gives ground for hope that our success will extend there.

J. Joffre

BIBLIOGRAPHICAL NOTE

The foundation of the present work has been laid upon the official histories of the four nations concerned, the French *Les Armées Françaises dans la Grande Guerre* (Tome I, Vols. I–III), the British *Military Operations-France and Belgium* 1914 (Vol. I), the Belgian *L'Action de l'Armée Belge. Période du 31 juillet au 31 décembre* 1914, and the German *Der Weltkrieg* 1914–1918 (Vols. I–IV). In Germany, the latter account has been supplemented by numerous other official publications, among which should be noted particularly, a series of monographs issued by the General Staff, *Die Schlachten des Weltkrieges*, including volumes dealing in detail with various important phases of military operations, *Das Marnedrama, Lüttich-Namur, Mons*, etc. ; a book, also prepared under the auspices of the General Staff, *Die Schlachten und Gefechten des Grossen Krieges* 1914–1918, giving the battles and engagements in which each German major unit participated, with details of their organization and command ; and finally other works relating to the more technical aspects of the campaign, such as *Das deutsche Feldeisenbahnwesen* (Vol. I).

In France, up to the time of the publication of the official history, of which the last volume appeared in 1932, the principal official document generally available was the record of the testimony taken before the Briey Parliamentary Commission of 1919, the commission which investigated the causes for the loss of the rich iron fields adjacent to the French eastern frontier, which the Germans seized at the outset of the war, almost without opposition, and worked for their own advantage until the end. This testimony constituted a primary source for many works written in France immediately after the war. While it must neither be ignored, nor its importance unduly minimized, its political back-ground should not be over-looked.

The official records are voluminous and on the whole indicate a conscientious effort in all countries to relate the facts dispassionately, but they cannot give the story of the Marne, any more than a collection of the chemical ingredients of the human body can be made into a man. To find the motives, opinions, aspirations and human relationships that give the breath of life to history, we must look elsewhere. Fortunately, most of those who took leading roles have left records of their activities. On the German side, five out of seven Army Commanders have published their accounts, Von Kluck, Von Bülow, Von Hausen, the German Crown Prince and Rupprecht of Bavaria, and two Army Chiefs of Staff, Von Kuhl and Von Dellmensingen, have done likewise ; while the point of view of the High Command is represented by the works of Von Stein,

Tappen, Gröner, Bauer and the rather inadequate memoirs of Von Moltke himself.   The French generals, though somewhat less prolific in their literary endeavours than their former adversaries, have not been idle. Joffre, Foch, Galliéni, Lanrezac, Sarrail and Dubail have given their versions, and the memoirs of Franchet d'Esperey are reported to be in course of preparation.   Of the principal British commanders, two out of three, French and Smith-Dorrien, have published memoirs, and it is said that Haig, at his death, left his in the hands of public trustees to be opened at some distant future date.   Many lesser figures have made contributions from their own experiences, Dupont, De Castelli, Legrand-Girarde, Huguet, Charteris, Spears, Von Gossler, Von Zwehl and Von Moser, among others.

It is obvious that all such books constitute primary source material of no less importance — and from the point of view of the general reader of considerably more interest — than the official records themselves.   Most of them were written several years after the events with which they deal, in many cases without the aid of records other than the writer's personal recollection or notes ; as a result minor inaccuracies abound, and occasionally important omissions are made.   These are hazards against which the seeker for facts must guard.

It is not unnatural that those who bore the responsibility for the development of events, should show a tendency to be strongly partisan, both in their nationalistic attitude and in describing their relations with their own compatriots.   Each commander has written from his own view-point and has striven to put his best foot forward, rarely admitting his own errors, laying the blame for failures, which in some measure were the common lot of all, occasionally upon the enemy, but more often, lest his warrior's prowess be diminished, upon the short-comings of his own subordinates, his colleagues or his superiors.   Exceptionally free in these respects and notably moderate in judgement are the memoirs of the two greatest of French leaders, Joffre and Foch, but in some instances, as in Lanrezac's *Le Plan de Compagne Français* for example, a desire for justification has led to such extremes as to constitute the resultant work a brief for personal vindication, rather than a serious contribution to history.

Another source of material, which deserves at least passing mention, is what may be described as the semi-official literature, the bumper crop of regimental, divisional and corps histories that has grown up in all countries.   In general, they are of necessity detailed chronicles, devoted to the achievements of individuals or of relatively small groups, and in them the reverse of the medal is rarely shown.   Many have been studied in the preparation of this book, however, and they have proved a fruitful source of information.

It is impossible to offer a detailed analysis, even of the most important books, nor does a formal bibliography seem necessary.   Reference is made in the foregoing text and in the foot-notes to many authorities which have been consulted and to which readers who wish to pursue the subject further may turn.   In connection with these references, however,

two points must be made clear. They are not exhaustive, for aside from
the exigencies of space, the number of books and articles, poured out
during the last twenty years in French, German and English, to say nothing of other languages, is so great that it is more than probable that many
— perhaps some of outstanding merit — have escaped the attention of
the present author. Neither must it be supposed that references cited
necessarily sustain the thesis of the text to which they appertain ; the
contrary is often the case, and not infrequently they may provide useful
ammunition to combat the soundness of the conclusions reached herein.

In spite of the records and all that has been written, there are certain
factors that must to the end of time remain uncertain, the imponderables
which the greatest soldiers have recognized as perhaps the most important
element in the art of war and certainly the most difficult with which to
deal. These confront a writer of military history, much as they do a
commander in the field, for the value of a history must greatly depend
on how they are judged and how they are treated. In the present work,
a conscientious effort has been made to weigh the evidence of official
records and of such accounts as are available, and to select judiciously
where there is a conflict. For the conclusions reached, no apology is
offered, but a wide field remains for honest difference.

LIST OF WORKS CITED IN THE TEXT

Alexandre, Gen., *Avec Joffre d'Agadir à Verdun* (Berger-Levrault, Paris, 1933).

Arthur, Sir George, *The Life of Lord Kitchener* (Macmillan, N. Y., 1930).

Ballard, Gen. C. R., *Kitchener* (Dodd, Mead, N. Y., 1930).

Bassompierre, Baron de, *La Nuit du 2 au 3 août 1914 au Ministère des Affaires Etrangères en Belgique;* Revue des Deux Mondes, February 15, 1915.

Bauer, Col., *Der Grosse Krieg in Feld und Heimat* (Osiander'sche Buchhandlung, Tubingen, 1921).

Baumgarten-Crusius, Gen. A., *Die Marneschlacht 1914* (Lippold, Leipzig, 1919); *Deutsche Heerfuhrung im Marnefeldzug 1914* (Scherl, Berlin, 1921).

Berthaut, Gen., *L' "Erreur" de 1914 — Réponse aux Critiques* (Van Oest, Paris, 1919).

Bertie, Lord, of Thame, *Diary 1914–1919* (Doran, N. Y., 1924).

Bienfait, Commandant, *Comme ceux de Quatre-vingt-treize* (Meiniger, Mulhouse, 1920).

Bircher, Col., *Die Krisis an der Marneschlacht; Die Schlacht am Ourcq* (Bücher, Leipzig, 1922).

Bird, Major-Gen. Sir W. D., *A Crisis of the Campaign in France 1914;* British Army Quarterly, April 1934.

Bizot, Gen., *A propos des Souvenirs 1914–1915 du Général Sarrail;* Revue Politique et Parlementaire, May 10, 1922.

Bloch, Prof. Camille, *Les Causes de la Guerre Mondiale* (Hartmann, Paris, 1933).

Bloem, Capt. Walter, *Vormarsch* (Grethlein, Leipzig).

Boelle, Gen., *Le 4ie Corps d'Armée sur l'Ourcq.*

Boucherie, Col., *Historique du Corps de Cavalerie Sordet* (Lavauzelle, Paris, 1924).

Bourgon, Gen. Nayral de, *Dix Ans de Souvenirs* (Chastanier, Nîmes).

Brandis, Lieut. von, *Die Stürmer von Douaumont* (Scherl, Berlin).

Brandt, Gen., *Moderne Kavallerie* (Mittler, Berlin, 1931).

Buat, Gen., *L'Armée Allemande pendant la Guerre de 1914–1918* (Chapelot, Paris, 1920).

Bujac, Gen., *Le Général Eydoux et le 11ie Corps d'Armée* (Nantes, 1924).

Bülow, Field Marshal von, *Mein Bericht zur Marneschlacht* (Scherl, Berlin, 1919).

Camon, Gen., *L'Effondrement du plan Allemand en septembre* 1914 (Berger-Levrault, Paris, 1925).

Canonge, Gen., *La Bataille de la Marne* (Fournier, Paris, 1918).

Carré, Commandant, *La véritable histoire des taxis de la Marne* (Chapelot, Paris, 1929).

Castelli, Gen. de, *Le 8ie Corps en Lorraine* (Berger-Levrault, Paris, 1925).

Charteris, Brig-Gen. J., *Field Marshal Earl Haig* (Scribners, N. Y., 1929) ; *At G.H.Q.* (Cassell, London, 1931).

Churchill, Rt. Hon. Winston, *The World Crisis* (Scribners, N. Y., 1923).

Clergerie, Gen., *Le rôle du Gouvernement Militaire de Paris* (Berger-Levrault, Paris, 1920).

Cochenhausen, Gen. von, *Von Scharnhorst zu Schlieffen* (Mittler, Berlin, 1933).

Colin, Gen., *La Division de Fer* (Payot, Paris, 1929).

Cordonnier, Gen., *L'Obéissance aux Armées* (Lavauzelle, Paris, 1924) ; *Ai-je Trahi Sarrail* (Les Etincelles, Paris, 1930) ; *A la droite de la 4ie Armée le 22 août* 1914 ; Revue Militaire Française.

D'Almeida, Prof., *L'Armée Allemande avant et pendant la Guerre de 1914–1918* (Berger-Levrault, Paris, 1919).

Dartein, Gen. de, *La 56ie Division au Feu* (Berger-Levrault, Paris, 1919).

Dellmensingen, Gen. Kraft von, *Die Führung des Kronprinzen Rupprecht von Bayern.*

Dubail, Gen., *Quatre Années de Commandement* (Fournier, Paris, 1922).

Dubois, Gen., *Deux Ans de Commandement sur le front de France* (Lavauzelle, Paris, 1921).

Duché, Commandant, *La Bataille de la Marne a-t-elle été engagée vingt-quatre heures trop tôt ? ;* Revue Militaire Française, June, 1925.

Dupont, Gen., *Le Haut Commandement Allemand en* 1914 (Chapelot, Paris, 1922).

Edmonds, Brig.-Gen. J. S., *The Scapegoat of the Battle of the Marne ;* British Army Quarterly, January, 1921.

Einem, Gen. von, *Erinnerungen eines Soldaten* 1853–1933 (Köhler, Leipzig, 1933).

Engerand, Fernand, *Le Secret de la Frontière, 1815–1871–1914. Charleroi* (Bossard, Paris, 1918) ; *La Bataille de la Frontière-Briey* (Bossard, Paris, 1920).

Fabry, Lieut.-Col., *Joffre et son destin* (Lavauzelle, Paris, 1931).

Fay, Prof. Sidney, *Origins of the World War* (Macmillan, N. Y., 1928).

Feldartillerie Regiment Nr. 4, Das, (Faber, Magdeburg, 1928).

Foch, Marshal, *Mémoires* (Plon, Paris, 1931).

Förster, Lieut.-Col., *Graf Schlieffen und der Weltkrieg* (Mittler, Berlin, 1921).

François, Gen. von, *Marneschlacht und Tannenberg* (Scherl, Berlin).

French, Viscount, of Ypres, *1914* (Constable, London, 1919).

Freytag-Loringhoven, Gen. von, *Generalfeldmarschall Graf von Schlieffen* (Leipzig, 1920).

Galet, Gen., *S. M. Albert I devant l'Invasion Allemande* (Plon, Paris, 1931).
Galliéni, Gen., *Mémoires* (Payot, Paris, 1920) ; *Carnets de Galliéni* (ed. by his son, Michel, Paris, 1932).
Gascouin, Gen., *L'Evolution de l'Artillerie pendant la Guerre* (Flammarion, Paris, 1920).
Gazin, Capt. F., *La Cavalerie Française dans la Guerre Mondiale* (Payot, Paris, 1930).
Gebsattel, Gen. von, *Generalfeldmarschall Karl von Bülow* (Lehmanns, Munich).
Genevoix, Maurice, *Sous Verdun.*
Gheusi, P-B., *Galliéni* (Fasquelle, Paris, 1922) ; *La Gloire de Galliéni* (Michel, Paris, 1928).
Giraud, Commandant, *Nos Grands Chefs — De Castelnau ;* Revue des Deux Mondes, August 1921.
Gossler, Gen. von, *Erinnerungen an den grossen Krieg* (Breslau, 1919).
Gothein, George, *Warum verloren wir den Krieg* (Deutsche Verlags-Anstalt, Berlin, 1919).
Grandidier, Guillaume, *Galliéni* (Plon, Paris, 1931).
Grasset, Col., *Virton* (Berger-Levrault, Paris, 1926) ; *Ethe* (Berger-Levrault, Paris, 1927) ; *Neufchâteau* (Berger-Levrault, Paris, 1930) ; *Rossignol-St. Vincent* (Berger-Levrault, Paris, 1932) ; *Comment fut livrée la Bataille de la Marne ;* Revue des Deux Mondes, September 1, 1933 ; *La Bataille des Deux Morins* (Payot, Paris, 1934).
Grey, Earl, of Falloden, *Twenty-five Years* 1892–1916 (Stokes, N. Y., 1925).
Gröner, Gen., *Das Testament des Grafen Schlieffen* (Mittler, Berlin, 1927) ; *Der Feldherr wider Willen* (Mittler, Berlin, 1930).
Grouard, Lieut.-Col., *La Conduite de la Guerre jusqu'à la Bataille de la Marne* (Chapelot, Paris, 1922).

Haldane, Viscount, *Autobiography* (Doubleday, Doran, N. Y., 1929).
Hannover Inf. Regt. Nr. 165 im Weltkriege, Das, (Fliess, Berlin, 1927).
Hanotaux, Gabriel, *La Bataille de la Marne* (Plon, Paris, 1922) ; *L'Enigme de Charleroi* (Ed. Française Illustrée, Paris, 1917).
Hart, Liddell, *Reputations Ten Years After* (Little, Brown, Boston, 1928) ; *The Real War* (Little, Brown, Boston, 1931).
Hausen, Gen. von, *Erinnerungen an den Marnefeldzug* (Köhler, Leipzig, 1919).
Herbillon, Col., *Le Général Alfred Micheler* (Plon, Paris, 1934).
Herr, Gen., *L'Artillerie* (Berger-Levrault, Paris, 1924).
Héthay, J. (Gen. de Cornulier-Lucinière), *Le rôle de la cavalerie française à l'aile gauche de la première Bataille de la Marne* (Perrin, Paris, 1919).
Hindenburg, Field Marshal von, *Aus meinem Leben* (Hirzel, Leipzig, 1920).

Hirschauer, Gen., in collaboration with Gen. Klein, *Paris en état de défense* (Payot, Paris, 1927).

Hosse, Karl, *Die englischen-belgischen Aufmarschpläne gegen Deutschland vor dem Weltkriege* (Leipzig, 1930).

Hötzendorf, Field Marshal Conrad von, *Aus Meiner Dienstzeit* (Rikola, Vienna, 1923).

Hübner, Capt. H., *Unter Emmich vor Lüttich. Unter Kluck vor Paris.* (Bahn, Schwerin).

Huguet, Gen., *L'Intervention militaire Britannique en 1914* (Berger-Levrault, Paris, 1928).

Immanuel, Col., *Siege und Niederlage im Weltkriege* (Mittler, Berlin, 1919).

Isaac, Prof. Jules, *Joffre et Lanrezac* (Chiron, Paris, 1922).

Jochim, Col., *Die Operationen und rückwartigen Verbindungen der deutschen I Armee in der Marneschlacht, 1914* (Mittler, Berlin, 1934).

Joffre, Marshal, *Mémoires* (Plon, Paris, 1932).

Justrow, Lieut.-Col., *Feldherr und Kriegstechnik* (Stalling, Oldenburg, 1933).

Kann, Reginald, *Le Plan de campagne Allemand de 1914 et son execution* (Payot, Paris).

Kluck, Gen. von, *Der Marsch auf Paris und die Marneschlacht 1914* (Mittler, Berlin, 1920).

Koeltz, Lieut.-Col., *La Garde Allemande à la Bataille de Guise* (Lavauzelle, Paris, 1928); *D'Esternay aux Marais de Saint-Gond* (Lavauzelle, Paris, 1930); *L'Armée von Kluck à la Bataille de la Marne* (Lavauzelle, Paris, 1931); *Le G.Q.G. Allemand et la Bataille de la Marne* (Payot, Paris, 1931); *La Bataille de Lorraine;* Revue de Paris, Sept.-Oct. 1923.

Köppen, Capt. Hans, *The Battle of the Marne, 8th and 9th September,* 1914; British Army Quarterly, July 1934.

Königliche Preuss. Inf. Regt. Nr. 127 im Weltkriege 1914–1918 (Bernard u. Grasse, Berlin, 1933).

Kracke, Dr. Otto, *Generalfeldmarschall von Bülow* (Scherl, Berlin).

Kräwel, Gen., Militar-Wochenblatt No. 74, 1919.

Kuhl, Gen. von, *Der Deutsches Generalstab* (Mittler, Berlin, 1920); Fr. trans. and commentary by Gen. Douchy, (Payot, Paris, 1922); *Der Marnefeldzug 1914* (Mittler, Berlin, 1921).

Langevin, Capt., *Cavaliers de France* (Crès, Paris).

Lanrezac, Gen., *Le Plan de Campagne Français* (Payot, Paris, rev. ed. 1929).

Larcher, Lieut.-Col., *Le 1er Corps à Dinant, Charleroi, Guise* (Berger-Levrault, Paris, 1932).

Lebas, Gen., *Places fortes et fortifications pendant la guerre de 1914–1918* (Payot, Paris).

402 LIST OF WORKS CITED IN THE TEXT

Leblond, M., *Galliéni Parle* (Michel, Paris, 1920).
Lefranc, Commandant, *Le 20^{ie} Corps à Morhange;* Revue Militaire Française, October, 1930.
Le Goffic, Charles, *Les Marais de Saint-Gond* (Plon, Paris, 1917).
Legrand-Girarde, Gen., *Les Operations du 21^{ie} Corps d'Armée* (Plon, Paris, 1922).
Legros, Gen., *La Genèse de la Bataille de la Marne* (Payot, Paris, 1919).
Lestien, Lieut.-Col., *L'Action du General Foch à la Bataille de la Marne;* Revue d'Histoire de la Guerre Mondiale, April, 1930.
Ligny, Col. de, *La Division de Maroc aux Marais de Saint-Gond* (Lavauzelle, Paris, 1933).
Lohrisch, Lieut. H., *Im Siegessturm von Lüttich an die Marne* (Quelle u. Meyer, Leipzig).
Lucas, Col., *Le 10^{ie} Corps à la Bataille de Charleroi* (Lavauzelle, Paris, 1930); *Le 10^{ie} Corps et la 42^{ie} Division à la Bataille de la Marne;* Revue Militaire Generale, October 1924.
Ludendorff, Gen., *Meine Kriegserinnerungen* (Mittler, Berlin, 1919).

Madelin, Louis, *La Victoire de la Marne* (Plon, Paris); *Devant Verdun;* Revue Hébdomadaire, October 1917.
Mangin, Gen., *Comment Finit la Guerre* (Plon, Paris, 1920); *Des Hommes et des Faits* (Plon, Paris, 1923).
March, Gen. Peyton C., *The Nation at War* (Doubleday, Doran, N. Y., 1932).
Marchand, A., *Plans de concentration de 1871–1914* (Berger-Levrault, Paris, 1926).
Maurice, Major-Gen. Sir Frederick, *Forty Days in 1914* (Little, Brown, Boston, 1919).
Mayer, Lieut.-Col., *Nos Chefs de 1914* (Stock, Paris, 1930).
Mazenod, Capt. de, *Dans les Champs de Meuse* (Plon, Paris).
Messimy, Gen., *Comment j'ai nommé Galliéni;* Revue de Paris, Sept. 15, 1921.
Michel, Commandant, *Monthyon* (Berger-Levrault, Paris, 1931).
Mierry, Commandant de, *Le Commandement allemand pendant les opérations d'Alsace-Lorraine;* Revue de France, May 15, 1922.
Moltke, Gen. von, *Erinnerungen, Briffe, Dokumente 1877–1916* (Der Kommende Tag A. G. Verlag, Stuttgart, 1922).
Mondésir, Gen. de, *Souvenirs et pages de guerre* (Berger-Levrault, Paris, 1934).
Moranville, Gen. de Selliers de, *Pourquoi l'Armée Belge s'est-elle retirée sur la position fortifiée d'Anvers le 18 août 1914?* (Dewit, Brussels, 1922); *Contribution à l'Histoire de la Guerre Mondiale 1914–1918* (Goemaere, Brussels, 1933); *Les inéxactitudes des Mémoires du Général de Ryckel;* Mercure de France, Paris, 1921.
Mortane, J., *L'Aviation a la Bataille de la Marne.*
Moser, Gen. von, *Feldzugaufzeichnungen 1914–1918* (Belserche, Stuttgart, 1920).

Muller, Commandant, *Joffre et la Marne* (Crès, Paris, 1931).

Müller-Loebnitz, Lieut.-Col., *Der Wendepunkt des Weltkrieges* (Mittler, Berlin) ; *Die Sendung des Oberstleutnants Hentsch* (Mittler, Berlin, 1922).

Normand, Gen., *Défense de Liége, Namur et Anvers en* 1914 (Fournier, Paris, 1923).

Osman, Prof. Sir Charles, *The Outbreak of the War* 1914–1918 (H. M. Stationery Office, London).

Palat, General (Pierre Lehautcourt), *La Grande Guerre sur le front occidental*, vols. I–VI (Chapelot, Paris).

Paleologue, Maurice, *Un Prélude a l'Invasion de Belgique ;* Revue des Deux Mondes, October 1, 1932.

Pelecier, Gen., *Un raid de cavalerie* (Lavauzelle, Paris, 1923).

Percin, Gen., *1914* (Michel, Paris, 1919) ; *Lille* (Grasset, Paris, 1919).

Pierrefeu, Jean de, *G.Q.G. Secteur* 1 (Ed. Françaises Illustrées, Paris, 1920).

Poincaré, Raymond, *L'Invasion* (Plon, Paris, 1928).

Poseck, Gen. von, *Die Deutsche Kavallerie in Belgien und Frankreich* 1914 (Mittler, Berlin, 1921).

Pugens, Lieut.-Col., *Rossignol ;* Revue Militaire Française, March, 1930 ; *La défense de la bréche Kluck-Bülow par les Corps de Cavalerie Marwitz et Richthoven ;* Revue de Cavalerie, May 1932 – November 1933.

Puyperoux, Gen., *La 3ie Division Coloniale dans la Grande Guerre* (Fournier, Paris).

Recouly, Raymond, *Joffre* (Ed. des Portiques, Paris, 1931).

Regnault, Gen., *La 3ie Division d'Infanterie en août* 1914 ; *L'Echec du Plan XVII ;* Revue de Paris, July 25, 1920.

Requin, Gen., *La journée du 9 septembre à la gauche de la 9ie Armée ;* Revue Militaire Française, November, 1930.

Revol, Gen., *Plan XVII* (Payot, Paris, 1920).

Risser, *Meine Erlebnisse als Mittkampfer* (Schiller, Berlin).

Robertson, Field Marshal Sir William, *From Private to Field Marshal* (Houghton Mifflin, Boston, 1921).

Rochs, Dr. Hugo, *Schlieffen* (Berlin, 1921).

Rolin, Charles, *La Bataille qui sauva Nancy – Champenoux* (Berger-Levrault, Paris, 1930).

Rouquerol, Gen. Gabriel, *La Bataille de Guise* (Berger-Levrault, Paris) ; *Le Canon Artisan de la Victoire* (Berger-Levrault, Paris, 1921).

Rouquerol, Gen. J., *Charleroi* (Payot, Paris, 1932).

Rupprecht, Crown Prince of Bavaria, *Mein Kriegstagebuch* (Deutscher National Verlag, Munich, 1928).

Ryckel, Gen. de, *Mémoires* (Chapelot, Paris, 1920).

Sarrail, Gen., *Souvenirs de* 1914–1915 ; Revue Politique et Parlementaire, May–July, 1921.

Schlieffen, Field Marshal Count von, *Gesammelte Schrifften* (Berlin, 1913) ; *Der Krieg in der gegenwart* (1909) ; *Cannae* (Berlin, 1925).

Schruyver, Gen., *La Bataille de Liége.*

Schubert, *Meine Erlebnisse auf d. Vormarsch d. I Armée* (Reinecke, Magdeburg).

Simonds, F. H., *They Won the War* (Harpers, New York, 1931).

Smith-Dorrien, Gen. Sir Horace, *Memories of Forty-eight Years Service* (Murray, London, 1925).

Spears, Brig.-Gen., *Liaison 1914* (Doubleday, Doran, N. Y., 1931).

Stein, Gen. von, *Erlebnisse und Betrachtung aus der Zeit des Weltkrieges* (Barth, Leipzig, 1919).

Steinhausen, Dr., *Die Gründfehler des Krieges und der Generalstab* (Perthes, Gotha, 1919).

Tanant, Gen., *Souvenirs d'Etat-Major ;* Revue de Paris, April 1, 1922.

Tappen, Gen., *Bis zur Marne* (Stalling, Oldenburg, 1920).

Thevenet, Gen., *La Place de Belfort* (Berger-Levrault, Paris, 1919).

Thomasson, Lieut.-Col. de, *Le Revers de 1914 et ses causes* (Berger-Levrault, Paris, 1919).

Times Documentary History of the War, Vol. II, Diplomatic, Part 2.

Tyng, S. T., *A French Cavalry Raid at the Marne ;* U. S. Cavalry Journal, Sept.-Oct., 1934.

Valarché, Col., *Le Combat d'Arsimont* (Berger-Levrault, Paris, 1926) ; *La Bataille de Guise* (Berger-Levrault, Paris, 1928) ; *Le Combat du Petit Morin* (Berger-Levrault, Paris, 1929) ; *Cannes et la Marche de von Kluck sur Paris* (Berger-Levrault, Paris, 1929) ; *La Bataille des Frontières* (Berger-Levrault, Paris, 1932).

Vauban, Marshal, *L'Importance dont Paris est à la France et le Soin qu'on doit prendre de sa Conservation* (Paris, 1821).

Villate, Capt. Robert, *Foch à la Marne* (Lavauzelle, Paris, 1933).

Wetzell, Gen., *Lehren aus der Kriegsgeschichte. Erinnerungen an die Marne 1914 ;* Deutsche Wehr, I. Jahrgang, Nos. 33–36.

Wilhelm, Crown Prince, of Germany, *Meine Erinnerungen aus Deutschlands Heldenkampf* (Mittler, Berlin, 1923).

Wilson, Field Marshal Sir Henry, *Diary* (Ed. by Gen. Sir C. E. Callwell, Scribners, N. Y., 1927).

Wirth, Capt. A., *Von Saale bis zur Aisne* (Hesse & Becker, Leipzig, 1920).

Zwehl, Gen. von, *Maubeuge, Aisne, Verdun* (Curtius, Berlin, 1921).

INDEX

A

INDEX